Lecture Notes of the Institute for Computer Sciences, Social Informatics and Telecommunications Engineering 377

More information about this series at http://www.springer.com/series/8197

Navid Shaghaghi · Fabrizio Lamberti ·
Brian Beams · Reza Shariatmadari ·
Ahmed Amer (Eds.)

Intelligent Technologies for Interactive Entertainment

12th EAI International Conference, INTETAIN 2020
Virtual Event, December 12-14, 2020
Proceedings

 Springer

Editors
Navid Shaghaghi (iD)
Santa Clara University
Santa Clara, CA, USA

Brian Beams
Santa Clara University
Santa Clara, FL, USA

Ahmed Amer
Santa Clara University
Santa Clara, CA, USA

Fabrizio Lamberti (iD)
INFN Sezione di Torino
Torino, Italy

Reza Shariatmadari
Santa Clara University
Santa Clara, FL, USA

ISSN 1867-8211   ISSN 1867-822X   (electronic)
Lecture Notes of the Institute for Computer Sciences, Social Informatics
and Telecommunications Engineering
ISBN 978-3-030-76425-8   ISBN 978-3-030-76426-5   (eBook)
https://doi.org/10.1007/978-3-030-76426-5

This Springer imprint is published by the registered company Springer Nature Switzerland AG
The registered company address is: Gewerbestrasse 11, 6330 Cham, Switzerland

Preface

We are delighted to introduce the proceedings of the 12th edition of the European Alliance for Innovation (EAI) International Conference on Intelligent Technologies for Interactive Entertainment (INTETAIN 2020). This conference brought together researchers, developers, and practitioners from around the world who are active in areas including art, science, design, and engineering for computer-based systems (algorithms, models, software, tools, etc.) and devices (digital cameras, Internet of Things components, Extended Reality equipment, etc.) that provide intelligent human interaction and/or entertainment experiences. This year's edition of the conference put emphasis on how technology is changing the way humanity interacts with reality, ranging from the usage of digital art in its many forms for entertainment to the usage of technology to provide a new lifeline to many segments of the human population who have been disenfranchised.

The technical program of INTETAIN 2020 consisted of 19 full papers in oral presentation sessions at the main conference tracks. The conference program included five sessions: Session 1 – Big Ideas and Ethics; Session 2 – Haptics, Audio, and Internet of Things (IoT); Session 3 – Industry and Government; Session 4 – Machine Learning (ML); and Session 5 – Extended Reality (XR) and Human Computer Interaction (HCI). Aside from the high-quality technical paper presentations, the technical program also featured three keynote speeches, one invited talk, four technical workshops, a demo, and a poster competition session with 10 finalists and 4 prizes in different categories.

The three keynote speeches were "Questions and Answers on Technology Ethics" by Brian Green, Director of Technology Ethics at Santa Clara University's Markulla Center for Applied Ethics, USA; "Maintaining the Ethics of Artificial Intelligence in the era of Over Digitization: Risks for Machines from Machines" by Abhishek Biswas, Senior Management Consultant at Protiviti Middle East, UAE; and "Leveraging Classical Mathematics for Computer Art and Design" by Frank Farris, Mathematics and Computer Science department chair at Santa Clara University's College of Arts and Sciences, USA. The four organized workshops were Workshop 1 "Prototyping for IoT Projects with Arduino and ProtoPie" instructed by Annie Sungkajun, Assistant Professor of Graphic Design and Creative Technologies in Wonsook Kim School of Art at Illinois State University; Workshop 2 "Basics of Gaze-based Interactivity with VIVE Pro Eye" instructed by Masson Smith, Lecturer and PhD Candidate at Texas A&M University; Workshop 3 "How to use VR Game Design to Teach Concepts in Sustainability" instructed by Brian Beams, Imaginarium XR Lab Manager and Lecturer at Santa Clara University; and Workshop 4 "How to use P5.js to Generate Ideas for your Art Practice" instructed by Krista Fay, an Independent, oil painter, digital artist, and art instructor. The invited talk titled "Art Access in Pandemic Times: 3D Digitization Process of an Art Gallery" was given by Rogério Augusto Bordini and Cesar Augusto Baio from the University of Campinas, Brazil. The demo entitled "MIST: You play, I draw" was given by Juliana Shihadeh from Santa Clara University's Computer Science and Engineering department.

The Organizing Committee did a tremendous job in putting together the three-day conference under the leadership of General Chair, Navid Shaghaghi, who envisioned this year's conference theme and direction with Steering Committee Chair, Imrich Chlamtac, and led the conference into new avenues not explored by previous iterations of the INTETAIN conference. Coordination with the Steering Committee Chair, Imrich Chlamtac, was essential for the success of the conference as his constant support and guidance were greatly appreciated especially given the global hardships faced due to the COVID-19 pandemic.

The outstanding Technical Program Committee (TPC), led by Co-chairs Ahmed Amer, Mehdi Dastani, Mohamad Eid, Brian Green, Mohd Sunar, and Shihan Wang, managed the peer-review process and put together a high-quality and high-impact technical program. Workshops Chair Brian Beams coordinated workshops that were truly exhilarating and informative. Local Co-chairs Reza Shariatmadari and Allan Baez Morales made the conference possible through well programmed and executed scheduling and video conferencing technology. Posters Track Chair Jaykumar Sheth put together a magnificent poster session and competition with a Healthcare Innovation Excellence award sponsored by SCU's BioInnovation and Design Lab, a Most Interdisciplinary and Innovative award sponsored by SCU's Ciocca Center for Innovation and Entrepreneurship, a Most Humanitarian award sponsored by SCU's Frugal Innovation Hub (FIH), and a Most Mathematically Rigorous award sponsored by SCU's Mathematics and Computer Science Department. Demos Chair Simon Flutur arranged for a most touching demonstration on the intersection of art and technology. Web Chair Yu Yang Chee, Publicity and Social Media Co-chairs Heidi Williams and Dagmar Caganova, and Sponsorship and Exhibits Chair Prashanth Asuri brought together authors, contributors, and participants from around the world.

Very special thanks are due to Publications Chair Fabrizio Lamberti, for making the contributions of INTETAIN 2020 accessible in this conference proceedings volume as well as to Conference Manager Viltare Platzner, for her extreme dedication and hard work in bringing INTETAIN 2020 to life; to all of the keynote speakers who awed and educated the conference attendees; and to all of the authors who submitted their papers and posters to the conference, without whom none of this would have been possible.

We strongly believe that INTETAIN 2020 provided a great forum for all researchers, developers and practitioners to discuss all science and technology aspects that are relevant to how technology is changing the way in which humans interact with reality. We also expect that the future iterations of the INTETAIN conference will be as successful and stimulating, as indicated by the contributions presented in this volume.

Organization

Steering Committee

Imrich Chlamtac — University of Trento, Italy

Organizing Committee

General Chair

Navid Shaghaghi — Santa Clara University, USA

Technical Program Committee Chair and Co-chairs

Ahmed Amer — Santa Clara University, USA
Brian Green — Santa Clara University, USA
Mohd Sunar — University of Technology, Malaysia
Mohamad Eid — NYU Abu Dhabi, United Arab Emirates
Mehdi Dastani — Utrecht University, Netherlands
Shihan Wang — Utrecht University, Netherlands

Sponsorship and Exhibits Chair

Prashanth Asuri — Santa Clara University, USA

Local Co-chairs

Reza Shariatmadari — Santa Clara University, USA
Allan Baez Morales — Santa Clara University, USA

Workshops Chair

Brian Beams — Santa Clara University, USA

Publicity and Social Media Chairs

Heidi Williams — Santa Clara University, USA
Dagmar Caganova — Slovak University of Technology in Bratislava, Slovakia

Publications Chair

Fabrizio Lamberti — Politecnico di Torino, Italy

Web Chair

Yu Yang Chee — Santa Clara University, USA

Posters and PhD Track Chair

Jaykumar Sheth   Santa Clara University, USA

Demos Chair

Simon Flutura   University of Augsburg, Germany

Technical Program Committee

Ruhiyati Idayu Abu Talib	Universiti Teknologi Malaysia, Malaysia
Mohamed Alborati	City University of New York, USA
Ryan Macdonell Andrias	Universiti Teknologi Malaysia, Malaysia
Mónica Aresta	University of Aveiro, Portugal
Hithesh Bathala	Santa Clara University, USA
Brian Beams	Santa Clara University, USA
Davide Calandra	Politecnico di Torino, Italy
Andres Calle	Santa Clara University, USA
Alberto Cannavò	Politecnico di Torino, Italy
Jorge Cardoso	Universidade de Coimbra, Portugal
Eva Cerezo	University of Zaragoza, Spain
Manuela Chessa	University of Genoa, Italy
Federico Delorenzis	Politecnico di Torino, Itally
Daja Evans	Santa Clara University, USA
Kenneth Feinstein	Sunway Education Group, Malaysia
Peter Ferguson	Santa Clara University, USA
Yolanda Fernández	University of Vigo, Spain
Silvia Figueira	Santa Clara University, USA
Matthew Gaudet	Santa Clara University, USA
Abdelwahab Hamam	Florida Polytechnic University, USA
Zeyad Abd-Algfoor Hasan	University of Mosul, Iraq
Bipin Indurkhya	University of Krakowie, Poland
Joseph Israel	Santa Clara University, USA
Ali Karime	Royal Military College of Canada, Canada
Ioannis Karydis	Ionian University, Greece
Fernando Koch	IBM, USA
Martin Lochner	University of Tasmania, Australia
John-Jules Meyer	Utrecht University, Netherlands
Braden Molhoek	Santa Clara University, USA
Joao Martinho Moura	Universidade Catolica Portuguesa, Portugal
Brinda Pabari	Santa Clara University, USA
Filipe Portela	University of Minho, Portugal

Contents

Big Ideas and Ethics

Designing Serious Games for the Mitigation of the Impact of Massive Shootings in a Mexican Environment

Juan Chacon Quintero[✉] and Hisa Martinez Nimi

Universidad de Monterrey, Monterrey, México
juan.chacon@udem.edu

Abstract. Serious games have proven to be effective methods of communication and learning. Qualities that had been taken advantage of in Disaster risk management by developing serious games that mitigate the impact of natural disasters by incurring in preparedness. Design Against Crime and its derived methodologies and tools have proven effective in the reduction of fear of crime in Mexican communities. By combining the approach previously applied in Disaster Risk Management (DRM) by game creators and researchers with Design Against Crime, the current research project proposes the use of the resulting methodology in the design of serious games as interventions for crime related incidents with similar characteristics to natural disasters like massive shootings in public spaces.

Keywords: Serious games · Disaster Risk Management · Design Against Crime

1 Introduction

Serious games, accompanied by simulations, present the opportunity to improve the information retention process through emotion and repetition. These activities act as metaphors in which users face artificial conflicts through defined rules and quantifiable results [1]. This can facilitate the measurement of these experiences' impact on mitigation in a potential disaster before the disaster occurs.

Since the beginning of the war against drug trafficking in Mexico, which began in 2006 [2], the population has lived in a situation of violence as the confrontation between the authorities and drug cartels has been recurrently provoked. This has generated a climate of insecurity and has had considerable impacts on the population, such as the increase in insecurity perception indices.

In crime sociology, insecurity perception can be defined as the emotional response to the perception of crime-related symbols, this implies that security perception is determined by the individual and collective perceptions of crime [3]. Fear of crime and insecurity perception can stimulate and accelerate communities' decay and provoke individuals to retire physically and psychologically from community life, weakening the informal process of social control that inhibits delinquency [4].

N. Shaghaghi et al. (Eds.): INTETAIN 2020, LNICST 377, pp. 3–14, 2021.
https://doi.org/10.1007/978-3-030-76426-5_1

Clashes in public spaces between members of organized crime and the authorities function as events that promote fear of crime and increase the perception of insecurity in the communities in which they occur. The consequences of this impact can be disastrous in the short term and long term since the fear of crime creates the risk of negatively impacting various aspects of life in the affected communities.

By matching intervention strategies to reduce the fear of crime in Mexican communities with interactive simulation experiences in the form of serious games, it was proposed to mitigate the situation from the perspective of disaster prevention as a result of the course. From the experience design of the player from the University of Monterrey, this research presents a methodology, as well as the initial documentation for the design of micro games in order to intervene in the positive mitigation of the problem.

During the project, a work methodology was developed. The steps to follow for developing this type of experience were selected, followed by a stage of conceptualization and defining the narrative elements to consider for the intervention.

2 Serious Games and Disaster Risk Management

Traditional Disaster Risk Management (DRM) methods tend to involve centralized decision processes, the responsibilities of which lie with members of the government and researchers [5]. These traditional strategies limit the participation of members of the affected communities. They tend to be perceived as imposed commands by affecting the existing culture and social participation in those communities [6].

However, the DRM strategies that have recently proven to be most successful involve community participation in the strategy and communication process [8]. By implementing these types of strategies, communities are treated as partners in co-creating products that reflect their participation, allowing these strategies to be better accepted and no longer perceived as impositions [7].

The application of interactive experiences such as serious games in these types of situations can facilitate the participation of communities, as they are perceived as tools capable of effectively and innately communicating essential concepts for disaster mitigation or prevention. It has been verified in different cases related to climate change mitigation and sustainable development, among others [8].

As highly interactive and social activities, games and simulations are able to activate a positive emotional response in players, transforming into convincing, memorable, and challenging learning experiences, making them fun and prolonging their impact on the user. Active learning methods have much greater information retention potential than passive or traditional methods. Studies show that only 5% of the information is retained in the case of reading, while in the case of an active experience, such as a training session, up to 75% of the information is retained [9]. Added to this is the evidence on adults' attention span, which is estimated to be 20 min, during which only in the first five minutes does the greatest learning impact occur [10].

Game-based learning strategies present a similar environment to those presented in problem-based learning. They are normally guided by a facilitator who provides the necessary information and determines the rules of the game. In this type of environment, participants face the collection of information by applying critical thinking, which allows participants to conclude with a broader picture of the issue presented to them, gaining a deeper understanding of systems or complex concepts [11].

Current interactive learning experiences like serious games present players with the opportunity for immersions in a simulated reality representing crucial elements of a particular process or problem. This environment allows the user or participant in the experience to take a specific role in the situation or problem, often inviting them to interact with other participants in the same environment, resulting in specific strategic decision-making, as well as consideration of the consequences produced by said decisions in the game environment [12]. This also allows players to explore and compare multiple causes and effects concerning the game's reality, which can then be extrapolated to other systems, resulting in players' ability to recognize the links between decisions made in the game.

Gaming and the mechanisms that govern reality turn serious games into practical tools for mitigation in DRM processes, both in the pre-disaster stages, such as mitigation, prevention, and preparedness, and in the post-disaster stages, such as response, reaction, and recovery, since it is entirely related to the main objectives of serious games, which are message broadcasting, training, and data exchange [13].

As cultural artefacts, Serious Games also represent an opportunity for those involved in an emergency situation to consider the ethical ramifications derived from their role and decision making during this type of situation. As experiences, video games in general can be used for developing ethical thinking skills [14].

Allowing players to reflect about the consequences derived from their actions. This is often achieved through assuming new identities that allow to experience these situations within the game space [15].

3 Design Against Crime and Serious Games

This research documents the work process followed in the conceptualization and design of an interactive micro-experience as a serious game to prepare a Mexican population sector to face a shooting situation in a public space. For this purpose, this study refers to strategies used in disaster prevention to mitigate the impact of natural disasters, as well as the design of interventions to mitigate the impact of crime in Mexican communities [16]. The use of a design methodology derived from the strategies above was conceptualized and put into practice, consisting mainly of involving stakeholders in the co-creation process directly or indirectly as well as a series of steps that have allowed for knowing the situation in relation to the needs derived from both the agents and the environment involved in the situation.

In the Design Against Crime, Crime Lifecycle Methodology [17], which has previously proven its effectiveness in the design of interventions to mitigate or prevent the impact of a crime situation by involving stakeholders in the planning and design process [18], community members or participants in various activities are invited to visualize and identify the most effective point at which to carry out an intervention so that the crime in question can be prevented, participants can react adequately to its occurrence, or, in the case of identifying a stage after the occurrence as the most relevant in the situation, participants can limit spread of the economic, emotional, or psychological impact of crime in the community.

Shootings in public spaces were selected as the central theme for the development of this project since these phenomena can be considered and analyzed from the perspective of both Design Against Crime and DRM, the latter being one of the fields in which the application of serious games has previously demonstrated its effectiveness as tools capable of mitigating such situations [19].

4 Designing Serious Games for the Mitigation of the Impact of Massive Shootings in a Mexican Environment

Once the topic was selected, the project participants undertook to investigate the background and registered cases of that type of occurrence and the main reactions of the participants or victims of said events in Mexico. Among the cases registered in the last decade, the situation derived from the capture of Ovidio Guzman in 2019 stands out, where the city of Culiacán and its surroundings were seized and virtually besieged by organized crime, resulting in dozens of shootings in public spaces and 14 deceased and 21 wounded people [20]. Something that stands out, in this case, is the high number of recordings resulting from this incident, due to the reaction of the witnesses and civilian victims who, contrary to what could be assumed, decided to react to the shootings by trying to follow their actions or staying immovable in the space of the action. However, despite keeping low to the ground or keeping cover, by broadcasting live on social networks or recording the situation, they put themselves even more at risk.

Such a reaction to this type of situation puts those involved physically at risk [21] and spreads the impact of the crime far beyond the environment and agents involved. When the captured images are disseminated, they end up affecting the perception of insecurity of all those inhabitants of nearby communities, possibly even affecting the indexes of security perception at state or national levels.

Although this case best exemplifies the lack of preparation or knowledge of the population when facing this type of situation, it is not isolated. Outdoor shootings have occurred both in Tamaulipas [22] and Coahuila [23], as well as in Nuevo León [24]. They show similar reactions and characteristics throughout the years.

Due to this type of reaction, as well as the fact that it is an apparently random and unexpected situation, out of control of the majority of those involved, it was decided to select the reaction to this situation as the stage for the intervention design. In this case, a serious game can teach potential victims how to react to this type of phenomenon. Derived from this, the city of Monterrey, Nuevo León, was selected to test this concept, and the students of the player experience design class, of the video game design master's degree from the University of Monterrey, were chosen to put the conceptualized methodology into practice. In order to put the participating students into the context and facilitate the assimilation of the process to follow in the design of the intervention against crime, the team opted to synthesize and replace the elements of the Crime Life Cycle [25] methodology, and the conjunction of criminal opportunity [26], previously used in the design of interventions against crime in Mexican communities [27], with procedures and elements related to or derived from the process of designing interactive experiences, as well as with video games. Both methods mentioned above consist of identifying the agents and environments involved in the crime situation, their needs and vulnerabilities, and the most important stage of the crime situation in which to apply an intervention capable of completely stopping or mitigating the impact of said crime, followed by designing the said intervention, applying it in the situation, and measuring its impact.

Following these guidelines as a basis, the students began by analyzing the agents involved in the situation, in this case, the profile of the potential victims, members of the general population of Nuevo León. A total of 12 participants, men and women with an average age of 26 years, were initially analyzed with a survey to determine from written text their profiles according to the traits of the Big Five Personality Model [28]. Previous research has used the relationship between these personality traits and gamer archetypes [29], so the same system was chosen to identify each participant's video game profile. Using this method determined those elements necessary to generate a greater emotional impact on the participants to facilitate the learning of the correct reactions or instructions to follow when facing a shooting in public spaces.

According to the Autonomous University of Hidalgo [21], if someone is in the middle of a shooting in a public space, hear gunshots from a distance, or have the shooter within sight range, it is recommended to drop to the ground, not to kneel nor bend down, and to let go of everything you're holding. Wait until you identify the shooter and withdraw from the area if possible. In the case of running, it is recommended not to run since you could be heading in the direction where the shots originate and running could also attract the shooter's attention. When hitting the ground, it is necessary to check where the shots have come from and how far away the shooter is and avoid any investigation. Use the ears and be prepared to stay away from the sound, if possible.

An attempt should be made to determine if the shots are directed at you or if there are immediate threats nearby. If you need to look, you should not raise your head, and it is recommended to look from the sides, taking into account that the shots can come from all directions. If there is an accessible escape route, you should try to evacuate the present people as long as you do not risk your life and that of others. It is recommended to leave belongings. As much as possible, prevent people from entering the area where the shooter is. Keep your hands visible and follow the instructions of any security officers or trained personnel present.

If evacuation is not possible, it is recommended to find a hiding place out of sight of the shooter, which protects you if shots are fired in your direction. Facing or trying to catch shooters is not recommended. If the shooter is close, it is recommended to silence your cell phone. Turn off any noise source, hide behind large objects, and stay calm. Stay calm and dial 911, if possible, to alert the police to the shooter's presence. If you cannot speak, leave the line open and allow the operator to hear you.

It is recommended that the player take action against the active shooter as a last resort. Only when your life is in imminent danger should you try to disrupt or incapacitate the active shooter. When the authorities arrive, it is recommended to stay calm and follow the instructions of the officers.

Following this stage, each participant's profile was developed with the results of the applied surveys. This profile included within it the elements the player archetype identified as the main ones, in this case, Mastermind–Manager, as well as the elements and characteristics of the most attractive video games for said profile.

Derived from said profile, the participants opted to propose a puzzle-like experience in the form of a maze. Users were confronted with the simulated situation of a street shooting and needed to find the route, making correct decisions to survive and complete their journey.

For the environment, the team chose the Monterrey metropolitan area. Considering previous occurrences of shootings and acts of violence by organized crime in the area [30], the municipality of Guadalupe, Nuevo León, was selected as a real space/location to be used as a basis for the design of the environment of the proposed experience.

In both DRM and Design Against Crime strategies, the background of the situation, the decisions available to those involved in the situation, and the possible consequences of making such decisions are taken into account. Following this scheme as a basis, the work team proposed using a similar structure for the construction of the message or complex concept to be transmitted as a form of teaching through interaction with the proposed experience. The students were invited to select the background, the possible decisions, and their consequences to be transmitted as a message, which was later used as the narrative basis of the proposed serious game, derived in the introduction, climax, and conclusion.

Once these narrative elements were determined, the students were invited to transfer these narrative elements into a real geographic area, using a digital map of the Guadalupe area (See Fig. 1), to distribute said elements, selecting three relevant points to use as base locations for the narrative, followed by a starting and an ending point. With this completed narrative, the team chose to start the creative conceptualization stage and the construction of the necessary elements for the execution of the experience.

Fig. 1. Map of Guadalupe zone, with narrative elements distributed and marked.

5 Life Oppression

As a result of this process, the students proposed "life oppression," a five-minute experience built using the Unity Engine [31], with the concept of run from the block. Here the players are immersed in a situation of being in-between an armed confrontation between the authorities and organized crime groups on the streets of Guadalupe, Nuevo León (See Fig. 2). The player must make correct decisions to survive, get out of the situation, and reach a safe area. The player can quickly visualize if their decisions are successful and have saved his life, or if they are incorrect and have led him to panic and die within the game (See Fig. 3).

Fig. 2. Game location inspired by Guadalupe Nuevo León

The game takes as inspiration the locations previously selected by the team and reinterprets them in a closed environment, like a labyrinth in which secondary agents are distributed, representing both members of organized crime and of the authorities. Members of organized crime may be able to directly shoot and "kill" the player by mistaking him for a member of the authorities, and in the same way, the authorities may mistake him for a member of organized crime. The player is also faced with situations where, depending on their decisions, they may find themselves in the crossfire and die amid accidental shooting. Along the way, the player receives messages that give her suggestions or, where appropriate, specific indications on how to react to survive the situation. To confront the player with different versions or cases in which a real victim can face an outdoor shooting, secondary agents are distributed so that the player can face different distributions and cases along the way. If the player makes the correct decisions and completes the route satisfactorily, fleeing the sound of the shots and trying to get as far away as possible within the confines of the available space, he ends up finding a safe area protected by the authorities where he can take refuge and conclude the experience

Fig. 3. Making the wrong decisions can lead to the player to death

satisfactorily, Fig. 4 shows the resulting environment map, player routes and agents' distribution.

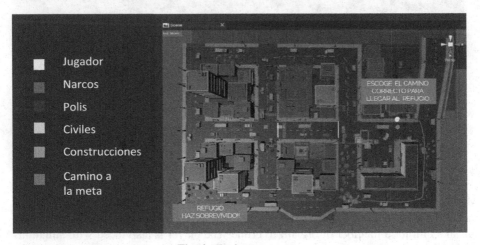

Fig. 4. Environment map.

For the evaluation of the experience in this stage of the project, the team opted to use a real-time facial recognition model, tensorflow-js in conjunction with a Single Shot Multibox Detector based on MobileNetV1 was used for face detection, while a depthwise separable convolutions and densely connected blocks model was used for emotion expression recognition, both models derived from the approach originally proposed by face-api.js [32]. The resulting tool estimates the players emotional impact that the experience has on them throughout their participation from their facial expression. At the end of the game, the participants were invited to provide feedback on their experience to improve future iterations of the game and to give a clearer idea of the learning impact it had on the participants. For the first test, a total of eight participants, men and women with an average age of 30 years, played the game.

Before interacting with the experience, the participants' profiles were evaluated using the same correlation method between the Big Five Personality Model and the player archetype to determine if there was a similarity between the profiles identified by the previous tests and the participants, with Mastermind–Manager being the profile identified among the participants. When analyzing the recordings of the different interactions, the participating students concluded that the participants showed sadness, anger, and disgust as the primary expressions of facial emotion throughout the experience when interacting with the game, such as surprise and sadness when dying and happiness when completing the game, Fig. 5 shows a participant interacting with the experience while their emotional reaction is being recorded. It should be noted that the fact that sadness, disgust, and anger were presented as the primary emotions may be related to the participants' lack of familiarity with the environment and the control of the experience, which must be improved in subsequent iterations.

Fig. 5. Participant interacting with the game.

There is a relationship between the characteristics of a video game and the level of excitement or satisfaction that users can obtain from that experience. Considering that the level of excitement can help maintain attention and improve learning through the experience, we opted for a type of game based on the personality and profile of the player identified among most of the participants.

6 Discussion and Conclusion

This research documents the background, the method and the process utilized to design and develop a 5-min interactive experience as a serious game, with the goal of teaching possible victims of street mass shootings how to react when confronted by such situation, potentially mitigating its impact. To achieve a meaningful impact in the situation, the Monterrey Nuevo Leon metropolitan area was selected as the environment for the project. A team of students from this area, specifically members of the game design master program of Universidad de Monterrey, which in a sense can be considered stakeholders because of their links to the local community, where selected to design the experiences and test the proposed work methodology. A first version of the conceptualized game, "Life Oppression", was developed in Unity Engine using stock assets and was consequently tested by members of the community, measuring the emotional impact by applying face recognition during their experience. Although the decision was made to measure users' emotional impact by interacting with the experience using real-time facial recognition, future elaboration of protocols and methods for quantification are required. Both based on the emotional impact of the participants' expressions, as well as the level of learning and retention of information after the experience. Further consideration and analysis should be directed towards the ethical ramifications and consequences derived from the interaction with the resulting game, particularly for members of the community that have been previous direct or indirect victims of a street shooting situation, which may be triggered by the simulation furthering the impact of the crime rather than mitigating it.

This research details the basis and methods applied in the first iteration of what is planned to be an annual recurrent program for the development of serious games that facilitate or promote the information necessary to mitigate the impact of this kind of violent situation. The possibility of expanding this method's application to other types of situations such as natural disasters or human-made disasters that plague communities in the same geographical area is not ruled out.

References

1. Salen, K., Zimmerman, E.: Rules of Play. MIT Press, Cambridge (2004)
2. Meschoulam, M.: Terror and fear: the Mexican case. In: Organized Crime, Fear and Peace-building in Mexico, pp. 29–44. Palgrave Macmillan, Cham (2019). https://doi.org/10.1007/978-3-319-94929-1_3
3. Jarząbek, L.: How game can help flood-prone communities (2016). https://games4sustainability.org/2016/08/18/flood-resilience-game-for-flood-pronecommunities/. Accessed 6 Jan 2019
4. Keating, A.: Playing at flood resilience: using games to help vulnerable communities. https://blog.iiasa.ac.at/2016/08/03/playing-at-flood-resilience-using-games-tohelp-vulnerable-communities/. Accessed 12 June 2019
5. World Bank United Nations: Natural hazards, unnatural disasters. The World Bank (2010). https://doi.org/10.1596/978-0-8213-8050-5
6. Mechler, R.: Reviewing estimates of the economic efficiency of disaster risk management: opportunities and limitations of using risk-based cost-benefit analysis. Nat. Hazards **81**(3), 2121–2147 (2016). https://doi.org/10.1007/s11069-016-2170-y

7. Roncoli, C.: Ethnographic and participatory approaches to research on farmers' responses to climate predictions. Clim. Res. **33**, 81–99 (2006)
8. Bachofen, C., Suarez P., Steenbergen, M., Grist, N.: Can games help people manage the climate risks they face? The participatory design of educational games, Red Cross Red Crescent Climate Centre (2012)
9. DeKanter, N.: Gaming redefines interactivity for learning. TechTrends **49**(3), 26–31 (2004).
10. Burns, R.A.: Information impact and factors affecting recall. Paper Presented at the Annual National Conference on Teaching Excellence and Conference on Administrators, 7th, Austin, TX, 22–25 May 1985 (1985)
11. Duke, R.: Gaming: The Future's Language. SAGE Publications, Thousand Oaks (1974)
12. Kwok, R.: Scientists are designing board, card and digital games to convey scientific concepts. Nature **547** (2017)
13. Djaouti, D., Alvarez, J., Jessel, J.: Classifying serious games: the G/P/S model. In: Felicia, P. (ed.) Handbook of Research on Improving Learning and Motivation Through Educational Games: Multidisciplinary Approaches, pp. 118–136. IGI Global
14. Schrier, K.: EPIC: a framework for using video games in ethics education. J. Moral Educ. **44**(4), 393–424 (2015)
15. Schrier, K., Gibson, D.: Ethics and Game Design. IGI Global, Hershey (2010)
16. Chacon, J.C., Martinez Nimi, H., Watanabe, M., Ono, K., Paskevicius, A.: Reducing fear of crime through design against crime. J. Sci. Des. **2**(1), 1_29–1_36 (2018). https://doi.org/10.11247/jsd.2.1_1_29. Japanese Society for the Science of Design
17. Ekblom, P.: Design Against Crime: Crime Proofing Everyday Products. Lynne Rienner Publishers, Boulder (2012)
18. Davey, C., Marselle, M.: Engaging young people in designing against crime. Swedish Des. Res. J. **1**(12), 29–38 (2012)
19. Barreteau, O., Le Page, C., Perez, P.: Contribution of simulation and gaming to natural resource management issues: an introduction. Simul. Gaming: Interdiscip. J. **38**, 185–194 (2007)
20. Infobae. Aumenta a 14 el numero de muertos por los tiroteos en Culiacan (2019). https://www.infobae.com/america/mexico/2019/10/23/aumento-a-14-el-numero-de-muertos-por-los-tiroteos-en-culiacan/. Accessed 06 Nov 2019
21. Universidad autonoma del estado de hidalgo: protocolos de seguridad antes, durante y despues de una balacera, Aniversidad Autonoma del estado de hidalgo (2019)
22. Diario 43. Viernes Negro; Persecuciones y Balaceras Ponen en Pánico a la Ciudad, 8 abatidos. https://eldiario43.com/2017/06/03/viernes-negro-persecuciones-y-balaceras-ponen-en-panico-a-la-ciudad-8-abatidos/. Accessed 06 Nov 2019
23. Digital, M.: Captan persecución y balacera en Piedras Negras, Coahuila, 06 November 2019. https://www.milenio.com/mileniotv/policia/captan-persecucio-balacera-piedras-negras-coahuila. Accessed 06 Nov 2019
24. Intento de secuestro desata balacera en Nuevo León, 07 April 2018. https://www.excelsior.com.mx/nacional/intento-de-secuestro-desata-balacera-en-nuevo-leon/1231010. Accessed 06 Nov 2019
25. Wootton, A., Davey, C.: Crime Lifecycle: Guidance for Generating Design Against Crime Ideas. The University of Salford, Salford (2003)
26. Ekblom, P.: The conjunction of criminal opportunity: a framework for crime reduction toolkits, Institute for Public Policy Research (2001)
27. Chacon, J.C., Martinez Nimi, H., Watanabe, M., Kenta, O., Paskevicius, A.: Reducing fear of crime through design against crime II. J. Sci. Des. 3 巻 (1) 号, 1_21–1_26 (2019). 公開日. https://doi.org/10.11247/jsd.3.1_1_21. https://www.jstage.jst.go.jp/article/jsd/3/1/3_1_21/_article/-char/ja. ISSN 2424-2217

28. John, O.P., Naumann, L., Soto, C.J.: Paradigm shift to the integrative Big Five trait taxonomy: history, measurement, and conceptual issues. In: John, O.P., Robins, R.W., Pervin, L.A. (eds.) Handbook of Personality: Theory and Research, 3rd edn., pp. 114–158. Guilford Press, New York (2008)
29. Lima, E.S., Feija, B., Furtado, A.: Player behavior and personality modeling for interactive storytelling in games. Entertain. Comput. **28**, 32–48 (2018). https://doi.org/10.1016/j.entcom. 2018.08.003
30. INEGI: Encuesta Nacional de Victimización y Percepción sobre Seguridad Pública 2019, Mexico (2019)
31. Unity3D (2014). https://unity3d.com/. Accessed 07 Dec 2020
32. Mühler, V.: https://github.com/justadudewhohacks/face-api.js. Accessed 07 Dec 2020

An Ethical Code for Commercial VR/AR Applications

Erick Jose Ramirez[1](✉), Jocelyn Tan[2], Miles Elliott[1], Mohit Gandhi[1], and Lia Petronio[1]

[1] Santa Clara University, Santa Clara, CA 95053, USA
ejramirez@scu.edu
[2] SisuVR, South San Francisco, CA 94080, USA

Abstract. The commercial VR/AR marketplace is gaining ground and is becoming an ever larger and more significant component of the global economy. While much attention has been paid to the commercial promise of VR/AR, comparatively little attention has been given to the ethical issues that VR/AR technologies introduce. We here examine existing codes of ethics proposed by the ACM and IEEE and apply them to the unique ethical facets that VR/AR introduces. We propose a VR/AR code of ethics for developers and apply this code to several commercial applications.

Keywords: ACM · IEEE · Applied ethics · Augmented reality · Professional ethics · Technology ethics · Virtual reality

1 Introduction

Virtual reality technologies have rapidly emerged into the consumer marketplace since the 2016 release of the HTC Vive and Oculus Rift systems. In 2019, aVR application, the motion game *Beat Saber*, was the first to sell over 1 million copies ("Virtual Reality 2019"). Late in 2019, Mark Zuckerberg announced that sales of VR content for the Oculus family of VR hardware had surpassed $100 million dollars ("Oculus" 2019).

With well over 1 million VR headsets connected monthly on the Steam platform alone, the VR marketplace is on a pace to expand radically as next generation hardware becomes wireless, more mobile, and more cost-effective. While we're not yet at the point where most households have access to VR and AR hardware, game and software developers are hoping that a day comes when this will be true. As a result, the need for deeper discussions on the ethics of VR and AR is imperative.

While significant attention has been given to its commercial potential, much less attention has been devoted to an examination of the potential ethical issues arising from VR and AR development. We examine these issues here and propose a new code of ethics for commercial VR and AR applications. This code draws upon existing frameworks provided by the IEEE and ACM professional codes and extends its applicability towards ethical issues surrounding unique features of VR/AR.

© ICST Institute for Computer Sciences, Social Informatics and Telecommunications Engineering 2021
Published by Springer Nature Switzerland AG 2021. All Rights Reserved
N. Shaghaghi et al. (Eds.): INTETAIN 2020, LNICST 377, pp. 15–24, 2021.
https://doi.org/10.1007/978-3-030-76426-5_2

2   Existing Codes of Ethics

Both the Association for Computing Machinery ACM) and Institute of Electrical and Electronics Engineers (IEEE) have developed codes of ethics to guide the members of their respective professional organizations (see Tables 1 and 2). We begin with these organizations in part because they are the largest international professional organizations which developers of VR and AR applications are likely to belong and thus they wield influence over how ethics gets incorporated into the project workflows of developers large and small.

Both codes of ethics stress professional duties to protect and promote public welfare, build public trust, and work toward the common good. The ACM code of ethics goes on to helpfully distinguish between ethical duties owed to consumers and the public from those developers owe themselves. The duty to be a good developer, in other words, extends beyond the duty to minimize harm, design for compliance, or to enhance social welfare. Being a good developer is, in itself, a moral virtue all developers should aim for.

In this section, we highlight what we believe are the most relevant aspects of each organization's code of ethics. In particular we will later draw upon both professional codes in order to create a code of ethics specifically aimed at developers of VR/AR applications. While there's significant overlap between being an ethical developer of traditional software platforms and that of VR applications, the unique features of VR/AR require we call specific attention to the virtues of good VR/AR design.

These codes of ethics include:

Table 1. IEEE Code of Ethics

• To hold paramount the safety, health, and welfare of the public
• To improve the understanding by individuals and society of the capabilities and societal implications of conventional and emerging technologies
• To seek, accept, and offer honest criticism of technical work, to acknowledge and correct errors, and to credit properly the contributions of others
• To avoid injuring others, their property, reputation, or employment by false or malicious action
• To assist colleagues and co-workers in their professional development and to support them in following this code of ethics

Retrieved from: https://www.ieee.org/about/corporate/governance/p7-8.html

One limitation of both the ACM and the IEEE codes is that, while both speak somewhat generally about harm avoidance and designing with the public good in mind, they do not make distinctions on methods by which different technologies can impact (and harm) individuals. Although some material harms (e.g., data privacy, physical safety) are easy enough to identify and to build protections around, emerging technologies are

Table 2. ACM Code of Ethics

• Avoid harm
• Be honest and trustworthy
• Be fair and take action not to discriminate
• Respect privacy
• Ensure that the public good is the central concern during all professional computing work
• Recognize when a computer system is becoming integrated into the infrastructure of society and adopt an appropriate standard of care for that system and its users

Retrieved from: https://ethics.acm.org/code-of-ethics/code-2018/

likely to bring with them new forms of harm that are especially important to protect consumers from in advance of launching a product.[1]

Virtual reality introduces several new variables into the equation of ethical game design that are unprecedented and require proactive attention. We must consider beforehand the potential harms of virtual reality to ensure that such technologies are neither intentionally nor accidentally misused. Accounting for these new forms of harm protects both the users and developers of VR/AR, who are both fundamental to the progression of good VR and AR technology.

In an effort to integrate VR/AR in a way that reflects the spirit of the ethical codes currently in play, as well as tailoring it to the unique features of the VR/AR landscape, we must look at the way people experience a virtually real environment. While there exist guidelines for the responsible creation of media like film and television, VR and AR are less researched, and they have more capacity to create psychologically real experiences. The interactivity, immersion, and the fact that VR and AR experiences are not screen-bound (experienced as being contained by a screen within the larger field of view of the user), means that events that occur in these virtual spaces will be more 'real' than in TV or film. As such, there is more responsibility to consider these impacts and mitigate any potential harms, especially because of a higher degree of similarity to real life experiences than in these more ubiquitous mediums.

One benefit of the ACM code is that it includes a special set of ethical considerations aimed at those technologies which are, or are poised to become, integrated into the infrastructure of society. We believe virtual reality hardware will be one of these technologies and thus should be subject to a higher level of ethical scrutiny. For example, in 2019, the Facebook Corporation (the parent company of the Oculus Corporation) announced a multimillion dollar effort to create Horizon, a VR social media environment, that it plans to roll out sometime in 2020 (Kaser 2019). We believe that the hardware and software investments being made by companies like Facebook are strong indicators that VR and AR technologies are likely to become a part of the social media infrastructure of the

---

[1] Most commercial developers (Oculus, HTC, etc) have their own internal codes for employees and other codes have been proposed (Madary and Metzinger 2016). We aim to incorporate and synthesize these codes into our own proposal here which builds on what we argue are unique psychological aspects of simulation design that are unique to VR/AR.

21st century and thus such technologies require an especially careful level of ethical assessment.

3 Ethical Issues in AR/VR

As the IEEE and ACM codes help us see, VR and AR technologies will inherit many ethical issues already familiar to those of us concerned with ethics and technology. In this section we briefly survey these issues before extending our analysis to ethical issues that are unique to emerging VR technologies and our research on the moral psychology of user experience.

3.1 Data Collection and Privacy

Virtual Reality devices are capable of collecting a great deal of personalized data that must be safeguarded. For example, VRand AR technologies are capable of collecting information about a user's location, the media they experience, hours spent in virtual space, virtual wallets, and other relevant data typically associated with virtual economies. AR technologies have the additional ability to track a user's location as they move about both virtual and real spaces.

Additionally, VR and AR devices are able to collect information about user height, motion, interaction choices, and avatar design choices. These devices are also able to track user gaze, record facial expressions, and store user audio input using the built-in cameras and microphones on newer generations of VR HMDs such as the Oculus Rift-S, the Vive Cosmos, and the Valve Index. Many developers in these spaces allow users to upload photos to allow their avatars to more closely resemble themselves (or others). These data could lead to a new, and more insidious, form of identity theft in which physical and audio avatar profiles can be cloned and used to deceive unsuspecting users (Slater et al. 2020).

Not only is the volume of data generated by virtual reality technologies larger than that provided by traditional consumer computing platforms, the haptic systems that make virtual reality technologies so immersive allows that data to be of a more intimate nature. Though data collection is used to enhance user experience, it introduces a potential invasion of privacy that players may not have explicitly consented to. Ethical commercial applications must make clear to users not only that such data can be collected but also take great pains to carefully encrypt collected data. Equally importantly, developers should aim not to collect more data than is absolutely necessary for particular applications. Furthermore, care must be taken to delete such data at the earliest possible time (minimizing the harm of a data breach). Users must also, to the degree allowed by the application, be empowered to opt out of data collection.[2]

---

[2] Although different in terms of their "opt-in" vs. "opt-out" structure, both the state of California's Consumer Privacy Act (CCPS) enacted in 2020 and the European Union's General Data Protection Regulation (GDPR) enacted in 2018 provide consumers with such a right and both serve as good models for ethical data collection.

3.2 Content

Like all media, some individuals may have concerns about VR and AR based on content that they may personally find objectionable. While this has been a concern raised about all forms of media, the interactive and especially immersive nature of VR and AR technologies, and the degree to which they more greatly affect user emotion, makes such concerns especially important.

Although content warnings, game ratings, and other advisories are now common in the industry, there may be instances in which the nature of immersion can add a new ethical dimension that should inform how developers, and rating agencies, respond to these content concerns. We address the special nature of content in section D below. The very same content should, we believe, often receive more conservative ratings (e.g., more adult ratings) when made for VR and AR than other forms of media. These ratings should explicitly convey that virtual reality may result in more severe psychological reactions to content that a player may otherwise find acceptable in less immersive mediums.

3.3 Nudges

Cambridge Analytica's approach to targeted advertising made the ethics of nudging salient in 2016. Nudges are intentional manipulations of a user's (real or virtual) environment that are meant to influence users (Sunstein 2015). As Cambridge Analytica's example helps demonstrate, nudges are sometimes morally problematic to design and use.

Because VR and AR technologies can be immersive, highly convincing, and emotionally engaging, they are an especially good tool for nudges. Already, such applications have been developed for the purpose of nudging users into being less racist, more sympathetic to homelessness, more caring about the environment, and to eating less meat. However, an ethical analysis of the design and development of such nudges has not followed suit. Tech ethicists have argued that a nudge is permissible so long as it avoids manipulating users (by deception or lack of transparency) and works to benefit users and social welfare whenever possible. VR and AR nudges can also be ethically appropriate ways of helping users develop good skills and habits (Sunstein 2015; Herrera et al. 2018).

Because experiences involving these technologies can blur the distinction between reality and simulation, developers should be especially cautious about developing nudges that leave users with the false impression that they understand what it's like to live the life of a different person (Ramirez 2018b).

3.4 User Experience/Harm

One of the unique features of virtual reality technologies is their ability to convince their users that they're physically located inside the virtual worlds instead of wherever they happen to be in reality. Psychologists refer to this phenomenon as the feeling of "presence" (Cummings and Bailenson 2016). While many forms of media can instill feelings of presence in their users, virtual reality technologies are capable of generating especially intense forms of presence known as "virtually real" experiences (Ramirez

2018a). Because virtual reality is capable of generating virtually real experiences (i.e., experiences that are treated by users, in the moment, as if they were real) developers of VR and AR applications should pay special care, in line with the ACM and IEEE codes, to avoid causing unintended harm to users.

Scott Stephan, director of games at FoxNext VR Studio (makers of TheBlu: Encounter), makes the same point when he cautions that he

...find[s] that scary experiences, horror experiences need to be really finely cali-brated. If you see a horror movie on a screen, you have the abstraction. It's not so frightening, and you know you're there for fun... I found that, in room-scale VR, things that might be fun on a TV screen, like jump scares...We actually have a rule that no creature should be larger than the size of a small dog. Anything above that and you get this primal, lizard-brain thing of, 'Oh, this isn't a fun scare. It's a survival scare. ("On Immersive Virtual Reality" 2018)

Commercial VR and AR applications need to be sensitive to the hardware's ability to generate virtually real experiences and need to think carefully about how to design simulations with them in mind. Specific design elements of simulations are known to affect the probability that a simulation will give its users virtually real experiences. An ethics for VR and AR applications requires that designers become sensitive to how these elements can be modified to decrease the risk of virtual trauma while increasing user engagement and enjoyment (see Fig. 1).

Less Virtually Real	More Virtually Real
3rd Person Perspective	1st Person Perspective
Non-Diegetic Sound	Only Diegetic Sound
Unrealistic Settings	Contemporary Settings
Impossible Physics	Naturalistic Physics
Poor NPC A.I.	Human-Like NPC A.I.

Fig. 1. A selection of features demonstrating the dimensional nature of virtually real experiences. Developers of VR/AR applications should adjust these parameters to tailor their simulations so as to avoid harmful or undesirable user experiences.

The success of virtual reality exposure therapies (VRET) support this point (Rizzo et al. 2017). VRET environments are created to simulate, as realistically as possible, real-world exposure therapy treatments for phobias and post-traumatic stress disorders. To date they show positive results, comparable to traditional treatments, demonstrating the power of virtually real experiences.

Best practice should focus on avoiding user harm through all phases of an appli-cation's design and development. We suggest that these practices should be aimed at following The Equivalence Principle (TEP) when it comes to ethical simulation design:

TEP: If it would be wrong to allow a person to have an experience of something in the real world, then it would be wrong to allow a person to a virtually real analogue of that experience. As a simulation's likelihood of inducing virtually-real experiences in its subject increases, so too should the justification for the use of the simulation (Bliznyuk 2019; Ramirez 2018a; Ffiske 2020; Ramirez and LaBarge 2018)

Ethical developers of VR and AR content should take care to fine-tune their application's parameters, in line with TEP, to enhance user experience and minimize user harm. Because these applications are more likely to give users virtually real experiences they should be subject to greater ethical scrutiny. For example, although virtually unreal simulations of murder or torture are common features of games, virtually real simulations of the same actions have the potential to harm users and, in rare cases, can affect real-world user behavior (Ramirez 2020). For this reason, developers of virtual reality simulations that include actions that would be bad for us to do in the real world need to be developed with special ethical care to avoid harming users. Also because of this, developers of applications for VR and AR should not use comparisons of violent content in non-VR/AR games to justify violent content in their own applications. These new media are psychologically unique and require their own ethical frameworks.

3.5 Dissociation/Derealization

Madary and Metzinger (2016) have cautioned that prolonged use of VR can affect a user's perception of reality. Dissociation (separating yourself from your experiences) and derealization (loss of a sense of reality) are concerns about long-term use of virtual reality technologies. There's evidence that supports Madary and Metzinger's concerns about the effects that VR and AR may have on our perception of reality and our ability to keep track of real and virtual experience (Aardema et al. 2010).

Madary and Metzinger (2016) also worry that long-term use of virtual reality technologies can have negative personal and social consequences if users neglect their real-world health, nutrition, home-life, and social obligations because they prefer to spend time in virtual worlds.

Ethical developers of commercial VR and AR applications should thus take care to prompt their users to exit or suspend use to minimize these problems. Such prompts have become more and more common in traditional media. Little research has been done, to date, on the severity of this problem and it's likely, given the immersive experiences that these technologies offer, that stronger nudges will be necessary to avoid the dangers of prolonged use.

3.6 The Special Case of Children

The Oculus Rift owner's manual recognizes that children raise a special set of ethical issues when it comes to VR. They caution owners that:

[t]his product is not a toy and should not be used by children under the age of 13, as the headset is not sized for children and improper sizing can lead to discomfort or adverse health effects, and younger children are in a critical period in visual development...Adults should monitor children age 13 and older who are using

or have used the headset for any of the symptoms described in these health and safety warnings ...and should limit the time children spend using the headset and ensure they take breaks during use. Prolonged use should be avoided, as this could negatively impact hand-eye coordination, balance, and multi-tasking ability. Adults should monitor children closely during and after use of the headset for any decrease in these abilities. (Oculus Health and Safety Manual)

VR and AR hardware and applications are likely to become deeply integrated into the future structure of society, and in line with the ACM code of ethics, special care and precaution need to be exercised when designing applications that may be attractive to children. Because very young children are especially likely to develop issues with derealization and depersonalization as a result of time spent in virtual environments, we believe that it would be wrong to develop VR/AR applications directly (or indirectly) for children. As we learn more about the effects of these technologies on developing brains and minds, such precautions may become less (or even more) necessary.

4   A Code of Ethics for VR/AR: Designing for the Common Good

Table 3. VR/AR Code of Ethics

• Design simulations to avoid being more virtually real than necessary
• The Equivalence Principle sets an upper limit on ethically acceptable virtual and augmented reality applications
• Take special care when designing VR and AR applications used by children 13 years or older and do not develop applications for children younger than 13 years
• Incorporate design elements into VR applications to avoid prolonged and sustained use
• Applications intended to change (nudge) user behavior must be transparent, avoid manipulation, and serve both the user and public goods
• Be mindful of the fact that content that may not be problematic if experienced using traditional media may *become* problematic if experienced as virtually real
• User data should only be collected as-needed for application functionality and should be encrypted and deleted as soon as is feasible to protect user privacy and identity-theft
• Simulated environments (social, educational, governmental) that aim to be integrated into the infrastructure of society should receive the highest level of ethical scrutiny

The code of ethics that we propose in Table 3 above draws from the decades of experience enshrined in the codes of both the ACM, the IEEE, and our own research on user responses to simulated environments. Developers of commercial VR and AR applications have ethical duties to avoid unnecessary harm to users and to consider the massive impact on basic social structures that these technologies are likely to have in the 21st century. Ethical VR and AR engineers (both software and hardware) must be mindful of both their impacts on users and society. The more axes in our code that a potential commercial application makes contact with (e.g., a VR app aimed at nudging teenagers toward healthy habits), the more ethical scrutiny such applications should be subjected to both internally, by development teams, and externally by government regulatory bodies. Understanding not only the role of virtually real experiences in the ethics of VR and AR but also how such experiences can be made more or less likely by concrete design choices, is essential to ethical VR and AR development.

To illustate a proper application of this code, we briefly look at one case of ethical virtual reality development, Sisu VR's sexual harassment VR training simulations. Sisu VR's simulations are aimed at both the user and public good. Sexual harassment not only harms individuals but also creates a workplace (and social) culture that, overall, generates negtive utility. Harnessing the perspective-taking and immersive capacities of VR, Sisu VR's simulations provide users with different points of view about how to confront, pacify, intervene, or even keep silent in those viewpoints helps ingrain ethical habits into the user. The simulations themselves aim to be virtually real enough (e.g., first-person, realistic settings, etc.) so that they engage users emotionally but not so virtually real that they traumatize them (e.g., text-box prompts artificially limit user choice as many VRET simulations do).

The objective of Sisu VR's product is to empower users to make morally civil decisions through "passive and active involvement…where the user is required to "hammer" home the activity or action" (Kenwright 2014). For example, the user is prompted to speak a variety of dialogue responses out loud to in-game characters. To complete the training, one has to select and speak a set of phrases containing both professional and ethical language. Practicing morally civil dialogue in a VR context may empower the user to eventually manifest such actions in a real life context.

5 Conclusion

Virtual reality technologies have been in development throughout the 20th century and are only now becoming widely available commercially. As consumers and developers explore the new spaces and possibilities opened up by VR and AR hardware, we must work proactively to avoid creating unethical applications of these technologies. As these technologies become more deeply integrated into the everyday fabric of our social, political, and educational institutions and as they become a part of the work-environment, we must make sure that such new developments are met with equally new and important ethical constraints. The code contained here represents one early attempt to express the most critical ethical considerations that VR and AR developers should build into all levels of their project workflows.

References

Aardema, F., O'Connor, K., Côté, S., Taillon, A.: Virtual reality induces dissociation and lowers sense of presence in objective reality. Cyberpsychol. Behav. Soc. Netw. **13**(4), 429–35 (2010)
Bliznyuk, A.: Ethical guidelines in virtual reality: towards a code of conduct in research, 5 February 2019. https://www.rm.wi.tum.de/fileadmin/w00bjc/www/Leaderschip_Learning_Innovation/Dokumente/Ethical_Guidelines_for_VR_TUM_11022019.pdf

Cummings, J., Bailenson, J.: How immersive is enough? A meta-analysis of the effect of immersive technology on user presence. Media Psychol. **19**(2), 272–309 (2016)

Ffiske, T.: Ethics in virtual and augmented reality in the 2020s. Virtual Perceptions (2020). https://www.virtualperceptions.com/ethics-vr-ar-2020/

Herrera, F., Bailenson, J.N., Weisz, E., Ogle, E., Zaki, J.: Building long-term empathy: a large-scale comparison of traditional and virtual reality perspective-taking. PLoS One **13**(10), e0204494 (2018). https://doi.org/10.1371/journal.pone.0204494

Hotchkiss, S.: In San Jose's Japantown, contemporary transience takes on historical weight. KQED, 18 June 2019. https://www.kqed.org/arts/13859833/transient-existence-artobjectgallery-san-jose-japantown

Kaser, R.: Ready player what? Facebook announces a new VR social network. The Next Web, 25 September 2019. https://thenextweb.com/facebook/2019/09/25/ready-player-what-facebook-announces-a-new-vr-social-network/

Kenwright, B.: Virtual reality: ethical challenges and dangers. Technology and Society, 14 January 2014. https://technologyandsociety.org/virtual-reality-ethical-challenges-and-dangers/

Matney, L.: Oculus eclipses $100 million in VR content sales. Tech Crunch, 25 September 2019. https://techcrunch.com/2019/09/25/oculus-eclipses-100-million-in-vr-content-sales/

Madary, M., Metzinger, T.K.: Real virtuality: a code of ethical conduct. Recommendations for good scientific practice and the consumers of VR-Technology. Front. Robot. AI **3**, 1–23 (2016). https://doi.org/10.3389/frobt.2016.00003

"Oculus Health and Safety" Manual. https://securecdn.oculus.com/sr/oculusrifts-warning-english. Accessed 27 Feb 2020

On Immersive Virtual Reality Technology and the Ethics Questions It Raises, VR Life, 8 October 2019. https://www.vrlife.news/immersive-experiences-virtual-reality-design-ethics/

Ramirez, E.: Ecological and ethical issues in virtual reality research: a call for increased scrutiny. Philos. Psychol. **32**(2), 211–233 (2018a)

Ramirez, E.: It's dangerous to think virtual reality is an empathy machine. Aeon, 26 October 2018 (2018b). https://aeon.co/ideas/its-dangerous-to-think-virtual-reality-is-an-empathy-machine

Ramirez, E., LaBarge, S.: Real moral problems in the use of virtual reality. Ethics Inf. Technol. **20**(4), 249–263 (2018). https://doi.org/10.1007/s10676-018-9473-5

Ramirez, E.: How to (dis)solve the gamer's dilemma. Ethical Theory Moral Pract. **23**(1), 141–161 (2020). https://doi.org/10.1007/s10677-019-10049-z

Rizzo, A., et al.: Virtual reality applications for the assessment and treatment of PTSD. In: Bowles, Stephen V., Bartone, Paul T. (eds.) Handbook of Military Psychology, pp. 453–471. Springer, Cham (2017). https://doi.org/10.1007/978-3-319-66192-6_27

Rogers, S.: 2019: The year virtual Reality Gets Real. Forbes, 21 June 2019. https://www.forbes.com/sites/solrogers/2019/06/21/2019-the-year-virtual-reality-gets-real/#1008d2296ba9

Slater, M., et al.: The ethics of realism in virtual and augmented reality. Front. Virtual Reality (2020). https://doi.org/10.3389/frvir.2020.00001

Sunstein, C.: The ethics of nudging. Yale J. Regul. **32**(2), 414–450 (2015)

On Trusting a Cyber Librarian: How Rethinking Underlying Data Storage Infrastructure Can Mitigate Risks of Automation

Maria Joseph Israel[1]([⊠]), Mark Graves[2], and Ahmed Amer[1]

[1] Santa Clara University, Santa Clara, CA 95053, USA
{misrael,aamer}@scu.edu
[2] University of Notre Dame, Notre Dame, IN 46556, USA
mgraves@nd.edu

Abstract. The increased ability of Artificial Intelligence (AI) technologies to generate and parse texts will inevitably lead to more proposals for AI's use in the semantic sentiment analysis (SSA) of textual sources. We argue that instead of focusing solely on debating the merits of automated versus manual processing and analysis of texts, it is critical to also rethink our underlying storage and representation formats. Further, we argue that accommodating multivariate metadata exemplifies how underlying data storage infrastructure can reshape the ethical debate surrounding the use of such algorithms. In other words, a system that employs automated analysis typically requires manual intervention to assess the quality of its output, and thus demands that we select between multiple competing NLP algorithms. Settling on an algorithm or ensemble is not a decision that has to be made a *priori*, but when made, involves implicit ethical considerations. An underlying storage and representation system that allows for the existence and evaluation of multiple variants of the same source data, while maintaining attribution to the individual sources of each variant, would be a much-needed enhancement to existing storage technologies, as well as, facilitate the interpretation of proliferating AI semantic analysis technologies. To this end, we take the view that AI functions as (or acts as an implicate meta-ordering of) the SSA sociotechnical system in a manner that allows for novel solutions for safer cyber curation. This can be done by holding the attribution of source data in symmetrical relationship to its further multiple differing annotations as coexisting data points within a single publishing ecosystem. In this way, the AI program allows for the annotations of individual and aggregate data by means of competing algorithmic models, or varying degrees of human intervention. We discuss the feasibility of such a scheme, using our own infrastructure model, (*MultiVerse*), as an illustrative model for such a system, and analyse its ethical implications.

Keywords: Intelligent systems · AI-Human problem · Semantic sentiment analysis · Artificial intelligence · Ethics of AI · Cyber curation of scholarship

N. Shaghaghi et al. (Eds.): INTETAIN 2020, LNICST 377, pp. 25–42, 2021.
https://doi.org/10.1007/978-3-030-76426-5_3

1   Introduction

Artificial Intelligence (AI) is increasingly touching and structuring our lives. AI helps enhance our ordinary experiences with its tailored news, real time traffic updates, more accurate weather forecasts, better personal time management, delivery of online meetings, global email communications, and cost-efficient healthcare diagnosis. Where the moral nature of the personal use of AI in these examples is largely beneficial, implicit and nominal, its impact becomes more direct and ethically ambiguous when employed essentially to judge people. Today AI is being used to predict one's ethnicity [29], credit-worthiness for a loan or mortgage [7,39], academic grade [38], or political leanings [54]. More recently, the literal judgement in court sentencing is increasingly influenced by "risk assessment" AI with potentially dire consequences to these developments [8,71,72]. Although seemingly innocuous, the application of algorithms for the micro-evaluations of a text demands moral explication. The use of Natural Language Processing (NLP) algorithms varies from its application to judge the veracity of a text's authorship, to the assessment of a written work's sub-text such as the writer's sentiment in the piece [20,60]. Because automated sentiment analysis and similar textual processing become more efficient as one increases the data available for the AI, it seems unlikely that this practice will cease, indeed it may be the only way to handle the exponential volume of automatically generated text flooding online media channels. The interconnectedness of data sets used by the AI mean there are no neutral or bias-free domains of knowledge. The need to automatically identify bad actors posting online news [2,49] or social media [58,75], can wrongfully limit an individual's freedom of speech or be gamed effectively by deliberate bad actors or states. These situations contextualize the ethical and professional domain of the hypothetical cyber-archivist, the AI librarian or scholarly assistant who processes written data and annotates it for further analysis or classification.

AI's usefulness for all such cyber-archivist tasks is undeniable, given its ability to quickly sift through massive datasets and to detect and trace patterns that would be impossible for a human to process with any efficiency [26,57]. For example, given human limitations and financial considerations, combing through online media posts to detect trends in public sentiment, or to detect spam in individual post comments, would require more personnel hours than could reasonably be brought to bear by any individual party or organization. As more and more data about our world becomes available and meets computing power to process it as never before, this apparent usefulness can only grow. But whether or not such usefulness is truly beneficial, or merely an invitation to hand over human judgment to fallible algorithms, given the potential for bias and error, is a topic of intense debate [33,36,41,47,67]. And when AI is used to process and pass judgment upon large data sets, attempts to improve the quality of an AI solution may be hindered by the very nature of the data that leads us to embrace such solutions – specifically, its vastness. For example, if an AI model that has processed vast volumes of data is found to be flawed, then correcting such a flaw and embracing a new model may be impossible without entirely reprocessing the vast datasets involved. This could mean that opportunities to embrace new, more trustworthy, AI models (or to simply tweak existing models to correct a minor flaw), would be lost to us without sufficient information being preserved regarding more than simply the results of prior processing.

To debate the merits and perils of applying such technologies without consideration for how the underlying technological infrastructure could be changed to promote or discourage risks, is a necessary ongoing ethical conversation, for any blinkered views could lead to an inaccurate and potentially harmful AI model.

Given the fundamental nature of this problem for all AI models we will consider the role of automated algorithms in rendering judgment without reference to a specific domain, that is, in its most general form as a processor of data that mimics human judgment. More specifically, we look to how artificial automation is analogous to an archivist or librarian citing, archiving, and scholarly critiquing data. We are, therefore, dealing with the question of whether or not a cyber-archivist can be both useful and safely trusted. In deciding whether or not to place AI technology in a position of trust, the question is not merely whether the AI can be trusted to offer good judgments, but also critical is how that technology, and the judgements it makes, is integrated into the broader system. The questions of whether or not an AI's judgment can be trusted is not therefore our focus, but rather we look at the manner in which it is best applied. We illustrate the potential to overlook this by illustrating how underlying infrastructure can impact the amount of trust placed in AI, and we do this by describing our system, *MultiVerse*[1], which allows us to support the coexistence and processing of multiple (competing, and potentially conflicting) decisions within the same archive. In other words, we argue that the ethical dilemma posed by whether or not AI can be trusted in roles of judgment can be mitigated by building better technological infrastructure underlying such AIs and affecting how AI and humans interact and collaborate. Specifically, we use the analogy of a flawed cyber-archivist, being trusted thanks to the construction of a suitably resilient library, rather than being the subject of attempts to create a flawless AI to serve as a trustworthy cyber-archivist.

---

[1] The term *"Multiverse"* is widely used in different domains to describe different concepts. In science, it refers to everything that exists in totality [13] - as a hypothetical group of multiple universes. In quantum-computation, it refers to a reality in which many classical computations can occur simultaneously [19]. In a bibliographic-archival system, referred to as "Archival Multiverse", it denotes "the plurality of evidentiary texts (records in multiple forms and cultural contexts), memory-keeping practices and institutions, bureaucratic and personal motivations, community perspectives and needs, and cultural and legal constructs" [24](Pluralizing the Archival Curriculum Group). In Information Systems, it deals with the complexity, plurality, and increasingly post-physical nature of information flows [31]. Our use of the term *"MultiVerse"* with a capitalized 'V' denotes a version of our proposed digital infrastructure for a richer metadata representation, which captures the nature of representing multiple versions of a source data object, and was named partially due to the system's earliest tests being focused on translated poetry verses.

The rest of the paper is organized as follows: Sect. 2 discusses the related work covering the efforts in tackling the trustworthiness of automated systems and the importance of human-computer interaction. Section 3 further leads the ethical discussions of AI/ML as understood by the proponents and opponents of cyber-archivists. Section 4 briefly describes our project, *MultiVerse*, as an illustrative example to discuss the importance of the underlying data storage infrastructure of an automated system, and broader ethical concerns. In particular, our focus in this paper is on the broader conflicting ethical implications that can be impacted by such focus on systems infrastructure (e.g., data privacy versus veracity, accuracy versus authenticity, efficiency versus transparency, and the ongoing need for more explainable AI)

2 Related Work: The Problem of Flawed Librarians

With our use of a library analogy and its focused use of text analysis and anno-tation, it is necessary to acknowledge the efforts that lead us to this work. In particular, there is a large body of works on automating the processing of tex-tual data and considerable recent efforts in tackling the trustworthiness of such automated systems. One particularly promising approach has been to consider how humans and AI can most beneficially interact. Our proposal, to focus more on the underlying storage infrastructure as a means of mitigating potential prob-lems, builds upon our ongoing work, and a considerable body of prior research, in the domain of data provenance.

Tools and techniques in automating data science, also known as AutoML/ AutoAI, are the subject of research in many companies and open source com-munities [22,46]. Given the speed and cost-effectiveness of AI for such tasks, there is optimism in the industry that AI/ML systems can eventually replace the thousands of human workers who are currently involved in making deci-sions, for example, automated comments moderation on social media [44]. Other examples of automated ML and NLP techniques for semantic sentiment anal-ysis include: financial microblogs and news [21], twitter [52,62,63], big social data [25], clinical analytics [59], specific language-based literature [3,48,50], and publishing domains [9,12,73]. These systems have the potential to perform mod-eration much faster than human moderators, which is attractive for more than simple performance/cost reasons (since removal of harmful content quickly can reduce the harm it causes). Automating humanly laborious tasks not only facil-itates scalability, it is also promoted for its potential to introduce consistency in performing allocated tasks/decisions. But this is not necessarily a good thing, if an error or a bias is consistently and reliably propagated across vast volume of data and large number of people.

Despite the many benefits of automated ML and NLP techniques, their use introduces new challenges. In an AI-automated system, identifying tasks that should be automated and configuring tools to perform those tasks is crucial. Perhaps there are those who view the biggest hurdle in accepting AI-generated models to be the lack of trust and transparency, given the potential for large-scale harm due to errors [46]. Attempting to understand an intelligent agent's intent, performance, future plans, and reasoning process is a challenge. Accurate automated systems are not an easy task. These challenges place a greater emphasis on how AI and humans interact, and prior research on this point – Computer Supported Cooperative Work (CSCW) research – has established that a fundamental socio-technical gap exists between how individuals manage information in everyday social situations versus how this is done explicitly through the use of technology [5,30]. Often, technical systems fail to capture the flexibility or ambiguity that is inherent in normal social conditions [1]. Concurrently, research findings reveal the deficiencies of AI in making decisions that require it to be attuned to the sensitivities in cultural context or to the differences in linguistic cues [1,65,73]. These failures to detect individual differences of context and content can have serious consequences, for example, in failing to distinguish hate speech and misinformation from newsworthiness in automated news feeds can have serious consequences. In fact, these failures to address context issues and misinformation on automated *Facebook* or *WhatsApp* content regulation arguably contributed to violence in Myanmar [66]. Overcoming these obstacles requires human ingenuity and the moral to engage artificial intelligent systems.

To overcome these challenges and to boost user's morale to act upon an artificial intelligent system requires human intervention. The Human-in-the-loop system or Human-guided machine learning [30] taps the speed and processing power along with human intuition and morality. Hybrid AI-Human systems forge a strong collaboration between artificial and organic systems and this opens a way to solve difficult tasks that were once thought to be intractable. To be ethical, this man-computer symbiosis must be characterised by the cooperation of machines with humans. The machine and AI systems should not be designed to replace the natural skills and abilities of humans, but rather to co-exist with and assist humans in making their work and lives more efficient and effective. Fortunately, some progress towards this goal has been made. Some works that combine human-in-the-loop collaboration with AI for solving difficult problems include, but not limited to: image classification [70], object annotation [61,69], protein folding [56,68], disaster relief distribution [28], galaxy discovery [43], and online content regulation [35].

Human-Computer Interaction (HCI) and in particular Computer-Supported Cooperative Work (CSCW) are not radically new concepts in spite of their current urgency. The concept of symbiotic computing has been around since the early 1960s "Man-Machine Symbiosis" work by J. C. R. Licklider [42]. Licklider envisioned computers serving as partners whose interactive design as intelligent agents would collaborate with human beings to solve interesting and worthy problems in computing and society. His view can be universally applied to any technologies that extend or enhance humans abilities to interact with their environments, and can therefore be considered a persistent question surrounding our interaction with AI.

More generally, as long as human operators and new automated systems simultaneously adapt, they will co-evolve. However, it remains important to remember that the socio-technical gaps that CSCW problems generalize, are never completely resolved and continued efforts to "round off the edges" [1] of such coevolution is necessary. Given the shortcomings of automated tools and the required careful human administration of these tools, we propose that instead of developing fully automated systems that require perfection for complete autonomy, researchers and designers should make efforts to improve the current state of mixed-initiative regulation systems where humans work alongside AI systems.

Since automated tools are likely to perform worse than humans on cases where understanding nuance and context is crucial, perhaps the most significant consideration is determining when automated tools should perform certain tasks by themselves and when results of such tasks need to be reviewed by human actors. We echo calls by previous studies for building systems that ensure that the interactions between automation and human activities foster robust communities that function well at scale [65].

MultiVerse looks at how an AI's improved infrastructure, for the preservation of both source data and its annotations (including AI generated annotations), can help grant greater resilience to decisions making capacities of AI-human systems. Our approach simplifies these decisions, as well as, allots for their safe reversal or delaying their implementation. In this way, a boon is made for explanatory data that supports these decisions of critical importance in the creation of accessible AI that also complies with the legislative demands for transparency like the EU's General Data Protection Regulation (GDPR) [32,34,64]. It does so by preserving more data regarding decisions/outcomes (i.e., automated results and judgments), their annotations as they are produced. In its support of the preservation of multiple versions of data, our approach is commensurate with both AI (XAI) algorithms used in a black box neural networks and those transparent box presentations of data such as decision trees. These features combine to grant greater flexibility in how humans verify the results or describe its data sources or when the results require explanation. To offer such a richer storage infrastructure, we leverage a novel architecture built upon our own extensions of data provenance research. Data provenance research is focused on the preservation and presentation of the origins and transformations of stored data, and has typically been narrowly employed for the management of project data like scientific workflow or code management [4,10,16,27,53].

3   The Proponents and Opponents of Cyber-Archivists

Opposing Camps of AI: While AI systems present enormous potential benefits, they are not without problems. As a result, there are opposing camps arguing extreme views on the acceptance or rejection of AI. The optimists of AI, like Ray Kurzweil, an inventor and futurist [40] and other AI enthusiasts [45], predict a utopian future of immortality, immense wealth, and all-engaging robotic assistants to humans, ushered in with the singularity AI help. These techno-optimists believe that Genetics, Nanotechnology and Robotics (GNR) with 'strong AI' will revolutionize everything "allowing humans to harness speed, memory capacities and knowledge sharing ability of computers and our brain being directly connected to the cloud" [40]. On the other hand, there are those who argue AI risks and its potential dystopian consequences. The critics of strong AI include the likes of Bill Joy, a computer engineer, co-founder of Sun Microsystems, and venture capitalist [37], Stephen Hawking, a theoretical physicist [14], and Nick Bostrom, a philosopher at the University of Oxford [11]. They believe that AI is "threatening to make humans an endangered species and second rate status" [45]. But there are others like Sam Altman, an entrepreneur and CEO of "OpenAI" and Michio Kaku, a theoretical physicist and futurist, who believe that AI could be controlled through "openAI" and effective regulation [55]. They believe that humans could learn to exploit the power of the computers to augment their own skills and always stay a step ahead of AI or at least not be at a disadvantage. The spectrum on this is expansive as it ranges between the extremes of reactive fear and complete embrace of AI. Both accounts fail to make a rational and ethical assessment of AI. The practical debate, the real question, is not *whether* AI technologies should be adopted, but *how* they can be most beneficially, and most safely, adopted.

Algorithmic Transparency: How algorithmic decisions are embedded in a larger AI system is difficult and specialized area of study. When an AI system produces outputs that can lead to harm, the likelihood of realizing that, let alone remedying it, can often be blamed on a lack of transparency regarding how the outcomes were reached. This has led to increasing demands for algorithmic transparency. But the immediate claim that these problems can be remedied by greater algorithmic transparency offers little more than the self-evident. Basically, any process or technology that does not offer perspective on its manner of operation is inherently suspect, and unlikely to be trusted. There is, of course, a place to discuss the philosophical notion of transparency as an ideal. Indeed, it can be argued that the genealogy for any one practical instantiation of the transparent is ultimately found in epistemological speculation concerning the nature of truth.

Recently, transparency has once again taken a prominent place in public governance systems, where social activists strive for greater government accountability. In AI, as with these practices, transparency is touted as a way to disclose the inherent truth of a system. In the context of AI, it is understood as taking a peek inside the black-box of algorithms that enable its automated operations. However, we view transparency for AI systems more broadly, not as merely seeing phenomena inside a system, but rather, across the system, as argued by Ananny and Crowford, and Crawford [6,15]. That is, not merely as code and data in a specific algorithm, but rather to see "transparency as socio-technical systems that do not contain complexity, but enact complexity by connecting to and intertwining with assemblages of humans and non-humans" [6]. In other words, it is better to take account of the more complete model of AI and this includes a comprehensive view of how humans and algorithms mutually intersect within the system [15]. Without a sound understanding of the nature of algorithmic transparency and decision making, a false conflation of the "algorithmic operation" and human policy failings is possible. This is an especially troubling occurrence when inherent bias in an AI model is applied to the judicial system as evident in the the scandalous *COMPAS* revelations about the Correctional Offender Management Profiling for Alternative Sanctions algorithm [8, 71, 72].

Accountability Beyond Algorithmic Transparency: In the ideal, algorithms are transparent when they are predicative, enable benefits given they are fundamentally neutral, unbiased. As stated previously, it is logically possible that deterministic, flawed or discriminatory algorithms may on occasion produce equitable outcomes – an AI system must be continuously evaluated [23]. On this reality, Dwork and Mulligan state concerning AI "the reality is a far messier mix of technical and human curating" [23]. AI has moral implications, but never in isolation of the context in which it is applied. When AI has a negative impact, the assumption of fault and responsibility differs based on your perspective and role.

If algorithms are presented as an open book, then the developers of algorithms have less responsibility when they are misapplied. On the other hand, if algorithms are constructed as a black-box, or an autonomous agent operating with an opaque logic, then the users are denied accountability for how algorithms make decisions that affect them. In essence, the developers of such systems are asking that their judgment be trusted blindly, and would therefore be expected to shoulder more responsibility for any future problems.

There are also different default assumptions depending on the role one plays. Generally speaking, the present legal system does not hold firms responsible for the misuse of algorithms they develop [46, 72], but they can be held responsible for systems they sell. From the perspective of software developers, their algorithms are neutral and so a failure is more likely assumed to be due to users' thrusting algorithms into fallible contexts of biased data and improper use. At the users' end, algorithms are difficult to identify and comprehend and therefore they aren't typically held accountable for the ethical implications of their use [46]. [18] and [74] suggest that as algorithms seem to be unpredictable and inscrutable, assigning the responsibility to developers or users is ineffective and even impossible, but firms could be better held responsible for the ethical implications of their products' use. [46] conceptualizes algorithms as value-laden in that algorithms create moral consequences, reinforce or undercut ethical principles, and enable or diminish stakeholder rights and dignity. In other words, ascribing responsibility for algorithms resulting in harm is very tricky. This lack of clarity is a hurdle to responsible and ethical adoption of algorithms in critical roles, e.g., when they are placed in roles that require them to pass judgment. But it is insufficient to say that these risks need only greater transparency of the algorithm, for the algorithm alone is never responsible for the outcome, and transparency needs to expose more than the workings of an individual algorithm to offer the most resilience and trust possible. Moreover, an algorithm's transparency and one's relevant faith in it involves the quality of data it processes, the structure of the AI from which it operates and larger socio-cultural considerations introduced with human involvement.

Without striving for transparency beyond the specific algorithm, i.e., striving for a broader, more holistic view of the system, we may miss opportunities to build better and more resilient AI-enhanced systems. Returning to our analogy of a cyber-archivist, we would argue that simply offering a view of the workings of a particular instance of such an AI is to pass on the opportunity to really understand the overall system and lessen later opportunities to harden it against failures. Specifically, imagine if one particular algorithm for processing a large dataset was deemed to be the best, and was employed for several years with acceptable performance (including full transparency regarding its implementation), but that it was discovered that its outputs were flawed for certain edge cases that could have been caught with a superior algorithm. The only way to remedy this, would seem to be to reprocess the entire dataset (assuming it is still available), and to compare the outputs of the algorithms. But if the data storage infrastructure had the facility to support the operation of both algorithms, and the maintenance of the provenance of their outputs, then this process would be feasible without a reprocessing of the potentially vast datasets (assuming they are still available). It's exactly this kind of increased accountability and accounting that is possible if we aim for transparency that goes beyond the algorithm alone, and is enabled with infrastructure that can support such a goal. Our *MultiVerse* system is an example of such an infrastructure.

4   Trusting the Cyber-Archivist – *MultiVerse*

MultiVerse is designed as a digital data infrastructure that preserves multiple perspectives, and thereby allows better support for multicultural digital content. We contend that in order to better support transparency, intercultural ethics, and more ethical digital media curation across cultures, such an infrastructure is needed. So, what is *MultiVerse*? *MultiVerse* is a digital data representation infrastructure intended to track provenance of multi-varied translations of scholarly texts and their derivatives. Provenance can be defined as the recording of the history of user activities that create and transform data. The *MultiVerse* infrastructure allows users to remix/combine existing translations and/or add one's own personal translations at will and add annotations to it. Annotations can be made regarding the scope, context, or other relevant metadata. *MultiVerse* is primarily concerned with the metadata needed to store such provenance alongside the data to which it refers. In this project, provenance tracking is done by capturing all translations (users' activities) without any preferences, prejudices, and prizes (value judgements/correctness), at the time of their composition.

To realize this concept, we have used the well known 13th century Italian poet Dante Aligheri's the *Divine Comedy*, and some of its many English translations [17]. We have combined these into a single repository that allows the remixing and composition of new translations, while offering detailed tracking of the origins and transformations of such texts. A user has the option of either collating different versions of verses or adding in his/her versions of verses from/to this repository to compose his/her unique version of translation of the *Divine Comedy*. Moreover, the user can tag richer semantic metadata like context, intent, scope, or tone/sentiment to his/her composition. Multiple versions of the *Divine Comedy* are thereby stored in a single repository with rich version histories. A high level architectural overview and the user API of *MultiVerse* are depicted in Fig. 1.

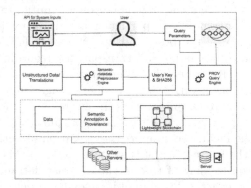

Fig. 1. *MultiVerse*'s architecture overview

The primary purpose of this project is to demonstrate the importance of a robust data storage technology, in the context of human-in-the-loop system, that captures and represents pluralistic views cutting across individuals' cultural, ethnic, religious, gender, social, political, economic, emotional, etc., stances/ viewpoints. At its very beginning, a key design principle of *MultiVerse* is to enhance technology to represent pluralistic multicultural perspectives of all users, rather than after-the-fact. This is achieved by designing *MultiVerse* which enables users to record not only their views irrespective of their correctness but also accommodate their contexts and intents.

We might ask, "what are the benefits of this technology design principle in the first place?" Without arguments, it can be stated that all voices (decisions/judgements) are preserved. Single versions can be presented on demand. But the history and identity of those who selected the individual versions and the provenance of the documents can be permanently stored using blockchain technology [51] and can not be tampered with in any way. By virtue of its immutability, *MultiVerse* becomes a means to establish the source of any loss of nuances, and makes arguments (by allowing future archaeology on such repositories) about the correct form moot. More precisely, while it does not eliminate contention over the ideal translation, it does not force that debate to be fought over the preserved version. There need be no permanent winner, and past mistakes can be corrected in future revisions. But this leads us to consider the broader ethical implications of such multicultural pluralistic digital infrastructures.

In the context of AI, it helps to record the decisions of users and machines, and to preserve them for as long as they might be needed. Such logs are useful in case we need to revisit them, whether to better understand past behavior or to further enhance future decisions. As the underlying data storage repository in *MultiVerse* preserves all versions of decisions in an immutable manner, any additions, deletions, and modifications may be made as annotations without corrupting original logs, or conflicting with their subsequent versions. It thereby helps by protecting their lineage/provenance.

4.1   Using *MultiVerse*

A user creates a resource (multi-varied translated texts in our initial example, *MultiVerse*), either by copying an existing resource, or by newly translating a resource. For this new resource, or for an existing resource we wish to add to the system, *MultiVerse* generates a few standard properties, also known as the structural metadata for that resource. This metadata describes the resource, such as its type, size, creation date, and creator, and adds this information to a provenance log. The *Semantic Metadata Module* extends this mechanism to allow generation of user-specified descriptive properties such as context, scope, and sentiments. These additional properties are a concrete example of what we mean by "richer semantic metadata." These properties will be based on the uploaded data as well as newly derived sources. Consequently it is possible to register new translations for existing resources and/or generate a new resource. This new resource can be described as a source, with its own location, i.e., context (which would be, for example, specified through a URL). It could, for example, be generated from an existing resource via a copy operation (where that existing resource would be the source for this copy). To help track a copied resource's origin, *Semantic Metadata Module* adds a source property, which becomes part of the provenance of the resource. This source property is added to the new copy, which links it to the original URL.

Once a user integrates a translated version of the data into his/her work space, the user can proceed to the next task in the plan. In the next task, if a user chooses to make his/her own translation, the *Semantic Metadata Module* generates a *hasTranslation* property and enables a user to tag information about the user-as-the-translator, its creation time, context, and scope of the translation. Using the provenance log, the *Semantic Annotation-Provenance Module* will help document the data's provenance into annotated provenance documents that contain both structural as well as user-specified descriptive metadata.

Given the final derived product's URL, anyone granted access to *MultiVerse* can trace backward following the links in *hasSource* and *hasTranslation* properties to discover the input data and relevant user-specified metadata entries. This kind of query would not be possible without the added metadata (i.e., the semantically-enrichable provenance framework we have proposed in *MultiVerse*). Adding this metadata would increase the storage demands of the system as a whole, but these would be increases in capacity demands (simply the volume of data stored, as opposed to the needed storage system performance), which is arguably a cheaper resource than the time, energy, and temporary storage demands of having to reconstitute such information at a later point in time. In other words, assuming that it is possible to reconstitute the varied versions of our data at a later date (which is not necessarily possible), then there is a tradeoff between efficient space utilization today, and the cost of future computation and data retrieval demands tomorrow. The decision to store such metadata thereby holds efficiency considerations, in addition to the added transparency it could provide.

MultiVerse is not just a repository of multivariate data, but a means of ensuring the preservation of those versions against malicious action attempting to rewrite history, hence the immutability requirement is incorporated into *MultiVerse*. To keep such a repository consistent, it is structured as an immutable data store, allowing the addition of new content and amendments, but disallowing any modification or deletion of data that has been committed to this store. The immutable aspect of *MultiVerse* is achieved by adapting a basic model of blockchain technology [51]. The technical details of blockchain technology is beyond the scope of this paper. The interactive aspects of *MultiVerse* are enabled by offering a user application programming interface (API) to annotate semantic analysis decisions and allow access to the repository in a secured manner. We discuss the ethical implications of the *MultiVerse* framework in the next subsection.

4.2   Ethical Considerations

A moral question that arises on *MultiVerse* is: How does *MultiVerse* change the ethical debate around allowing an algorithm to judge/annotate and provide an actionable opinion? Our approach, illustrated through the *MultiVerse* example, shows that it is possible to construct systems whose impacts are more easily reviewed and evaluated against each other (since multiple versions are readily accessible for comparison), or that allow decisions taken by an automated algorithm to be less permanent in their effect (since alternative results that have been preserved, can be retroactively embraced). In other words, by allowing for one of three outcomes:

1. The decisions can be undone by preserving results of the prior decision and superseding it by adopting an alternate decision at a later date;

2. If undoing is not possible, then perhaps it allows us to defer making the decision at all, if we delay the aggregation or selection amongst alternative annotations (judgements) until the latest possible point in time, we would have guaranteed the adoption of the best and fairest technology available for that decision; or finally,

3. Assuming that decisions can neither be undone nor delayed, it is still beneficial to have on hand the results of competing models, if only to aid the more rapid analysis and evaluation of new and improved models, and to improve and accelerate our understanding of where and how defunct models may have failed.

On the contrary, leaning too heavily on an ability to defer or delay decisions, or a false sense of immunity to bad decisions, can lead to more reckless human adoption of algorithmic decision-making technologies.

However, one view of what distinguishes human intelligence from AI in decision-making is our ability to make connections in ways that are not formalizable (through unconscious processes, for example, or by involving emotions). When seen from that perspective, an AI algorithm would be a tool enacting what is ultimately a human will. That human will may be inexplicable, but the algorithms can and should be transparent and open to revision, making it easier to adopt in an informed manner. The use of an infrastructure like *MultiVerse* may aid in documenting such open algorithms, or may host the results of more opaque algorithms. It does not dictate taking one approach or the other.

The moral considerations of *MultiVerse* are slightly different than the moral considerations of using AIs for sentiment analysis. Harm is mitigated by potentially making sure that no decision is necessarily permanent, or that bad decisions can be attributed to specific sources (allowing for greater accountability), but this still leaves concerns. It is possible to confuse the mitigation of harm with the elimination of the possibility of harm, which of course is not the case here. A decision can be revised if enough provenance data is available to retroactively consider alternatives, but the effects of decisions might not be reversible (e.g., we can learn to improve a sentencing algorithm, but cannot expect any data storage system to restore a single day of unjustly lost freedom. While it may be possible to retroactively determine what a sentence algorithm could have recommended, it is definitely not possible to undo a sentence that has already been served). A potential harm that could be introduced arises if users of *MultiVerse* are lulled into a sense of complacency, such that human errors that would result in poor decisions might be made more often. *MultiVerse* provides the ability to mitigate harms and add greater accountability, but it is still up to individual deployments of systems to actually monitor the performance of their "cyber-librarians" and to temper their decisions when there is doubt about the quality of their outputs.

A significant portion of the potential harm of automated systems can arise as a result of those systems shifting the focus of responsibility away from humans. In other words, when we lose accountability, harm caused by acting on AI-provided data would not necessarily be blamed on those who should have maintained human oversight of how we got there. A mechanism that can improve the accountability of such systems, improving tracking of problems to failures of algorithm selection or oversight, would therefore have the potential to encourage both system builders and system adopters, to be more conscientious and ethical (thanks to an awareness of provenance tracking), but may also be helped in their oversight tasks thanks to the long term evaluation and auditing of the performance of different algorithms. The different choices regarding whether we defer to the algorithms, when and how often we defer to the algorithms, or when and how often we defer to the algorithms that are deployed for a specific problem is a question related to best practices around auditing and system improvements.

Finally, one might perceive *MultiVerse* as a system that is deliberately designed to record too much metadata, thereby creating an unnecessary information overload; or as a scientific apparatus to dissect the intellectual work of others; or as a blockchain mechanism to prevent the ability to edit what is stored. This leads to the issue of (data) privacy in the context of immutability of stored information about persons interacting with *MultiVerse*. To prevent these undesired consequences, there is a choice, by design, for users either to opt out from recording all their creative activities or to opt in to reveal as much as it is needed or to choose documenting the synthesizing process of a digital product. Such decisions regarding opting in or out would affect what data is recorded by the system, but it's important to recognize that when it comes to the question of an individual's right to be forgotten, such a question is not simply decided by the presence or absence of data, but is a question of the retrievability of such data. A data store can be immutable, and hold data that is never completely removed, and yet can still honor an individual's right to be forgotten within such a system, for example, adapting users' data access and retrieval rights and policies as appropriate.

To return to the use a library analogy, we go beyond prior efforts by focusing less on making librarians less flawed, but instead highlighting how an improved library could perhaps lessen the risk of harm posed by less-than-perfect librarians, and help all who support and benefit from librarians to better support and improve the library.

5   Concluding Remarks and Further Applications

To demonstrate how rethinking underlying technical infrastructure can reshape the questions we face with AI, we illustrated an example of one such "rethought" realization of a data storage system. By combining elements of version control systems, trusted immutable stores, and provenance technologies, *MultiVerse* shows that we can defer and revise decisions between human and automated analysis.

Such an infrastructure functions as an example of how to critically rethink the either/or decision regarding the applicability of AI. In fact, this infrastructure is useful for any AI domain that involves NLP and text processing/classification of texts, etc. While we've used the analogy of a librarian, to emphasize that our focus is on systems that automate the processing and tagging of textual information, our arguments should hold for any data processing task that could involve AI. It, therefore, would have applications beyond scholarly articles and references, including domains like managing fake news, social media, synthetically generated media, legal and governmental processes, materials in the broader arts and sciences (beyond simple workflow management), and can encompass more than purely textual media and materials.

References

1. Ackerman, M.S.: The intellectual challenge of CSCW: the gap between social requirements and technical feasibility. Human-Comput. Interact. **15**(2–3), 179–203 (2000)
2. Al Asaad, B., Erascu, M.: A tool for fake news detection. In: 2018 20th International Symposium on Symbolic and Numeric Algorithms for Scientific Computing (SYNASC), pp. 379–386. IEEE (2018)
3. Alowaidi, S., Saleh, M., Abulnaja, O.: Semantic sentiment analysis of Arabic texts. Int. J. Adv. Comput. Sci. Appl. **8**(2), 256–262 (2017)
4. Altintas, I., Barney, O., Jaeger-Frank, E.: Provenance collection support in the kepler scientific workflow system. In: Moreau, L., Foster, I. (eds.) IPAW 2006. LNCS, vol. 4145, pp. 118–132. Springer, Heidelberg (2006). https://doi.org/10.1007/11890850_14
5. Amershi, S., Cakmak, M., Knox, W.B., Kulesza, T.: Power to the people: the role of humans in interactive machine learning. AI Mag. **35**(4), 105–120 (2014)
6. Ananny, M., Crawford, K.: Seeing without knowing: limitations of the transparency ideal and its application to algorithmic accountability. New Media Soc. **20**(3), 973–989 (2018)
7. Angwin, J., Parris Jr, T., Mattu, S.: Breaking the black box: when algorithms decide what you pay. ProPublica (2016)
8. Angwin, J., Larson, J., Mattu, S., Kirchner, L.: Machine bias: there's software used across the country to predict future criminals and it's biased against blacks (2016). https://www.propublica.org/article/machine-bias-risk-assessments-in-criminal-sentencing. Accessed 2019
9. Athar, A., Teufel, S.: Context-enhanced citation sentiment detection. In: Proceedings of the 2012 conference of the North American chapter of the Association for Computational Linguistics: Human Language Technologies, pp. 597–601 (2012)
10. Bavoil, L., et al.: Vistrails: enabling interactive multiple-view visualizations. In: VIS 05. IEEE Visualization, pp. 135–142. IEEE (2005)
11. Bostrom, N.: Superintelligence: Paths, Dangers, Strategies. Oxford University Press, Oxford (2014)
12. Cambria, E., Olsher, D., Rajagopal, D.: SenticNet 3: a common and commonsense knowledge base for cognition-driven sentiment analysis. In: Proceedings of the Twenty-Eighth AAAI Conference on Artificial Intelligence, pp. 1515–1521 (2014)
13. Carr, B., Ellis, G.: Universe or multiverse? Astron. Geophys. **49**(2), 2–29 (2008)
14. Cellan-Jones, R.: Stephen hawking warns artificial intelligence could end mankind. BBC News **2**(2014), 10 (2014)
15. Crawford, K.: Can an algorithm be agonistic? Ten scenes from life in calculated publics. Sc. Technol. Human Values **41**(1), 77–92 (2016)
16. Davidson, S.B., Freire, J.: Provenance and scientific workflows: challenges and opportunities. In: Proceedings of the 2008 ACM SIGMOD International Conference on Management of Data, pp. 1345–1350 (2008)
17. (DDP), T.D.D.P.: Multiple translations of comedia di dante degli allaghieri col commento di jacopo della lana bolognese, a cura di luciano scarabelli (bologna: Tipografia regia, 1866–67), as found on dante lab (2013). http://dantelab.dartmouth.edu
18. Desai, D.R., Kroll, J.A.: Trust but verify: a guide to algorithms and the law. Harv. JL Tech. **31**, 1 (2017)

19. Deutsch, D.: The structure of the multiverse. Proc. R. Soc. London. Ser. A: Math. Phys. Eng. Sci. **458**(2028), 2911–2923 (2002)
20. Dos Santos, C., Gatti, M.: Deep convolutional neural networks for sentiment analysis of short texts. In: Proceedings of COLING 2014, the 25th International Conference on Computational Linguistics: Technical Papers, pp. 69–78 (2014)
21. Dridi, A., Atzeni, M., Recupero, D.R.: FineNews: fine-grained semantic sentiment analysis on financial microblogs and news. Int. J. Mach. Learn. Cybern. **10**(8), 2199–2207 (2019). https://doi.org/10.1007/s13042-018-0805-x
22. Drozdal, J., et al.: Trust in automl: exploring information needs for establishing trust in automated machine learning systems. In: Proceedings of the 25th International Conference on Intelligent User Interfaces, pp. 297–307 (2020)
23. Dwork, C., Mulligan, D.K.: It's not privacy, and it's not fair. Stan. Law Rev. Online **66**, 35 (2013)
24. The Archival Education and Research Institute (AERI), Pluralizing the Archival Curriculum Group (PACG): Educating for the archival multiverse. The American Archivist, pp. 69–101 (2011)
25. El Alaoui, I., Gahi, Y., Messoussi, R., Chaabi, Y., Todoskoff, A., Kobi, A.: A novel adaptable approach for sentiment analysis on big social data. J. Big Data **5**(1), 12 (2018)
26. Fayyad, U., Piatetsky-Shapiro, G., Smyth, P.: From data mining to knowledge discovery in databases. AI Mag. **17**(3), 37 (1996)
27. Freire, J., Koop, D., Santos, E., Silva, C.T.: Provenance for computational tasks: a survey. Comput. Sci. Eng. **10**(3), 11–21 (2008)
28. Gao, H., Barbier, G., Goolsby, R.: Harnessing the crowdsourcing power of social media for disaster relief. IEEE Intell. Syst. **26**(3), 10–14 (2011)
29. Garfinkel, P.: A linguist who cracks the code in names to predict ethnicity. New York Times (2016)
30. Gil, Y., et al.: Towards human-guided machine learning. In: Proceedings of the 24th International Conference on Intelligent User Interfaces, pp. 614–624 (2019)
31. Gilliland, A.J., Willer, M.: Metadata for the information multiverse. In: iConference 2014 Proceedings (2014)
32. Goebel, R.: Explainable AI: the new 42? In: Holzinger, A., Kieseberg, P., Tjoa, A.M., Weippl, E. (eds.) CD-MAKE 2018. LNCS, vol. 11015, pp. 295–303. Springer, Cham (2018). https://doi.org/10.1007/978-3-319-99740-7_21
33. Grove, W.M., Meehl, P.E.: Comparative efficiency of informal (subjective, impressionistic) and formal (mechanical, algorithmic) prediction procedures: the clinical-statistical controversy. Psychol. Public Policy Law **2**(2), 293 (1996)
34. Holzinger, A., Kieseberg, P., Weippl, E., Tjoa, A.M.: Current advances, trends and challenges of machine learning and knowledge extraction: from machine learning to explainable AI. In: Holzinger, A., Kieseberg, P., Tjoa, A.M., Weippl, E. (eds.) CD-MAKE 2018. LNCS, vol. 11015, pp. 1–8. Springer, Cham (2018). https://doi.org/10.1007/978-3-319-99740-7_1
35. Jhaver, S., Birman, I., Gilbert, E., Bruckman, A.: Human-machine collaboration for content regulation: the case of reddit automoderator. ACM Trans. Comput.-Human Interact. (TOCHI) **26**(5), 1–35 (2019)
36. Johnson, C., Taylor, J.: Rejecting technology: a normative defense of fallible officiating. Sport, Ethics Philos. **10**(2), 148–160 (2016)
37. Joy, B.: Why the future doesn't need us. Wired Mag. **8**(4), 238–262 (2000)
38. Katwala, A.: An algorithm determined UK students' grades (2020)
39. Kharif, O.: No credit history? No problem. Lenders are looking at your phone data. Bloomberg.com (2016)

40. Kurzweil, R.: The Singularity is Near: When Humans Transcend Biology. Penguin, New York (2005)
41. Lehner, P.E., Mullin, T.M., Cohen, M.S.: A probability analysis of the usefulness of decision aids. In: Machine Intelligence and Pattern Recognition, vol. 10, pp. 427–436. Elsevier (1990)
42. Licklider, J.C.: Man-computer symbiosis. IRE Trans. Human Factors Electron. **1**, 4–11 (1960)
43. Lintott, C.J., et al.: Galaxy zoo: morphologies derived from visual inspection of galaxies from the Sloan digital sky survey. Mon. Not. R. Astron. Soc. **389**(3), 1179–1189 (2008)
44. Madrigal, A.: Inside facebook's fast-growing content-moderation effort. The Atlantic (2018)
45. Makridakis, S.: The forthcoming artificial intelligence (AI) revolution: its impact on society and firms. Futures **90**, 46–60 (2017)
46. Martin, K.: Ethical implications and accountability of algorithms. J. Bus. Ethics **160**(4), 835–850 (2019). https://doi.org/10.1007/s10551-018-3921-3
47. Mateos-Garcia, J.: To err is algorithm: algorithmic fallibility and economic organisation (2017)
48. Molina-González, M.D., Martínez-Cámara, E., Martín-Valdivia, M.T., Perea-Ortega, J.M.: Semantic orientation for polarity classification in Spanish reviews. Expert Syst. Appl. **40**(18), 7250–7257 (2013)
49. Monti, F., Frasca, F., Eynard, D., Mannion, D., Bronstein, M.M.: Fake news detection on social media using geometric deep learning. arXiv preprint arXiv:1902.06673 (2019)
50. Mukku, S.S., Choudhary, N., Mamidi, R.: Enhanced sentiment classification of Telugu text using ML techniques. In: SAAIP at IJCAI, vol. 2016, pp. 29–34 (2016)
51. Nakamoto, S.: Bitcoin: a peer-to-peer electronic cash system, p. 4 (2008). https://bitcoin.org/bitcoin.pdf
52. Nakov, P.: Semantic sentiment analysis of twitter data. arXiv preprint arXiv:1710.01492 (2017)
53. Oinn, T., et al.: Taverna: a tool for the composition and enactment of bioinformatics workflows. Bioinformatics **20**(17), 3045–3054 (2004)
54. O'neil, C.: Weapons of math destruction: How big data increases inequality and threatens democracy. Broadway Books, Portland (2016)
55. Peckham, M.: What 7 of the most world's smartest people think about artificial intelligence. Time Magazine (2016)
56. Peng, J., Mit, C., Liu, Q., Uci, I., Ihler, A., Berger, B.: Crowdsourcing for structured labeling with applications to protein folding (2013)
57. Piateski, G., Frawley, W.: Knowledge Discovery in Databases. MIT Press, Cambridge (1991)
58. Rafiq, R.I., Hosseinmardi, H., Han, R., Lv, Q., Mishra, S.: Scalable and timely detection of cyberbullying in online social networks. In: Proceedings of the 33rd Annual ACM Symposium on Applied Computing, pp. 1738–1747 (2018)
59. Rajput, A.: Natural language processing, sentiment analysis, and clinical analytics. In: Innovation in Health Informatics, pp. 79–97. Elsevier (2020)
60. Redhu, S., Srivastava, S., Bansal, B., Gupta, G.: Sentiment analysis using text mining: a review. Int. J. Data Sci. Technol. **4**(2), 49–53 (2018)
61. Russakovsky, O., Li, L.J., Fei-Fei, L.: Best of both worlds: human-machine collaboration for object annotation. In: Proceedings of the IEEE Conference on Computer Vision and Pattern Recognition, pp. 2121–2131 (2015)

62. Saif, H., He, Y., Alani, H.: Semantic sentiment analysis of Twitter. In: Cudré-Mauroux, P., et al. (eds.) ISWC 2012. LNCS, vol. 7649, pp. 508–524. Springer, Heidelberg (2012). https://doi.org/10.1007/978-3-642-35176-1_32
63. Saif, H., He, Y., Fernandez, M., Alani, H.: Contextual semantics for sentiment analysis of Twitter. Inf. Process. Manag. **52**(1), 5–19 (2016)
64. Samek, W., Montavon, G., Vedaldi, A., Hansen, L.K., Müller, K.R.: Explainable AI: Interpreting, Explaining and Visualizing Deep Learning, vol. 11700. Springer, Heidelberg (2019). https://doi.org/10.1007/978-3-030-28954-6
65. Seering, J., Wang, T., Yoon, J., Kaufman, G.: Moderator engagement and community development in the age of algorithms. New Media Soc. **21**(7), 1417–1443 (2019)
66. Stecklow, S.: Why Facebook is losing the war on hate speech in Myanmar (2018). https://www.reuters.com/investigates/special-report/myanmar-facebook-hate
67. Taylor, T.B.: Judgment day: big data as the big decider. Ph.D. thesis, Wake Forest University (2018)
68. Vijayanarasimhan, S., Grauman, K.: What's it going to cost you?: Predicting effort vs. informativeness for multi-label image annotations. In: 2009 IEEE Conference on Computer Vision and Pattern Recognition, pp. 2262–2269. IEEE (2009)
69. Vondrick, C., Patterson, D., Ramanan, D.: Efficiently scaling up crowd sourced video annotation. Int. J. Comput. Vis. **101**(1), 184–204 (2013). https://doi.org/10.1007/s11263-012-0564-1
70. Wah, C., Van Horn, G., Branson, S., Maji, S., Perona, P., Belongie, S.: Similarity comparisons for interactive fine-grained categorization. In: Proceedings of the IEEE Conference on Computer Vision and Pattern Recognition, pp. 859–866 (2014)
71. Wexler, R.: How companies hide software flaws that impact who goes to prison and who gets out. Washington Monthly (2017)
72. Wisser, L.: Pandora's algorithmic black box: the challenges of using algorithmic risk assessments in sentencing. Am. Crim. L. Rev. **56**, 1811 (2019)
73. Yousif, A., Niu, Z., Tarus, J.K., Ahmad, A.: A survey on sentiment analysis of scientific citations. Artif. Intell. Rev. **52**(3), 1805–1838 (2019). https://doi.org/10.1007/s10462-017-9597-8
74. Ziewitz, M.: Governing algorithms: myth, mess, and methods. Sci. Technol. Human Values **41**(1), 3–16 (2016)
75. Zinovyeva, E., Härdle, W.K., Lessmann, S.: Antisocial online behavior detection using deep learning. Decis. Supp. Syst. **138**, 113362 (2020)

ToDI: A Taxonomy of Derived Indices

Maria Joseph Israel[✉], Navid Shaghaghi, and Ahmed Amer

Ethical, Pragmatic, and Intelligent Computing (EPIC) Laboratory,
Santa Clara University, Santa Clara, CA, USA
{misrael,nshaghaghi,aamer}@scu.edu

Abstract. Advancements in digital technology have eased the process of gathering, generating, and altering digital data at large scale. The sheer scale of the data necessitates the development and use of smaller secondary data structured as 'indices,' which are typically used to locate desired subsets of the original data, thereby speeding up data referencing and retrieval operations. Many variants of such indices exist in today's database systems, and the subject of their design is well investigated by computer scientists. However, indices are examples of data derived from existing data; and the implications of such derived indices, as well as indices derived from other indices, pose problems that require careful ethical analysis. But before being able to thoroughly discuss the full nature of such problems, let alone analyze their ethical implications, an appropriate and complete vocabulary in the form of a robust taxonomy for defining and describing the myriad variations of derived indices and their nuances is needed. This paper therefore introduces a novel taxonomy of derived indices that can be used to identify, characterise, and differentiate derived indices.

Keywords: Data indices · Index derivation · Metadata hierarchy · Referential data · Taxonomy

1 Motivation

Advancements in digital technology have eased the process of gathering, generating, and altering digital data at large scales. As a result, publishing, intellectual property, or moderation of data raises questions of proper attribution, ownership, and fair use. These questions are further complicated when dealing with data that refers to other data, *i.e.*, referential data, metadata, indices, *etc.* and it would be impossible to speak rigorously and meaningfully about solutions to problems in this space (which will only increase as the volume of digital corpora increases) without a clear taxonomy of the different dimensions of metadata and its derivation. To address this issue, we have developed a taxonomy to assess the nature and shape of all the different forms and collections that such referential data can take. At the time of this writing, to the best of our knowledge, the Taxonomy of Derived Indices (ToDI) presented in this work is the first of

© ICST Institute for Computer Sciences, Social Informatics and Telecommunications Engineering 2021
Published by Springer Nature Switzerland AG 2021. All Rights Reserved
N. Shaghaghi et al. (Eds.): INTETAIN 2020, LNICST 377, pp. 43–61, 2021.
https://doi.org/10.1007/978-3-030-76426-5_4

its kind to provide a clear and rigorous vocabulary for describing instances of derived or referential data in the form of indices.

The focus of this paper is not so much on the specific implementations of different index types, but rather on the basic variations in the relationship between indices (and similar metadata) and the data from which it is derived. We make some basic assumptions regarding data and metadata, but attempt to keep our definitions as broad and inclusive as possible.

The key question is whether a datum is solely a primary representation of data, or whether it was a result of derivation from existing indices. This brings about complex questions regarding originality, authorship, ownership/intellectual property, attribution, responsibility, and privacy. We cannot be confident in rigorous analyses of such questions, let alone ethical evaluation, if we cannot describe clearly the relationship of data to its derivatives. The presented taxonomy here is an attempt at laying the foundation for others to achieve all of that.

The rest of this paper is structured as follows: Sect. 2 introduces basic terminology such as data, metadata, and index, as way of providing background for discussing other key terms of the taxonomy and Sect. 3 details related work. Section 4 describes the structure of the proposed taxonomy and key descriptors and Sect. 5 explores the future work on ethical frameworks which this taxonomy contributes to. And lastly, Sect. 6 provides some closing remarks.

2   Background

This section provides a brief overview of some basic but important terms and terminologies such as data, metadata, and index, in order to set the background for describing a taxonomy as these terms are implicitly referred to in describing the taxonomy.

2.1   Data

We live in an era of big-data with unfathomable amounts of data everywhere. Data is often associated with electronic data produced by and stored on the informational technology innovations of the twentieth century, though the use of the term "data" is much older. Datum, a singular element of data, can be understood as a basic unit of information. When it is aggregated it forms the bedrock of knowledge. Data differs from information and knowledge, in the sense that it is discrete and descriptive, and is dependent on interpretation for it to hold meaning (and thus become information). To this, Gitelman prepends other characteristics such as abstractness, aggregativeness, and graphicalness [8] when he discusses the origins and economy of modern data and offers the following rationale: Data is abstract, because it requires material expression. Data is aggregative because it can pile up into larger datasets or be reduced into smaller datasets. Data is graphical because it can be visualized by diagrams and graphs as part of an explanation of one's argument as well as to inform us of what we already know or ought to know, and drive us either to action or inaction depending on circumstances (such as data-driven government policies, financial investments, scientific experiments, medical and health practices, ecological claims, personal decisions, *etc.*). Data is therefore a symbolic, aggregatable, abstraction of the concepts that we interpret it to represent.

While the underlying idea of data remains the same, the relationship between data, data creation, and data consumption has radically changed. This is a result of our increased ability to generate and process ever greater quantities of data. That is to say, we have moved from passive data consumers to active data creators, as today's information technology makes it easy and relatively cheap or even free to create, manipulate, accumulate, store, and transmit data at high speed and large quantities. This characteristic nature of data has also reversed the role of data from being subject to us, waiting upon our interpretation of small amounts of data, to we being subject to the data, given that every click and every move has the potential to count for something for someone somewhere, meaning that every individual can produce such vast quantities of data, that no individual can reasonably consume or process it all. For example, the Google Search Engine collects information on user's interests and behaviors [19], Amazon's Alexa gathers user's personal information and interactions [15], Facebook tracks user's social friends and their activities [4], just to name a few. There is a radical shift in contemporary conception of data and its economy on everyday life activities and interactions. This raises complex questions of naming such data for what they are, let alone ethical questions raised by the use and abuse of such data. Descriptive language for all this data is complicated based on activities that alter data creation, collection, and its subsequent custodianship or ownership.

2.2 Metadata

Closely related to data is the concept of metadata that is gaining currency in the field of big-data and online social media. Metadata, generally defined as "data about data" [11], describes additional information about data and its movement and modification among individuals, organizations, disciplines, and machines. Paradigmatic metadata use cases include library catalogs, table of contents, and inventories. With the advent of information technologies, metadata is gaining popularity and is widely used both by information professionals in cataloging, classifying, and indexing data, and by information consumers in social networks' tag clouds, folksonomies, photo captions, and social bookmarks. Therefore, metadata can be understood as the sum total of value-added information/description of any information object's content, context, and structure at any level (*i.e.*, individual, aggregate, or system) [7]. Often metadata elements are structured as explicit information, compiled in standardized categories, and tightly controlled vocabularies in order to establish common ground for researchers and users [13] and to enable authoritative, inter-operable, scalable, achievable, preservable record-keeping systems [7]. For example, archival and museum metadata contain information such as indices, abstracts, and bibliographic records adhering to data content standards like Anglo-American Cataloging Rules (AACR), Machine-Readable Cataloging (MARC), and Library of Congress Subject Heading (LCSH). Scientific metadata datasets specific to Earth System Science comply with, among many others, the Open Archival Information System (OASIS) Reference Model and the Network Common Data Form (NetCDF). With the advent of RDF and semantic technologies, rich metadata are not only manually generated/curated, but automated through metadata mining, metadata harvesting, and web crawling.

However, the origin of metadata goes back to when humans began using language to communicate their feelings, thoughts, and plans. One of the earliest recorded examples of metadata is the use of meta tags, at the great library of Alexandria in 280 C.E., attached to the end of each scroll containing information like title, subject, and author, assisting library users to search through the scrolls without having to unroll all the scrolls and to return a scroll to its right position after usage [5]. This practice evolved into standard library catalogs in the eighteenth and nineteenth centuries and evolved into online catalogs with the emergence of information technology in the late twentieth century [5]. The modern metadata requirement was introduced via meta language by MIT's Stuart McIntosh and David Griffel [9] and metadata standards by the International Press Telecommunications Council [20]. In the early twenty-first century, the National Information Standards Organization introduced metadata for libraries [17] and Adobe's Extensible Metadata Platform (XMP) made use of XML and RDF for metadata representation [2]. Eventually metadata became a pivotal tool for marketing by companies (like Google and Amazon) and leveraged machine learning techniques to automate metadata mining and harvesting [18]. The usage of such vast stores of metadata has thus raised countless privacy and intellectual property concerns to levels that have not yet been fully regulated nor even understood. One attempt to counter the misuse of metadata collection and its management, for instance, the European Union introduced the General Data Protection Regulation (GDPR) compliance law [21].

2.3   Index

Another term that needs to be defined is index which is now generally understood as a mechanism to optimise access to certain data records within a file. The modern use of index traces back to the mid 18th century [22]. In today's digital database context, a database index is a structure similar to a book's table of content utilized for quick data retrieval operations achieved by minimizing table traversal and maximizing performance [1]. In other words, an index is associated with a table and used to efficiently locate data without having to investigate every row in a database table. An index is a routine way of maximizing performance of the databases, at the cost of extra replicas of data.

An index file consists of index entries of the form search key value and pointers to blocks of data in a data file. There are two types of indices: ordered indexes and hash indexes. In the former, search keys are stored in a sorted order and in the latter, the search keys are distributed uniformly across buckets/slots using a hash function. The hash function $f(k, n)$ denotes the key k and the number of buckets n, and maps the key k to the corresponding bucket of the hash index. There are many more types of indices such as primary, secondary, clustering, dynamic, B-Tree, and bitmap indices available to achieve various performance and storage requirements. However, ToDI is not dependent in the 'form' of the index as listed above, but rather in the 'nature' of the index. Section 4 explicates the assumptions, structure, and descriptors of the new proposed taxonomy.

3   Related Work

Given the new ground explored in this work, it is insufficient to focus on a single area of related works; thus a discussion of relevant historical usage and contexts is included.

Before the modern adoption of the term index, tracing back to its classical usage in the mid 18th century, the term index had the same indication or meaning as words like: Table, Register, Calendar, Summary, and Syllabus, and conveyed the meaning of a discoverer, discloser, informer, catalogue or list, inscription, title of a book, and the fore or index-finger [22]. Index was meant to be an indicator, pointing out the position of the desired information. As observed by Wheatley [22], some early usages of (English) indices as tables of references arranged in alphabetical order placed either at the beginning or end of a book, include: Biblical concordances (e.g., an earliest one dedicated to Edward VI by John Marbec in 1550); indices to publications of societies; indices of atlases; indices to statutes; indices of parliamentary papers; indices to the journals of the houses of lords and commons; and indices of periodicals. In other words, an index of the historical uses and forms of indices would not be short.

In more modern usage, within the domain of digital databases and storage systems, an index helps retrieve data from a database system quickly by minimizing data structure traversal and physical access demands, thereby maximizing performance [1]. As a result, most technical researches on indices have looked at their use for performance improvement in various contexts. Several studies have addressed factors concerning the speed and storage efficiency of various index structures like T-Trees, B-Trees, and etc., for main memory databases [3,14] as well as disk-based database systems [10,12,16]. There are also works that focused on the sequential/single dimensional and multidimensional features of index structures in relational database systems [6]. Some examples of the former include: dense index, sparse index, multilevel index, secondary index, B-Tree index, and hash tables; and examples of the latter include hash-like structure based index, tree-like structure based index (k-d tree, Quad tree, R-tree, etc.), and bitmap indices [6]. These classifications of indices deal with data storage and retrieval performances of mostly relational database systems. Unlike such a technical focus on index form and performance, the proposed taxonomy presented in this paper is technology agnostic, and is therefore not restricted to any specific realization or application. It also deals particularly with the nature of derived indices, as distinct from base indices.

4   Taxonomy: Assumptions, Structure, and Derivatives of Referential Data

For the design and development of ToDI, the life cycle of data is assumed to include creation/capture, modification, transmission, storage, update, access, archive, restore, and delete. The focus of this research paper is on the modification and access of data by a user or a software agent that operates on it. Naturally, any modification and transformation of original data brings forth another set of data, a derived data. Therefore, derived data is defined as data that has come about either partially or fully from other data sources. Though a data source can be literally anything, for the purpose of this paper, the (main) source of referential data is the actual data without which an index or other related metadata could not exist. It is therefore the primary corpus of digital data without which any derived metadata is not defined, as it would have no context. Depending on the instance of derived data the source may vary. For example, when the first instance of any index or metadata is further abstracted, then the source of the newly derived data is the immediate metadata, not the original data upon which it was defined. Similarly, referential data is defined as data that performs the functions of pointers, indicating where or how to reference other data.

This is different from the main content of a data repository. For example, chapters in a book can be considered as the main content of the book, whereas an index at the end of the book, by its very nature, does not form the primary data of the book, but rather helps reference content/concepts in the main body of the book. In the database domain, a data repository is the actual data, but indices are typically pointers to the main data, structured in some useful manner. Similar to a book's table of contents, some indices can be a part of the book itself, while others, like a bibliographical index, could typically be seen as a separate entity. Either way, there is a logical distinction between the base data, and the data that is derived from it (*e.g.*, a table of contents or bibliographic index), regardless of whether that derived data is typically found along, or apart from, the data from which it was derived.

4.1   Taxonomy Assumptions

The following assumptions determine the scope of the taxonomy:

A1. The types of data that are considered in this paper are indices, also known as referential data, metadata, or pointers/derivatives of original data.

A2. The type of classified index in this taxonomy refers to the nature of the derived indices depicting implicit relationships between original data and derived data, and not based on any data storage and retrieval performance factors.

A3. The proposed taxonomy is generic and tech-agnostic in nature, meaning that it is not restricted to any specific type of data or database architecture. In other words, it is applicable to all heterogeneous data types and database systems.

4.2 Taxonomy of Derived Indices (ToDI)

The different types of indices are categorized based on the nature of their derivation. Figure 1 illustrates the taxonomy of derived indices graphically and Table 1 summarises key characteristics of each of the derived indices. This section describes the taxonomy and presents a case for each type of the derived indices by discussing the logic behind the structure of the taxonomy. Each node of the taxonomy is illustrated with examples as appropriate.

The taxonomy is based on the premise that indices ares a kind of metadata and metadata is itself data. Moreover, like raw data, metadata can be generated directly from data or from modifying, combining, or altering existing metadata. The taxonomy follows a successive hierarchical refinement approach in simplifying the classification of child nodes in the taxonomy. Different taxonomies can be created depending on the different premises. However, the presented taxonomy is the first of its kind and even though it may require further refinement by including finer types to make it more comprehensive, this does not diminish its usefulness and significance.

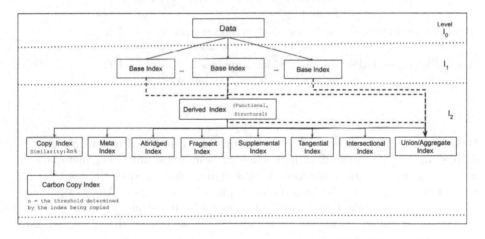

Fig. 1. A Taxonomy of Derived Indices (ToDI)

The root of the taxonomy is a data node which represents a collection of raw data. An example of a dataset which will be used throughout this section is the information housed within a book. A book is usually defined as a set of sheets or pages comprising of sentences containing fictional or nonfictional information that is organized in sections, chapters, and paragraphs.

Table 1. Derived indices: types, definitions, and examples

Index type	Description	Example reference
Base Index	An immediate index of a data set	BI
Derived Index	An index that is derived from an existing index	DI
Functional Derivation	Refers to the functional aspect of the index	FD
Structural Derivation	Refers to the structural aspect of the index	SD
Copy Index	An index that duplicates a portion of an existing index (beyond a threshold)	DI0
Carbon Copy Index	An index that duplicates a hundred percent of an existing index	DI0
Meta Index	An index of an index	DI1
Abridged Index	A briefer version of an existing index	DI2
Fragment Index	An incomplete portion of an index	DI3
Supplemental Index	An index which supplements an existing index	DI4
Tangential Index	An index which indexes related data to data already indexed in an existing index	DI5
Inter-sectional Index	An index which combines parts of existing indices into a single index	DI6
Union/Aggregate Index	An index which combines 2 or more indices in their entirety into a single index	DI7

Base Index (BI). A base index is an immediate index of a data set that is derived directly from the data it indexes without using any other metadata or indices about the data it indexes. All the indices described in the background and related works sections above are examples of base indices. An example base index for a book could be the table of contents included in the book, which is used to index the location where each chapter or section of the presented data in the book can be found.

Derived Index (DI). Derived indices are the result of indexing an existing index or the duplicating, summarizing, supplementing, and/or combining of several indices (be they base or derived) to form a new index of a data set. Derived indices may be the result of structural or functional derivation, or a combination of the two.

Functional Derivation (FD) of an index refers to the derivation of the functionality and purpose of the index that is being derived from. The result of a functional derivation of an index is a derived index that in some way indexes or duplicates, summarizes, supplements, and/or combines existing indices' functionality. Meaning the derived index copies, limits, or enhances the indexing capability of an existing index's referential purpose and functionality regardless of whether it is structured similar to or different from the index or indices it is derived from.

Structural Derivation (SD) on the other hand, refers to indexing or duplicating, summarizing, supplementing, or combining an existing index in precisely the same way that the existing index indexes the data. Meaning the derived index in some way mimics the look and feel (a.k.a. structure) of the index or indices it is derived from. This type of derivation has the potential to violate the copyright and patent protections of the original index if any exist. But this discussion is beyond the scope of this paper and will be explored in a future paper by the authors.

ToDI distinguishes a set of eight basic types of derived indices ($DI0..DI7$): Copy & Carbon Copy, meta, abridged, supplemental, tangential, intersectional, and union/aggregate indices. Each of which is explored below:

DI0. Copy & Carbon Copy Indices. A copy index, is a derived index that is created through any process that duplicates (copies) some or all of an existing index's functionality, structure, or both; but which need not result in a perfect structural and/or functional duplicate of the original index. The amount of the original index which needs to be duplicated in the derived index before that derived index is considered to be a copy index is dependent on the context of the original data and differs from case to case. A copy index may vary from a carbon copy index to a certain degree of cloning of an index which could be distinguished by a degree of (intentional) similarity of the index. In other words, the degree of similarity of a copied index with the original index is a range between some lower bound and 100%. The lower bound is dependent on the data and the purpose of the index being created and thus varies from index to index. A 100% copy is a carbon copy index, similar to the olden days dittoed blue carbon copy paper. That is to say, since the degree of similarity of a copied index to the original index is defined within a range, when the degree of similarity is exactly at 100% of its function and/or structure, then the copy is a carbon copy index. For this reason, a carbon copy index can also be called a clone index.

A copy (and as an extension a carbon copy or clone) index can be a functional copy and/or structural copy, based on the properties of the derived index from which a copy is made. A functional copy of an index functions similarly to the original index, but its design and specific purpose may be different. It may differ in structure, but aid the same functions as the original index. Alternatively, it could be a duplicate of a partial or complete structure, making it a structural copy, that in turn need not be used for the same functions.

An example of a carbon copy or clone index would be a table of contents copied from a book. Since a publisher may have produced a table of contents included with the text, it is possible for another party (such as an online bookseller) to simply copy all of the chapter title and page number information from that table of contents, hence producing a structural carbon copy of that index, or replicating the same work to produce an informationally equivalent but structurally different table of contents, thus producing a functional carbon copy of that index. The former is a base index created by a third party (publisher) from the original data (from the author), while the latter is a derived index.

A more complex example of a structural copy index could be using a traditional book index to produce a table of keyword page occurrence counts. The data from a traditional word index, listing the pages on which the word occurs, would be copied and used to serve a different function, which in this case could be to offer a count of the number of pages on which the word occurs. This is an example of a different functional use of structurally identical data. On the other hand, an example of a functional copy index might be a data structure listing the locations of words in a book organized in ascending order of occurrence (instead of alphabetically), or arranged in a sequence dependent on a numerical hash of the word letters thereby creating a hash table of the words, as opposed to the more traditional alphabetical listing that would be found in a book. Such an index would be derived from the existing index and used to serve the identical function as the existing index but with a fundamentally different structure.

As this example also demonstrates, it is possible for a derived index (such as a carbon copy index) to be indistinguishable structurally and/or functionally from the base index it is derived from. Therefore, it is not the content or functionality of the index itself but rather the manner of its creation that defines its characteristics. It is possible for two people to independently come up with structurally similar (relatively unlikely) or functionally similar (more likely) copies of a derived index. What then makes such indices carbon copy indices is the manner in which these indices are created. If they are created independently then they are both base indices of the same data but if one is created off of (*i.e.*, copied from) another then the one that was produced via copying is a derived copy index of the other index.

DI1. Meta Index. A meta index is an index of an index which in turn refers to the data being indexed. An index of indices occurs in many contexts, and is not directly based on the original data. Sticking with the book analogy, a bibliography of books and book chapters in a particular subject area is effectively a meta index of indices. But such an index, built upon data that is a set of existing indices, need not simply be a higher-level implementation of the same functionality as its underlying indices. One usage domain for such an index, that is not concerned with locating individual indices but rather quite the opposite, it's obfuscation, is the removal of "personally identifiable data elements" in an index of a users' data records. The use of a meta-index as an additional layer of indirection, doubly distances the user from the original data records, and thereby is a means of obfuscation rather than location of data. This is an implicit goal in building general purpose recommendation systems based on individual tracking of user behavior. The result is a broader indexing of indices, intended to provide a wider view of the original data, while simultaneously obfuscating individual behaviors (indices) that contributed to that broader view.

DI2. Abridged Index. An abridged index is an index that focuses on certain select aspects/sections of an existing index. An example of an abridged index is seen in books which poses two indices: one that only lists the chapters and another which lists the chapters along with every section and subsection of each chapter. If the more detailed index is for example assumed to be the base index, then the chapters-only index is a shortening (abridgement) of that index.

DI3. Fragment Index. A fragment index is an incomplete portion of an index, which differs from an abridged index in that it was not necessarily constructed deliberately as an abridged index, and thus is inconsistent in its missing components. An index is therefore fragmentary if it is created through an inconsistent or unplanned process of abridgement. An example of such an index is a table of contents of a book which is missing a page. This table of contents thus might include an incomplete selection of subsections for one chapter, while being complete for all the preceding and following chapters. Any salvaged part of an index of an ancient book is thus also an example of a fragmented index.

DI4. Supplemental Index. A supplemental index is an index that supplements an existing index. In other words, it is a value-added index as it adds additional information to the existing index. In terms of our taxonomy, this would differ from the other derivations in that it is an index that merges additional data that is not inferrable from the original data or the index from which it was derived. An example of a supplemental index in a book is seen in various paper copy textbooks which include several additional (not included on paper) chapters on either an included digital media such as a disk or the textbook's/author's/publisher's website. The added chapters are accompanied with new index entries which supplement the existing index.

DI5. Tangential Index. A tangential index is an index which indexes related data to data already indexed in an existing index. Unlike the Supplemental index, this type of index merely links data that already exists in the original data corpus with existing index data. Since it does not add data from an external source, it is therefore tangential, touching on more of the existing data, but not supplementing it with additional information that could not be derived solely, albeit with extra work, from the existing index. For example, a book word index, listing the pages upon which a word occurs, can be enhanced with a tangential index that adds the line number or numbers in that page wherein the word occurs.

DI6. Intersectional Index. An intersectional index is an index that combines certain parts of other indices into a single index. For example, a table of contents in a book that is an editorial work which brings together parts of several books and lists several chapters, sections, and subsections of each in one uniform index, is an intersectional index.

DI7. Aggregate/Union Index. An aggregate/union index is one that combines two or more existing indices in their entirety into a single index. Any book series which after completion is then republished in a single volume edition may contain a master index which brings together the indices of each of the books together in a single index. That union of indices is an aggregate or union index and not an intersectional index because it includes all of the individual book indices in their entirety.

The taxonomy described is not limited to books and applies equally well to all indices in their varied forms and incarnations. Furthermore, these categories are not mutually exclusive as combinations are easily possible. For example, a separate tangential page occurrence index for all words that are included in each novel written by the Brontë sisters (Anne, Emily and Charlotte) could be created. Then these indices could be aggregated into a master union index which is used as a basis for a supplemental derived index that lists synonyms and antonyms for each word in the novels to produce a thesaurus specific to this body of work. In other words, this would produce a literal Brontë-saurus[1] which is a supplemental aggregate index of tangential indices to each of the table of contents (base indices) in Brontë sisters' novels.

4.3   Taxonomy's Structure and Hierarchy

ToDI deals with referential (anything to which we can refer) data, which by its nature is data that refers to anything, but typically that to which it refers is itself data. This means that referential data is relative to some starting point, that may well be arbitrary. An example could be a single digital data word (or a single binary datum, *i.e.*, a bit) which represents the smallest, simplest, unit of data to which a reference can be made. If debating the nature of scholarly publication indices, it would be reasonable to call a single published paper the atomic datum in such a context. If, however, we are talking about indices built upon a textual database like a book, then the smallest item to which one can refer can be an individual character or symbol within the book. Where one chooses to start, answers the following question of what the lowest level of granularity is within the system, *i.e.*, level 0 or the source data itself, as opposed to any reference to it. If one were to build a higher-level index, not of papers, but of existing scholarly indices, and cared not for any individual paper, then level

---

[1] We use this particular example to point out that such an index can have surprisingly comical uses. This example, and terrible pun, was inspired by the works of British writer and comedian John Finnemore.

zero would be a single index, with its data items being the entries of the index
(which may seem clearly referential data, but would not be considered level 0
if one does not ever actually refer to any individual papers within the system).
A table of contents of a conference proceedings is a simple example of a level 1
index, which in this case does not make use of any of the referential data that
could be decoded from the papers (*i.e.*, the bibliographies and citations).

In the proposed taxonomy, there are many levels of indices based on the
nature of the derived index/indices. To determine the order of these different
types of indices, the formula: $I_{(i+1)}$ can be used. Here, I indicates the index and
$i + 1$ indicates the current order of the index which is the result of incrementing
the order of I's parent index (i) by 1 to arrive at the order of the index. This
simply means that the raw data is I_0, the first (base) index of the raw data is
denoted by $I_{0+1} = I_1$ to indicate that it is of the first order level, and a derived
index from it is denoted by $I_{i+1} = I_2$ to indicate that it is of the second order
level, and so on ad infinitum. That is, any index that is derived from index order
i, is a derived index of the order $i + 1$. The different types of indices and their
relative order is depicted in Fig. 1 and enumerated in Table 1.

5   Future Work

Given the advancement in digital technology, it is not only easy to generate and
alter data at large scale, it is also feasible to add, modify, and delete underlying
metadata that point to the location of original data/information. Such metadata
can be of index types which could be further abstracted to distance/alter from
the original data, or otherwise transcribed, translated, or modified to varying
degrees from the original data and the original index. Descriptive language for all
this data, and the nature of their potential links and associations, is complicated
based on activities that automated data creation, collection, and alteration, in
such a manner as to bring into question its rightful custodianship, ownership,
or even authorship. This raises ethical questions concerning the use and abuse
of such data, especially issues of proper attribution, ownership, and fair use of
such digital data and derivatives thereof. While there are efforts to address the
ethical and legal dimensions of these issues, a consensus regarding their desired
properties is yet to emerge. In this context, this new taxonomy can be used to
guide, compare, or differentiate, the different ethical and legal frameworks that
have been, and may yet be, proposed. This could be very beneficial for the clear
communication of arguments and proposals regarding ownership and attribution
of metadata for instance.

The ethical question "Is data about you yours, or should it be?" is an important one for discussing the nature of ownership of data in general, but any such
discussion is incomplete if it does not address derivative and referential data as
well. For example, how would we describe the data in the following scenarios: Is
data about person X, when X's personally identifiable information is included

within the metadata, considered the data of person X? What if the personally identifiable data was not included in the corpus, but could be inferred by processing derivative metadata? Would the anonymized data be of person X with or without the metadata? Is the metadata considered to be about person X if it alone would not identify the person? To address these questions, and to coherently discuss questions of identification, in addition to attribution, custodianship, and ownership, the vocabulary provided by the proposed taxonomy of derived indices would become very useful. Further exploration of this space, including comparative analysis of case studies of intellectual property arguments involving metadata, and privacy arguments surrounding the use of metadata, is warranted. Such explorations would be direct applications of the presented taxonomy, and would be expected to demonstrate its usefulness for providing a coherent common language when describing data that described data.

6   Concluding Remarks

This paper delineates a novel taxonomy of derived indices and explains its potential usefulness in exploring ethical questions surrounding metadata. The motivation for the research is the confluence of big data, specifically the increasing ability to manipulate and manage ever-larger datasets, which in turns aids the increasingly easy modification, abstraction, and duplication or recreation of metadata. Such data, whether ubiquitously captured from users' interactions on social media, or mined from ever-growing logs of transactions and activities, is increasingly vast, but so is our ability to generate more useful representations, summaries, and references to the data. So far the focus of discussion has naturally been concentrated on the original preserved data, and less on the derived metadata (*i.e.*, indices). The presented taxonomy specifically focuses on this easily overlooked form of data, which with ever-larger datasets becomes increasingly valuable, but which also is – by its very nature – a derivation with varying degrees, of the original data.

The objective was therefore to present a taxonomy of derived indices that provides a basis for systematically understanding the complexity of different forms of referential metadata, and thereby introducing a useful vocabulary to discuss them. And the proposed taxonomy is an initial offering which may well require further iterations of refinement and development to ensure that it is comprehensive and complete.

Acknowledgement. Many thanks are due to the departments of Mathematics and Computer Science (MCS) and Computer Science and Engineering (CSEN) for their continued support of the project. And to reviewers of ToDI's drafts for their helpful comments without which this work could not have been improved.

A   Appendix

A.1   Taxonomy and Associated Descriptors

Term	Description
Term Name	Base Index
Label	Base Index
Definition	A base index is an immediate index of a data set
Comment	A base index is different from other derived indices in that it is base/source of all other derived index (indices). All the indices described in the related work section of this paper are examples of base indices. An example of a base index is for a book could be the table of contents, which is used to index the location where each chapter or section of the presented data in the book can be found
Type of Term	Base index

Term	Description
Term Name	Derived Index
Label	Derived Index
Definition	A derived index is an index that is derived from an existing index
Comment	Derived indices may be the result of structural or functional derivation, or a combination of the two
Type of Term	Derived Index

Term	Description
Term Name	Functional Property
Label	Functional Property
Definition	Functional property refers to the functionality and purpose of the index that is being derived from
Comment	A functional property is different from other properties of an index in that it is in some ways indexes or duplicates, summarizes, supplements, and/or combines existing indices' functionality
Type of Term	Property

Term	Description
Term Name	Structural Property
Label	Structural Property
Definition	Structural property refers to the structural aspect of the index
Comment	A structural property is different from other properties of an index in that it is in some ways mimics the look and feel of the index or indices it is derived from
Type of Term	Property

Term	Description
Term Name	Copy Index
Label	Copy Index
Definition	A copy index is an index that duplicates a portion of an existing index
Comment	Copy index is different from Carbon copy index and from other derived index in that it copies some or all of an existing index's functionality, structure or both
Type of Term	Derived index

Term	Description
Term Name	Carbon Copy Index
Label	Carbon Copy Index
Definition	A carbon copy index is an index that duplicates an existing index a hundred percent
Comment	Carbon Copy index is different from copy index and other derived index in that it is an exact copy of an existing index or indices
Type of Term	Derived index

Term	Description
Term Name	Meta Index
Label	Meta Index
Definition	An index of an index, meaning an index that is abstracted from the original index without revealing identifiable information, that may be doubly distanced from the original base index or other derived index
Comment	Meta index is different from other derived index in that it is meta of derived index. An example of a meta index is a bibliography of books and book chapters in a particular subject area. It is a meta index of indices
Type of Term	Derived index

Term	Description
Term Name	Abridged Index
Label	Abridged Index
Definition	An abridged index is a briefer version of an existing index
Comment	Abridged index is different from other derived index in that it is shorted version of a derived index. An example of a abridged index can be seen in books which poses two indices: one that only lists the chapters and another which lists the chapters along with every section and subsection of each chapter...
Type of Term	Derived index

Term	Description
Label	Fragment Index
Term Name	Fragment Index
Definition	A fragment index is an incomplete portion of an index
Comment	Fragment index is different from other derived index in that it is an incomplete derived index. An example of a fragment index is a table of contents of a book which is missing a page
Type of Term	Derived index

Term	Description
Label	Supplemental Index
Term Name	Supplemental Index
Definition	A supplemental index is an index which supplements an existing index
Comment	An example of a supplemental index in a book is seen in various paper copy textbooks which include several additional (not included on paper) chapters on either an included digital media such as a disk or the textbook's/author's/publisher's website
Type of Term	Derived index

Term	Description
Label	Tangential Index
Term Name	Tangential Index
Definition	A tangential index is an index which indexes related data to data already indexed in an existing index
Comment	For example, a book word index, listing the pages upon which a word occurs, can be enhanced with a tangential index that adds the line number or numbers in that page wherein the word occurs
Type of Term	Derived index

Term	Description
Term Name	Intersectional Index
Label	Intersectional Index
Definition	An intersectional index is an index which combines parts of existing indices into a single index
Comment	For example, a table of contents in a book that is an editorial work which brings together parts of several books and lists several chapters, sections, and subsections of each in one uniform index is an intersectional index
Type of Term	Derived index

Term	Description
Term Name	Union/Aggregate Index
Label	Union/Aggregate Index
Definition	A union/aggregate index is an index which combines 2 or more indices in their entirety into a single index
Comment	Any book series which after completion is then republished in a single volume edition will contain a master index which brings together the indices of each of the books together in a single index
Type of Term	Derived index

References

1. Ahmed, I., Fayyaz, A., Shahzad, A.: PostgreSQL Developer's Guide. Packt Publishing Ltd., Birmingham (2015)
2. Ball, A., Darlington, M.: Briefing paper: the adobe extensible metadata platform (XMP). UKOLN research organization (2007)
3. Choi, K.R., Kim, K.C.: T*-tree: a main memory database index structure for real time applications. In: Proceedings of 3rd International Workshop on Real-Time Computing Systems and Applications, pp. 81–88. IEEE (1996)
4. Dwyer, C.: Privacy in the age of google and facebook. IEEE Technol. Soc. Mag. **30**(3), 58–63 (2011)
5. Foote, K.D.: A brief history of metadata. Online (Data Varsity) (2019)
6. Garcia-Molina, H., Ullman, J.D., Widom, J.: Database System Implementation, vol. 672. Prentice Hall, Upper Saddle River (2000)
7. Gilliland, A.J.: Setting the stage. Introduction Metadata **2**, 1–19 (2008)
8. Gitelman, L.: Raw Data is an Oxymoron. MIT Press, Cambridge (2013)
9. Griffel, D.M., McIntosh, S.D.: Admins: a progress report. Technical report. Center for International Studies, Massachusetts, Cambridge (1967)
10. Heumann, K., Mewes, H.W.: The hashed position tree (HPT): a suffix tree variant for large data sets stored on slow mass storage devices. In: 3rd South American Workshop on String Processing, pp. 101–114 (1996)
11. Hey, T., Trefethen, A.: The data deluge: an e-science perspective. In: Grid Computing: Making the Global Infrastructure a Reality, pp. 809–824 (2003)

12. Japp, R.: The top-compressed suffix tree: a disk-resident index for large sequences. In: Proceedings of the Bioinformatics Workshop at the 21st Annual British National Conference on Databases (2004)

13. Lawrence, B., Lowry, R., Miller, P., Snaith, H., Woolf, A.: Information in environmental data grids. Philos. Trans. R. Soc. A: Math. Phys. Eng. Sci. **367**(1890), 1003–1014 (2009)

14. Lehman, T.J., Carey, M.J.: A study of index structures for main memory database management systems. Technical report, University of Wisconsin-Madison, Department of Computer Sciences (1985)

15. Orr, D.A., Sanchez, L.: Alexa, did you get that? Determining the evidentiary value of data stored by the Amazon® echo. Digit. Investig. **24**, 72–78 (2018)

16. Phoophakdee, B., Zaki, M.J.: Genome-scale disk-based suffix tree indexing. In: Proceedings of the 2007 ACM SIGMOD International Conference on Management of Data, pp. 833–844 (2007)

17. Riley, J.: Understanding metadata. National Information Standards Organization, Washington DC, United States, p. 23 (2017). http://www.niso.org/publications/press/UnderstandingMetadata.pdf

18. Şah, M., Wade, V.: Automatic metadata mining from multilingual enterprise content. J. Web Semant. **11**, 41–62 (2012)

19. Schmidt, D.: Google data collection. Digital Content Next [Online] (2018)

20. Smith, J.R., Schirling, P.: Metadata standards roundup. IEEE Multimed. **13**(2), 84–88 (2006)

21. Voigt, P., Von dem Bussche, A.: The EU general data protection regulation (GDPR). A Practical Guide, 1st edn. Springer, Heidelberg (2017). https://doi.org/10.1007/978-3-319-57959-7

22. Wheatley, H.B.: What is an Index?: A Few Notes on Indexes and Indexers, vol. 1. [for the Index Society]. Longmans, Green (1879)

Haptics, IoT, and Audio

Plug-and-Play Haptic Interaction for Tactile Internet Based on WebRTC

Ken Iiyoshi[1] , Ruth Gebremedhin[1] , Vineet Gokhale[2] ,
and Mohamad Eid[1]([⊠])

[1] New York University Abu Dhabi, Abu Dhabi, UAE
{ki573,rgg282,mohamad.eid}@nyu.edu
[2] Delft University of Technology, Delft, Netherlands
V.Gokhale@tudelft.nl

Abstract. *Tactile Internet* promises a widespread adoption of haptic communication over the Internet. However, as haptic technologies are becoming more diversified and available than ever, the need has arisen for a plug-and-play (PnP) haptic communication over a computer network. This paper presents a system for enabling PnP communication of heterogeneous haptic interfaces. The system is based on three key features: (i) a haptic metadata to make haptic interfaces self-descriptive, (ii) a handshake protocol to automatically exchange haptic metadata between two communicating devices, and (iii) a multimodal (haptic-audio-visual) media communication protocol. Implemented using WebRTC, the PnP communication is evaluated using a Tele-Writing application with two heterogeneous haptic interfaces, namely Geomagic Touch and Novint Falcon. Our findings demonstrate the potential of the system to be employed in any Tactile Internet scenario.

Keywords: Tactile Internet (TI) · Haptic-Audio-Visual (HAV) handshake · TI Metadata (TIM) · WebRTC · Request/response

1 Introduction

Tactile Internet (TI) [16] – deemed as the *Internet of Skills* [12] – is anticipated to redefine the nature of human interactions with remote environments. TI extends the human capability to effectively control and manipulate remote environments by providing haptic (touch) experience in an ultra-responsive and ultra-reliable fashion [6]. This enables humans to experience remote environments as if they are located there. This has opened up a world of new opportunities with potential to impact every aspect of human lives [18]. Some examples include telesurgery [7], remote disaster management, online shopping [31], gaming and entertainment, and long-distance inter-personal communication.

The inclusion of haptic media as an integral element of TI presents several challenging communication requirements that are unique to TI, and hence need to be separately addressed. For example, design of schemes for robust control

© ICST Institute for Computer Sciences, Social Informatics and Telecommunications Engineering 2021
Published by Springer Nature Switzerland AG 2021. All Rights Reserved
N. Shaghaghi et al. (Eds.): INTETAIN 2020, LNICST 377, pp. 65–81, 2021.
https://doi.org/10.1007/978-3-030-76426-5_5

and communication, inter-media (haptic, audio, and video) as well as intra-media (haptic sensors and actuators) synchronization, and so on. To address these challenges, IEEE established the IEEE P1918.1 TI standards Working Group (WG) [18] for defining a standard framework encompassing a generic TI reference model and architecture. It also aims to standardize the interconnections between multitude of interfaces featured in the framework. Further, in order to identify and standardize the TI modules specific to haptic communication, a sub-WG – P1918.1.1 – has been created. This has spawned a string of activities with specific focus on design and development of:

1. *haptic codecs* for perception-based haptic signal compression
2. *plug-and-play (PnP) communication* for interoperability under heterogeneous environment settings.

While the former has witnessed significant progress, the latter is still in its nascent stages of development.

Design Challenges: Designing a PnP communication system for TI comes with several challenges. We list the most important ones here.

1. **Application-level heterogeneity**: TI applications manifest a diverse range of requirements. For instance, while in a haptic-based VR game a single point device with 3 Degrees of Freedom (DoF) suffices, complex interactions, such as a telesurgery, require several sensors and actuators possibly with heterogeneous Quality of Service (QoS) requirements. A PnP communication system should be capable of detecting these interfaces and start communication on the fly with zero or minimal configurations.
2. **Interoperability**: PnP communication system for TI should be cross-platform and work without requiring installation of any software/firmware.
3. **Quality of Service**: TI applications demand extremely stringent QoS requirements, such as a round trip time (RTT) 10 ms [16]. PnP communication system should be capable of strictly complying to such requirements.

In this work, we attempt to fuel this direction of advancement in TI by proposing a WebRTC-based system for enabling PnP haptic communication for TI interactions. Our contributions in this paper are the following:

1. We propose a system for haptic interaction between multiple TI nodes in a PnP fashion. Our system is robust to the characteristics of applications and the haptic interfaces used.
2. We present the design details of our PnP communication system developed using WebRTC API. The efficacy of our design lies in the fact that we achieve haptic communication by leveraging only the built-in features of WebRTC, thereby posing no demands for modifications to the standard WebRTC structure.
3. We test the proof-of-concept of the proposed system through a tele-writing application using both homogeneous and heterogeneous haptic interfaces connected via a real-network. The latency measurements of our system demonstrate its potential to be employed in any TI scenario.

The remainder of the paper is organized as follows. In Section 2, we present a review of the related literature. In Sects. 3, 4, we present an overview of our PnP system and discuss its implementation details, respectively. We present our experimental results and discussions in Sect. 5. Finally, we state our conclusions in Sect. 6.

2   Related Literature

Standardizing haptic communication interfaces has been a pervasive challenge in the haptic research community. This primarily requires (i) comprehensive definition of haptic metadata format, (ii) exchanging and negotiation of metadata, and (iii) exchange of media payload.

Several works exist in the literature that have looked at definition and exchange of haptic metadata. In order to systematically describe various attributes of a haptic interface, researchers have proposed a structured data format. Early studies proposed an XML-based approach to represent generic haptic applications [8]. Cha et al. extended MPEG-4 Binary Format for Scenes (BIFS) [29] to support the synchronization and communication of haptic-audio-visual (HAV) media streams [9]. Others [14] have proposed HAML, a haptic applications metadata language, to describe haptic-related information, including haptic interfaces, haptic development APIs, and quality of experience requirements. A HAML-based authoring tool has also been developed [13] to facilitate the development of haptic applications for various haptic interfaces for non-programmer developers or artists. The work in [24] explored the use of Session Initiation Protocol (SIP), used commonly in VoIP sessions, for establishing haptic interactive sessions.

Only a handful of works have addressed the latter challenge of exchanging media payload using standardized protocols/tools. An example is the work in [24] that considered Real-time Transport protocol (RTP), which forms the cornerstone of VoIP applications, for haptic interactions.

A recent work in [20], presents Tactile Internet Metadata (TIM) and a haptic handshake protocol, the implementations of which were realized using WebRTC. This study is a continuation of our previous work where we evaluate the PnP system with heterogeneous haptic devices in a realistic tele-haptic application (Tele-writing). This design choice of using a browser-based API enabled the authors to develop the protocol in a cross-platform manner. In this work, we make significant enhancements to the work in [20] to come up with a PnP communication system for TI that we present in the following section.

3   Proposed PnP Communication System

In this section, we provide an overview of the proposed PnP communication system. The system consists of three tightly coupled components: Tactile Internet Metadata (TIM) scheme, haptic handshake protocol, and a real-time haptic-audio-video communication protocol to support network applications. While a preliminary implementation of these components was done in the recent work [20], we have enhanced it significantly in order to make the communication system plug-and-play. Nevertheless, we will provide a holistic view of the proposed system here.

3.1 HAV Handshake

We propose a three-way handshake protocol for the exchange of haptic-audio-video (HAV) metadata between TI nodes, as shown in Fig. 1. The TI node initiating the TI session (node A) advertises all of its capabilities/requirements to the other participant (node B) through the *request* message. For example, node A could be capable of supporting a set of haptic codec types and certain maximum haptic refresh rate. In response, node B chooses a feasible option out of the advertised specifications. For example, only a subset of the advertised codecs and a lower refresh rate could be supported. Node B transmits the *response* message carrying the chosen parameters. Upon reception of the *response* signal, node A transmits *ACK* message indicating that the consensus on metadata is reached. The packet structures of these messages are discussed in Sect. 3.2.

The reception of ACK marks the completion of HAV handshake phase where the advertisement and negotiation of metadata happens. This is then followed by the *media communication* phase in which the exchange of media and control data corresponding to the live TI interaction is carried out. We discuss further details on this in Sect. 3.3.

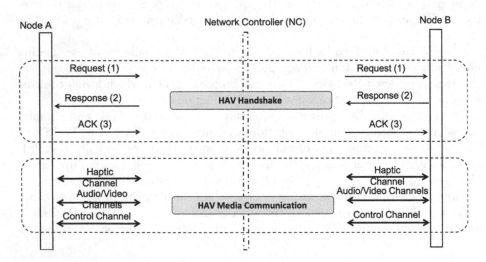

Fig. 1. Schematic of the proposed HAV handshake. HAV synchronization involves a simple 3-way handshake consisting of request, response, and acknowledgment.

3.2   Tactile Internet Metadata (TIM)

TIM is designed to provide a technology-neutral description of the various characteristics and requirements of TI systems in terms of session attributes. As
shown in Fig. 2, the session attributes are organized into two broad categories:
Quality of Experience (QoE) and *haptic*. QoE captures the essential parameters
that are crucial for an immersive perception of the remote haptic interaction
by the human operator. This category is further sub-divided into *Quality of
Experience (QoS)* and *user experience*. QoS specifies the end-to-end network
requirements for guaranteeing transparency between the TI nodes. For example,
latency and *jitter* fields specify the maximum tolerable end-to-end delay and
jitter, respectively. User experience specifies the perceptual attributes that will
be used to describe the current quality of human perception, such as the quality
of user immersion or telepresence.

On the other hand, the haptic category represents the haptic modality in
terms of the properties of the *media* (data) and the haptic *interface* attributes.
While the former describes the attributes for source coding and communication
of the haptic data, the latter describes the capabilities of the haptic interface
being employed in the TI session. These include the number of degrees of freedom, ranges of displayable force and torque, and position resolution, among
others.

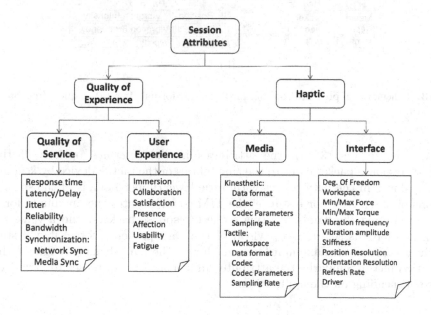

Fig. 2. Haptic session attributes as defined in TIM.

The TIM structure is adapted for various types of haptic handshake and communication messages, including the schema for the request/response messages
and the data/control messages.

As for the haptic handshake, two types of messages are defined, namely the request and the response (Fig. 3 (a)). The message header consists of a *packetType* identifier for indicating the type of handshake message – request, response, or ACK. The header also include a packet sequence number for unique identification of the packet. The request/response message payload carries the metadata advertised/selected by the transmitting TI node. In order to support evolving requirements, *CustomHapticAttributes* field is provided in which several user-defined attributes may be added. The payload of the message is formatted in accordance with the TIM definition (Fig. 1).

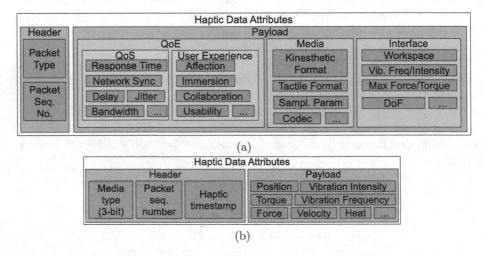

(a)

(b)

Fig. 3. Schematic representation of TIM packet format for (a) request/response, (b) data.

As seen in Fig. 3 (a), the attributes in the *interface* options of the request/response packet cater to the capabilities of the tactile device by keeping the attributes in the data packet within the lower/upper bounds of the specifications of the device. For instance, the TIM communicates the maximum force attribute during the handshake (via request/response packets) and a value for maximum force is set. If the payload of the data packet is force, it will stay within the bound of maximum force set during the handshake throughout the operation phase. Similarly, the attribute "immersion" could be set to "true" or "false" depending on the application.

3.3 HAV Media Communication

The media communication phase starts once the haptic handshake phase completes. In Fig. 1, this is shown as the operation state, consisting of haptic, audio-visual, and control channels. In the phase, two types of messages are exchanged: data message shown in Fig. 3 and (b) control message which is a combination of fields in Fig. 3 (a). The data message simply carries a header and a payload. The header defines the media type (haptic, audio, video, or combination), the packet sequence number, and the haptic timestamp (utilized for intra- and inter-media synchronization). The payload comprises the corresponding haptic media data (such as position, force, torque or velocity for kinesthetic haptic interaction or vibration frequency, location, intensity for tactile feedback, etc.). On the other hand, the control messages are used to deal with dynamic control parameter adjustments during the data communication, such as change in network characteristics, addition of a new media type or user.

In this work, while we implement the handshake and media communication of haptic-related messages, for communicating AV-related messages, we simply invoke the de-facto standards – Real-time Transport Protocol (RTP) and Session Description Protocol (SDP) for data and control, respectively.

4 Implementation on WebRTC

In this section, we will provide the implementation details of our PnP communication system using Web Real Time Communication (WebRTC) – an open-source peer-to-peer cross-platform and cross-browser communication API [23].

4.1 TIM

A sample request packet of TIM is shown in Fig. 4. As can be seen it contains several attributes and their corresponding values. This particular example configures the deadband parameter for velocity signals ("VelocityDeadbandParameter") to 0.1, the manufacturer of the haptic device used ("manufacturerName") as "3D Systems", and the device model ("modelName") as "Geomagic Touch". Note that this excerpt of response packet is being taken from a real TI experiment of tele-writing that we discuss in detail in Sect. 4.4. Here, we used the kinesthetic codec [19] to smoothly interface haptic devices to the TI nodes. Other attributes related to QoS, media, and interface fields are specified in detail. The fields are arranged in JSON format. TIM is extensible and the exact attributes can be easily defined by the developers depending on their application needs. This can include any attributes related to handshake/data/control packets. For AV metadata, we simply leverage the SDP implementation of WebRTC.

4.2 HAV Handshake

Haptic handshake and communication requires open source protocols for accessibility, flexibility, and maintenance. For these reasons, commercial and proprietary services such as Skype and Google Hangout are challenging to adopt, although their texting features can certainly be re-purposed for haptic handshake. Due to these reasons, we resort to WebRTC for realizing our proposed system.

```
{"packetType":"request",
 "payload"    :{"QoS"      :{"CommandDelay":0},
                "Media"    :{"ControlMode":true,
                            "FlagVelocityKalmanFilter":false,
                            "ForceDeadbandParameter":0,
                            "PositionDeadbandParameter":0,
                            "RecordSignals":false,
                            "VelocityDeadbandParameter":0.1},
             "Interface":{"actuatedGripper":false,
                          "actuatedPosition":true,
                          "actuatedRotation":false,
                          "gripperMaxAngleRad":0,
                          "leftHand":true,
                          "manufacturerName":"3D Systems",
                          "maxAngularDamping":0,
                          "maxAngularStiffness:0,
                          "maxAngularTorque":0,
                          "maxGripperAngularDamping":0,
                          "maxGripperForce":0,
                          "maxGripperLinearStiffness":0,
                          "maxLinearDamping":4,
                          "maxLinearForce":3.3,
                          "maxLinearStiffness":400,
                          "model":14,"modelName":"Geomagic Touch",
                          "rightHand":true,
                          "sensedGripper":false,
                          "sensedPosition":true,
                          "sensedRotation":true,
                          "workspaceRadius":0.075}}}
```

Fig. 4. Sample TIM Request generated when TI node is connected to Geomagic Touch Device.

WebRTC handles AV data through Secure Real-Time Transport Protocol (SRTP) and non-AV data, which can be re-purposed for haptic data, through UDP-based, DTLS-encapsulated SCTP [RFC4960]. Supported by major browsers, it is being standardized through the World Wide Web Consortium (W3C) and the Internet Engineering Task Force (IETF) [23,25]. These features make WebRTC the most versatile solution among other open source options such as easyRTC [26], Jitsi [21], Linphone [2], Jami [1], Riot [4], and Retroshare [3].

AV Handshake: We leverage the standard AV handshake handled by WebRTC's *MediaStream* for handling AV handshake and communication. Figure 5 outlines the AV handshake. First, each TI node involved in the TI interaction creates a *PeerConnection* for the AV channel. These nodes then connect with each other through signaling messages. The request/response/ACK generations are automated, and the SDP exchange process between the nodes can be implemented using any third-party services such as emails, SMS, and external servers. After these steps are executed, the *PeerConnection* objects of the interacting nodes get attached to each other and the AV communication starts between the nodes.

Haptic Handshake: WebRTC provides a generic object *RTCDataChannel* that can be employed for any non-AV data communication. We make use of this for haptic data. Figure 6 outlines the haptic handshake. First, both TI nodes obtain TIM described earlier in Sect. 4.1. This is then encapsulated in SDP packets that are exchanged through the haptic handshake *RTCDataChannel*. Note that the haptic handshake leverages the *PeerConnection* that was established

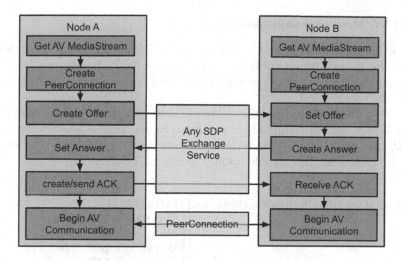

Fig. 5. Schematic of AV handshake carried out by WebRTC.

during the AV handshake. Hence, there are no more processes to be executed before the SDP exchanges can begin.

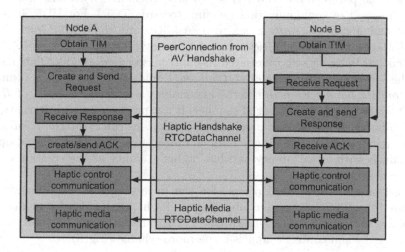

Fig. 6. Schematic of haptic handshake after completion of AV handshake.

AV and haptic media are intentionally handled in separate channels so that third party developers can use different AV codecs based on their own application needs. Note that the haptic metadata exchange happens separately from the AV metadata, however, haptic media communication may or may not happen with RTP.

4.3   HAV Media Communication

After the handshake, the *RTCDataChannel* that was used for haptic handshake is reused for control communication, and a second *RTCDataChannel* is opened to be used for haptic media communication, thus triggering the comprehensive HAV media communication.

RTCDataChannel objects exist in WebRTC to address communication needs of various data, not only limited to haptic data. Hence, although not exactly TCP or UDP, they can be configured to protocols within those two ends of transport layer spectrum. The configurable options are listed below in Fig. 7:

```
const mediaChannelOptions = {[[Ordered]],
                             [[MaxPacketLifeTime]],
                             [[MaxRetransmits]],
                             [[DataChannelProtocol]],
                             [[Negotiated]],
                             [[DataChannelId]]};
```

Fig. 7. Different configuration options offered by the general *RTCDataChannel* object.

When the parameter *Ordered* is set to true (default), it means choosing a reliable method of communication (leaning towards TCP). For UDP, it is set to false and *MaxRetransmits* is set to 0. Additionally, *RTCDataChannel* can control *MaxRetransmits* or *MaxPacketLifeTime* attributes but not both. *RTC-DataChannel* is by default negotiated in-band between two nodes. This means that the local node calls *createDataChannel()*, and the remote node connects to the *ondatachannel EventHandler*. This enables a dynamic creation of *RTC-DataChannel* where the number of channels is not predetermined. Alternatively, they can be negotiated out of-band, where both sides call *createDataChannel()* with a predetermined ID to create data channels statically. This method opens the channels with lower latency and has higher stability as the creation of the channels is symmetric.

Based on the above descriptions, for the purpose of our experiments, we configured the *RTCDataChannel* objects used for haptic handshake, media, and control are to be UDP-like as shown below. Of course, there is flexibility to set the handshake and control channels to be more reliable (Fig. 8).

4.4   Tele-Writing Demonstration

To evaluate the performance of the proposed PnP communication system, we developed a tele-writing application where a human can write something phys-ically on a piece of paper present in a remote location. For this demonstration, we attached a pen to the remote haptic device (Node A). The human user con-trols it through another device in his/her location (Node B). The two nodes are connected to each other through a star connection of category-5e RJ45 ethernet

```
const handshakeChannelOptions = {Ordered: false,
                                  MaxRetransmits:0,
                                  negotiated: true,
                                  id: 0}};

const mediaChannelOptions = {Ordered: false,
                             MaxRetransmits:0,
                             negotiated: true,
                             id: 1}};
```

Fig. 8. Setting of the *RTCDataChannel* objects that are used for haptic signaling in the proposed communication system.

cables and gigabit desktop switch. The interface for the haptic device was programmed in C++ language. A schematic diagram of the complete tele-writing setup is shown in Fig. 9. The implementation of the tele-writing setup is divided into two programs at each node: a C++ program interfacing with the haptic device and a WebRTC simulation written in HTML, CSS, and JavaScript. Node A can be connected to either Geomagic Touch or Novint Falcon for controlling the Node B device, which uses a pen-mounted Novint Falcon. This allows demonstrations of the PnP system for both homogeneous and heterogeneous TI nodes. It should be noted that for the sake of simplicity we mount the pen to only one type of haptic device. However, the tele-writing application can be directly extended to any other haptic device as well.

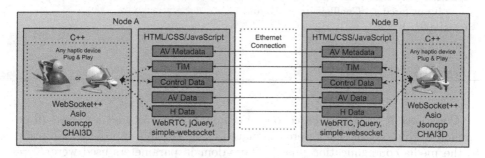

Fig. 9. Schematic diagram of PnP communication system for tele-writing application.

As noted in Fig. 9, the HAV WebRTC simulator was built by combining HTML, CSS, and JavaScript files from WebRTC's Munge SDP sample program with those from C++ WebSocket Server Demo's client project [5,28]. The client project consists of jQuery and simple-websocket [15,30]. jQuery simplifies traditionally verbose JavaScript expressions while simple-websocket is used to receive WebSocket data. The C++ haptic interfacing programs consist of C++ WebSocket Server Demo project and a simplified version of kinesthetic codec provided by the works in [17,19,28]. The WebSocket server projects consist of

WebSocket++ [27], Asio [10], and Jsoncpp [11]. The layout of the nodes are identical. The only difference is in how the signaling process is handled on each node. Node A first generates its own TIM, and based on this, Node B generates its own TIM. Node A, upon receiving this information, sends an acknowledgement to Node B and begins data communication.

Kinesthetic Codec Reference Software. We use the kinesthetic codec reference software, proposed by IEEE Haptic Codecs Work Group, to interface the C++ programs with the haptic devices, particularly in a well-controlled, stable manner [19]. It uses Chai3D engine to sense and actuate the haptic interface, queue-based haptic packet management for smooth communication, and Winsock's UDP mode to communicate between localhost-simulated TI nodes. To reduce congestion, it uses the perceptual deadband haptic data reduction.

Since UDP is not supported on browsers due to security issues, this was replaced with the WebSocket functionalities. Thus, the Chai3D-obtained haptic data are converted into stringified JSON via Jsoncpp and WebSocket++, and are then sent to the WebRTC simulator.

It is worth mentioning that the communication involved Node A sending timestamped velocity data to Node B. Based on this data, Node B device's force data is calculated through Algorithm 1 and sent back to Node A along with its own timestamp.

Algorithm 1: Slave force calculation algorithm.

Data: Newly read position p. Received velocity v. Previously stored error e_p and input force f_p. Coefficients A, B, and C.

$e \leftarrow 0.001 \cdot v - p$;
$f \leftarrow A \cdot e - B \cdot e_p - C \cdot f_p$;
$e_p \leftarrow e$;
$f_p \leftarrow f$;

Constants A, B, C are based on z-domain PD control and low pass filter applied to this system. They were calculated using Tustin's approximation prior to the media communication phase. The s-domain parameters used were $K = 1000$, $K_e = 5$, $T = 0.001\,\text{s}$, and $\tau = 0.0016\,\text{s}$. The s-domain transfer function was:

$$F = \frac{Ke + K_e\dot{e}}{\tau s + 1}$$

where, K, K_e, and τ respectively were Proportional Gain, Derivative Gain, and Low pass filter parameter. The resulting z-domain functions were:

$$A = \frac{2K_e + KT}{2\tau + T}, \quad B = -\frac{-2K_e + T}{2\tau + T}, \quad C = \frac{-2\tau + T}{2\tau + T}$$

The coefficients above can be modified to support applications with different control needs. These parameters can be included in the TIM packets if needed.

Figure 10 shows both homogeneous and heterogeneous modes of the tele-writing application along with C++ console for displaying the contents of request and response packets.

Figure 10 (a), Novint Falcon was used for controlling Node B, whereas in Fig. 10 (b), was used Geomagic Touch. In Fig. 10 (c), the C++ console log and web GUI from the Node A is shown, which, content-wise, was identical to Node B. Figure 10 (C). The C++ console log displaying packet communication rates, and the web GUI from Node A displaying SDP request and response from Node A and B, as well as their video data. The setup allowed the user to choose the audio, video, and haptic source devices before setting up the session. In this case, the AV data was provided from webcams connected to the nodes. Once the user began the WebRTC signaling process, the HAV communication commenced automatically.

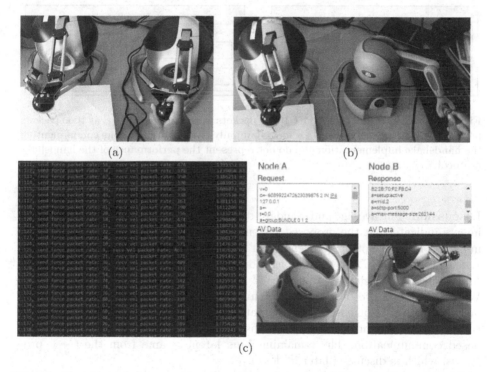

Fig. 10. Two heterogeneous nodes experimental setup. (a) Novint Falcon to Novint Falcon. (b) Geomagic Touch to Novint Falcon. (c) C++ console log displaying packet communication rates, and web GUI from Node A displaying SDP request and response from Node A and B, as well as their video data. Its content is identical to the other node.

5 Experimental Results

In this section, we present the latency findings of the tele-writing experiment. The mean and the standard deviation of the handshake latency is measured to be 47.25 ms and 23.38 ms, respectively. The performance of the bidirectional HAV communication was assessed through its mean roundtrip time (RTT) measured over the tele-writing experiment with a duration of 10 s. The standard packet rate of 1000 (consequence of 1 kHz sampling rate), leads to measuring RTT of 10000 packets. It was observed that the mean and standard deviation of RTT were 3.57 ms and 1.81 ms, respectively. The breakdown of the mean RTT is shown in Fig. 11. We observed a high level of consistency in these RTT measurements over several runs of the application.

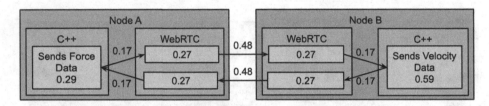

Fig. 11. Breakdown of 3.57 ms RTT 10000 packets were sampled in 10 s, at 1000 packets per second. Note that the C++ segments are only sample applications complimenting the handshake implementation and do not represent the performance of the handshake protocol.

Discussion: The average and standard deviation of RTT measured in our experiments indicate that the proposed system can provide stable bidirectional communication under both heterogeneous or homogeneous haptic interfaces. Around 1 ms of the total RTT, is the propagation delay between the TI nodes. Another 1 ms came from delays within the TI node browsers. This is attributed to WebRTC-related protocol handling. This is expected since the browsers are in high-level JavaScript-based implementation. Around 0.6 ms additional latency came from interfacing the C++ programs with the browsers through WebSocket-based communication. The remaining 1 ms latency came from the C++ programs, which is discussed later in detail.

Latency for some of these segments could potentially be eliminated. For example, switching from JavaScript Web API to native C++ implementation would address synchronization of AV data with haptic data. It will also allow the haptic interface setup to be integrated with WebRTC. This will eliminate any unnecessary cross-language latency. HAV handshake and communication latency between TI nodes will further reduce once WebRTC extends *RTCDataChannel* transport configuration option to pure UDP.

It should be noted that the latency for each of these segments are heavily dependent on the size of the haptic information being communicated. The

C++ programs are designed to send a set of timestamp and velocity/force data upon significant haptic device movement, with processing delays as low as around $1\,\mu s$. When they are wrapped in JSON formatting and converted to strings for communication, their sizes are typically around 120 bytes in length. If other types of data such as rotation, gripper movement, and button press also need to be communicated, the data size would further increase. The processing delay may then increase, thereby congesting the system. The communicated data should therefore be minimized by using compression mechanisms. Xu et al. effectively addresses such issues by demonstrating a combination of the perceptual-deadband haptic data reduction approach and the time domain passivity approach (TDPA) [32]. The size of the programs also affect the processing delay. As the C++ programs run multiple threads within themselves and the browser programs are executed asynchronously, adding more features could increase RTT proportionally more than when they are run on a single thread or run through a synchronous language. In addition to this, using browsers other than Chrome is known to increase the processing delays [22].

Lastly, the hardware-level performance of TI nodes might have contributed to the RTT as well. To our surprise, the latency in Node B's C++ program was twice as much as that of Node A, as seen in Fig. 11. These programs were developed to exchange different form of data, namely force or velocity, and while Node A requires calculation of force data based on the received velocity data, Node B has to simply actuate the received force data. Hence, the latency difference was most likely due to the fact that the Node A and B's haptic loop frequency were around 2 and 0.5 MHz respectively, as measured by Chai3D's frequency counter. This made Node A four times more responsive than Node B at handling possible congestions. To address this limitation, faster running programs or hardware should be used.

Taking these into account, the RTT is specific to the software and hardware environment it was implemented in. It is therefore recommended that for more complex TI applications, more efficient applications and hardware should be used. In addition, more types of haptic devices and applications can be tested to ensure that the PnP system is agnostic to multitude of scenarios. The above discussion suggests that as long as these recommendations are met, the system can be used to construct practical TI applications. These application will meet the sub-10 ms requirement for safe haptic control, and will be near the 1 ms average human haptic reaction time [16]. To our knowledge, this implementation is the only openly available WebRTC-based HAV communication system, and will therefore serve as an integral part of future TI application development.

6 Conclusions

In this paper, we presented the design of a WebRTC-based PnP communication system for TI interactions encompassing haptic feedback. We described in detail the TI Metadata (TIM) devised for conveying the haptic metadata of various TI nodes, the handshake protocol, and communication protocol for HAV interaction. Through implementation of the proposed PnP system on a WebRTC-based platform and heterogeneous haptic interfaces, we provided a proof of concept of its operation. Further, the average and standard deviation of RTT were 3.57 ms and 1.81 ms, respectively. This paves way for sub-10 ms RTT crucial for TI interactions. As the system substantiates its usefulness for TI applications, it has been made open-source for further TI application development. The system will thus serve to form the foundation of TI application development. Such progress will drive innovation in global products and services, changing societies for the better. As for future work, we would like to evaluate the PnP system with a wider range of haptic interfaces, such as interfaces with multi-points of haptic interaction.

The proposed PnP communication system is aimed to be used by a broad set of audience. Hence, in future, we plan to make the project resources publicly available to fuel the explosive growth of TI.

References

1. Jami. https://jami.net/
2. Linphone. https://www.linphone.org/
3. Retroshare. https://retroshare.readthedocs.io
4. Riot. https://about.riot.im/
5. Webrtc samples munge SDP. https://webrtc.github.io/samples/src/content/peerconnection/munge-sdp/
6. Aijaz, A., Dohler, M., Aghvami, A.H., Friderikos, V., Frodigh, M.: Realizing the tactile internet: haptic communications over next generation 5G cellular networks. IEEE Wirel. Commun. **24**(2), 82–89 (2016)
7. Anderson, R.J., Spong, M.W.: Bilateral control of teleoperators with time delay. IEEE Trans. Autom. Control **34**(5), 494–501 (1989)
8. Carter, J., et al.: The gothi model of tactile and haptic interaction. In: Proceedings of GOTHI-05 Guidelines on Tactile and Haptic Interactions, pp. 93–95 (2005)
9. Cha, J., Ho, Y.S., Kim, Y., Ryu, J., Oakley, I.: A framework for haptic broadcasting. IEEE Multim. **16**(3), 16–27 (2009)
10. Kohlhoff, C.: Asio C++ library (2020). https://think-async.com/Asio/
11. Dunn, C.: open-source-parsers/jsoncpp (2020). https://github.com/open-source-parsers/jsoncpp
12. Dohler, M., et al.: Internet of skills, where robotics meets AI, 5G and the tactile internet. In: 2017 European Conference on Networks and Communications (EuCNC), pp. 1–5. IEEE (2017)
13. Eid, M., Andrews, S., Alamri, A., El Saddik, A.: HAMLAT: a HAML-based authoring tool for haptic application development. In: Ferre, M. (ed.) EuroHaptics 2008. LNCS, vol. 5024, pp. 857–866. Springer, Heidelberg (2008). https://doi.org/10.1007/978-3-540-69057-3_108
14. Fayez, R., Eid, M., Orozco, M., El Saddik, A.: Haptic applications meta-language. In: 2006 Tenth IEEE International Symposium on Distributed Simulation and Real-Time Applications, pp. 261–264. IEEE (2006)
15. Aboukhadijeh, F.: feross/simple-websocket (2020). https://github.com/feross/simple-websocket
16. Fettweis, G.P.: The tactile internet: applications and challenges. IEEE Veh. Technol. Mag. **9**(1), 64–70 (2014). https://doi.org/10.1109/MVT.2013.2295069

17. Conti, F.: Chai3d (2020). https://www.chai3d.org/
18. Holland, O., et al.: The IEEE 1918.1 "tactile internet" standards working group and its standards. Proc. IEEE **107**(2), 256–279 (2019). https://doi.org/10.1109/JPROC.2018.2885541
19. IEEE P1918.1.1 Haptic Codecs for the Tactile Internet Task Group: Kinesthetic reference setup (2018). https://cloud.lmt.ei.tum.de/s/8ol5mX6TCDBS8t4
20. Iiyoshi, K., Tauseef, M., Gebremedhin, R., Gokhale, V., Eid, M.: Towards standardization of haptic handshake for tactile internet: a WebRTC-based implementation. In: 2019 IEEE International Symposium on Haptic, Audio and Visual Environments and Games (HAVE), pp. 1–6. IEEE (2019)
21. Ivov, E.: Jitsi. The architecture of open source applications, pp. 121–132 (2011)
22. Jansen, B., Goodwin, T., Gupta, V., Kuipers, F., Zussman, G.: Performance evaluation of WebRTC-based video conferencing. SIGMETRICS Perform. Eval. Rev. **45**(3), 56–68 (2018). https://doi.org/10.1145/3199524.3199534
23. Johnston, A.B., Burnett, D.C.: WebRTC: APIs and RTCWEB protocols of the HTML5 real-time web. Digital Codex LLC (2012)
24. King, H.H., Hannaford, B., Kammerly, J., Steinbachy, E.: Establishing multimodal telepresence sessions using the session initiation protocol (SIP) and advanced haptic codecs. In: 2010 IEEE Haptics Symposium, pp. 321–325. IEEE (2010)
25. Loreto, S., Romano, S.P.: Real-time communications in the web: issues, achievements, and ongoing standardization efforts. IEEE Internet Comput. **16**(5), 68–73 (2012). https://doi.org/10.1109/MIC.2012.115
26. Pelton, D.: Easyrtc framework tutorial (2013)
27. Thorson, P.: zaphoyd/websocketpp (2020). https://github.com/zaphoyd/websocketpp
28. Rehn, A.: Websocket server demo (2020). https://github.com/adamrehn/websocket-server-demo
29. Signes, J., Fisher, Y., Eleftheriadis, A.: Mpeg-4's binary format for scene description. Sig. Process.: Image Commun. **15**(4–5), 321–345 (2000)
30. The jQuery Foundation: jquery (2020). https://jquery.com/
31. de Vries, R., Jager, G., Tijssen, I., Zandstra, E.H.: Shopping for products in a virtual world: Why haptics and visuals are equally important in shaping consumer perceptions and attitudes. Food Qual. Prefer. **66**, 64–75 (2018)
32. Xu, X., Panzirsch, M., Liu, Q., Steinbach, E.: Integrating haptic data reduction with energy reflection-based passivity control for time-delayed teleoperation. In: 2020 IEEE Haptics Symposium (HAPTICS), pp. 109–114 (2020)

SwingBeats: An IoT Haptic Feedback Ankle Bracelet (HFAB) for Dance Education

Navid Shaghaghi$^{(\boxtimes)}$ (iD), Yu Yang Chee, Jesse Mayer, and Alissa LaFerriere

Ethical, Pragmatic, and Intelligent Computing (EPIC) and Creative, Augmented, and Virtual Environments (CAVE) Laboratories, Santa Clara University, Santa Clara, CA 95053, USA
{nshaghaghi,ychee,jdmayer,alaferriere}@scu.edu

Abstract. Dance choreography is often synchronized with music. Thus, a major challenge for learning choreography is moving the correct body part to a signified rhythm in the music surrounding the beat. However, the rhythm is often more complex than a metronome. SwingBeats is a real time, haptic feedback system under research and development with the goal of helping learners of any dance style to a) focus on learning the various dance moves, steps, patterns, and dynamics without the need to keep constant track of the music's beat pattern, and b) to condition any choreography for the dance through custom built Internet of Things (IoT) wearables.

This paper is to report on the development and preliminary success of custom Haptic Feedback Ankle Bracelets (HFABs) for the SwingBeats system. HFABs enable learning the footwork for any dance through conditioning the learner to move their feet in accordance to the choreography which follows the beat of the music. Thus HFABs condition muscle memory in the same way learning to play the piano conditions the musician's finger muscles to anticipate each move ahead of time and play the notes in perfect harmony. Thus far, the custom HFABs have been tested with Tap dancing because this style of dancing is predominantly focused on footwork and includes a relatively small degree of freedom in the directions each foot can travel during dancing. The results are thus easily generalizable to any footwork with the addition of more haptic actuators as needed per degrees of freedom.

Keywords: Haptic feedback · Internet of Everything (IoE) · Internet of Things (IoT) · Rhythmic metronome · Tap dance education · Wearable technology

1 Introduction

Dancing is a form of human expression consisting of purposefully selected sequences of bodily movement, each with aesthetic or symbolic values, most

© ICST Institute for Computer Sciences, Social Informatics and Telecommunications Engineering 2021
Published by Springer Nature Switzerland AG 2021. All Rights Reserved
N. Shaghaghi et al. (Eds.): INTETAIN 2020, LNICST 377, pp. 82–101, 2021.
https://doi.org/10.1007/978-3-030-76426-5_6

often synchronized with music. Since dancers must land specific movements on specific beats, it is crucial to maintain a constant awareness of beat and rhythm while dancing. However, many have issues remembering the order of steps and rhythm of choreography. They may forget what step comes next or what part of the music that step occurs on. Since proper steps and timing are key for properly performing a dance, they are currently conditioned into muscle memory by endless practice in leading up to a performance for instance. This is similar to how practicing playing the piano conditions the musician's finger muscles to anticipate each move ahead of time and to play the notes in perfect harmony on the night of the performance. For the case of pianists, research has shown promise in being able to enhance their practicing experience as well as to shorten the time needed for practicing by using Passive Haptic Learning (PHL) gloves as seen in [6]. Thus, it stands to reason that haptic feedback assistance can be provided for conditioning muscle memory for other tasks such as dancing.

To address this issue for dancing, the SwingBeats project has developed IoT Haptic Feedback Ankle Bracelets (HFABs) to signal learners when and how to move their feet to the beat of the music. This can provide the learner with immediate feedback, thus improving the learning experience. Tap dance was chosen as the first dance style to test the HFABs. Tap dance is a style of dance focused on rhythmic footwork which is characterized by the sounds of the metal taps affixed under the toes and heels of the dance shoes striking the floor. Tap dance is the perfect style of dance for this phase of the system's development as this style focuses on the feet rather than the whole body. This paper will discuss the usage of HFABs for tap dance education only, but HFABs are usable for any style of dance without loss of generality. Future work will include further development and testing of HFABs for additional dance styles.

Section 2 will provide a background overview as well as the motivation for the development of HFABs and Sect. 3 will explore existing products. Section 4 will detail the design and development of SwingBeats' HFABs and Sect. 5 will detail the testing methodology, logistics, and results for the system with Alpha testers. The, Sects. 6 and 7 will delineate the currently under development features and future targets for the development of HFABs respectively. And lastly, Sect. 8 will offer some concluding remarks.

2 Background

At the time of this writing, the SwingBeats system has been under research and development for two years.

2.1 History

As was reported in HAVE 2019, the SwingBeats system began as an iOS metronome application that acquires a song's beat pattern from Spotify's API [10] and vibrates an iPhone and/or a smart watch to the beat of the music [7].

While the mobile app works great as a metronome, it does not teach learners how to dance or to follow a specific choreography. With the addition of HFABs, the SwingBeats app can now wirelessly transmit a set of instructions to an HFAB in order to actuate the correct vibrators at the correct times. This guides dancers' footwork by communicating the exact part of the foot they are supposed to move at that exact point in the choreography.

2.2 Motivation

Dancers usually learn choreography in a dance studio with an instructor that can observe their movements from all angles and give them feedback on how they are doing as well as how they could improve. With tap dance for instance, this feedback usually pertains to their rhythm and whether they are using the correct part of the correct foot at the correct time to produce that rhythm.

Remembering a dance involves a lot of practice which frequently takes place at home without an instructor. However, if a student does not remember the dance choreography from class, missed a rehearsal, or is unable to attend a weekly dance class due to cost, availability, or other factors such as a pandemic, they will not be able to practice effectively. Furthermore, at the time of this writing, due to the COVID-19 pandemic most dance studios are closed and students are taking dance classes via video conferencing applications, which does not offer the same learning experience as the instruction and feedback they would have received in person from a dance instructor. Video conferencing does not allow for watching instructors from multiple angles nor is it suitable for receiving feedback from instructors as they are unable to observe the learners from all angles.

Closing this learning gap is one of SwingBeats' main motivations which is achieved by allowing learners to transmit the choreography they need to practice from their SwingBeats mobile phone app to their SwingBeats HFABs. The HFABs vibrate the correct actuators located on the correct part of each foot at the correct times and thus help condition the learners' muscle memory - in effect helping learners practice and learn the choreography.

3 Existing Products

As reported in [7] not many products for assisting in dance education exist.

3.1 Metronomes

Most existing metronome applications such as WatchHapticMetronome [4], and "Pulse - Metronome & Tap Tempo" [5] and hardware metronomes such as Soundbrenner Pulse [9] and Core [8] are simple metronomes meant for helping musicians stay in sync with the beat. As such, they do not have any real application in dance education beyond helping dancers stay in sync with the beat of the music. This however, is not enough as learning how to dance requires awareness and conditioning of complex choreography.

3.2   Haptic Socks

As part of Georgia Tech's 2018 "Get a Move On" hackathon, a team of graduate students prototyped a pair of haptic socks with three sample elementary tap routines [2]. The socks sent vibrations to individual legs in order to instruct the dancer which foot to move when. However to the best of the author's knowledge, this product was never followed upon nor commercialized.

4   SwingBeats Haptic Feedback Ankle Bracelets (HFABs)

Haptic Feedback Ankle Bracelets (HFABs) depicted in Fig. 1 are custom IoT addons for the SwingBeats system [7] designed and built to assist in the learning of the footwork for any dance. This is done by triggering the movement of the feet in accordance with the programmed choreography which is in sync with the beat of the music. The main two use cases for HFABs are to 1) help condition the learner's muscle memory to remember choreography during learning and practice and 2) to allow a dancer to dance to any choreography on the spot even without having learned or practiced a choreography in the past.

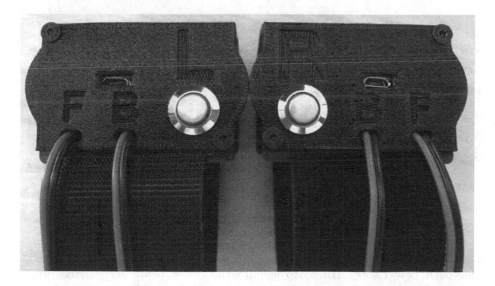

Fig. 1. SwingBeats Haptic Feedback Ankle Bracelets (HFABs)

4.1   Hardware

The HFAB circuitry depicted in Fig. 2 centers around the ESP32 series of System on a Chip (SoC) development boards and includes vibration motors, a rechargeable battery and charging apparatus, and an on/off push button.

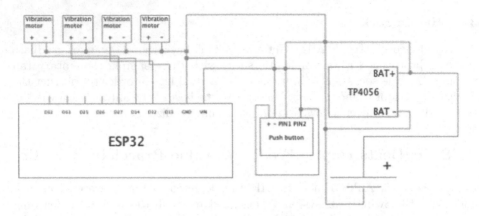

Fig. 2. HFAB schematic

All of the HFAB's circuitry is mounted and interconnected on a soldered Printed Circuit Board (PCB) that as depicted in Fig. 3 sits in a 3D printed drawer that slides in and out of a 3D printed casing for easy access.

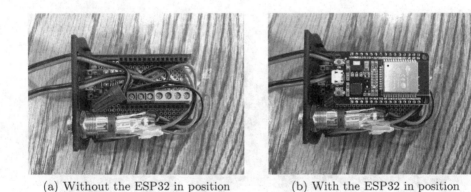

(a) Without the ESP32 in position   (b) With the ESP32 in position

Fig. 3. Internals of an HFAB

Communication: SwingBeats' HFABs communicate with a mobile phone via Bluetooth Low Energy (BLE) to acquire the music beats and choreography queues. There are no wires between the two HFABs nor between the devices and the phone, as a truly wireless setup is essential to maximize mobility and degrees of freedom when dancing.

For the first prototype, the number of BLE connections to the phone are limited. The HFAB mounted on the left ankle (referred to as the primary device) establishes a connection with the iPhone via BLE to receive instructions. It then forwards the instructions to the one mounted on the right ankle (referred to as the secondary device) via WiFi. The secondary device only listens to the primary device and never the iOS application.

Actuation in the Form of Vibration: As dancing shoes are quite tight, it could be a problem if the vibration motors used are too thick. As a result the micro (10 mm diameter × 3 mm thickness) flat coin vibration motors depicted in Fig. 4 were used which have a DC voltage rating of 3 V and an operation speed of 12,000 RPMs.

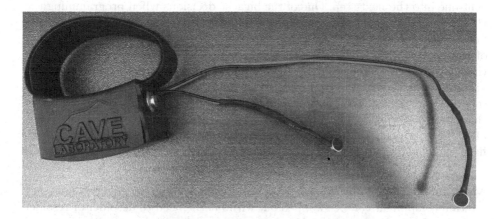

Fig. 4. HFAB with micro, flat coin vibration motors

Two different levels of vibrations for the toes and a single level of vibration for the heal actuators were incorporated in order to help learners distinguish between certain steps. A lighter vibration on the toes indicates when the learner is supposed to strike their toes on the ground but not transfer any of their body's weight onto that foot (a.k.a. not step onto that foot). A stronger vibration on the toes indicates when the learner is supposed to step onto that foot.

Tap dancers stand on the balls of their feet which means their heels are off the ground. This is so they are able to drop their heels to make a tap sound instead of having to first lift their heel off the ground and then drop it to get the same sound. The importance of this increases as the rhythms being created with the tap sounds get faster and faster. It would thus be impossible to produce such fast rhythms otherwise. Therefore for now, only one vibration level has been programmed for the heel actuators which indicates when the dancer needs to drop their heel to the ground. Different heel vibration levels will be programmed in the future to incorporate more advanced tap moves.

Since beginner tap dancers struggle with remembering to stand on the ball of their feet, if the dancer is meant to step (meaning lift their foot and drop it to the ground), as aforementioned only the toe actuators will vibrate so they do not drop their heal when they take the step and thus remain on the balls of their feet. There are however times during tapping that the dancer needs to use their entire foot such as when the dancer strikes the floor with their entire foot for a louder sound but does not step onto that foot, jumps to the other foot, or hops (jumps and lands on the same foot). To indicate these instances, both the front and back actuators vibrate. When the dancer is to strike their foot, but not step onto it, a lighter vibration occurs; and when the dancer is to jump or hop, a stronger vibration occurs. Both feet will vibrate if the dancer is meant to jump with both feet.

The vibrations, regardless of level, occur for 200 ms which is long enough for the dancer to feel and recognize them, but not long enough that they would continue into the next step. One of the biggest decisions when programming the HFABs was deciding if the vibration should start right on the beat or slightly before the beat. If before the beat, the HFABs can not vibrate too far ahead of the beat so the dancer can still distinguish when they are meant to strike the ground. After testing out both methods, it was decided to have the device vibrate 100 ms before the beat. This is so the dancer's brain has time to react to what part of the foot vibrated and perform the correct footwork. Therefore the HFAB will vibrate 100 ms before the beat starts and finish vibrating 100 ms after the beat occurs. Meaning the HFAB vibrates through the beat so dancers have enough time to react to the vibration and step on the beat.

Modularity: The HFABs have been designed and built to ensure that every internal component can be swapped out without the need to desolder or resolder anything. This allows for speed and ease in repairing and upgrading each and every one of the components. Furthermore, the modular approach to SwingBeats' hardware design is especially important for future applications, as different dance styles will require slightly different set ups. For example, while tap dance only requires a vibration motor on the front and back of each foot, other styles will require four vibration motors on each foot's front, back, left, and right. To this end, terminal block connectors were used to connect the vibration motors to the ESP32 development board, and two extra connectors were included to enable easy expansion.

Power: HFABs are powered by a LiPO 3.7 V 1500 mAh battery. A McIgIcM TP4056 battery charger is used to enable usb charging of the battery.

Cost: Table 1 details the cost of each hardware component. Due to economies of scale however, all of these components can be purchased for a fraction of the prices listed here when purchased in bulk from overseas vendors. It should be noted that the total coast does not include the extra wires, heat shrink tubing, and solder used in each HFAB. Since it is extremely difficult to truly ascertain these components' cost due to their bulk availability in the lab. Hence, to roughly incorporate their cost, the total cost of an HFAB's circuitry is rounded to $14 USD.

Table 1. Cost of items

Components for a single HFAB	Count	Cost
MELIFE ESP32	1	$5.07
YDL 3.7 V 1500 mAh 603959 Lipo battery	1	$4.50
McIgIcM TP4056 battery charger	1	$0.59
Linkstyle 12–24 V 12 mm ON/OFF Latching Push Button Switch	1	$2.00
YXQ 1030 Flat Vibration Motor Coin	2	$0.63
Blank PCB	1	$0.40
Total		$13.82

4.2 3D Printing

The HFAB's circuitry is encapsulated by a 3D printed case consisting of a main body and a slide in drawer as seen in Figs. 5, 6 and 7. The case is 3D printed using Polyethylene Terephthalate Glycol (PETG) filament to provide a high level of durability without making the case brittle [3]. At a 0.2 mm layer height, making a complete set of two cases (one for each of the left and right ankles) takes 11 h and 22 min, uses 103 g of filament, and costs roughly $3.8 USD to produce. This brings the hardware cost of producing a single HFAB to $14 (for circuitry) + $3.8/2 (for 3D-Printing) = $15.9 which is rounded to $16 USD once the cost of the Velcro is assumed to be $0.10 due to its availability in bulk at the lab.

The casing dimensions are 55 mm × 45 mm × 70 mm (L × W × H) in order to maintain a low profile on the user's leg. As can be seen in Figs. 5a and 6b, the main body of the capsule is curved to comfortably fit around the dancer's leg right above the ankle joint. An opening on the ankle side of the case holds a Velcro strap used for securing the HFAB to the dancer's leg. This opening has a tight tolerance in order to provide resistance so that the device does not freely shift on the strap, while still enabling easy user adjustments.

(a) Side profile of switched Off HFAB   (b) Switched on HFAB

Fig. 5. Assembled HFAB in custom 3D-printed case with heal and toe actuators

The use of Velcro also enables the mounting of the HFABs at almost any distance above the ankles based on the dancer's preference. The length of the actuator cables can be adjustable and custom built but for this first prototype have been kept to a minimum length to reduce tangling. In order to ensure that the heal actuators have the shortest cables as possible, the HFABs are designed to be mounted with their actuator cable holes facing backwards. To this end, the left and right ankle HFAB cases have small variations in order to help easily distinguish them from each other: when mounted around the ankle, the power toggle switch and actuator cables on each need to be facing backwards as seen in Fig. 6a and the Creative, Augmented, and Virtual Environments (CAVE) Laboratory's logo on each case faces upward as can be seen in Fig. 6b.

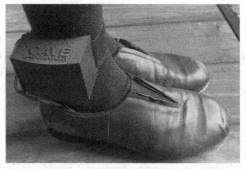

(a) Front view: Power switch and cable holes face backwards

(b) Side View: Creative, Augmented, and Virtual Environments (CAVE) laboratory logo faces upward

Fig. 6. HFABs mounted above dancer's ankles

If that fact is forgotten, the case also has an "L" or "R" carved out right above the power switch in order to further indicate whether the HFAB is for the left or right ankle, which can be seen back in Fig. 1. The letters "B" and "F" are placed above cable holes for the actuators to indicate whether the actuator should be placed on the back (heel) or front (above the toes) of the foot. The front also contains a hole for the micro-USB charging port. An incline around the charging port provides room for charging cables of various housing dimensions to be accommodated. The interior of the capsule has a tight tolerance so that the PCB is right against the interior wall, preventing movement of the PCB when pushing in the charging cable. Two mounting holes diagonal from one another secure the slide in drawer to the main body using M3 × 6 mm screws.

Inside the capsule, the removable drawer has a two sided tray. On the side facing the user's leg, the tray has small ridges on its two edges that act as a slide mechanism allowing the PCB and its hardware to be slid into position and secured due to their tight tolerance. This mechanism can be partially seen back in Fig. 3. The other side of the tray has another similar slide in mechanism for the battery, as can be easily seen in Fig. 7a. The use of these slide in mechanisms ensures that the device's hardware is secured and does not rattle in the case when in use. In addition, the tray acts as a barrier between the PCB hardware and the battery, ensuring no damaging interactions occur between the two. This tray also makes assembly and disassembly significantly easier, as all the HFAB's hardware is directly mounted on the slide-in tray and can be easily inserted or removed from the casing as is conveyed in Fig. 7b.

(a) Battery compartment under slid-in tray of HFAB along with connector for easy replacement of battery.

(b) Hardware compartment tray partially slid out of HFAB case in order to expose circuitry.

Fig. 7. HFAB slide-in tray mechanism

4.3   Software

The software necessary to make everything work is divided into two locations: the SwingBeats (currently iOS only) mobile application and the ESP32 microcontroller.

iOS: The basic flow of the application which can be seen in Fig. 8 is as follows: First, the user taps a button on the screen to establish a connection between the SwingBeats application and the Spotify application. SwingBeats checks if the Spotify application is installed and if the user has a Spotify premium subscription. This step is required as Spotify iOS SDK requires the user to have a Spotify premium account for remote playback. Next, the user turns on the HFABs by pressing the toggle button on the device. A ring light around the button will illuminate when the device is powered on as depicted in Fig. 5b. Once the HFAB is on, the user can scan for the device in the SwingBeats phone application and connect it via BLE. Connection between the left and right device is automatic assuming both devices are turned on. Once a connection is established between the iPhone and the device, the user can choose between four choreographed dances. Each dance is labeled by the song used when performing. When the song is selected by the user, the application runs an algorithm that converts the dance moves into compressed instruction sets for the HFABs. Finally, the user can tap the start button when he/she is ready to begin. The start button sends the instructions to the HFABs to start the vibration in sync with the song playing on Spotify.

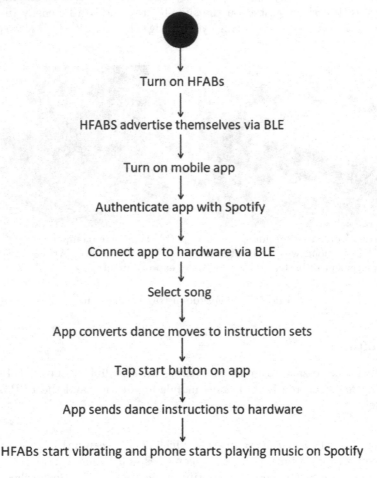

Fig. 8. SwingBeats HFAB connection and utilization sequence diagram

ESP32: One priority of the HFABs' design is for them to be as small and light as possible in order to prevent disruption of any of the dance moves when being worn. This makes the ESP32 series of SoC perfect for HFABs due to their small size and wireless communication features. Furthermore, ESP32 microcontrollers come with a dual core processor which enables the parallel processing of the vibration instructions and the timings of the beats without the need for multi threading and context switching between the two processes.

The software on the primary HFAB is in one of two modes: waiting or dancing. In waiting mode, the primary HFAB listens for instructions from the phone.

The moment it receives dance instructions, it processes and forwards that message to the secondary HFAB. In dancing mode, the HFAB's ESP32 uses core 0 to read timings and adjust the amount of time to delay until the next vibration, and uses core 1 to manage turning the vibrations on and off. Each vibration is turned on for 200 ms.

5   User Testing

For the initial round of testing, advanced tap dancers with 8–20 years of experience were recruited. While this may not be the eventual key demographic that will take advantage of SwingBeats' HFABs, feedback from people with a lot of tap experience is crucial for successful product development. These individuals know what is most important when learning to tap dance, thus will be able to provide the most useful feedback on how the HFABs are helpful and what can be done to improve them as they have past learning experiences to compare this experience to. Given the pandemic, however, many were not available to test the HFABs or did not have the resources such as tap shoes and a suitable floor to dance on in order to participate. Thus, only 7 testers were recruited for this round of testing. However, even given this small number, the feedback provided was invaluable for how the HFABs performed and how they could be improved. Once the COVID-19 pandemic subsides, the upgraded HFABs will be tested with larger numbers of participants from the introductory tap dancing class on campus.

5.1   Methodology

Each participant took part in 4 rounds of testing where each round consisted of a different tap dance choreography. Every dance was 14 eight-counts long (112 beats) and consisted of beginner basic tap moves. Each dance incorporated the same steps in different orders and the songs were approximately the same beats per minute (bpm) thus all dances were at the same level of difficulty. The dances incorporated portions with slower and portions with faster rhythm. The four tests involved learning the dance, practicing the dance with the music while watching the instructor, and filming themselves perform the dance. The participants were on a video conference call with the instructor while they filmed themselves performing the dance to ensure that they recorded the video immediately after learning the choreography. In one round, participants practiced and recorded with the HFABs. In another round, they practiced with HFABS but recorded without using them. In a third round they practiced without the HFABS but recorded with their assistance. And finally in the last round they practiced and recorded without using the HFABs. Each group did each of these rounds in a different order with different choreography in order to ensure that no environmental bias enters the results from any of those factors.

All the testing except for one participant occurred over video conferencing with one of the authors who has years of experience tap dancing and teaching tap dancing. Each round took 30 min including learning, practicing, and performing the dance. Teaching participants how to use the system and app for the first time also took about 30 min. Participants learned the dance without the music. They were allowed to ask any questions they had on the dance at any time. Then, they were able to practice the dance with music and feedback from the instructor 4 times before filming themselves perform the choreography without the instructor guiding them. With beginner tap dancers it is expected that testing will take much longer. However, since the choreography for these tests were basic and the participants were advanced, they did not need much time to learn the choreography prior to recording.

5.2   Results

Everyone in the testing had a different skill level. Thus their videos were compared and judged solely against their own videos from their various rounds of testing. When analyzing the videos, the main criteria for judging were correct timing, performing the correct step, and whether they started and stopped the dance move at the correct time. Then, their dances were ranked from the one they performed most accurately to the one they performed least accurately considering those criteria. In order to rank the testing setup, 4 points were given for performing the best, 3 for second best, 2 for third best, and finally 1 point for worst. If the dancer did the same on two dances, each dance was given the same amount of points. There were multiple cases where it was too hard to distinguish between someone's second best and third best performance. When adding up the points, as can be seen in Table 2 practicing and performing with HFABs was the most effective. No HFAB usage was second in effectiveness. Only practicing with HFABs but not performing with them was third effective. And finally only performing with HFABs was least effective.

Table 2. Testing results: HFAB usage vs. performance

HFAB usage/performance	Best	Second	Third	Worst
HFAB used during both practice and performing	3	3	1	0
HFAB only used during practice	0	5	0	2
HFAB only used during performing	1	2	3	1
HFABs not used for practice nor performing	3	1	1	2

Based on the feedback elicited via a survey from the participants, testers found practicing and recording with the HFABs helpful as they were able to get used to the vibrations of the dance and thus allow it to guide them in performing. However, many felt that as experienced dancers used to learning without HFABs, they were more comfortable learning and performing as they normally would without HFABs in comparison to using HFABs for only the practice or recording portions but not both. Future testing with less experienced dancers will provide a better perspective for seeing how prior dance expertise affects the results.

5.3   Feedback

After testing was completed, each participant was asked to fill a survey on the strengths, weaknesses, and ways to improve the HFABs. Some of their most important overall thoughts are summarised here.

On Vibration Initialization Time: About 71% of participants thought the system should vibrate a little ahead of the beat (as programmed) in order to have time to react. 15% thought it should vibrate on the beat, and 15% could see benefits in both ways. Given that 86% are happy with the current design, no future modification is planned for this feature.

On Vibration Strength: Every tester noted that the vibrations needed to be stronger in order to be more useful. They also noted that because of the low intensity of the vibrations they were unable to differentiate between the softer and stronger vibrations. 57% of participants thought the device helped them get back on track if they lost their place, know what foot to use, keep track of when the choreography got slower or faster, know when the dance started and stopped, and learn the musicality and timing. The other 43% of participants thought that the vibrations need to be stronger for the HFABs to be as helpful as intended in helping them learn and remember the dance choreography. This issue has already been resolved as will be discussed in the Work in Progress section below.

On Usage Purpose: 43% of participants found using the device for both practicing and performing most helpful. 23% found just practicing with the device most helpful. And the remaining 23% found just performing with the device most helpful. All participants thought the system would be beneficial for beginning tap dancers especially to be used for them to practice between classes. Further testing with beginners will provide more clarity on the most effective use of the HFABs.

6   Work in Progress

6.1   Increasing Vibration Intensity

The current version of SwingBeats is capable of producing stronger and weaker vibrations by controlling the speed of the vibration motors. This is done by using Pulse Width Modulation (PWM) on output pins of the ESP32, and simulating more or less voltage for the vibration motors. However, participant's commented that because the vibrations were not strong enough, they could not distinguish them from one another as easily as they should or at times not at all. Since the ESP32 output pins are not capable of producing voltage higher than 3.3 v the circuitry is being redesigned using transistors to have the output pins act as on/off switches that connect/disconnect the vibration motors to/from the battery directly which can supply higher voltages up to 3.7 v. Initial testing in the lab has proven significant increase in the vibration intensity of the actuators.

6.2   Addition of a Second Dimension of Vibration

Another improvement to the actuation is to add a variation in length of vibration depending on the speed of the choreography. For example assume a dance has steps 500 ms apart in some parts and 250 ms apart in other parts. The actuators would have to vibrate for longer to signify that the rhythm is slower and shorter to signify the rhythm is faster. And since as aforementioned the actuators vibrate through the step, in this way, the HFABs will be able to communicate more than only which part of which foot to move and when but also how fast to perform that movement.

6.3   SwingBeats Phone Application UI Improvements

Currently, little effort has been put into the design of the mobile app beyond what was reported on in this paper and in [7]. The application needs to include individualized features that allow for users to create and add their own choreographies and to get valuable diagnostics data such as battery life, etc. as well as sensor date (more on this later) from each of the HFABS.

6.4   Direct BLE Connection Between Phone and both Left and Right HFABs

The current version of HFABs designates the left leg's HFAB as the primary and the one for the right leg as the secondary. Only the primary HFAB communicates with the phone and relays the instructions for the right HFAB through a WiFi connection between the two. This is inefficient as it causes unnecessary communication which drains battery life and pollutes the airwaves, but more impotently prevents the usage of the right HFAB by itself. This is being rectified by revamping the mobile application to establish two concurrent BLE connections and disseminating the choreography for the left and right HFABs separately.

6.5   Programming Warm Ups

A common feedback received from many testers was that they did not have enough time to get used to the system. They didn't have time to get used to how different steps felt with the vibration. Thus, while learning the dance it was hard to rely on the vibrations to guide them. One way to fix this problem is to program warm up dances into the system. A warm up consists of repetitive steps to help beginners learn certain steps and get advanced dancers ready for more advanced combinations of those steps. Every dance class begins with a warm up. Thus it makes sense for SwingBeats to incorporate them. For example, an instructor may begin all of the tap classes she teaches with a shuffle warm up. This warm up occurs in most tap classes as a shuffle is a fundamental tap step used in most dances. The warm up includes doing the step 8 times on one leg then 8 times on the other. The dancer then repeats this multiple times at different speeds. Using SwingBeats' HFABs during this warm up for instance would allow dancers to get used to the vibrations indicating a shuffle. That way when they felt that vibration during a dance they would know exactly what step to perform. And similarly for all other moves that show up in warm us. Furthermore, by adding a body temperature sensor, the HFABs will be able to sense when the dancer's body has warmed up and is ready for transitioning to the actual dance. This can be one of the data points which is sent back to the mobile/watch app in order to signal to the dancer that they have warmed up and are ready for transitioning from the warm ups into their dance routine.

6.6   Dance Intensity Measurement

Through the addition of a Pulse Oximeter and Oxygen Saturation (SPO_2) sensor, the HFABs will be able to monitor the heart rate and oxygen levels of the dancer throughout a dance. Not only does this allow the graphing and maintenance of the workout intensity experienced by the dancer, but also the ranking of dances by their level of intensity and thus difficulty. This can further help determine what warm ups are needed before attempting a certain choreography or even what level of dance proficiency may be needed to attempt a certain choreography. Furthermore, this can help determine when the blood oxygen level of the dancer has reached its needed level during warm up which would be due to the muscles having reached their ready (warmed up) state so that the dancer can move on to the dance.

7   Future Work

7.1   Recording Dances

The current prototype relies on hand transcribed choreography. This is a manageable solution at the moment but impossible to scale. Therefore, gyroscopes and accelerometers are being worked into the HFABs' design in order to enable the recording of dances when performed by a professional or instructor. This addition is very important as it would massively increase the size of SwingBeats' repository of dances and enable the addition of dance choreography by users without any programming or even knowledge of the inner workings of the system. Some other implications of this include being able to compare different dances, visually represent some dances using only the motion data, and to measure dance expertise levels needed to perform a certain dance or choreography. Furthermore, with quantified dances, the dance performance can be recorded as has been shown to be possible in ballet dancing [11].

7.2   Real Time Instruction

Enabling the real-time transmission of the choreography from an instructor to a learner will enable a whole new world of possibilities. Instructors could in real-time lead individual or groups of learners in their class regardless of whether the class is conducted in person in a dance studio, or over video conferencing anywhere on earth.

The ability to transmit general dance movements through a tactile language has been demonstrated in work done by a team of researchers at Universidad de las Américas Puebla where they developed a rudimentary tactile language prototype consisting of 9 tactile vocabulary for assisting in the transfer of motor skills [1]. Participants in their study had a 90% recognition rate for the haptic signals, highlighting the viability of haptic feedback in dance instruction.

The goal with SwingBeats' HFABs would however be to transmit nuanced bodily movements from the instructor to the learner in order to not only convey the movement but also help teach the movement. The communications channel between the instructor and learner's systems should also be full-duplex in order for the learner to also be able to transmit their movements to the instructor so the instructors can provide even more feedback based on how the movements feel rather than only how they look or sound (in the case of Tap dance). This is important because even though a dance move can look correct, it may not be of the correct intensity for instance and thus for example fail to lead a follower correctly in a partnered dance.

7.3   Enabling Group Choreography

Currently, each set of HFABs are controlled by a single instance of the Swing-Beats phone application. It stands to reason that the SwingBeats app can control many more sets of HFABs simultaneously. This can be done in two modes: all HFAB sets being in sync or each having their distinct instructions. These modes are explored more below:

Staying in Sync: As of this writing, the HFABs used by an individual are not in sync with anyone else's. If the HFABs were capable of being in sync, this could help groups of dancers make sure they are all in sync with one another. This is extremely important in tap dance because of the sound of the steps. It is very obvious when someone is off from the rest of the group, which diminishes the performance significantly. This becomes especially important during A Capella group dancing, when a group tap dances with no music, as they are creating the music with the sound of their taps striking the floor. In this application, it is even more important that dancers are in rhythm as there is no music to cover up when someone is off. During A Capella it is extremely difficult for groups to stay in sync because without the music keeping a consistent beat that all can hear and synchronize with, many may begin to count the beats incorrectly in their head. However, Swingbeats' metronome [7] and HFABs would fill the gap created by a lack of music and vibrate to the beat for all dancers to follow. This will ensure they all stay in sync.

Puppeteering Group Performances: Using the SwingBeats application to puppeteer every dance move of every dancer in a performance has the ability to revolutionize the performing arts industry. A choreographer will be able to record each individual dancer's movements using SwingBeats' recording feature and then bring them all together under a single harmonized performance where the moves of each individual need not be similar. The dancers would all use SwingBeats for warm ups and once practice of the performance begins, each will receive the haptic feedback specific to their moves from their HFABs. This will reduce the time needed to individually train each dancer and to harmonize each with the group. Without such puppeteering capabilities, this process can take months depending on the complexity of the choreography and number of dancers involved.

Furthermore, the choreographer can easily change the tempo for all dancers at once without having to retrain each individual dancer. The faster or slower vibrations will convey that to the dancers as they practice. Even more beneficial, the choreographer can easily modify or even drastically change or add movements to each dancer's choreography without having to retrain the dancer with the new moves and then reharmonize them with the group. SwingBeats will thus in essence enable the puppeteering of any dance performance with ease, speed, and precision.

7.4 Real Time Choreography Puppeteering

The use of HFABs can allow a whole new performing art or sport: Real-Time Dance Puppeteering. Imagine the ability of choreographers to create/change choreographies on the spot during a live performance where they can build off of the mood of the audience and/or the abilities of the dancers. Or a dance or athletic instructor/coach puppeteering a group of dancers or attendees who simply show up with their HFABs and after warm ups are sent choreography or exercises moves. Or even dance-offs where two coreographers and two sets of dancers show up and compete with one another to the cheering of the audience.

7.5 Case Improvements

Reducing 3D-printing Time: 3D Printing at the 0.2 mm layer height provides quick print times for the device's casing but at the expense of printing resolution and thus aesthetics. Future iterations of the device will have their cases printed at a variable layer height. This would mean thick fast to print layers around the case, with thin slow to print layers around the connector ports, the drawer's sliding mechanism for the circuitry and battery, and the CAVE Laboratory's logo. As a result, the case will print faster than it normally would at a high resolution while maintaining a high level of detail where it matters most.

Incorporating Connectors for Actuators into the Drawer: Currently, the drawer includes two holes for the actuator cables to enter. This does not allow for the on-the-spot customization of the cable lengths, colors, etc. by the user nor allows the upgrading of the actuators without opening the case should new or different type of actuators become available. Furthermore, the ability to disconnect actuators will enhance the packaging and carrying ability of the HFABs without the worry that the cables could get bent or damaged in the process. And it enables dancers to use only the actuators they want. For instance if a dancer is trying to use an HFAB to cue a certain move she keeps forgetting or which she does not have time to condition into muscle memory through a long practice period, then she could remove all the other actuators which do not engage in that particular movement or sequence without having to change the vibration choreography in the mobile SwingBeats application.

7.6 Custom PCB

By using a custom Printed Circuit Board (PCB) for mounting and interconnecting the HFABs' electronics, the length and height of the casing can be shrunk. As a result, the HFABs will be smaller and lighter which will make long-term wearing of the device much more comfortable for the user. Furthermore, this will significantly reduce the assembly time for each HFAB's circuitry and thus enable their mass production with more precision and efficiency.

8 Conclusion

The SwingBeats HFABs provide an effective way to learn Tap dance footwork as the results indicate. Without any loss of generality, it can be argued that such haptic devices can not only easily be used to teach/learn other dance styles' footwork but also athletic footwork such as for soccer, physical therapeutic guidance, or even walking assistance for patients suffering from cerebral palsy or recovering from a stroke. However, much more development and testing are needed for the tuning of the system to these other domains.

Furthermore, as the proliferation of haptics continues, and the size, energy usage, and cost of readily available haptic components continue to shrink, it becomes more realistic and aesthetic to produce such devices for not only the ankles but also for all other parts of the body.

Acknowledgements. Many thanks are due to Santa Clara University's department of Mathematics and Computer Science for their generous grant for student summer research through the College of Arts and Sciences' REAL program even during the COVID-19 global pandemic. To Richard Mora for inspiring the SwingBeats project as a whole and his continued involvement with the project. To the Mora family, Santa Clara University's Frugal Innovation Hub, and Santa Clara University's department of computer Engineering for their continued support of the project. And lastly to all of the remote alpha testers from the Dynamic Rhythm Tap dancing performing arts student organization on campus: Natalie Sheridan, Chloé Stedman, Ashley Costa, Mikaela Wentworth, Sarah Zasso, Jada Lawson, and Alexis Morris; without whom validation of the system would not have been possible.

References

1. Camarillo-Abad, H.M., Sanchez, J.A., Starostenko, O., Sandoval, M.G.: A basic tactile language to support leader-follower dancing. J. Intell. Fuzzy Syst. **36**(5), 5011–5022 (2019). https://doi.org/10.3233/jifs-179047

2. Georgia Institute of Technology College of Computing: Bust a move: Ic ph.d. student caitlyn seim tests passive haptic learning for dance at get a move on hackathon—college of computing, March 2018. https://www.cc.gatech.edu/news/604288/bust-move-ic-phd-student-caitlyn-seim-tests-passive-haptic-learning-dance-get-move

3. MakeShaper: Important advantages of petg filament in 3d printing (2016). https://www.makeshaper.com/2016/11/15/important-advantages-of-petg-filament-in-3d-printing/

4. Perfect World Programming, LLC: Apple watch app. http://watchaware.com/watch-apps/1037103227

5. Radman, S.: Pulse - metronome & tap tempo, April 2016. https://apps.apple.com/us/app/pulse-metronome-tap-tempo/id1097323003

6. Seim, C., Estes, T., Starner, T.: Towards passive haptic learning of piano songs. In: 2015 IEEE World Haptics Conference (WHC), pp. 445–450. IEEE (2015)

7. Shaghaghi, N., Chee, Y.Y., Howser, E., Mora, R.: Requirements analysis and preliminary development of swingbeats: a real-time haptic beat tracking system for dance education. In: 2019 IEEE International Symposium on Haptic, Audio and Visual Environments and Games (HAVE) (2019). https://doi.org/10.1109/have.2019.8921326, https://ieeexplore.ieee.org/abstract/document/8921326

8. Soundbrenner Inc.: Soundbrenner core. https://www.soundbrenner.com/core

9. Soundbrenner Inc.: Soundbrenner pulse. https://www.soundbrenner.com/pulse

10. Spotify Inc.: (2020). https://developer.spotify.com/documentation/web-api

11. Thiel, D.V., Quandt, J., Carter, S.J., Moyle, G.: Accelerometer based performance assessment of basic routines in classical ballet. Procedia Eng. **72**, 14–19 (2014). https://doi.org/10.1016/j.proeng.2014.06.006

Mona Prisa: A Tool for Behaviour Change in Renewable Energy Communities

Olivia De Ruyck[1,2,3]([envelope]) [iD], Peter Conradie[1] [iD], Lieven De Marez[1,3] [iD], and Jelle Saldien[1,2] [iD]

[1] imec-mict-UGent, Ghent, Belgium
{olivia.deruyck,peter.conradie,lieven.demarez,
jelle.saldien}@ugent.be
[2] Department of Industrial Systems Engineering and Product Design, Ghent University, Kortrijk, Belgium
[3] Department of Communication Sciences, Ghent University, Ghent, Belgium

Abstract. Innovative construction projects, such as Energy Communities, are crucial to meet challenging climate objectives. However, currently residents of shared energy projects receive no feedback about the real-time consumption in the building and they cannot adjust their behaviour according to the needs of the community. In this paper we introduce the "Mona Prisa", an interactive prototype dashboard with the looks of a painting at the entrance of a building which is part of an Energy Community. The design is based on the results from 51 interviews with 37 experts living or involved in an energy community and 14 non-experts. We question the level of openness of participants to energy behavior change and how this information should be visualized for a community, not on an individual level. We present the translation of these insights into a prototype with real-time energy, water and heat flows. The content is based on three important features of energy consumption feedback: awareness, action-based feedback and gamification. Interaction with the prototype is possible by infrared sensors and a camera for face detection. In this paper we focus on the design process and components of the product. We conclude with future development ideas.

Keywords: Energy consumption feedback · Prototype · Energy community · Feedback · Information · Interface · Behaviour change

1 Introduction

As a result of depletion of fossil fuel resources, technological and institutional changes and increased awareness about climate change, the energy systems are going through a radical transformation. Progressive cities, such as the city of Ghent in Belgium, want to be climate neutral by 2050 and in the meantime reduce 40% of its CO_2 emissions by 2030 [10]. New CO_2 neutral construction projects that meet strict environmental standards are crucial to meet these objectives. Renewable energy communities (RECs) where citizens, business or other community organizations invest, produce and use renewable energy,

N. Shaghaghi et al. (Eds.): INTETAIN 2020, LNICST 377, pp. 102–117, 2021.
https://doi.org/10.1007/978-3-030-76426-5_7

are viewed as one way of reducing fossil fuel dependency [23, 35]. While the behaviour of people living in RECs impact the water, energy and heat balance (e.g. energy usage is preferable low on energy shortage moments, and high when much energy is produced and batteries are full), they have low control and feedback over the system. Energy analysis has focused largely on the technological aspects of energy use and on the effects of price fluctuations; limited research however, looks at the human perspective [26]. While Strengers describes a "Resource Man" [36], an ideal type of smart energy consumer seen as a knowledgeable micro-resource manager; other research contests this view with a passive and carefree energy consumer who is not engaged with energy consumption and becomes inattentive to energy feedback platforms over time [37]. Furthermore, there is a lack of research that looks beyond individual housing and meters, and that gives users information about a broader living context [17] and engages with emerging energy systems such as distributed or renewable generation [32].

We present the "Mona Prisa", an interactive design for increased awareness and pro-environmental behaviour based on energy, water and heat consumption of habitants of renewable energy communities. Instead of an app or desktop based solution which are currently the standard, it presents energy feedback on a screen, framed like a painting. The prototype attempts to move an individual from the previous described careless category into the "Resource Man", who desires to reduce carbon emissions and create an energy efficient power generation. The remainder of this paper is structured as follows. First, we review prevalent research within the domain of energy feedback. Secondly, we discuss the methods used in this study, results of our interviews and present our tangible design. We conclude by highlighting attributes of the design leading to ecologic behaviour change.

2 Related Work

2.1 Renewable Energy Community

The Renewable Energy Directive (EU) 2018/2001 in the European Union [11] aims to support the increase of locally, community-driven production of renewable energy. The most common energy model today is called a centralized energy distribution model. The participant is called a consumer. He is connected to an energy supplier and network operator. Energy is produced centrally, such as in nuclear power plants or large wind farms. Large energy plants are switched on and off to keep the energy supply and demand in balance. In new, distributed energy models, energy can be generated and consumed locally. Participants are called prosumers, they produce, share and store energy with e.g. solar panels, wind mills, and (community) batteries. Such Renewable Energy Communities (REC) are viewed as an alternative to traditional energy production [22]. They accelerate the transition towards carbon-free energy [5, 35]. Renewable Energy Communities (REC) are also known under terms such as low-carbon communities [20], clean energy communities (CEC) [7, 30] and community renewable energy' (CRE) [21].

The transition towards renewable and sustainable energy is being accompanied by a transformation of communities and neighbourhoods [2]. Since Energy Communities are new, participants are scare. Existing research focussing on the participants of such projects question motivations and barriers [3,21,28]; willingness to actively be engaged, co-create and share energy [25] and the design of such systems [39].

2.2 Energy, Water Feedback and Smart Meters

The compulsory roll-out of smart meters in many European countries led to a great deal of research into smart metering (SM). A smart meter has proven his effectiveness in raising energy awareness and creating behaviour change in the form of reduced energy consumption [3, 16, 40]. Early trails reported expected energy saving of 5 to 15% when feedback on energy meters or associated displays is provided to the user [9]. More recent large-scale studies lower the change in energy usage to around 3% [1]. Important reasons for limited energy reductions and fall backs in old habits after a short time are the lack of interest of householders, difficult or confusing feedback, and an overemphasis on financial motivations [6, 19].

Energy and Water Feedback Guidelines

Clear energy feedback, is a necessary element in learning how to control energy usage and eventually achieve an ecologic behaviour change [9]. Energy feedback literature addresses two questions: how to visualize feedback? And how to create behaviour change through feedback [29]. For the visualisation of feedback, Fisher [12] describes in a study on household electricity consumption that most successful energy feedback combines the following features: data is given frequently and over a long time, provides an appliance-specific breakdown, is presented in a clear appealing way, and uses computerized and interactive tools. When looking at guidelines for in-home water consumption, Froehlich [13] identifies four eco-feedback design elements that should be used: data granularity (e.g. breakdown of data per individual fixture, fixture category or activity); time granularity (time window with which data is calculated and presented such as per day, week or month); comparison (to reveal whether usage is normal) and measurement unit (metrics used to present usage data such as litres, or monetary).

Above mentioned visualization guidelines lead to better comprehension and follow up, but they do not necessary lead to behaviour change. Next to guidelines on visualisation, following research suggests ways of changing consumption behaviour. First, the provision of action-oriented tips is a common strategy used in both water as energy applications [13, 14, 29]. Second, increased awareness has a proven effect to eventually stimulate behaviour change [1, 4]. Finally, gamification appears to be a frequently used tool within the domain of energy consumption leading to positive behaviour change [24].

However, the guidelines and tools described above are designed for in-home, single family consumption feedback. They do not encounter more complex settings such as energy communities where - example given - data granularity is not shared on a personal level due to privacy reasons. Moreover, the pursued behaviour change in the mentioned research only focusses on a reduction of the total energy or water usage. Sharing of energy and water and reduced usage of energy at peak moments -which can be explored in amongst others energy communities- are not taken into account. The three mentioned tools to stimulate behaviour change in energy behavior are action-oriented tips, increased awareness and gamification will be further used as guidelines during the design of the concept (Table 1).

Table 1. Overview of literature energy feedback guidelines (EFG)

Type of EFG	Guidelines	Sources
Visualization guidelines of energy feedback	Use data granularity (per fixture, category) Use time granularity (per hour, month) Use comparison (social) Use of measurement unit (euro, liter)	Froehlich et al. [13]
	Give data frequently, over a long time Appliance-specific breakdown Present data in a clear appealing way Use computerized and interactive tools	Fischer et al. [12]
Behavior change guidelines of energy feedback	Increase awareness	Fischer et al. [12]
	Feedback on consumption should be action oriented	Froehlich; Gamberini; Micheel [13, 14, 29]
	Use gamification of consumption stimulate competition	Johnson et al. [24]

Energy Feedback Prototypes

"Energy is doubly invisible" [8]. It is not experienced directly but is best experienced by its absence, such as realizing the importance of electricity when the power is off. Devices that generate, manage and monitor energy at the household level make electricity visible. Making energy visible might be crucial for future energy communities that rely on smart users: being flexible, responsible and engaged in the electricity system's functioning. The majority of the papers in the literature review on energy related work in Human–Computer Interaction (HCI) by Paulos and Pierce [32], focus their work on electricity consumption feedback "feeding back" electricity consumption data to users via a computational display. Next to these energy displays such as screens, apps and web platforms to give energy feedback, we take a short look at three energy artefacts which are designed to create awareness about energy, water or heat consumption and aim for a positive behaviour change.

First, "The 'Power-Aware Cord' [18] is a re-design of a common electrical power strip that displays the amount of energy passing through it with electroluminescent wires moulded into the transparent electrical cord." The power-aware cord, lays the focus on awareness, but does not give an answer on how preferred behaviour to reduce energy consumption can be achieved. A second example is The Shower Calendar [27]. When showering, a dot –visualizing 60L of water- becomes smaller until it almost disappears. Aesthetic, large visualizations can be obtained when less water is used. This prototype on the contrary gives real-time feedback on the location of consumption (water usage in the shower) which opens up the possibility for the user to adjust his behaviour. Last, much commented, energy related design example is the Energy Babble [15]. It is an automated talk-radio that is obsessed with energy and the environment. Is has been developed with, and deployed to, a number of existing 'energy communities' in the UK. The Babble can be considered both as a product and as a research tool, in which role it worked to highlight issues, understandings, practices and difficulties in communities. From the review of energy feedback prototypes, we can conclude that the large majority of the energy prototypes are designed for an individual user or appliance. To our knowledge, only the last example addresses broader communities.

ICT Platforms

Next to previously discussed individual smart meters and prototypes, recent studies focus on interfaces for energy, heat or water sharing in groups. Three found examples communicate personal data through an ICT platform. Anda and Temmen [3] demonstrate that the use of advanced metering infrastructure coupled with community based social marketing (CBSM) can achieve a reduction in peak demand and overall energy consumption in an urban electricity meter replacement program. From a second study with an ICT platform for energy sharing in the Netherlands, we learn that participants engage with energy through the concept of energy practice [37]. E-practices go beyond managing energy with smart devices, and can include being actively involved in an energy collective, generating, trading, storing or discussing energy. A third, Swiss pilot study, implements an ICT platform for water sharing. First results indicated reduced water consumption, positive user feedback and suitability of the designed incentive model [31].

Conclusion

From previous research we can conclude that Renewable Energy Communities are relatively new in the energy domain. Current studies focuses on motivations and barriers, they describe the concept from a technical perspective and are less concerned about the needs of the people living in them. When energy feedback is provided to participants, a positive effect on reduction of consumption can be noticed. Guidelines on visualization and feedback to increase awareness and behavior change of the participants have been formulated. However current guidelines focus on individual houses. They don't take newer types of living into account such as projects with collective energy production and sharing or energy management systems where energy can be stored when there is over production in a common battery and use it at a later moment. Therefore we find that guidelines for the design of an interface for a Renewable Energy Community are lacking. Based on interviews, we want to understand

- the openness of REC participants to change energy consumption behavior and how energy consumption feedback guidelines can be applied
- their information needs and the way they want this information to be presented.

These insights will be translated in a design suited for energy, water and heat feedback in a Renewable Energy Community in the city of Ghent, Belgium.

3 Method

3.1 Context of the Renewable Energy Community

Prior to the design, workshops took place with potential habitants of a Renewable Energy Community (REC) and people who recently bought an apartment in the new development. The "Nieuwe Dokken" ("New Docks") is a real-estate development realized in the old harbour of the city of Ghent, in Belgium. The phased construction site will be completed in 2025 and will settle 400 new apartments and houses, shops, offices and various public facilities. In 2020, first residents move in. At full deployment, the district will be an example of a circular economy. It strives to be self-sustaining on 3 levels: water, heat and energy. On a water and heat level, the district will amongst others yearly re-use over 30.000 m^3 of city water (which is over 90% of the total consumption), use of over 500 MWh of waste heat from wastewater of a neighbouring soap factory and produce biogas from local organic waste. On an energy level, the district will supply and store renewable energy with the possibility to store surpluses in a community battery. It will balance energy and avoid dependence on the energy grid. Electrical vehicles will be loaded depending on the supply and demand.

As sources of renewable energy, water and residual heat are scarce for a crowded neighbourhood; consumption is smartly controlled through an Energy Management System (EMS) based on the expected solar energy and the trends in energy demand during the day. Currently, studies take place to demonstrate an economically viable innovative business model. However, the future habitant is not actively involved. He is currently seen as a passive subject, information about consumption balances are shared with them through yearly meetings, newsletters and can be consulted on a website, which is still under construction.

3.2 Focus Groups

To gather information about the user needs and interactions, we used generative focus groups [42]. We give preference to this technique, because as noted by Visser et al. [38], generative techniques give access to latent and tacit knowledge, while techniques like observations and interviews are more likely to reveal explicit and observable knowledge. In total, n = 51 people participated in a total of five focus groups. Of these, n = 35 consisted of people already living, or are actively involved in an energy community.

Since Renewable Energy Communities are very novel in Belgium, participants are scarce. Recruitment of the REC participants was organised by the managers of two RECs that where just running at the moment of the interviews. Participants had already signed for their participation in the community, but they did not experience it yet since the building was still under construction. The 14 remaining respondents were recruited through an online platform. No knowledge about the topic of energy communities was required, but participants needed to own or rent a dwelling. A majority of participants were male (59%), average age was 42 years.

Beside this, n = 2 additional expert interviews with the building promotor specialized in environmental technologies of the district and the company responsible of the ICT platform were held to better understand the technical specifications. The focus groups took a maximum of two hours, and participants where offered a small compensation for their time. The goal of the workshop was twofold. First, we wanted to understand the motivations and barriers to participate in a REC. Respondents actually living or involved in a REC (37 of the 51 participants) could share their experience, others shared how they think and wish to participate in one. Secondly, we questioned their intention to change their behavior being part of an Energy Community and how they would like to be interact with it. The focus groups all followed the same structure and were executed by two researchers. The workshops started by open questions and a discussion on participation in a REC, followed by an exercise with pictures of small and big appliances such as an iron, a dishwasher, an electric vehicle... Participants indicated on the pictures how they would be willing to adapt their consumption according to energy peaks. This, in order to obtain "peak shaving", achieve auto-consumption and production of energy within the district. Finally, potential interfaces to communicate this information were discussed.

4   Development of the Prototype

4.1   Focus Group Results

Main conclusions and their impact on design requirements for a tool to inform and change behavior of participants in an energy community are discussed below in four points.

Knowledge about the Working Principle of a REC
Participants of the newly built REC do not indicate the energy community as the primary reason to purchase a dwelling in the building. The location of the project was generally the main reason for their participation in an energy community, the REC was for the majority of them seen as a nice extra. Consequently, the knowledge about energy communities, functioning and suited behaviour of the people participating in a REC was often low. Participants feel proud to be involved in an ecologic sustainable project and are interested to learn more about it.

> "I bought a property in the "Nieuwe Dokken"project. The location was the main reason for that. But if I had the choice between two residents on the same location, one with and one without sustainable energy, I would definitely choose the sustainable one." – woman, REC participant

A barrier for many, however, is the fear for the technical aspect. "What if it breaks? How does it work?" Participants want to be unburdened. Habitants wish that technical problems are taken care off by experts. Currently, participants are informed about the technicalities and the infrastructure through a yearly meeting with all habitants. In the future they will also be informed by newsletters. There is a concern that habitants are not well informed; this due to newcomers moving in the building in the following years that didn't receive the same information; or people not attending the meetings. This will result in frequent reparations, low efficiency of the system and high maintenance costs.

> "Living in this REC comes with certain obligations. An example are the vacuum toilets installed in every apartment. Disposal of e.g. sanitary pads can block the

whole system and will cause high reparation costs. Another example is that the disposal of paint or other chemicals in the sinks could cause an imbalance in our water filtration system. We count on the participation of all habitants to let the community work efficiently". – expert REC project

Motivation to Participate in Peak Balancing

Participants question the effort that the switch to a REC will mean for them. The minority of the participants is willing to change the usage of small electric appliances to decrease their energy consumption (e.g. no use of appliances as TV, radio…). They do not want to lose out on comfort for a minimal financial benefit or for the purpose of a more efficient system. Energy shift of larger energy consuming appliances, however, poses less of a problem. Changing the moment of consumption of devices such as a washing machine, tumble dryer, dishwasher, electric cars is acceptable for most of the participants.

"I don't want to lose out on comfort. Charging a small device like a camera on a later moment, depending on the energy supply at that time? No way. I'm a professional photographer, I wouldn't allow this"-man, participant REC project.

"I want to go reasonably far in adapting my consumption to the energy offering: I see myself cooking at 3 p.m. for a meal in the evening or making Paella outside on a fire to be self-sustaining. I find this need to adapt myself really cool. I find it important to see predictions. Will there be a surplus of energy tomorrow? Then I could prepare myself for this and I will postpone the laundry to the next day."– woman, participant REC project

Type of Information Needed

Residents are interested to be informed about incoming and outgoing water, heat and energy flows of the whole district. Also about information which individual habitants can't control such as the litres of water being exchanged with the neighbouring company. They feel proud to be part of such a special project, and wish to understand their impact.

"I would like to know what the impact is of our community. I would feel proud to know that my ecologic footprint is 10 times lower than the one of someone else in the city, living in a regular home. It would motivate me to behave well." – man, participant REC project

In the building all kinds of devices are being monitored in real time: they number of rotations of a pump, the litres of water filtered, the number of cars charged a day, the percentage of the community battery that is filled at the moment… Displaying all the information however would be impossible. The type and depth of information (going from general explanation of the concept to detailed numbers) participants are interested in varies. They are interested to see real-time data and the evolution over time.

"Today, through my app, I can see my personal data. I would like to know what the largest energy consumers are in the whole building, if we did well, and how I can help in this whole system." – man, non-REC participant.

A minority has knowledge about terms like Mega Watt hours (MWh) or m^3 to communicate about the water consumption. There is a general preference to be informed in a rather playful way and receive tips on how to behave. Organising the information by the 3 most important flows: heat, water and electricity responds to the needs of the majority. Clear messages like "don't do the laundry now, but wait until tomorrow morning" will allow people to better adapt their behavior to the needs of the district.

"I wouldn't look at graphs and numbers: 30.000 m^3 of city water or 500 MWh. No idea how much this is. For me, the information should be simple and fun to look at. Not telling me the number we have saved, but translating it into Olympic pools of water we have saved or example given in a number of polluting cars less on the road." -woman, non REC participant

Communication to Involve all Habitants
During the expert interviews with the building promoter and ICT manager, insights on the applied technologies, available sensors, data and the existing communication platform in the building were shared.

Today, they choose to share information through apps, website or message systems. In addition, every apartment will be equipped with a display on which the consumption of all appliances can be consulted. Privacy is respected by showing this on an individual level. Nevertheless, participants indicated that they want information about the entire building. Data about joint achievements are not shared with residents, but participants show their interest and mention the possible positive feeling and motivational effect.

"An example of interesting information for me would be the amount of bio waste coming from the wasted shredded in the kitchen that is collected. This would motivate me to sort and give me a positive feeling. These common achievements are not communicated today." -woman, REC participant

Participants want personal information on a personal device (smartphone, or display in the apartment). However, these displays need to be consulted pro-actively and don't enable them to understand the working of a REC. The need for a public screen with information, tips, realisations of the community are suggested from both community management as habitant side.

Especially older participants prefer having information presented to them instead of looking it up. The entrance of an apartment building, with the possible extension of the same product at other entrances such as the garage or bicycle shed are preferred locations to present the information.

4.2 Focus Group Conclusion and Design Requirements

Based on the most important conclusions of the interviews we want to list up the following requirements. We conclude that there is a need both from the habitants as from the management of the building, to inform people about the working principle of the REC. This to avoid reparations of the recycling system, increase the efficiency and increase awareness about the impact of behavior on the whole system. Currently there exists no such tool. The tool should focus on the information of the district, not about personal data since this could violate privacy and this data is already available on a personal level for the habitants. The participants are motivated to adapt their consumption to current availability of energy resources. Therefor real time data and previsions should be provided. The information should be grouped by topic: heat, water and energy and vary in the depth of information. The majority wants the information presented in a playful way with recommendations on actions to take. On a lower level, more specific data can be shared. Gamification, especially by comparing the own results with results of neighbouring areas is appealing. Finally, participants believe that active participation and awareness will increase by displaying this on a larger interface, instead of having it on a personal device like a smartphone or desktop (Table 2).

Table 2. Translation of interview conclusions into design requirements

Conclusions interviews	Design requirements
Knowledge of the working principle of a REC is low	Habitants should be informed about not only their personal use, but also about the joint achievements of the whole community
Participants are motivated to adapt consumption to the energy offering	Information should be real-time and provide previsions
Information needs of the habitants differ	Information should be grouped by topic (e.g. heat, water, energy) and vary in depth of the information
	Information should contain tips and actions
Need to involve and inform all habitants	Information should be communicated in a playful way, gamification helps to reach these means Information should be displayed on a larger interface, which pulls the attention of all habitants

4.3 Content Development

Based on the results from the interviews and literature, we proceeded with the development of our prototype, the Mona Prisa. The name is a wordplay on the artwork Mona Lisa by Leonardo da Vinci and the French word "prise" (socket). The Mona Prisa is not just a screen, it is a real-time dashboard for renewable energy communities of the future. It displays energy, water and heat flows and informs habitants about ideal consumption patterns based on the expected solar energy and the trends in energy demand during the day. The prototype is designed to be located at the entrance of an CO_2 neutral building with around 100 Units that are part of the Renewable Energy project described above. It will display information about the whole district. Personal information on the consumption (such as the energy usage of every appliance in an apartment, the amount of water used a day) is already foreseen to be displayed by unit, this on a fixed display in the entrance of a dwelling (Figs. 1 and 2).

Fig. 1. Face detection to attract the attention to the screen.

Fig. 2. Background of the painting adapts according to the current energy balance in the district

When a resident enters the hall, the screen switches on by detection with a motion sensor. First, the resident sees an image of the painting. We chose for the Mona Lisa as this is an internationally renowned work, it is characterized by its mysterious smile and creates some curiosity. In addition, the background is a pure, natural landscape. Through capacitive buttons at the bottom of the frame, the user can browse through consumption data in the district and scroll through the pages for more detailed information. We continue to describe the concept based on 3 important features of energy consumption feedback: awareness creation, action-based feedback and gamification.

Awareness Creation

Static images receive less attention. Moving images will better capture the attention of the passing person. The resident's attention is drawn to the digital painting because he sees himself in an environment reflecting the current air pollution. In normal conditions, The Mona Lisa is located in greenery. However, she will be covered in a grey mist when water, heat or energy resources outside the community need to be exhausted to meet the consumption needs of the community at the time of viewing. Research on the long-term use of more traditional smart meters shows inattentive participants over time. Without triggers or invitation to take part in specific activities, the average user loses interest to take part in learning activities to reduce or shift energy consumption [37]. To retain the novelty aspect, we plan updates on the screen. For example, the Mona Lisa can be on a beach in the summer, in a snowy landscape in the winter. Or she could make way for Santa Claus or other moment-bound characters.

The face detection by camera is only used to replace the Mona Lisa face on the painting by the face of the participant. There was a suggestion to use the face recognition to show personal data such as your score compared to the neighbours... Due to privacy reasons, and due to the fact that also many other non-residents will enter the building, this option was not selected.

Action Based Feedback

Real-time data allows for real-time actions. There are 4 buttons (Fig. 5, 6) representing the data categories: a building (for general information), a lighting (energy balance), a water drop (water balance), and fire (heat balance). For all of the data categories there are 3 types of visualisations: an animation with coloured dots moving over the screen visualising the source and consumption, real-time data, and action tips. By turning the knob, the habitant scrolls through the different screens. The real-time data of amongst others the solar panels, car chargers, battery storage and water consumption are displayed to provide the residents with accurate information (Fig. 3). Example given: Is there an energy shortage? Then the building will give instructions on how energy usage can be reduced or postponed in time. Froelich [13] describes the need for granular data, so that data about water consumption in a home should e.g. be divided per faucet. However, interviews revealed granular data on a personal level is not suited for shared buildings. Furthermore, interviewed experts felt it could violate the privacy and lead to an overload of data. Following information is very valuable to the respondents. They would like to be informed and behave according to the needs:

Energy: level of energy production of solar panels and wind mills, level of the community battery which stores energy and number the of electrical vehicle that are disposable to (dis)charge, largest energy consuming devices in de building, tips to adapt consumption in case of low or high production.

Water and Heat: Production of soap by the neighbouring company from which water and heat is exchanged, communication about possible low production due to technical failure or holidays, percentage of water and heat being recycled and reused, largest water and heat consumers in the building, tips to adapt consumption.

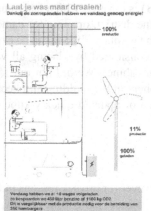

Fig. 3. Action based feedback with real-time data

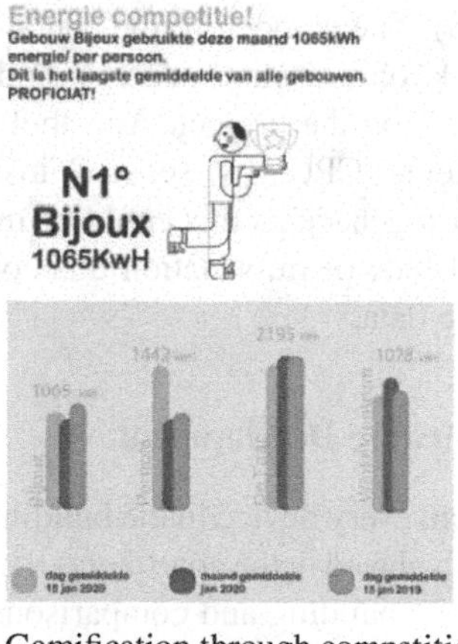

Fig. 4. Gamification through competition between the buildings

Gamification

Sustaining environmental behaviour isn't easy. As an additional motivation to maintain an ecological behaviour, the Mona Prisa adds a gamification element. The gamification element in this prototype has not fully been implemented yet. Currently a simulation is made (Fig. 4). Our expert interviews revealed that comparison between buildings of an energy community will need a corrective factor due to difference in use of the buildings. If one building has a residential purpose and consumes a lot especially in the evenings and weekends. Another building houses a primary school with a very different users. This comparison is perceived unfair by the participants. In a final prototype it might therefor be more appropriate to compare the consumption of the whole district with a regular neighbourhood in the city. This will allow and have a view on how much better the community scores. Next to comparing, it is also possible to set goals that the community wants to reach. example is obtaining a reduction of 2% of water consumption compared to the same month in the previous year. It facilitates comparison of energy consumption between the buildings and enables a fun competition between the residents of the different buildings. The tool does not only compare consumption with neighbouring buildings, but will also compare its consumption with the average consumption of people in the city of Ghent.

4.4 Hardware Development

In the following we give an overview of the different hardware components used in the prototype. Four IR sensors and a rotation encoder (Fig. 5C, D) – read in by Arduino (Fig. 5E)- are used to scroll through the different pages. Main reason not to choose for a large touch display was the price. By holding the hand in front of the icons, the IR sensor switches to the according page.

For face detection, necessary to paste the image of the face of the visitor on the face of the "Mona Lisa" painting, a basic computer Logitech Camera is installed at the top (Fig. 5A). The standard 28-inch TV screen (Fig. 5B) is covered with a laser-cut frame (Fig. 5G). The wooden frame contains the logo of the district, opening for camera and rotation knob and water-, energy- and heat- icons. The number of icons can be expanded depending on the project. Anti-theft measure was considered by placing all valuable components (CPU, TV, sensors) inside the wooden cabinet. We did not opt for extra auditory feedback as this could be disturbing for others in the building and because of the multitude of information this could not be given or updated quickly enough with real-time data.

4.5 Software Development

Data from every device in the building is logged, however for privacy reasons individual data is displayed in the apartments themselves. In the entrance hall, on the prototype, only data of the building and comparisons with the district are showed. The program Unity [41] is used to make the different pages each with their own animations. Running this program was too demanding for the Raspberry Pi, therefor an Intel stick PC' was added. The real-time data used in the animations is recalled from the Api's of the company managing the EMS system; this at a refresh rate of 1 Hz. For the face detection and animation of the Mona Lisa painting filter, a program called Lens Studio was used.

Fig. 5. IR sensors behind the cut-outs and rotation encoder to scroll through the pages.

Fig. 6. Components (clockwise) A. camera for face detection, B. 28-inch TV screen, C. capacitive sensors, D. rotation encoder, E. Arduino, F. Intel CPU, G. laser-cut wooden frame

5 Conclusion and Future Work

In this paper, we present the "Mona Prisa", an interactive design for increased awareness and pro-environmental behaviour for habitants of renewable energy communities (REC). Instead of an app or desktop based solution which are currently the standard, it presents energy feedback on a screen, framed like a painting. The prototype attempts to move an individual from being careless about resource consumption to a caring one "Resource Man" who desires to reduce carbon emissions and create an energy efficient power generation. We discuss the user research and literature that were at the basis of the design. Our goal was to understand the openness of participants of Renewable Energy Communities to change their behavior and the type of information that would be suited to help them. Conclusions of 51 interviews have been translated into design requirements for interfaces in energy communities and form the basis of the prototype. Participants of RECs currently have no view on the achievements of the community. An accessible screen, in the entrance of the building with information about the achievements of the community will encourage them to be more aware and change energy behavior. We highlighted 3 features used in the prototype: increased awareness, real-time data and gamification and describe the software and hardware development.

However, the prototype has not been tested with habitants since the building is not fully occupied yet and not all sensor data can be requested. Future tests with the prototype in the hallway of the building, will enable us to better understand which data habitants appreciate most and the impact on their conservation behaviour. Later, the prototype will be refined based on the new acquired insights. Finally, we want to mention that we included non-REC participants to expand our sample due to the limited existence of REC participants. We did not find significant differences of opinion between the groups. However REC participants could be more specific in mentioning the type of interface since they better know the location and the type of information that could be displayed. We aim to continue our collaboration with experts and participants to improve our understanding of design needs for Energy Communities.

Acknowledgements. Funding for this research was provided by Flux50, HBC.2018.0527. We are grateful for the help of the electronica and engineering students of Ghent University, department of Industrial Systems Engineering and Product Design in the materialization of the prototype. We thank the experts and participants for their participation in the user research.

References

1. AECOM: Energy demand research project: final analysis. Engineering. pp. 16–17, June 2011
2. Akella, A.K., et al.: Social, economical and environmental impacts of renewable energy systems. Renew. Energy **34**(2), 390–396 (2009)
3. Anda, M., Temmen, J.: Smart metering for residential energy efficiency: the use of community based social marketing for behavioural change and smart grid introduction. Renew. Energy **67**, 119–127 (2014)
4. Barnicoat, G., Danson, M.: The ageing population and smart metering: a field study of householders' attitudes and behaviours towards energy use in Scotland. Energy Res. Soc. Sci. **9**, 107–115 (2015)
5. Bomberg, E., McEwen, N.: Mobilizing community energy. Energy Policy **51**, 435–444 (2012)
6. Buchanan, K., et al.: Feeding back about eco-feedback: how do consumers use and respond to energy monitors? Energy Policy **73**, 138–146 (2014)
7. Burch, S.: In pursuit of resilient, low carbon communities: an examination of barriers to action in three Canadian cities. Energy Policy **38**(12), 7575–7585 (2010)
8. Burgess, J., Nye, M.: Re-materialising energy use through transparent monitoring systems. Energy Policy **36**(12), 4454–4459 (2008)
9. Darby, S.: The effectiveness of feedback on energy consumption a review for DEFRA of the literature on metering, billing and Environ. Chang. Inst. Univ. Oxford, 22 April, pp. 1–21 (2006)
10. European Commission: EU. 2030 framework for climate and energy policies
11. European Union: Directive (EU) 2018/2001 of the European Parliament and of the Council of 11 December 2018 on the promotion of the use of energy from renewable sources (2018)
12. Fischer, C.: Feedback on household electricity consumption: a tool for saving energy? Energy Effic. **1**(1), 79–104 (2008)
13. Froehlich, J., et al.: The design and evaluation of prototype eco-feedback displays for fixture-level water usage data. In: Conference on Human Factors in Computing Systems - Proceedings, pp. 2367–2376 (2012)
14. Gamberini, L., et al.: Saving is fun: designing a persuasive game for power conservation. In: ACM International Conference Proceeding Series, pp. 1–7 (2011)
15. Gaver, W., et al.: Energy babble: mixing environmentally-oriented internet content to engage community groups. In: Conference on Human Factors in Computing Systems - Proceeding 2015-April, April 2016, pp. 1115–1124 (2015)
16. Gölz, S., Hahnel, U.J.J.: What motivates people to use energy feedback systems? A multiple goal approach to predict long-term usage behaviour in daily life. Energy Res. Soc. Sci. **21**, 155–166 (2016)
17. Goulden, M., et al.: Smart grids, smart users? The role of the user in demand side management. Energy Res. Soc. Sci. **2**, 21–29 (2014)
18. Gustafsson, A., Gyllenswärd, M.: The power-aware cord: Energy awareness through ambient information display. In: Conference on Human Factors in Computing Systems - Proceedings, pp. 1423–1426 (2005)
19. Hargreaves, T.: Beyond energy feedback. Build. Res. Inf. **46**(3), 332–342 (2018)

20. Heiskanen, E., et al.: Low-carbon communities as a context for individual behavioural change. Energy Policy **38**(12), 7586–7595 (2010)
21. Hicks, J., Ison, N.: An exploration of the boundaries of 'community' in community renewable energy projects: navigating between motivations and context. Energy Policy **113**, 523–534 (2018). https://doi.org/10.1016/j.enpol.2017.10.031
22. Hoffman, S.M., High-Pippert, A.: Community energy: a social architecture for an alternative energy future. Bull. Sci. Technol. Soc. **25**(5), 387–401 (2005)
23. Interreg Europe: Policy brief: Renewable Energy Communities, Brussels (2018)
24. Johnson, D., Horton, E., Mulcahy, R., Foth, M.: Gamification and serious games within the domain of domestic energy consumption: a systematic review. Renew. Sustain. Energy Rev. **73**, 249–264 (2017)
25. Kubli, M., et al.: The flexible prosumer: measuring the willingness to co-create distributed flexibility. Energy Policy **114**, 540–548 (2018)
26. Lainter, J.A.: The contribution of the social sciences to the energy challenge. In: American Council for an Energy-Efficient Economy. ACEEE, Washington (2007)
27. Laschke, M., et al.: "Annoying, but in a nice way": an inquiry into the experience of frictional feedback. Int. J. Des. **9**(2), 129–140 (2015)
28. Mendes, G., et al.: Local energy markets: opportunities, benefits, and barriers. In: Proceedings of the CIRED Work, vol. 0272, pp. 7–8 (2018)
29. Micheel, I., et al.: Visualizing & gamifying water & energy consumption for behavior change. In: Fostering Smart Energy Applications (FSEA) 2015 at Interact 2015, At Bamberg, German, pp. 1–8 (2015)
30. Moloney, S., et al.: Transitioning to low carbon communities-from behaviour change to systemic change: lessons from Australia. Energy Policy **38**(12), 7614–7623 (2010)
31. Novak, J., et al.: Behaviour change and incentive modelling for water saving : first results from the SmartH2O project behaviour change and incentive modelling for water. In: Proceedings of the 8th International Congress on Environmental Modelling and Software, July 2016
32. Pierce, J., Paulos, E.: Beyond energy monitors: interaction, energy, and emerging energy systems. In: Proceedings of the SIGCHI Conference on Human Factors in Computing Systems, pp. 665–674 (2012)
33. Sanders, E.B.-N., Stappers, P.J.: Co-creation and the new landscapes of design. CoDesign **4**(1), 5–18 (2008)
34. Sanders, E.B.-N., Stappers, P.J.: Probes, toolkits and prototypes: three approaches to making in codesigning. CoDesign **10**(1), 5–14 (2014)
35. Van Der Schoor, T., Scholtens, B.: Power to the people : local community initiatives and the transition to sustainable energy. Renew. Sustain. Energy Rev. **43**, 666–675 (2015)
36. Strengers, Y.: Smart energy in everyday life: are you designing for resource man? Interactions **21**(4), 24–31 (2014)
37. Verkade, N., Höffken, J.: Is the Resource Man coming home? Engaging with an energy monitoring platform to foster flexible energy consumption in the Netherlands. Energy Res. Soc. Sci. **27**, 36–44 (2017)
38. Visser, F.S., et al.: Contextmapping: experiences from practice. CoDesign **1**(2), 119–149 (2005)
39. De Vries, G.W., et al.: User-led innovation in civic energy communities. Environ. Innov. Soc. Transit. **19**, 51–65 (2016)
40. Wood, G., Newborough, M.: Dynamic energy-consumption indicators for domestic appliances: environment, behaviour and design. Energy Build. **35**(8), 821–841 (2003)
41. Unity. https://unity.com/

GrainSynth: A Generative Synthesis Tool Based on Spatial Interpretations of Sound Samples

Archelaos Vasileiou, João André Mafra Tenera, Emmanouil Papageorgiou, and George Palamas$^{(\boxtimes)}$ ⓘD

Aalborg University Copenhagen, Copenhagen, Denmark
{avasil19,jtener19,epapag19}@student.aau.dk, gpa@create.aau.dk

Abstract. This paper proposes a generative design approach for the creative exploration of dynamic soundscapes that can be used to generate compelling and immersive sound environments. A granular synthesis tool is considered based on the perceptual self-organization of sound samples by utilizing the t-Stochastic Neighboring Embedded algorithm (t-SNE) for the spatial mapping of sonic grains into a 2D space. The proposed system was able to relate the visual stimuli with the sonic responses in the context of the generic gestalt principles of visual perception. According to user evaluation, the application operated intuitively and also revealed the potential for creative expressiveness both from the user's perspective and as a standalone, generative synthesizer.

Keywords: Granular synthesis · Gestalt principles · Data visualization · Generative sound · Perlin force field · Machine learning for audio

1 Introduction

Granular synthesis is based on the same principle as sampling. The samples are split into small pieces of around 1 to 50 ms. These small pieces are called grains. Multiple grains may be layered on top of each other, and may play at different speeds, phases, volume and frequency, among other parameters, in order to create what can be thought as "sound clouds". The theory of granular synthesis was initially proposed, in conjunction with a theory of hearing, by the physicist Dennis Gabor [15]. Gabor referred to the grains as acoustical quanta, and he postulated that a granular or quantum representation could be used to describe any sound. Iannis Xenakis, [16], explicated a compositional theory of grains of sound. His theory describes a possible approximation to Gabor's model in the context of an analog synthesis implementation, where he suggested that the grained wave forms could be calculated directly on an appropriately programmed digital computer [10]. Recording a set of sound grains and mapping them as a data visualization could allow the performer to explore the sonic

© ICST Institute for Computer Sciences, Social Informatics and Telecommunications Engineering 2021
Published by Springer Nature Switzerland AG 2021. All Rights Reserved
N. Shaghaghi et al. (Eds.): INTETAIN 2020, LNICST 377, pp. 118–130, 2021.
https://doi.org/10.1007/978-3-030-76426-5_8

space in new ways of musical performance that could integrate a multi-modal, perception based framework, that could fuse both sonic and visual ques, at the same time. In order to make a consistent map of the various samples, these would have to be sorted and organized by a measure of perceptual familiarity. The aim of this study is to explore how the visualization match up with the user's intuitive sensibility of where the various samples should be positioned in space. This sensibility is influenced by the fact that humans associate the listening experience with simultaneous experiences obtained through non-auditory organs. This phenomenon is called synaesthesia [20].

2   Background

2.1   Generative Art

Generative art, as an artistic approach, utilize an autonomous system controlled by a set of predefined properties, balancing between unpredictability and order. This behavior arises out of the dynamics of a complex system. This system can be analysed in individual procedures and can be given a mathematical description which can be modelled and simulated. Thus, the generative system produces artworks by formalizing the uncontrollability of the creative process [18]. According to [19] "Generative art refers to any art practice where the artist uses a system, .., which is set into motion with some degree of autonomy contributing to or resulting in a completed work of art". The use of a generative approach provides new ways of expressing the artistic intent and purpose. Some supporters of generative systems consider that the art is not anymore in the achievement of the formal shape of the work but in the design of a system that explores all possible permutations of a creative solution [17]. Generative Art range from simple probabilistic procedures, to highly complex models that learn from a set of sample examples. Moreno [23] demonstrates a method to generate original bird vocalizations using a Variational Convolutional Autoencoder trained on a dataset of bird songs and call recordings. Training can be autonomous or might include a human in the loop. In their work [22] describe a human motion tracking system, from surveillance cameras on New York Time Square, that was used to feed a generative design algorithm in order to generate emotionally expressive 3D visualizations.

2.2   Audio Visualization

Audio visualizations, based on perceptual similarity of sound, have been used and implemented in various ways, for a variety of applications. The "Bird Sounds" interface [1] created at Google Creative Lab, applied the t-SNE algorithm to self-organize thousands of different bird songs, with a goal to depict their sonic relationships in a two dimensional grid. A similar application, "the infinite drum machine" [2], use a similar topological mapping as a spatial exploration tool of sound similarity. Selected sound samples could then be used to generate drum loops. The "Audio Explorer" interface by Leon Fedden [3], is a project exploring an audio data-set visualization by mapping a multi-dimensional feature space represented by Mel-frequency cepstral coefficients (MFCCs), into a 2D space. The study considered a variety of dimensionality reduction algorithm such as the UMAP, t-SNE and the PCA. Another project on interactive exploration of musical space [4] build a music-space of 20,000 songs, visually rendered in a way that could enhance music navigation in a way similar to a recommender system.

2.3   Feature Extraction

Dimensionality describes the potential perplexity of a given data-set such as audio samples. A term often used is the "curse of dimensionality" which describes the exponential growth of the space of possible hypotheses as the dimensionality becomes higher [21]. This in effect creates sparse data representations that render the hypothesis statistically insignificant. The procedure of compressing a data-set by crafting new features from the existing ones and afterwards discarding the original set of features, is called feature extraction. The new data-set should be more comprehensive and inclusive in terms of information provided, as a summarized version of the original set.

MFCCs. Mel-frequency cepstral coefficients are commonly used as features in speech recognition systems as well in music information retrieval (MIR) applications such as genre classification and audio similarity measurement for recommender systems. MFCCs are perceptually motivated and spectrally smoothed representations of sound. The mel scale describes the non-linearity of the human ear, where each scale of pitches is perceived as equal in distance from one another [6]. This perceptually meaningful representation could be more comprehensive and inclusive in terms of information provided, as a summarized version of the original set.

2.4   Dimensionality Reduction

Principal component analysis is a popular technique for dimensionality reduction. PCA is essentially a multivariate data analysis method involving transformation of a number of possibly correlated variables into a smaller number of uncorrelated variables known as principal components. However, its effectiveness is limited by its global linearity [7]. Another popular choice that overcome the limitation of PCA is the Stochastic Neighbor Embedding algorithm (t-SNE) [9].

t-SNE. (t-Stochastic Neighbor Embedding) is a manifold learning technique used to visualize high-dimensional data by giving each data-point a location in a two or three dimensional map and it was introduced by van der Maaten and Hinton in 2008 [8]. The t-SNE requires tuning of parameters regarding initialization and visualization. It can be initiated randomly, or even through PCA, and can have its perplexity adjusted. Van der Maaten & Hinton suggests a perplexity value between 5 and 50 [9] The distribution of points obtained by t-SNE may be misleading when clusters form but practice may develop an intuition on how to interpret these observations. Looking at a t-SNE map, one of the first things to notice would be arbitrarily shaped clusters of data-points; this usually mean that data-points who are further in distance are considered to be dissimilar, while data-points appearing to be closer in space are considered to be more similar. Depending on their position, in a 2D plane for example, one may be able to recognize the patterns of the distribution and get to know the data-set better and maybe conclude to some solid observations [14] (Fig. 1).

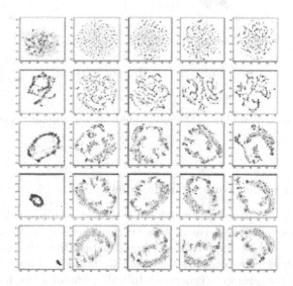

Fig. 1. t-SNE parameters test, with Perplexity (Y-axis) = [2, 5, 30, 50, 100] and Number of Iterations (X-axis) = [250, 500, 1000, 2000, 5000]. The Learning rate was set to 200

2.5   Gestalt Theory of Perception

The Gestalt school of psychology describes how we naturally perceive the world as perceptual groups [13]. Two Gestalt grouping principles, which pose a central role to this study, are the similarity and proximity rules. Ideally, sonic similarities among the sound grains would correspond with their visual proximity. In addition, there are principles describing connectivity and continuation, where points that form lines or other shapes are perceived as a whole. The various Gestalt principles can override each other, which means that in some cases the perceived sonic similarity can outweigh the importance of the visual grouping, and vice versa. Other times the principles are complementary, pulling in the same perceptual direction.

3   Creative Workflow

A modified version of the Audio t-SNE Viewer [5] was used as the basis of this system. The system consists of 4 discrete parts as can be seen in Fig. 2, which are further analysed below.

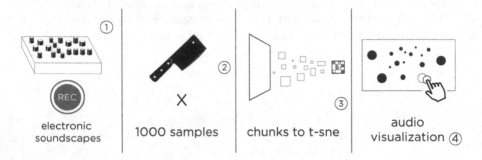

electronic
soundscapes

1000 samples

chunks to t-sne

audio
visualization ④

Fig. 2. Workflow of the sound analysis and visualization

3.1   Generating Electronic Soundscapes

Analog electric soundscapes generated and recorded with a synthesizer that has been built from our research team. This single voice semi-modular synthesizer designed as a tool for the exploration of soundscapes through a variety of sound synthesis techniques. The recording lasted for about an hour and as a result more than a thousand samples were generated. Initially, fundamental frequencies were recorded, then periodic frequencies were generated from a Voltage Controlled Oscillator (VCO), controlled by a Low Frequency Oscillator(LFO). The first step was to record every waveform format that could be produced by the oscillator in order to get different timbres. Next step was to repeat the same method and lead the same signal both to the VCO and to a Voltage Controlled Filter (VCF). Moreover, drum timbers were generated by mixing white noise together with a very low frequency and lead them into the filter which was modulated at the same time by a very short Envelope Generator (EG).

3.2   Sample Generation

Next step was to create a set of sound chunks, with 1000ms duration each and a sample rate of 44.1 kHz/24bit. A set of 1063 sound files were generated and an overlap of 1.5ms was used to create a continuous feeling when samples would be played in a sequence.

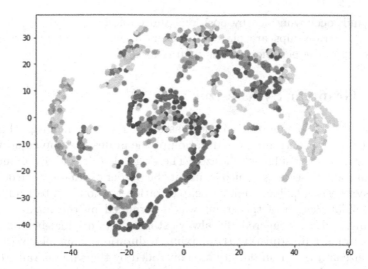

Fig. 3. Spatial mapping of sound samples based on the t-SNE algorithm. Sounds that appear to have a similar color, belong to the same sequence and probably have similar sound content. Different sections (e.g. teal and orange) appearing clustered together as well. This suggests those two sections may have similar audio content.

3.3   Chunks to t-SNE

Mel-frequency cepstral coefficients are a common choice in speech recognition systems as well in music information retrieval (MIR). The mel scale describes a scale of pitches perceived as equal in distance from one another [6]. For each audio chunk the first 13 mel-frequency cepstral coefficients have been calculated along with their first- and second-order derivatives, and concatenated into a single 39-element feature vector which would characterize each clip and is standardized so that each feature had an equal variance.

3.4   Visualizing the Sound Manifold

The t-SNE algorithm, as a manifold learning technique, was used to reduce the dimensionality of the initial (N × 39) data-set to only two dimensions (N × 2), where N = 1063 is the number of sound grains. Additionally the results were normalized between 0 and 1. The t-SNE requires tuning of two hyper-parameters, the perplexity and the learning rate. The perplexity parameter relates with the number of nearest neighbors; As a rule of thumb, Van der Maaten and Hinton suggest a perplexity value between 5 and 50 [9]. Learning rate was taken into consideration, as if set too high it might cause the data to be hard to analyse due to excessive proximity as well as if too low where most points may get clustered in exaggeration. These considerations take into account the Kullback-Leibler cost function for preventing it to get stuck in a local minimum [11]. In a t-SNE map, clusters might form corresponding to individual sound chunks, with similar sounds occupying nearby positions and dissimilar sounds positioned far away. Thus, certain clips are placed together in clouds of varying size, while others end up in the periphery of the map (Fig. 3).

4   The Granular Synthesizer

A functionality for looping the samples has been added in the original application. That way, by controlling the duration of the grains the app could work in a similar way as a granular synthesizer. The original code had a minimum clip duration of 100 milliseconds, which is just at the border of what can be defined as granular synthesis [12]. The minimum clip duration was lowered to 1 millisecond and the window length of the grains was determined by the maximum duration parameter. Each triggered clip always starts at its original beginning, and loops at a rate set by adjusting the maximum duration. This means that both the grain size and the grain density are controlled by the same parameter. This density only applies horizontally over time, while the vertical density depends on how many grains the user plays at the same time. Since the grains are all regularly placed over time, this should be characterized as synchronous granular synthesis [10]. However, there is no grain spacing, since they are all played in continuous loops with no spaces in between. A panning gives the application space to breathe in the stereo field. It is used lively and interactively by identifying the spatial position of performative gestures. The technique that has been used identifies the user's relative position in the visualization and multiplies it by 45°. The angle is normalized by $[-1, +1]$ and is converted into radians.

Human Computer Interaction. A common way to generate sounds from a synthesizer is through a MIDI controller, typically by triggering sounds and control parameters during a music performance. A quite different way is to use natural gestures on a touch screen or input from haptic sensors. Sparse distributions and data positions throughout the screen would allow for navigation through these sounds, inviting energetic exploration and improvisation. Moreover, different t-SNE parameter can affect the spatial navigation and perception of sonic stimuli. We have found that distributions with values greater than 30 in perplexity and greater than 500 in number of iterations, could form distributions that visually imposes a good navigational structure for exploring the spatial formations of the samples.

Generative Design Scheme. In order to aid the creative exploration of the synthesis of soundscapes a flow field was used to control a number of particles within it. These moving particles, influenced from this force field could trigger successive grains along their pathways. Flow fields are especially useful for modeling chaotic movement, such as fluid dynamics, for procedurally generated textures and for the control of the movement of autonomous agents. A flow field is an area of usually 2D or 3D space divided up into a grid of cells. Each cell contains a velocity vector which represents a direction and speed of movement Fig. 5. When a particle enters a cell, its direction is transformed to match that of the vector in the cell. As it moves through the field it will enter other cells containing velocity vectors that change its movement again. The crucial factor in a velocity field is the arrangement of the vectors. We use a special case of a flow field that is based on a perlin noise texture (grid). Each cell of the flow field represents a single, animated, force field vector. The vector is represented by three values, the angle, the magnitude of the vector at the given position and a global time t value that represents the evolution of the process. Thus, two different Perlin textures are needed to describe an animated force field. When a particle is crossing over a sample point, the sound would be triggered by it. That way, a high number of particles could trigger many samples at once, which could generate aesthetically pleasant, polyphonic sequences (Fig. 4). As the sound samples are not evenly distributed to cover all the available space, a lot of empty space forms, surrounding the grains. This neutral space serves as silent "white space" that simplifies the scene, according to the Gestalt approach, into figure and ground.

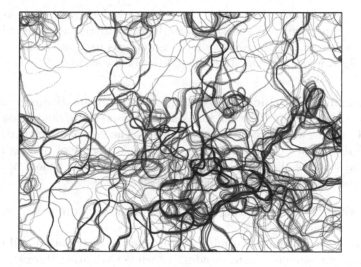

Fig. 4. Ten particles spawned at the center of the canvas, moving under the influence of a perlin based flow field, formed by a grid of size 32×22.

4.1   User Experience Testing

Eleven (11) Participants, with previous experience in synthesizer practices, were asked to explore the interface and customize the available parameters after being briefly instructed on the system's controls. There was no specific time frame in which the user had to complete the evaluation. The users were prompted then

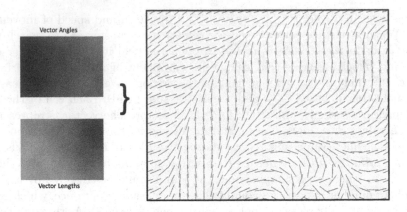

Fig. 5. Two different textures were used to form a perlin noise flow field. The first texture (up) used to store the vector angles of the vectors in radians, while the second texture (down) used to store the magnitude of the force vector. The size of the textures is 32×22 pixels.

to answer a questionnaire in which they were asked to rate some aspects of the interface's performance and their overall user experience, along with some additional commentary. Moreover, a focus group was used as the main method for the evaluation of the generative capabilities of the system.

Gestalt Grouping Principles Testing. A second questionnaire was conducted as a non-parametric test and was addressed to a random sample of twenty (20) people with no cognitive perquisites. The non-parametric test aimed to explore the efficacy of the application to achieve a sense of playing intuition through the scope of the grouping principles of the Gestalt School of thought. Five basic principles were interpreted as questions:

- **perplexity**: "Do neighbouring dots in the visualization represent sonic similarities in sonic space?"
- **Closure**: "Did you notice forming patterns in the distribution and if so, did the sound correspond to sonic landmarks while navigating through them?"
- **Continuity**: "Did the distribution of points suggest a path to navigate through and if so, did the sound correspond to a sonic gesture?"
- **Common Region**: "Did the samples' position display correspond to their position in the sonic space?"
- **Similarity**: "Were similarly sounding samples, visually grouped together in the distribution?"

4.2   Results

Tables 3 and 1 presents the average score on a ten-point scale in regards to each of the system's performance overview and the user experience's aspects respectively. Most participants reported highly satisfied with the interface control response. Regarding the interface's parameter customization layout, it has been reported that being able to adjust the parameters while producing sound simultaneously, would be a useful and creative feature. As far as the user experience is concerned, none of the participants got the impression of being able to anticipate the audio samples they were triggering, so as a result, they rated the playing intuition and the ability to trigger the desired sounds the lowest. However, after an initial navigation period the participants were able to anticipate the sounds being triggered. This finding might suggest the formation of cognitive spatial maps that could possibly help the user navigate within a previously experienced topological map of sounds. The synth controlling novelty was rated high and five out of six participants with experience in music production, reported that they would use the current interface in a music production project of their own. Moreover, regarding the generative approach the overall aesthetics was rated as good with temporal coherence although some irregularities have been spotted.

Non - parametric Test. The outcome of the second experiment would provide evidence on whether or not the application achieved its goal of providing the user with a novel and intuitive way of playing with a synthesizer. Table 2 demonstrates the average scores of the application's compliance with Gestalt's principles while Fig. 6 provides a histogram of the score of the individual ratings of the grouping principles against the number of occurrences. All collected data underwent the Kolmogorov - Smirnov Test of Normality and found not to differ significantly from that which is normally distributed.

5   Future Work

There are many possibilities of extending the functionality of this application by utilizing the user interface for ultimate expressiveness and better performance. A desirable way would be to use tactile sensors or human motion, such as input from live camera feed, to trigger and manipulate the samples. Within this example, the application would have more potential of being used not only by musicians, but also from dancers or performers. For the moment, our team is focusing on utilizing this system with an optical flow system, based on real time camera feed. Our intention is to integrate a real-time sound generation system, for dance performance, with a motion expressiveness visualization system. (https://vimeo.com/220138824).

Moreover, adding new generative algorithms such as a flocking boid [21] is under development. Flocking boid is similar, in a sense, with a perlin flow field, however within a flocking boid the set of individual agents is capable of interacting with each other. In a similar fashion, when a flocking agent would cross over a sample point a sound would be triggered by it. That way, a population would trigger an arbitrary amount of samples, generating interesting and stochastically rich soundscapes.

Table 1. Average ratings of their user experience on a 10 point scale (sound engineering students).

User experience	AVG score
1. Playing intuition	6.9
2. Desired sounds triggering	5.09
3. Panning correspondence	8.09
4. Sample distribution scheme	7.45
5. Synth controlling novelty	8.18

Table 2. Average ratings of the application's compliance to Gestalt's grouping principles on a hundred point scale.

Gestalt grouping principles	AVG score
1. Perplexity	79
2. Closure	62
3. Continuity	63
4. Common region	69
5. Similarity	75

Table 3. Average ratings of the application's performance efficiency on a 10 point scale (sound engineering students).

Performance overview	AVG score
1. Navigation triggering efficiency	8.18
2. Click-looping efficiency	7.54
3. System latency	9
4. Navigation and loop synergy	7.72
5. Parameter customization	7

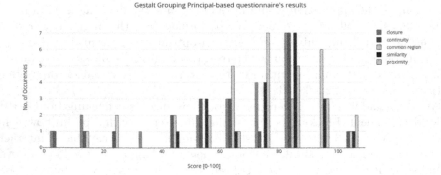

Fig. 6. Histogram of the non-parametric Evaluation Test

6 Conclusion

The proposed system augmented the artistic capabilities of a semi-modular analog synthesizer. A data-set of 1000ms audio clips were self-organized using different visualization techniques, according to their musical content. As has been demonstrated the dimensionality reduction capabilities of t-SNE is a rewarding approach for shaping a "playable" visualization. Perceptually, the application achieved to connect the visual stimuli and aural sound based on the generic gestalt principles of grouping and continuation as well as the figure-ground principle. According to user evaluation, the application operated quite intuitively. The evaluation also revealed the potential for creative expressiveness both from the users perspective and as a standalone, generative synthesizer.

References

1. Tan, M., McDonald, K.: (2006). https://experiments.withgoogle.com/bird-sounds
2. McDonald, K., Tan M., Mann Y.: The infinite drum machine (2018). https://experiments.withgoogle.com/ai/drum-machine/view
3. Fedden, L.: Comparative audio analysis with wavenet, MFCCs, UMAP, t-SNE and PCA (2017). http://bitly.ws/8E26
4. Lionello, M., Pietrogrande, L., Purwins, H., Abou-Zleikha, M.: Interactive exploration of musical space with parametric t-SNE. In 15th Sound and Music Computing Conference (SMC 2018) Sound & Music Computing Conference, pp. 200–208. Sound and Music Computing Network (2018)
5. Kogan, G.: (2018). http://ml4a.github.io
6. Sahidullah, M., Saha, G.: Design, analysis and experimental evaluation of block based transformation in MFCC computation for speaker recognition. Speech Commun. **54**(4), 543–565 (2012)
7. Gewers, F.L., et al.: Principal component analysis: a natural approach to data exploration (2018). arXiv preprint arXiv:1804.02502
8. Maaten, L.V., Hinton, G.: Visualizing data using t-SNE. J. Mach. Learn. Res. **9**(Nov), 2579–2605 (2008)
9. Wattenberg, M., Viégas, F., Johnson, I.: How to use t-SNE effectively. Distill **1**, 10 (2016)
10. Roads, C.: Microsound. MIT Press, Cambridge (2004)
11. Kullback, S., Leibler, R.A.: On information and sufficiency. Ann. Math. Stat. **22**(1), 79–86 (1951)
12. Park, T.H.: Introduction to Digital Signal Processing: Computer Musically Speaking. World Scientific, Singapore (2009)
13. Wertheimer, M.: Gestalt theory (1938)
14. Lunterova, A., Spetko, O., Palamas, G.: Explorative visualization of food data to raise awareness of nutritional value. In: Stephanidis, C. (ed.) HCII 2019. LNCS, vol. 11786, pp. 180–191. Springer, Cham (2019). https://doi.org/10.1007/978-3-030-30033-3_14
15. Gabor, D.: Theory of communication. Part 1: the analysis of information. J. Inst. Electr. Eng.-Part III: Radio Commun. Eng. **93**(26), 429–441 (1946)
16. Xenakis, I.: Formalized Music: Thought and Mathematics in Composition. Pendragon Press, New York (1992)

17. Kaspersen, E.T., Górny, D., Erkut, C., Palamas, G.: Generative choreographies: the performance dramaturgy of the machine. In: Proceedings of the 15th International Joint Conference on Computer Vision, Imaging and Computer Graphics Theory and Applications, vol. 1: Grapp, pp. 319–326. SCITEPRESS Digital Library (2020)
18. McCormack, J., Bown, O., Dorin, A., McCabe, J., Monro, G., Whitelaw, M.: Ten questions concerning generative computer art. Leonardo **47**(2), 135–141 (2014)
19. Galanter, P.: Generative art theory. In: A Companion to Digital Art, pp. 146–180 (2016)
20. Parise, C., Spence, C.: Audiovisual cross-modal correspondences in the general population (2013)
21. Bellman, R.: Dynamic Programming. Princeton University Press, Princeton (1957)
22. Billeskov, J.A., Møller, T.N., Triantafyllidis, G., Palamas, G.: Using motion expressiveness and human pose estimation for collaborative surveillance art. In: Brooks, A.L., Brooks, E., Sylla, C. (eds.) ArtsIT/DLI -2018. LNICST, vol. 265, pp. 111–120. Springer, Cham (2019). https://doi.org/10.1007/978-3-030-06134-0_12
23. Moreno, J.A., Bigoni, F., Palamas, G.: Latent birds: a bird's-eye view exploration of the latent space. In: Proceedings of the 17th Sound and Music Computing Conference, Torino, June 2020

Modeling Audio Distortion Effects with Autoencoder Neural Networks

Riccardo Russo$^{(\boxtimes)}$, Francesco Bigoni, and George Palamas

Aalborg University Copenhagen, Copenhagen, Denmark
{rrusso19,fbigon17}@student.aau.dk, gpa@create.aau.dk

Abstract. Most music production nowadays is carried out using software tools: for this reason, the market demands faithful audio effect simulations. Traditional methods for modeling nonlinear systems are effect-specific or labor-intensive; however, recent works yielded promising results by black-box simulation of these effects using neural networks. This work aims to explore two models of distortion effects based on autoencoders: one makes use of fully-connected layers only, and the other employs convolutional layers. Both models were trained using clean sounds as input and distorted sounds as target, thus, the learning method was not self-supervised, as it is mostly the case when dealing with autoencoders. The networks were then tested with visual inspection of the output spectrograms, as well as with an informal listening test, and performed well in reconstructing the distorted signal spectra, however a fair amount of noise was also introduced.

Keywords: Autoencoders · Convolutional autoencoders · Audio distortion · Audio effects modeling · Black box modeling · Machine learning for audio

1 Introduction

Through audio effects, one can manipulate an audio signal in order to shape its characteristics to fit the desired purpose. These tools have important creative and industrial applications in areas such as music production or telecommunications. In the music field, audio effects are generally divided into macro-categories which either refer to the audio feature being transformed or to the method used, e.g. *dynamic range compressor, distortion, pitch shifter, phase vocoder*, etc. Among all, distortion effects aim to increase the amplitude and enrich the spectral content of the input by making use of nonlinear components. In the digital domain, this kind of transformations entails the use of nonlinear functions to process the incoming waveform into a different shape, which depends on the amplitude of the incoming signal.

While audio processing devices were originally based on analog circuits, most music production nowadays is carried out using digital audio workstations

© ICST Institute for Computer Sciences, Social Informatics and Telecommunications Engineering 2021
Published by Springer Nature Switzerland AG 2021. All Rights Reserved
N. Shaghaghi et al. (Eds.): INTETAIN 2020, LNICST 377, pp. 131–141, 2021.
https://doi.org/10.1007/978-3-030-76426-5_9

(DAWs) and audio plugins: for this reason, the demand for accurate digital emulations of analog audio effects is always high. The field of virtual analog (VA) modeling is concerned with creating these emulations, and over time many commercial solutions have been proposed, such as AmpliTube from IK Multimedia[1] or Guitar Rig from Native Instruments[2]. A common approach for analog modeling is the so-called *white-box modeling* [3]. This technique involves analysing the circuitry of the device and simulating it through discrete-time mathematical models. White-box modeling is a widely used method and can be very accurate, but has some drawbacks. First, it requires a exhaustive knowledge of the circuit under exam, which is not always possible. Second, the simulations can be computationally demanding, especially if the circuit contains many nonlinear components. Lastly, this technique requires intensive labor for the design of a single effect.

An alternative approach is *black-box modeling* [3], which is based on measuring the response of the system to particular input signals, in order to create an input-output map. Since this technique is based on measurements of the device under test, it is easier to adapt it for the simulation of different effects. However, black-box modeling comes with drawbacks too, e.g. if user controls are required, one has to measure the system response for every parameter configuration. A nonlinear system cannot be modeled using classic frequency response analysis, since this assumes linear and time-invariant systems; for this reason, different mathematical methods have been proposed for addressing this task over time [14]. More recently, deep learning [5] methods have been explored, showing increasingly good results [2–4,8–10,16]. This paper is organized as follows: Sect. 2 explores two techniques for audio distortion modeling, both based on convolution. In Sect. 3 two models of distortion effects are presented, and the results are discussed in Sect. 4. Conclusions are drawn in Sect. 5.

2   Background

As stated above, neural networks have found many applications in audio signal processing. However, common practice has been to not work directly in the time domain, but rather use time-frequency representations (e.g. spectrograms) as input [7]. Despite its many applications, this approach involves discarding the phase information, which is an important feature of audio distortion. The nonlinear phase behaviour of many audio effects, including distortion, causes the partial cancellation of some frequencies, affecting the sound quality in a perceivable manner. For this reason, only models that take raw audio as input were considered in this work. Recurrent neural networks (RNNs) are a common way to approach the task of generating data with a definite temporal structure, and many works on audio effects have been using this technique [2,15,16]; an extensive evaluation of these methods is behind the scope of this paper. Moreover, WaveNet demonstrated that it is possible to achieve significant results by using only convolutional layers [12].

---

[1] www.ikmultimedia.com/products/amplitube4.
[2] www.native-instruments.com/en/products/komplete/guitar/guitar-rig-5-pro.

2.1   WaveNet

WaveNet is a generative model operating directly on raw audio waveforms. It is *autoregressive*, meaning that the output variable depends linearly on its own previous values. Based on this technique, WaveNet shapes the discrete probability distribution of the next sample given a series of past samples. Both input and the output have the same dimensions, as the model outputs a probability distribution over the current sample x_t using a softmax layer. An entire sequence of samples is produced by sequentially feeding the previously generated samples back into the model. The probability of a waveform $\mathbf{x} = \{x_1, \dots, x_T\}$ is given by the following relation:

$$p(\mathbf{x}) = \prod_{t=1}^{T} p(x_t | x_1, \dots, x_{t-1}) . \tag{1}$$

Looking at Eq. 1, it is clear that the probability of the sample x_t is conditioned on all the past samples x_n. WaveNet has demonstrated state-of-the-art performances in the field of speech generation, and studies has been made to adapt its structure for other purposes; as an example, Damskägg et al. developed a WaveNet-based model for the simulation of tube amplifiers [4] and distortion effects [3]. The network structure is similar to the one proposed by Rethage et al. and used for speech denoising [13]. These tasks differ from the one for which the original WaveNet architecture was developed. While WaveNet aimed at generating a new audio output, these adaptations are made for processing an existing input. For this reason, these works modify the architecture for a regression task, eliminating the softmax output layer: hence, the model is trained to predict the current audio sample, based on a series of past samples and the current one, as shown in Eq. 2:

$$\hat{y}[n, \theta] = f(x[n], \dots, x[n - N], \theta) , \tag{2}$$

where x is the input, N is the receptive field, θ are the network parameters and f is the nonlinear transformation learned by the model.

The model consists of a series of convolutional layers, which take the original waveform as input and apply a linear filter along with a nonlinear activation function. The layers include residual connections between them.

The loss function used is the *normalized mean squared error (NMSE)*: the model parameters are learned by minimizing the squared error between the output signal and the target, divided by the square of the target, as follows:

$$NMSE = \frac{\sum_{n=0}^{\infty} (y[n] - \hat{y}[n, \theta])^2}{\sum_{n=0}^{\infty} y[n]^2} \tag{3}$$

The tube simulation model described in [4] includes a conditioning control. This feature helps to overcome one of the previously mentioned drawbacks of black-box simulation: the difficulty of including user-controllable parameters. Previous studies on this approach, have yielded promising results [3].

2.2 Autoencoders

Autoencoders (AEs) [6] are data-specific lossy compression algorithms. They are used to obtain a compressed representation of an input, which is stored in the so-called *latent space* and are typically employed for dimensionality reduction and data denoising [7], however, they have been also used for more artistic purposes [11]. Although these networks obtained significant results in the field of audio denoising, the applications in the area of nonlinear effects simulation are still not thoroughly explored. In addition, the simplicity of their structure and the smaller training effort compared to WaveNet-like methods makes them easier to adapt for different tasks. AEs consist of a front end, or *encoder*, a latent space representation, and a back end, or *decoder*. The encoder and decoder usually have the same structure (mirrored, as seen in e.g. Fig. 1). AEs are trained in a self-supervised fashion: since the input values are also the target, the network learns to encode data in order to reconstruct it from its latent space representation. These models can make use of different layer types: for example, we talk about *deep AEs* when encoder and decoder contain more than one dense hidden layer, or *convolutional AEs* when they employ convolutional layers.

Recently, Martìnez Ramìrez et al. proposed a convolutional AE for nonlinear audio effect simulation [10], based on their previous model for performing automatic equalization [9]. This model is entirely time-domain based and is divided into three parts: adaptive front end, synthesis back end and latent-space deep neural network (DNN). The front end consists of two convolutional layers, one pooling layer and a residual connection. The first convolutional layer contains 128 one-dimensional filters with a kernel size of 64, and an *absolute value* activation function. The second layer is equal to the first one, but it is locally connected, meaning that it resembles a filter bank structure; it also applies a *softplus* activation function, i.e. a smoothed version of the *rectified linear unit* (ReLU) function, to the input.

The pooling is obtained through a *max-pooling* layer with a window of 16 samples (i.e. the layer returns the maximum value between the 16 analysed). The latent space consists of a locally-connected dense layer of 64 units, and a fully-connected one of 64 units, both followed by a *softplus* function. The back end is made of an unpooling layer, a DNN with nonlinear activation functions, and a convolutional layer which is exactly the same as the input layer of the front end. The loss function used is the NMSE, same as Eq. 3.

3 Design and Implementation

We developed two models in order to test the performances of different types of AEs: firstly, we implemented a deep AE, using only dense layers; secondly, we replaced some of the dense layers with convolutional layers in a convolutional AE. Both models were implemented using the Keras library[3].

---

[3] www.keras.io.

3.1   Deep Autoencoder

The deep AE is built with dense layers only, as shown in Fig. 1. An overview of the architecture is presented here:

- The encoder contains 1 input layer (579 units) and three hidden layers (256, 128 and 64 units respectively),
- The latent space is made of a single layer (32 units),
- Finally, the decoder has the same structure as the encoder, but mirrored, so that the output has the same dimensions as the input.

The optimal number of hidden layers was determined empirically by considering different combinations of sizes and number of layers. Each layer applies a ReLU activation function, except for the last layer of the decoder, which has a linear activation function. This approach was chosen rather than re-normalizing the output samples between 0 and 1, as our initial tests showed that it would produce an output amplitude range similar to the input range. In addition, our experiments showed that the data squeezing performed by the ReLU resulted in amplified background noise, making the musical structure in the output sound almost indistinguishable to the ear; by applying a linear function to the last layer instead, we obtained significantly better results.

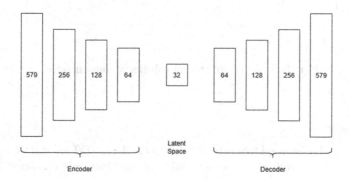

Fig. 1. Structure of the deep autoencoder. The numbers indicate the quantity of fully connected units.

3.2   Convolutional Autoencoder

The convolutional AE was built by taking the deep AE and substituting some dense layers with convolutional layers. Our architecture is depicted in Fig. 2:

- The encoder is made of 1 dense input layer (256 units) and a convolutional layer (128 one-dimensional filters of size 64),
- The data are then flattened to fit a latent space made of a single dense layer (512 units),

- The decoder contains 1 convolutional layer (same hyperparameters as the one in the encoder),
- Lastly, the data are flattened to fit the output dense layer (256 units).

This structure was chosen in order to re-implement some parts of the model proposed by Ramìrez et al. [10]. At a first stage, a max-pooling and an un-pooling layer were included, but we chose to remove them since they prevented the network from learning. As for the deep AE, all layers except the last one apply a ReLU activation function to the data (as opposed to Ramìrez et al., that makes use of *softplus* functions). This change was necessary, as testing using softplus yielded far more noisy results than with ReLU.

As for the deep AE model, the last layer of the convolutional AE applies a linear function, for reasons described in the previous subsection.

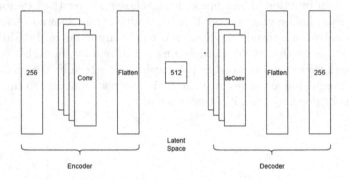

Fig. 2. Structure of the convolutional autoencoder.

3.3 Dataset

Our input data is obtained from the *IDMT-SMT-Audio-Effects* dataset [1], which is made of 2-second long single tones and two-note bichords recorded from various 6-string electric guitars and 4-string bass guitars, and covers the common pitch range of these instruments. The recordings include the clean notes and their respective effected versions. The dataset includes eleven different effects with different settings for each effect: more specifically, three different settings for each tone are present for the distortion effect. Since including user controls falls outside the scope of this paper, only the instances for the first of the three settings were used for training. The training procedure differs from self-supervised learning, which is more commonly used when dealing with autoencoders: unprocessed (clean) monophonic notes were given as input, and the corresponding processed (distorted) notes were set as target. Thus, the network learned to apply the distortion effect to the clean sound. A part of the monophonic set was used for validation, and the trained model was tested on single notes, as well as two-note bichords. The files in the dataset were recorded at a sample rate 44100 Hz (16-bit, mono).

3.4   Training

Figure 3 shows a diagram of the training process. The models were trained using clean sounds as inputs and distorted sounds from the dataset (same pitch as the input) as targets. Both models were trained using the Adam optimizer and a normalized mean squared error (NMSE) loss function was used to compare the processed and target output (Eq. 3). The training was performed on a workstation with three Nvidia TITAN X GPUs and an Intel Xeon CPU.

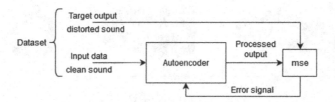

Fig. 3. Diagram of the training process: the processed output is compared to the target distorted sound using a normalized mean squared error loss function.

Deep AE. We trained on 13 min of audio, which corresponds to the length of all the distorted notes data with the chosen setting. The sample rate 44100 Hz and a mini-batch size of 128 was used. The audio was cut in slices of 579 samples each (i.e. 13.1 ms) in order to feed the input layer of the network.

Convolutional AE. Only a smaller part of the entire dataset could be used before running out of memory: the training was performed on 3 min of audio, with a mini-batch size of 64. The input data was divided in frames of 256 samples (i.e. 5.8 ms), in order to feed the input layer of the network.

4   Results and Analysis

After the model is trained, a clean input is fed into the AE, which returns a processed (i.e. distorted) output.

We tested the models with a sequence of clean single notes and two-note bichords. The reconstructed audio was compared to the corresponding target from the dataset through informal listening tests and visual inspection of the spectrograms. As an example, we compare time-domain plots (Fig. 4) and spectrograms (Fig. 5) of three single notes as output of our two architectures vs the target signal from the dataset. In this case, we choose single notes rather than bichords as they allow an easier visual inspection. As the outputs of both models contained broadband noise, we applied lowpass filters with a cutoff frequency of 10 kHz in order to cancel the spurious high frequencies outside the guitar/bass

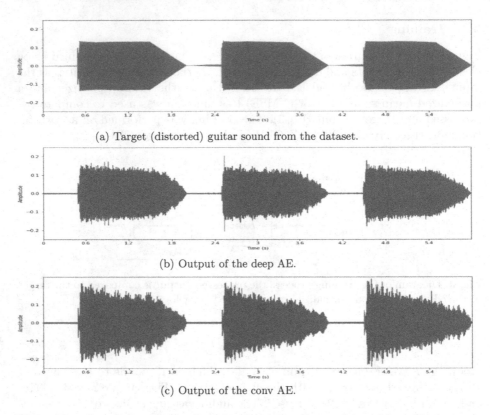

(a) Target (distorted) guitar sound from the dataset.

(b) Output of the deep AE.

(c) Output of the conv AE.

Fig. 4. Time-domain comparison between target (i.e. distorted sound from the dataset) and the outputs of the deep AE and convolutional AE. Here, three 2-second notes (E2, F2, F#2) played with an electric guitar are shown.

range. The time-domain plots (Fig. 4) show that the model outputs present a rougher shape compared to the target sound, with clear ripples in the case of the convolutional AE. The peak amplitude is larger (again, especially the output of the convolutional AE): this is probably due to the additional noise which can also be heard in the processed sound.

4.1   Deep AE

Figure 5b shows the spectrogram of one output from the deep AE. By comparing with the spectrogram of the target sound in Fig. 5a, it can be noted that the reconstructed data are noisy, but the desired spectral content is present almost in its entirety. However, conversely to the target signal, some undesired frequency content is added between the tones: our listening tests suggest that this corresponds to the guitar pickup hum, which is amplified by the distortion effect. In the real world, this sound is usually less intense that the guitar sound and disappears quickly after the attack. This difference may be due to the fact that

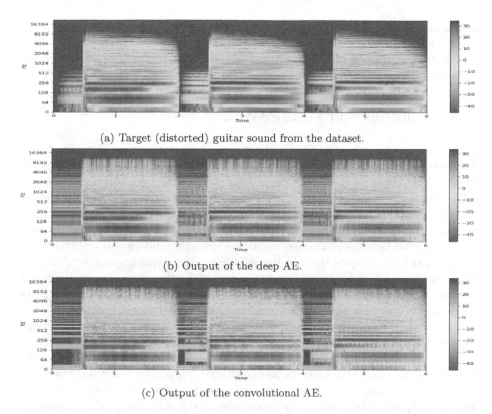

(a) Target (distorted) guitar sound from the dataset.

(b) Output of the deep AE.

(c) Output of the convolutional AE.

Fig. 5. Spectrograms of the signals represented in Fig. 4. It should be noted how the most relevant frequency content is reliably reconstructed, but a fair amount of noise is also introduced by the networks.

the network has not been properly trained to generate silence, as it hasn't been trained on instances that contained silence: a further analysis is left for future work. The comparison between waveforms (Figs. 4b and 4a) shows that, despite the aforementioned discrepancies (which contribute in hiding the sharp decay clearly visible in the target signal), the network seems able to approximate the correct amplitude envelope.

4.2   Convolutional AE

Figure 5c shows the spectrogram of the output from our convolutional AE. The spectral reconstruction does not seem to be improved with respect to the deep AE, and our output results even noisier than in the previous case. However, this model performs better while reconstructing the frequency content of the pause between two notes, i.e. the "silent" parts of the signal mentioned above. An inspection of the waveforms (Figs. 4c and 4a) shows that the convolutional AE does a worse amplitude envelope reconstruction than the deep AE: the first peak is smaller than in the target sound, whereas the main peak is higher, and the envelope exhibits clear ripples. This might be explained with the fact that this model was trained on a less amount of data that the previous one: a more thorough investigation is left for future work.

5   Conclusions and Future Work

In this paper, we gave a background on previously implemented methods for black-box modeling of nonlinear audio effects. We have implemented two models with different hyperparameters: a deep autoencoder and a convolutional autoencoder. These were then trained in a different way with respect to the standard self-supervised manner: clean sounds were used as input and distorted sounds were used as target. Our results show that, despite the noise in the output, even simple architectures as deep autoencoders are valid implementations for the required task. Despite the added complexity, our convolutional autoencoder did not achieve noticeable improvements in terms of either reconstructed spectral content or noise amount when compared to the deep autoencoder: this suggests that a proper deep learning virtual analog model based on convolutional layers requires a more complex structure than the one we implemented, and perhaps a larger training set. However, a more extensive comparison on these results should be performed in order to test the performance of both models properly. As far as noise is concerned, an additional deep autoencoder could be trained on the task of removing it, using the distorted sound from the dataset as target. A further analysis of the number and structure of the convolutional layers might improve our results, as well as an investigation on what made the pooling layers prevent the learning process. Residual connections could also be implemented to help the decoder reconstructing the input. A real-time implementation could also be considered.

Audio samples for this work can be found on GitHub: github.com/Rickr9 22/dist-nNet.

References

1. Idmt dataset. www.idmt.fraunhofer.de/en/business_units/m2d/smt/audio_effects. html
2. Covert, J., Livingston, D.: A vacuum-tube guitar amplifier model using a recurrent neural network. In: Proceedings of IEEE SOUTHEASTCON 2013, pp. 1–5 (2013)
3. Damskägg, E.P., Juvela, L., Välimäki, V.: Real-time modeling of audio distortion circuits with deep learning. In: Proceedings of International Sound and Music Computing Conference (SMC), Malaga, Spain, pp. 332–339 (2019)
4. Damskägg, E.P., Juvela, L., Thuillier, E., Välimäki, V.: Deep learning for tube amplifier emulation. In: Proceedings of IEEE International Conference on Acoustics, Speech and Signal Processing (ICASSP), Brighton, UK, pp. 471–475 (2019)
5. Goodfellow, I., Bengio, Y., Courville, A.: Deep Learning. MIT Press (2016). http:// www.deeplearningbook.org

6. Hinton, G.E., Zemel, R.S.: Autoencoders, minimum description length and Helmholtz free energy. In: Proceedings of the 6th International Conference on Neural Information Processing Systems, NIPS 1993, pp. 3–10. Morgan Kaufmann Publishers Inc., San Francisco (1993)
7. Lu, X., Tsao, Y., Matsuda, S., Hori, C.: Speech enhancement based on deep denoising auto-encoder. In: Proceedings of Interspeech 2013, pp. 436–440 (2013)
8. Martínez Ramírez, M.A., Benetos, E., Reiss, J.D.: A general-purpose deep learning approach to model time-varying audio effects. In: 22nd International Conference on Digital Audio Effects (DAFx-19) (2019)
9. Martínez Ramírez, M.A., Reiss, J.: End-to-end equalization with convolutional neural networks. In: Proceedings of International Conference on Digital Audio Effects (DAFx) 2018, Aveiro, Portugal, pp. 296–303 (2018)
10. Martínez Ramírez, M.A., Reiss, J.D.: Modeling nonlinear audio effects with end-to-end deep neural networks. In: Proceedings of IEEE International Conference on Acoustics, Speech and Signal Processing, ICASSP 2019, Brighton, United Kingdom, pp. 171–175 (2019)
11. Moreno, J.A., Bigoni, F., Palamas, G.: Latent birds: a bird's-eye view exploration of the latent space. In: Proceedings of 17th Sound and Music Computing Conference, Torino, 24th–26th June 2020 (2020)
12. van den Oord, A., et al.: WaveNet: a generative model for raw audio (2016). https://arxiv.org/abs/1609.03499. Accessed 01 Nov 2019
13. Rethage, D., Pons, J., Serra, X.: A wavenet for speech denoising. In: Proceedings of 2018 IEEE International Conference on Acoustics, Speech and Signal Processing, ICASSP 2018, Calgary, AB, Canada, pp. 5069–5073 (2018)
14. Schattschneider, J., Olzer, U.: Discrete-time models for nonlinear audio systems. In: Proceedings of the 2nd COST G-6 Workshop on Digital Audio Effects (DAFx99) (1999)
15. Schmitz, T., Embrechts, J.J.: Real time emulation of parametric guitar tube amplifier with long short term memory neural network. In: Proceedings of Conference on Image Processing and Pattern Recognition (IPPR 2018), pp. 149–157 (2018)
16. Zhang, Z., Olbrych, E., Bruchalski, J., McCormick, T.J., Livingston, D.L.: A vacuum-tube guitar amplifier model using long/short-term memory networks. In: Proceedings of IEEE SOUTHEASTCON 2018, pp. 1–5 (2018)

Industry and Government

Investors Embrace Gender Diversity, Not Female CEOs: The Role of Gender in Startup Fundraising

Christopher Cassion, Yuhang Qian, Constant Bossou,
and Margareta Ackerman$^{(\boxtimes)}$

Santa Clara University, Santa Clara, CA 95050, USA
mackerman@scu.edu

Abstract. The allocation of venture capital is one of the primary factors determining who takes products to market, which startups succeed or fail, and as such who gets to participate in the shaping of our collective economy. While gender diversity contributes to startup success, most funding is allocated to male-only entrepreneurial teams. In the wake of COVID-19, 2020 is seeing a notable decline in funding to female and mixed-gender teams, giving raise to an urgent need to study and correct the longstanding gender bias in startup funding allocation.

We conduct an in-depth data analysis of over 48,000 companies on Crunchbase, comparing funding allocation based on the gender composition of founding teams. Detailed findings across diverse industries and geographies are presented. Further, we construct machine learning models to predict whether startups will reach an equity round, revealing the surprising finding that the CEO's gender is *the* primary determining factor for attaining funding. Policy implications for this pressing issue are discussed.

Keywords: Gender bias · Venture capital · Diversity · Entrepreneurship

As gender equality continues to make strides across a wide range of industries from STEM to medicine, there is a critical sphere where bias persists: Compared to their male counterparts, women have little access to startup funds, restricting them from engaging in our economy at this critical level. According to Pitchbook, in 2019, female founders raised just 2.7% of the total venture capital funding invested and mixed gender founding teams received 12.9% [1].

The economic impact of the COVID-19 pandemic is having severe consequences for female entrepreneurs. Compared with 2019, the first quarter of 2020 saw a decline in the proportion of deals made with female and mixed-gender teams and funding allocated to female teams. In the third quarter of 2020, funding given to female-only teams dropped to 1.8% with mixed-gender teams receiving just 11.1% [1]. There is an urgent need for understanding the nature of this persistent bias and uncovering effective solutions for systemic change.

N. Shaghaghi et al. (Eds.): INTETAIN 2020, LNICST 377, pp. 145–164, 2021.
https://doi.org/10.1007/978-3-030-76426-5_10

In the United States, only 10–15% of startups are founded by women [2]. Yet, the number of women starting companies is not the primary issue, the far more important problem is their lack of access to capital [3]. The funding gap between male and female founders is particularly high at the early stage of a venture, with an analysis of California and Massachusetts startups revealing that female-led ventures are 63% less likely than male-led ones to obtain VC funding [4].

While it is generally well-known in the venture community that men have an easier time raising funds, much remains unclear. In order to ascertain effective solutions, it is necessary to gain insight into the nature of the problem. For instance, does having a woman on a founding team increase or decrease fundraising outcomes? What role does the gender of the CEO play compared to the gender of other founders? If funding is successfully raised, how does gender impact the amount raised? How much does gender matter in different geographic regions and across industries?

We perform an in-depth data analysis of over 48,000 companies on Crunchbase. Our analysis suggests the presence of bias against women across geographies and industries, which extends not only to female-only but also to mixed-gender teams with female CEOs. We also construct machine-learning models (Decision Tree, Random Forest, Logistic Regression, Gradient Boosted Trees, and Multi-layer Perceptron (MLP)) to predict whether a founding team will reach a priced funding round.[1] Our findings show the CEO's[2] gender to be the most important founder characteristic for predicting fundraising success, beating critical features including whether the founders attended top universities and the number of prior exits. We discuss the implications of these findings to the utilization of machine learning models in venture capital allocation, and make recommendations for systemic change.

1   Background

Gender plays a key role across the lifetime of an entrepreneurial journey: Women are less likely to become entrepreneurs than men [5] and less likely to get external funding once a new venture is founded [6]. The funding gap between male and female founders is higher at the early stage of the venture than at later stages [7]. Women are 65% less likely to get funded at early stages and 35% less likely to be funded at later stages, when strong signals of growth are available [4].

Consequently, women-owned businesses rely heavily on internal funding (ex. personal finances) rather than funding from others, both debt and equity, to finance their firms [7]. Even though the number of women-owned firms is increasing rapidly [8], they are still left behind compared to their male counterparts in receiving external founding.

Previous work provides valuable insight into the role of gender in the allocation of Venture Capital funds. However, the data used in previous studies,

---

[1] Raising a priced round is a major milestone that offers startups the means to succeed.

[2] In startups, the role of CEO is most often taken by one of the founders. This is nearly ubiquitous at early stages.

such as those above, tends to be geographically limited (focusing on individual countries, often the US), or consisting of only several hundred instances. Many questions remain to be answered: How wide is the gender gap in the allocation of venture capital funding across geographic regions and industries? Does gender diversity help or hinder fundraising outcomes? Does the gender of the CEO play a special role compared to other founders?

In order gain a broader understanding into the nature and prevalence of gender bias in VC, we perform the most comprehensive analysis to date on the impact of gender on startup funding across geographies and industry verticals, utilizing both statistical methods and machine learning techniques. We are careful to account for the potential influence of the pipeline problem, whereby fewer women seeking to engage in entrepreneurship.[3] The data analysis helps inform our policy recommendations, and we hope that it will support future research on resolving gender bias in startup funding allocation.

2 Methodology

We rely on Crunchbase data to attain a data set of over 48,000 companies along with founder information. We consider four gender compositions: founding teams consisting entirely of male founders (male-only), founding teams consisting entirely of female founders (female-only), teams with at least one female and at least one male founder led by a male CEO (mixed male-led), and teams with at least one female and at least one male founder led by a female CEO (mixed female-led). Companies with these gender and leadership compositions are subsequently compared, with emphasis on funding raised across a variety of industries and geographies. We then construct machine learning models to ascertain the importance of the team's gender composition and the leader's gender in funding outcomes.

2.1 Data Collection

The data was obtained from Crunchbase, which prides itself for being "the leading destination for company insights from early-stage startups to the Fortune 1000."[4] Crunchbase provides two majors types of data: Information on companies and data on individuals in leadership positions. We separately retrieved both types of data as they include some non-overlapping features. For instance, gender information is only available as a founder attribute and is absent from the company description.

---

[3] The pipeline problem is often perceived as the primary cause of the gender gap in startup funding allocation, suggesting that the gap would be eliminated if women were as interested as men in pursuing entrepreneurship. We devise and apply analysis methods that shed light into these issues in a manner that cannot be reduced to the pipeline problem.

[4] https://www.crunchbase.com/.

Our final dataset is an integration of the company and founder data. We first downloaded data of 224,000 companies and 175,000 founders with attributes of interest to our analysis. We then combined the two datasets by matching the Company's Website attribute in both the founders and companies dataset to produce a new dataset of 63,462 data points. The combined dataset contains all the attributes of the companies and all the aggregated attributes of the founders dataset. We dropped all rows with missing values in the key attributed (head-quarter region, total funding raised, and industry) and obtained a final dataset of 48,676 entries. 58.14% of the companies are led by multi-member founding teams. It is worth noting that companies ranked higher by Crunchbase tend to have fewer missing values.

While not all founders are present in the founders dataset, founders names are present in the company dataset as comma separated attributes. Whenever a founder's gender is missing from the founder data set, we rely on a machine-learning model for gender classification based on names.[5]

Another important aspect is identifying who is leading the startup. We define the leader as either the CEO, or the sole founder for one person founding teams. In order to determine leadership, we inspect the job titles of all of the founders found on Crunchbase that have the company as their primary organization. We set if the company is male or female led based on the gender of the identified founder. Female-only and male-only companies are respectively female and male led.

We reclassified the industries attribute values by reducing over one hundred industries down to thirty by combining closely related industries, from amongst which twenty industries with over 300 companies each were selected. We then picked the first industry that each company provides as its primary industry. The company's headquarter region was used to identify its location.

2.2   Attribute Statistics

Before delving into extensive analysis, we share some basic statistics about the data. As shown in Fig. 1, overall founder gender distribution of the 48,676 companies in our dataset consists of 7.13% female-only companies, 80.22% male-only companies, 3.26% mixed female-led companies, and 9.39% mixed male-led companies (see Fig. 1).The average funding by gender composition is shown in Fig. 2.

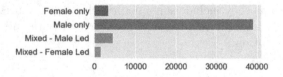

Fig. 1. Number of companies of each gender composition type

---

[5] We utilized the following name-based gender classifier: https://github.com/clintval/gender-predictor. We retrained the model, achieving an accuracy of 97.10%.

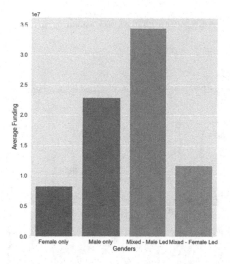

Fig. 2. Average funding by gender composition of founding teams. Values in tens of millions of USD.

Our analysis includes 20 industries, each consisting of at least 300 companies (See Fig. 3 for the list of industries). We omit locations with fewer than 1,500 companies, resulting in three major geographic regions, consisted of North America, Europe, and Asia-Pacific. Since 64.01% of companies are located in North America, we also include a detailed analysis focusing on companies based in the top four US startup hubs: Silicon Valley Bay Area, Greater New York Area, Greater Los Angeles Area, and Greater Boston Area. Lastly, 94.84% of the startups in our data were founded on or after the year 2000. Please see the Appendix for additional information about the data set.

3   Data Analysis

In this section, we analyse the funding allocated to founding teams with different gender compositions. Results are reported across diverse industries and geographic regions.

3.1   Analysis by Industry

We begin with an analysis of funding allocation by industry across the 20 most dominant industries identified in our data. As shown in Fig. 3, there are far more male-only companies than female-only and mixed-gender companies across all industries. The industries Data, Commerce and Apps have the largest number of companies while Gaming, Agriculture and Farming and Administrative Services have the fewest. In all but 5 out the 20 industries, the next biggest category is male-led, mixed-gender groups.

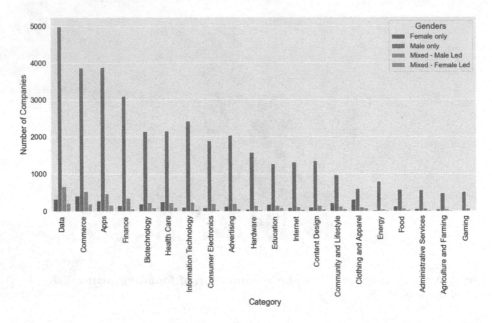

Fig. 3. Number of companies for each gender composition type by industry. All 20 industries are dominated by male-only teams.

As shown in Fig. 4, male-only and male-led mixed-gender teams receive the great majority of funding. In particular, male-only teams receive significantly 31 times more funding than female-only teams (statistic $= 11.0715$, $P < 0.0001$). Male-only teams also get significantly 47 times more funding than mixed-gender female-led teams (statistic $= 5.8197$, $P < 0.0001$). Similarly, mixed-gender male-led teams also receive significantly 8.5 times more funding than mixed-gender female-led (statistic $= 3.5987$, $P < 0.0001$) and female only teams (statistic $= 4.2129$, $P < 0.0001$).

Male-only teams receive more funding in 19 of the 20 industries. In 18 of the 20 industries, there is a significant difference between the amount raised by male-only teams compared with female-only teams, the exceptions being agriculture & farming and biotechnology, where the difference is not significant. On the other hand, the difference between male-only and male-led is often insignificant, with a significant difference found in only 4 of the 20 industries.

For example, in the Data industry, male-only teams get significantly more funding than mixed female-led teams (statistic $= 6.0181$, $P < 0.0001$), and female only teams (statistic $= 4.6942$, $P < 0.0001$), and insignificantly more than mixed male-led teams (statistic $= 0.6319$, $P = 0.5276$). Similarly, in Commerce, male-only teams get significantly more funding than mixed female-led teams

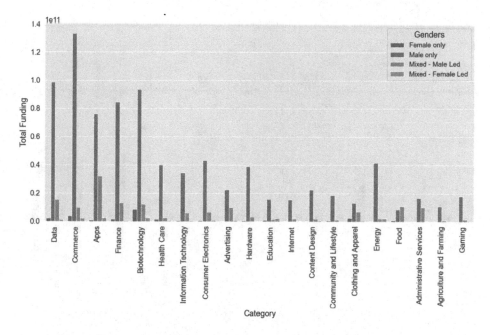

Fig. 4. Total funding allocation for founding teams with different gender composition across industries. Values in hundreds of billions of USD. Total funding across all twenty one industries are dominated by companies founded by male-only founders except in the Food industry where mixed-gender male-led teams raised more funding than any other group type.

(statistic $= 3.4581$, $P = 0.0005$) and female only teams (statistic $= 3.7047$, $P = 0.0002$) and significantly more than mixed male-led teams (statistic $= 2.6360$, $P = 0.0084$). Of the industries studies, Food is the only one where male-only teams did not raise the largest amount of total funding, however, the difference between male-only and mixed male-led teams was not significant (statistic $= 0.9567$, $P = 0.3427$).

3.2   Average Funding by Industry

The pipeline problem, the fact that fewer women engage in entrepreneurship, is often perceived as the primary factor in the discrepancy in funding allocation. In order to gain insight into the nature of the issue beyond the pipeline problem, we consider the average funding allocated to teams that have successfully raised funds, comparing the amounts raised against the gender of the founding teams. This analysis helps gain insight while offering an accessible demonstration of a potential gender gap to lay audiences.

As shown on Fig. 5, male-only founding teams and male led founding teams lead in average funding, receiving the highest amount of average funding across most industries (18 out 20). In 11 of the 20 industries, mixed-gender male-led

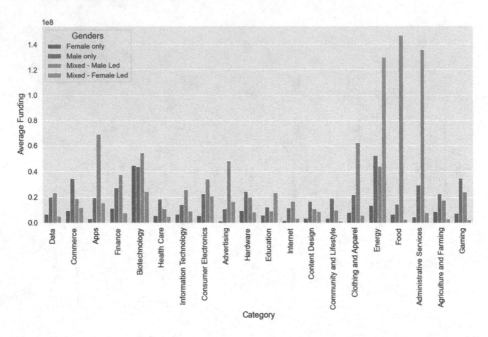

Fig. 5. Average funding allocation for founding teams with different gender composition across industries. Values in hundreds of millions of USD. Of the 20 industries, average funding is highest for mixed-gender male-led teams in 11 industries and for male-only teams in 7 industries.

team achieve the highest average funding, compared with 7 industries where male-only teams raise the most average funding. In industries including Food and Administrative Services there is a substantial gap between average funding given to mixed male-led led teams and male-only, with the mixed teams raising a greater amount of funding.

Of the twenty industries, there are only two industries (Energy and Education) where female-led teams receive more average funding. Notably, there are no industries where female-only teams raise the greatest amount of average funding. Unlike total funding, this persistent gap in average funding to startups that successfully raise funds cannot be explained by low numbers of women entrepreneurs.

Comparing companies led by women, we find that in 9 of the 20 industries female-only teams receive more average funding than mixed-gender female-led startups.

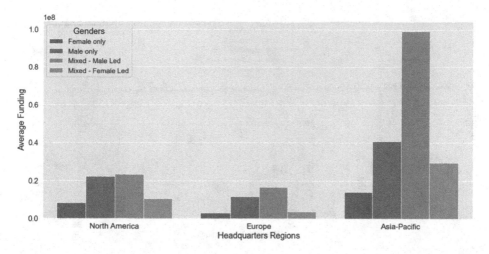

Fig. 6. Average funding allocation to founding teams with different gender composition across dominant continents. Values in hundreds of millions of USD. All continents under consideration reveal the same raking, with male-led mixed-gender teams receiving the highest average funding, followed by male-only teams, then female-led mixed-gender teams, and finally female-only teams receiving the lowest amount of average funding.

3.3 Analysis by Geography

Considering average funding allocation, shown in Fig. 6, we see the same raking by average funding allocation across all continents, with female-only teams receiving the lowest average funding, followed by female-led mixed-gender teams, then male-only teams, and finally mixed-gender male-led teams receiving the highest amount of average capital.

Analyzing startup hubs in the United States, shown in 7, we discover that in Silicon Valley and New York male-only teams receive the highest average funding, narrowing beating mixed-gender male-led teams. LA and Boston follow the global trend of giving mixed-gender male-led teams the highest amounts of average funding, followed by male-only teams. In Silicon Valley, New York, and LA, female-only teams receive the least amount of average funding, followed by mixed female-led teams. However, in Boston, female-only teams receive more average funding than mixed-gender female-led teams.

In summary, companies with male CEOs receive greater funding across all continents and US startup hubs compared with companies with female CEOs. Mixed-gender teams perform well with respect to fundraising, often better than male-only teams, when they are led by male-CEOs.

When comparing total funding for different gender composition teams across continents (see Fig. 8), we find that mixed-gender teams receive the great majority of funding in the three continents considered. Europe appears to be exhibiting the greatest preference for male-only teams, where such groups receive significantly over 65.5 times more funding than female-only companies (statis-

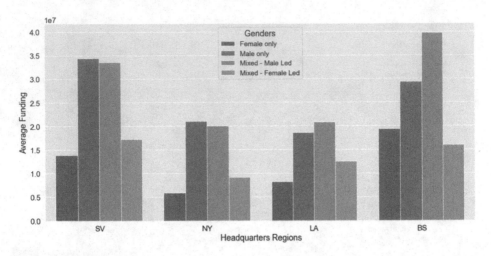

Fig. 7. Average funding allocation to founding teams with different gender compositions across US startup hubs. Values in tens of millions of USD. In the US, Silicon Valley Bay Area and New York allocate the highest average funding to male-only teams, whereas male-led mixed-gender groups in Greater Los Angeles Area and Boston receive more average funding than all other group types.

tic $= 6.5061$, $P <$ 0.0001). European male-only teams raise significantly 92.9 more money than mixed female-led teams (statistic $= 7.6873$, $P <$ 0.0001). Comparing mixed gender teams, those led by men raise 15.3 more funding than female-led groups (statistic $= 2.0306$, $P =$ 0.0427). Male-only companies in Europe raise non-significantly 6 times more total funding than mixed-gender teams led by men (statistic $= 0.6232$, $P =$ 0.5327).

In Asia-Pacific, male-only companies receive significantly over 37 times more funding than female-only companies (statistic $= 5.1950$, $P <$ 0.0001). Male-only teams raise insignificantly over 43 times more than mixed-gender female led teams (statistic $= 1.0063$, $P =$ 0.3157). Comparing mixed gender teams, those led by men raise insignificantly 12 times more funding than female-led groups (statistic $= 1.8761$, $P=$ 0.0611). Finally, male only teams raise 3.5 time more than male-led mixed-gender teams, not statistically significant (statistic $= 1.6322$, $P =$ 0.1032).

When looking at total funding for different gender composition teams across US startup hubs (see Fig. 9), similar to the continental analysis, male only teams receive the great majority of funding for the four major hubs. Silicon Valley exhibits some of the greatest preference for male founders, with male-only companies receiving significantly over 27 times more funding than female-only companies (statistic $= 2.9081$, $P <$ 0.0038) and significantly over 35 times more than mixed-gender female-led companies (statistic $= 2.7921$, $P <$ 0.0054).

In Los Angeles Area, male-only companies significantly receive over 23 times more funding than female-only companies (statistic $= 3.3092$, $P <$ 0.0010). Comparing male-only to mixed female-led companies, male-only raised insignificantly

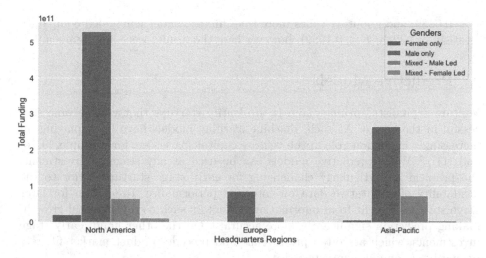

Fig. 8. Total funding by major geographic regions. Values in hundreds of millions of USD. Male-only founding teams receive the greater amount of funding in all regions considered, while female-only teams and female-led teams receive the least founding.

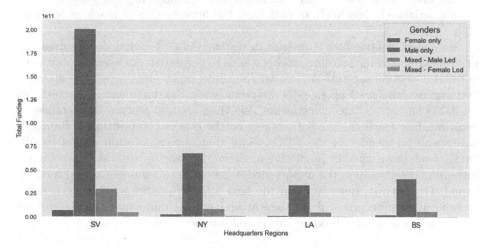

Fig. 9. Total funding by major US startup hubs. Values in hundreds of billions of USD. Male-only founding teams receive the greater amount of funding in all regions considered, while female-only and female-led teams receive the least.

over 30 times more (statistic $= 1.0888$, $P = 0.2787$). New York gives male-only companies over 21 times more funding than female-only companies (statistic $= 6.8847$, $P < 0.0001$) and over 37 times more than mixed-gender female-led companies (statistic $= 3.4533$, $P = 0.0006$), both results being significant.

Finally, analysis of Boston area shows that male-only companies receive about 16 times more funding than female-only companies (statistic $= 1.8629$,

$P < 0.0639$) and about 41 times more than mixed-gender female-led companies (statistic $= 1.4243$, $P < 0.1599$), however here the results were not significant.

4   Predictive Models

Venture capitalists? primary aim is to identify startups that will become successful in the future. As such, machine learning models have been playing an increasingly important role in the venture capital space (see, for example, [9,10] and [11]).[6] While predictive models can be used at any stage of investment, the problem is particularly challenging for early stage startups, prior to the availability of qualitative data on company performance. Prediction for later stage startups benefit from information on factors such as revenue and growth, making prediction significantly more accurate. On the other hand, early stage investments, which are often pre-revenue and precede product market fit, rely primarily on founder characteristics.

One of primary risks with the utilization of machine learning models from an ethical perspective is the perpetuation and even amplification of existing biases. For instance, in the context of credit markets, Black and Hispanic borrowers are disproportionately less likely to gain from the introduction of machine learning [12].

How much gender bias is present in startup data? To what degree does the utilization of machine learning models stands to perpetuate, or even amplify, gender bias in venture capital? We explore this direction by creating several machine learning models based on founder characteristics, the dominant characteristics available for early stage investments. We then analyze feature importance to ascertain how much the predictions rely on the gender composition of founding teams and the gender of the CEOs. Note that our exploration differs significantly from prior work in predictive modeling for startup success, since we are interested specifically in the importance of gender for attaining a priced funding round. By contrast, most work in the field aims to predict startup success by incorporating information about the startup itself, including quantitative success indicators such as total funding raised and number of employees.

4.1   Feature Selection

In order to ascertain investor behaviour prior to having clear success indicators available, we focus exclusively on founder characteristics[7]. However, it is essential to avoid including features that would be heavily altered by the target variable. For instance, social media presence stands to alter for founders who successfully raised funding. Similarly, information regarding investments made

---

[6] Further, many venture capital firms built their own custom models which they do not make public in order to maintain a competitive advantage.

[7] As mention above, while a gender gap exits at all startup stages, investors are most reluctant to invest in women in the early stages, where female ventures are 65% less likely to receive funding [4].

by the founders is heavily influenced by their entrepreneurial success, and are as such also omitted.

Training Features. To build the model, we first extract a set of features related to the founders from the aggregated dataset discussed in Methodology. The following features have been selected:

- **Male Led:** Boolean variable that is True if the CEO or sole founder is Male, False otherwise
- **Gender Composition:** If the founding team is male-only, female-only, mixed male-led, or mixed female-led
- **Total Previously Founded Organizations:** Total number of companies previously founded by members of the founding team
- **Average Previously Founded Organizations:** The average number of companies previously founded by the founders
- **Has Previously Founded Organizations:** Boolean variable indicating True if any of the founders previously founded an organization
- **Total Number of Exits:** Total number of exit events in which the founders participated
- **Average Number of Exits:** Average number of exit events for the company founders
- **Has Exits**: Boolean variable indicating True if any of the founders had previously founded a company that had an exit event
- **Total Number of Founders:** Number of founders of the company
- **Multiple Founders:** Boolean variable set to True if the founding team consists of two or more founders
- **Same Alma Mater:** Boolean variable indicating True if all of the founders went to the same university, False otherwise
- **% from Top School:** Percentage of founders that went to a top 100 school [13]
- **Top School Attended:** Boolean variable set to True if any of the founders went to a top 100 school [13]

Target Feature. The goal of these experiments is to determine if a startup reached an equity funding round based on its founders. An equity round is when a startup sells shares of the startup in exchange for a large investment (generally well over a million). Equity rounds are important to the life cycle of startups largely because they provide a significant monetary influx into the company and represents a vote of confidence from the Venture Capital community, which helps with subsequent rounds.

We separate the dataset into two funding stage groups, pre-equity rounds and post-equity rounds. We define pre-equity rounds as those whose latest funding stage is an Angel Round, Pre-Seed, Seed Round, or Convertible Note. We define post-equity rounds as those that whose latest funding stage is Series A, Series B or beyond, or Corporate Rounds. Using that, we construct models to predict whether a founding team has reached a priced round.

4.2   Model Analysis

Using hyperparameter grid-search to obtain the best model of each type, we constructed the following models: (1) Decision Tree (DT), (2) Random Forest, (3) Logistic Regression (LR), (4) Gradient Boosted Trees (GBT), and (5) Multi-layer Perceptron (MLP), for each of the worldwide and US data. MLP had the highest accuracy on worldwide data, at 63.73%. Similar results were found for US data with MLP giving the highest accuracy of 63.61%. Table 1 and Table 2 summarize the results for worldwide and US data, respectively. All models performed comparably, with worldwide accuracies varying by only 0.86% (Table 1).

Table 1. Predictive model results for worldwide data.

Model	AUC	Precision	Recall	Accuracy
Decision Tree	53.30	59.90	53.23	62.91
Random Forest	53.20	59.78	53.17	62.86
Logistic Regression	52.70	61.38	52.73	63.00
Gradient Boosted Trees	53.00	60.04	53.04	62.88
Multi-Layer Percepton	**53.80**	**63.92**	**53.80**	**63.72**

Early stage predictions are known to be highly challenging. It is essential to emphasize that no information about the companies has been provided beyond founder features, in order to ascertain the impact of gender on early stage investing. It is unlikely that much higher accuracy is possible without incorporating features beyond the scope of founder characteristics.

Table 2. Predictive model results for the US dataset.

Model	AUC	Precision	Recall	Accuracy
Decision Tree	54.20	58.36	54.17	60.68
Random Forest	54.70	58.90	54.70	61.00
Logistic Regression	55.80	60.97	55.83	62.08
Gradient Boosted Trees	55.00	60.15	55.00	61.52
Multi-Layer Percepton	**57.60**	**63.63**	**57.59**	**63.61**

Feature Importance in Tree Based Models. Considering feature importance enables us to ascertain how significant are gender-related characteristics compared with other founder attributes, such as prior exits or whether founders attended top schools. Table 3 and Table 4 detail the feature importance for the

Table 3. Decision Tree and Random Forest feature importance for top 5 features for worldwide data. Whether the company is led by a male CEO is the most important feature for both the decision tree and random forest models, more important than the features addressing the number of prior exits and founders' alma mater.

Feature	Decision Tree	Feature	Random Forest
Male Led	25.62%	Male Led	15.50%
% from top school	18.81%	Total Number of Founders	12.97%
Has Exits	18.81%	% from top school	11.26%
Same Alma Mater	10.10%	Same Alma Mater	9.12%
Total Number of Founders	6.99%	Has Exits	7.86%

Table 4. Predictive model feature importance on US data. According to both the decision tree and random forest models, the most important feature for reaching a priced round in the US is whether the company consists of only male founders.

Feature	Decision Tree	Feature	Random Forest
Male Led	19.34%	Male Led	18.40%
Number of Exits	19.29%	Number of Founders	13.78%
% from top school	14.81%	% from top school	9.38%
Same Alma Mater	12.46%	Same Alma Mater	7.91%
Number of Founders	8.22%	Avg Number of Exits	7.21%

Decision Tree and Random Forest models.[8] The results show that whether a company is led by a male CEO is by far the most important feature in the decision tree model, and also the top feature in the random forest model for both the worldwide and US-only datasets.

For the Gradient Boosted Tree (GBT) model on US data, the top 5 features are ranked as follows: whether the founding team is male-only (14.46%), number of founders (13.04%), percent of founders from top schools (12.03%), number of exits (11.46%), and if all the founders have graduated from the same university (10.07%). For the worldwide GBT model, where GBT achieved the second lowest accuracy of the models created, the top feature is the number of founders.

In summary, feature importance analysis for the tree-based models indicates that in most instances, for both worldwide and US-only datasets, gender is key to fundraising success. We find that the main indicator of whether a startup will reach a priced funding round centers on gender, either the gender of the CEO or whether the team consists entirely of male founders.

---

[8] We report feature importance for the interpretable tree-based models, emphasizing that all models obtained comparable accuracy. Importance analysis for other models are left for future work.

5 Conclusions and Recommendations

Our analysis suggests the presence of a pervasive and substantial bias against female-led startups across geographies and industries. Looking at average funding, where only startups that have raised funds are considered, lets us eliminate the pipeline problem as a primary explanation for discrepancies in funding allocation. The analysis reveals that, across all but 2 of the 20 industries considered, male-led teams received the highest average funding. Across all three continents in our analysis, North America, Europe, and Asia-Pacific, the highest average funding went to mixed-gender teams led by male CEOs. In all three continents, the least average funding went to female-only teams, followed by female-led mixed-gender teams.

Among US startup hubs, Silicon Valley and New York gave the highest average funding to male-only teams, while LA and Boston gave greatest average support to mixed-gender teams led by male CEOs. As in the continental analysis, female-only teams receive the lowest average funding, following by mixed-gender teams with female CEOS.

Our ML-based analysis reveals gender characteristics to be of highest importance amongst founder features for reaching a prices round, in particular, more important that traditionally prized characteristics pertaining to whether the founders have attended top universities or had prior exits. Worldwide analysis reveals the gender of the CEO to the most important feature. On US data, machine learning modelling shows that the most important characteristic tends to be whether all founders are male.

In summary, we find that across all geographic regions and the great majority of industries, companies a male CEO have much better funding outcomes those with female CEO. The gender of the CEO appears to be *the most* important factor in fundraising. With no exceptions across geographies and industries, our results show that startups led by male CEOs raise more money than startups raised by female CEOs, irrespective of the gender of the rest of the founding team. On the other hand, having women as founders but not CEOs improves funding results in some (but not all) cases, sometimes by a substantial margin. Across all geographies (but not all industries), female-led companies achieve better funding outcomes when they include a male co-founder.

5.1 Implications for Machine Learning Modeling for Investment Decisions

Our machine-learning analysis reveals that CEO's gender to be the most important amongst founder characteristics for attaining a priced funding round. In particular, gender composition was found to be more important than characteristics that are known to be prized by venture capitalists, such as the number of prior exits or the founder's alma mater. This surprising finding not only reveals the primary role of gender in venture capital allocation, but also warns of potential pitfalls when applying machine learning models to investment decisions.

Machine learning models in other spheres, such as credit markets, have already been shown to inflate biases [12]. We recommend exercising caution when building machine learning models for startup success prediction, in order to reduce the impact of gender on the resultant decision making. Most importantly, features directly capturing the gender of the founders should be omitted.[9]

Further, we observe that features such as prior exits, while not directly capturing bias, may play an important role in perpetuating it. With longstanding low access to startup funding, women have much lower chances of having had previous exits.

5.2   Discussion and Policy Implications

One of the most important findings of this analysis is the critical role of a CEO's gender for fundraising outcomes, even in mixed-gender teams. This is notable because in startups, particularly at early stages, division of labour amongst founder is a less clear cut than in mature companies. Thus, it unlikely that a mixed-gender company's performances in terms of investor returns will be impacted on the basis of whether a male or female co-founder is designated as the CEO.

Yet, fundraising is often handled by the CEO, making the founder identified as such the primary link between the startup and any potential investors. Even when other founders are present, the CEO is expected to lead the discussion on behalf of their startup. Consequently, any bias against women, implicit or otherwise, is likely to manifest most strongly if the CEO is female.

The critical role of the CEO in funding outcomes may thus be reduced to differences in how investors treat men and women. Prior research points to desperate treatment of men and women during startup pitches. In a study on interactions at TechCrunch Disrupt in New York City, investors asked men to expand on how the plan to reach success, whereas women were asked to defend themselves against failure [14], which hindered women's ability to raise funds. Notably, both male and female investors exhibited this bias against female founders.[10] Further research is needed to elucidate the impact of implicit gender bias on fundraising outcomes and uncover the reasons behind ubiquitous lower propensity towards investing in female CEOs across the globe.

Our findings show that across all continents considered and some US startups hub mixed-gender are given higher average funding, when they are male-led. This likely stems from the inherent advantage of mixed gender teams. Gender balanced teams perform better than male-dominated teams in terms of sales and

---

[9] Gender information has been incorporated into previous ML models for startup success, see, for example [11].

[10] There is a prevalent notion that the key to eradicating gender bias in startup investing lies in increasing the number of female investors. This view is oversimplified and potentially misleading. Both men and women are highly prone to bias against women [15]. While increasing gender diversity amongst investors is important for a variety of reasons, tackling gender bias against female founders calls for more comprehensive solutions.

profits [16], and gender diverse executives teams are 21% more likely to yield higher financial returns [17]. The venture capital firm First Round reported that their investments in companies with at least one female founder were meaningfully outperforming their investments in all-male teams [18]. In fact, their investment in companies with a female founder performed 63% better than their investments with all-male founding teams [18].

The benefit of a gender diversity helps mixed-gender teams raise funding, but only when they are led by a male CEO. The consistently lower funding allocation, both in total and on average, to mixed-gender teams when they are led by women CEOs points to the severity of gender bias in startup capital allocation.

In recent years, a number of Venture Capital firms emerged with the mandate to invest in teams with at least one female founder. However, these investment firms tend to be (1) late stage, and (2) utilize a "follow" investment strategy, investing only after another VC firm makes a substantial investment and sets the deal terms. This does little to help increase the number of female founders.

Our findings suggest that importance of investing in female-led companies to correct the gender bias in capital allocation. We recommend the formation of venture capital firms with the mandate to invest in companies with female CEOs. Investing in women-led, mixed-gender teams should allow investors to benefit from the performance boost of gender diversity, while helping to correct the long standing bias against female business leaders. Investors with expertise to lead early stage deals applying such practiced can further reap the benefit of early investing, receiving large equity in promising deals.

A   Appendix

This appendix includes additional information on the data used in our analysis (Tables 5, 6 and 7).

Table 5. Global startup hubs total number and percentage of companies per region

Geography	# of companies	Percentage
North America	30,212	62.07%
Europe	8,932	18.35%
Asia-Pacific	7,968	16.37%
Latin America	1,308	2.69%
Gulf Cooperation Council	256	0.53%
Total	48,676	100.0%

Table 6. US startup hubs total number and percentage of companies per region

Geography	# of companies	Percentage
Silicon Valley Bay Area	7,611	46.98%
Greater New York Area	4,420	27.28%
Greater Los Angeles Area	2,416	14.91%
Greater Boston	1,754	10.83%
Total	16,201	100.0%

Table 7. Total and percentage of companies per industry

Verticals	# of companies	Percentage
Data	6,200	12.74%
Commerce	5,008	10.29%
Apps	4,789	9.84%
Finance	3,679	7.56%
Information Technology	2,822	5.80%
Health Care	2,755	5.66%
Biotechnology	2,663	5.47%
Advertising	2,442	5.02%
Consumer Electronics	2,236	4.59%
Hardware	1,826	3.75%
Education	1,690	3.47%
Content Design	1,670	3.43%
Internet	1,575	3.24%
Community and Lifestyle	1,388	2.85%
Clothing and Apparel	1,107	2.27%
Energy	884	1.82%
Food	828	1.70%
Administrative Services	729	1.50%
Gaming	613	1.26%
Agriculture and Farming	612	1.26%
Others	3,160	6.49%
Total	48,676	100.0%

References

1. Pitchbook. The VC female founders dashboard (2020). https://pitchbook.com/news/articles/the-vc-female-founders-dashboard
2. Ewens, M., Townsend, R.R.: Are early stage investors biased against women? J. Financ. Econ. **135**(3), 653–677 (2020)

3. Forbes. Does gender bias have an impact on venture funding? (2019). https://medium.com/@EventerpriseAG/does-gender-bias-have-an-impact-on-venture-funding-fba3375a5bb. Accessed 25 Oct 2019
4. Guzman, J., Kacperczyk, A.O.: Gender gap in entrepreneurship. Res. Policy **48**(7), 1666–1680 (2019)
5. Ruef, M., Aldrich, H.E., Carter, N.M.: The structure of founding teams: homophily, strong ties, and isolation among us entrepreneurs. Am. Sociol. Rev. **68**(2), 195–222 (2003)
6. Yang, T., Aldrich, H.E.: Who's the boss? Explaining gender inequality in entrepreneurial teams. Am. Sociol. Rev. **79**(2), 303–327 (2014)
7. Coleman, S., Robb, A.: Sources of funding for new women-owned firms. W. New Eng. L. Rev. **32**, 497 (2010)
8. Greene, P.G., Brush, C.G., Hart, M.M., Saparito, P.: Patterns of venture capital funding: is gender a factor? Venture Cap.: Int. J. Entrep. Finance **3**(1), 63–83 (2001)
9. Krishna, A., Agrawal, A., Choudhary, A.: Predicting the outcome of startups: less failure, more success. In: 2016 IEEE 16th International Conference on Data Mining Workshops (ICDMW), pp. 798–805. IEEE (2016)
10. Halabí, C.E., Lussier, R.: A model for predicting small firm performance: increasing the probability of entrepreneurial success. Documentos de Trabajo **3** (2010)
11. Arroyo, J., Corea, F., Jimenez-Diaz, G., Recio-Garcia, J.A.: Assessment of machine learning performance for decision support in venture capital investments. IEEE Access **7**, 124233–124243 (2019)
12. Fuster, A., Goldsmith-Pinkham, P., Ramadorai, T., Walther, A.: Predictably unequal? The effects of machine learning on credit markets. SSRN Electron. J. (2017)
13. The world's top 100 universities, June 2020. https://www.topuniversities.com/student-info/choosing-university/worlds-top-100-universities
14. Kanze, D., Huang, L., Conley, M.A., Higgins, E.T.: We ask men to win and women not to lose: closing the gender gap in startup funding. Acad. Manag. J. **61**(2), 586–614 (2018)
15. United Nations Development Programme (UNDP): Tackling Social Norms: A Game Changer for Gender Inequalities. United Nations Development Programme (UNDP) (2020)
16. Hoogendoorn, S., Oosterbeek, H., Van Praag, M.: The impact of gender diversity on the performance of business teams: evidence from a field experiment. Manag. Sci. **59**(7), 1514–1528 (2013)
17. Hunt, V., Prince, S., Dixon-Fyle, S., Yee, L.: Delivering through diversity. McKinsey & Company Report (2018). Accessed 3 Apr 2018
18. First Round. 10 Years (2019). http://10years.firstround.com/. Accessed 1 Nov 2019

A Tool for Narrowing the Second Chance Gap

Navid Shaghaghi[1]($\boxtimes$)(iD), Zuyan Huang[1], Hithesh Sekhar Bathala[1],
Connor Azzarello[1], Anthony Chen[1], and Colleen V. Chien[2]

[1] Ethical, Pragmatic, and Intelligent Computing (EPIC) Laboratory,
Santa Clara University, Santa Clara, CA, USA
`{nshaghaghi,zhuang5,hbathala,cazzarello,achen11}@scu.edu`
[2] Santa Clara Law School, Santa Clara University, Santa Clara, CA, USA
`cchien@scu.edu`

Abstract. The United States has the largest prison population in
the world with more than 650,000 ex-offenders released from prison
every year, according to the United States Department of Justice. But
even after time has been served, criminal records persist, limiting their
bearer's ability to qualify for job, rental, loan, volunteering, and other
opportunities available to citizens. It is thus not surprising that the
US Department of Justice also reports that approximately two-thirds
of those released are rearrested within three years of release. In recent
years, many laws have been passed to shield past criminal records from
future background checks. The Second Chance Gap Initiative at the
Santa Clara University's Law School (paperprisons.org) uses empirical
research and analysis to draw attention to the millions of Americans
that remain stuck in "the second chance gap" of being eligible for but
not receiving their second chance in the realms of expungement, reinfranchisement, and resentencing. In the case of criminal records, it finds that
tens of millions of people that have completed their formal sentences are
stuck in a "paper prison,"s held back, not by steel bars but bureaucratic
and related hurdles that prevent them from assessing a cleaned record.
In support of this initiative, the SCU Ethical, Pragmatic, and Intelligent
Computing (EPIC) laboratory has developed a flexible tool for ascertain-
ing expungement eligibility. The project hopes to assist those seeking to
determine if they qualify via a user-friendly web application containing
a rule engine for expungement qualification determination.

Keywords: Criminal records expungement · Digital humanity ·
Justice · Legal technology · Paper prisons · Petitioning · Rule engine ·
Second chance gap

1 Introduction

The United States has the largest prison population in the world [35]. The single
greatest force behind the growth of the US prison population is the 1971 national

© ICST Institute for Computer Sciences, Social Informatics and Telecommunications Engineering 2021
Published by Springer Nature Switzerland AG 2021. All Rights Reserved
N. Shaghaghi et al. (Eds.): INTETAIN 2020, LNICST 377, pp. 165–174, 2021.
https://doi.org/10.1007/978-3-030-76426-5_11

"War on Drugs" [1]. Which as of the year 2020 has resulted in 49% of the prison population to be due to drug offences [19].

According to the United States Department of Justice, more than 650,000 ex-offenders are released from prison every year [34]. But people released from prison can find themselves not only stripped of their ability to provide for themselves and their loved ones, but also with a criminal record that ensures employers, landlords, bankers, and others can disqualify them from receiving any opportunities due to a mistake they made possibly decades ago and have already served their time or paid other penalties for. These rehabilitated members of our society are thus only released from their physical confinements yet still trapped in a "paper prisons" in which their criminal records precede them in job, rental, and loan applications [6]. It is thus not surprising that the US Department of Justice also reports that approximately two-thirds of those released are rearrested within three years of release [34].

"Over the last decade, dozens of states have enacted 'second chance' reforms that increase the eligibility of individuals charged or convicted of crimes to, upon application, shorten their sentences, clean their criminal records, and/or regain the right to vote" [6]. On average, ex-offenders that clear their records experience a 12% net gain in employment by the end of their first year with a clean record [30]. But "while much fanfare has accompanied the increasing availability of 'second chances,' little attention has been paid to their delivery" [6]. Chien 2020 [7] defines the concept of a "Second Chance Gap" as the difference between eligibility and delivery of one's second chance, and measures the "second chance gap" across a number of regimes including resentencing, reinfranchisement, and expungement. After analyzing the laws of the 50-states and applying it to data provided by a background check provider, it estimates that tens of millions of people are eligible under the new laws but have not had their records expunged [7].

Building on Chien 2020 and the Paper Prisons Project (paperprisons.org), this paper reports on the uses of technology to help narrow the second chance gap. The prototype helps individuals with criminal histories in the states of Washington (WA) and New York (NY) to determine their possible eligibility through a series of questions, and points them to the resources that are available for them to utilize, if they wish to pursue expunging their record.

2   Terminology

This section contains legal terminology used throughout this paper, and is largely adapted from [6].

- *Charge:* In a criminal case, the specific statement of what crime the party is accused of committing (charged with) which is contained in the indictment or criminal complaint [21].
- *Conviction:* A legal finding by a court that the defendant is guilty of the crime with which he or she was charged, either through an adjudication, default judgement, or plea.

- *Eligible:* A legal determination that, based on application of the law to the ascertainable record, a record is eligible for expungement, sealing or related remedy.
- *Expungement:* The removal, sealing (defined below), or other state process for rehabilitating one's criminal record.
- *Second Chance Expungement Gap:* The number of people who are eligible for record expungement/sealing but that have not yet taken advantage of the enacted laws.
- *Gap Sizing:* The process of computing/estimating the number of people in the expungement gap.
- *Sealing:* A weaker form of clearing the criminal record history in comparison to expungement where instead of the records being permanently deleted, they are removed from background checks though are still available to those connected with law enforcement. This is the usual practice for the criminal records of under-age offenders which cannot be examined without a special court order [32]. And can sometimes be stipulated as part of a settlement in order to keep the terms of the settlement from public scrutiny [32].

3   Gap Sizing Methodology

Chien 2020 defines a process of "gap sizing" in order to estimate the size - in terms of criminal histories (people), charges, and incidents - of a given second chance gap. That process of gap sizing is summarized below in order to help describe how it is leveraged in building the automated Tool.

Although Chien 2020 focused primarily on developing a national estimate of the number of people eligible for relief from non-convictions, because the consequences of convictions are more severe than non-convictions, a series of related reports have applied the gap sizing approach described above to size the second chance convictions gap in a number of states. At the time of this writing, reports for the 10 states of Connecticut [14], Iowa [9], Minnesota [11], Missouri [12], North Carolina [13], New York [15], Oregon [16], Rhode Island [10], South Carolina [8], and Washington [17] are available. Each report follows a similar approach as is detailed in the methodology page of the paperprisons.org [29].

Each state has its own set of laws dictating what charges are eligible for clearance. The set of laws are first summarized into concise statements by staff lawyers and law students of the Paper Prisons project. Concise statements of the law are then organized into if/then logic rules, translated into Python code, and run on the data to generate an eligibility determination for each charge in the dataset. Lastly, using the known count of the people in the state's criminal history database, the eligibility size is estimated. The details of this work can be found in [6,7], and the Methodology page of the Paper Prisons website [29].

4   Motivation for Automation of Expungement Eligibility Determination

The clearing of criminal records exhibits significant beneficial effects on society. Expungement is shown to "increase wages by 25%" [2]. From a broader perspective, employment penalties for people with a criminal charge can cost the country's GDP up to $87 billion [3]. Similar benefits were apparent through Detroit's *Project Clean Slate*, which conducts a variety of initiatives to increase expungement participation. The project found that for every $1 spent on the project, there was a potential $3.70 return in the form of potential annualized wage gains which translate to local, state, and federal employment tax revenue. Furthermore, the financial returns on expungement programs outpaced job training by 3.8 to 1 [22]. In an ideal world, those who are eligible to have their records expunged should be able to do so, and their record should reflect as such. However, this is not always the case.

In many jurisdictions, the records are *sealed*, rather than wholly expunged, and retained for law enforcement purposes [24]. In this case, the records should not be available to third parties, such as employers, but will still be retained by the government entities involved. Furthermore, the internet presents a significant hindrance to an offender's ability to remove their information from the public eye altogether. In 2009, journalist Paul Silva said, "getting out of Google's grip is harder than clearing the legal record – newspapers cannot be in the business of erasing the past." [4].

One of the key findings from Gap Sizing the 10 states aforementioned is the sheer size of the gap in each state. A significantly large proportion of the people with charges in each state are eligible to have their charges cleared. However, only a small subset of people take any action to have them cleared every year. One possible explanation for this discrepancy is the lack of awareness of this opportunity or their eligibility as they may not have kept track of the passage of new laws or be aware of the eligibility criteria for the state they have a record in. Many of them may also not know that they can consult or do not have access to advocates which can help them determine their eligibility. Given that, most do not have the resources to consult or heir a lawyer for that purpose either. Therefore, an automated tool that helps individuals determine their eligibility for expungement and connects them with resources to do so, is crucial.

5   Related Work

Over the recent years several expungement eligibility web tools have been developed by advocacy groups in several states such as California, Maryland, Montana, and Texas.

California: "Clear My Record" is a free service by Code for America for helping people with a criminal record in certain counties in California which is accessible at clearmyrecord.org [18]. This tool is different from all the other tools delineated below in that it is not an anonymous tool meant to allow users to determine if they are eligible and then connect them with resources. Instead, it starts with a comprehensive form asking the users for their name, phone number, address, email, etc. and then a series of questions regarding their criminal history. The idea seems to be to immediately get the users into their database and thus be able to guide and track their progress throughout the process. This is truly helpful for making sure that individuals do not get lost in the system and have an advocate to help them throughout the process. However, it may pose as a barrier for entry. It may make individuals stop once they see the form asking for all of their personal information as they may just want to test the tool and see if they may be eligible but not necessarily commit to doing anything. This will potentially pose a problem for many individuals who are in the gray area with regard to expungement as they would not feel comfortable providing all of their personal and criminal history information out of the fear that they may just get a non-eligibility result in the end yet create another database record of their unexpungable criminal history in the process.

Maryland: At the time of this writing the authors have been able to find two separate web applications for expungement eligibility determination for the state of Maryland:

1. The Warnock Foundation has produced an expungement eligibility determination web tool accessible at cxpungemaryland.org/b0 that asks yes/no questions one at a time in order to determine whether the user is eligible to expunge a criminal record in Maryland [33].
2. Maryland Legal Apps, LLC has created a web application accessible at MDExpungement.com that takes a completely different approach: The web tool asks users to enter their case number in order to get started and then looks up their charge in a state database and determines its eligibility. This may at first seem as an obstacle since many may not remember their case numbers especially if a long time has passed since their incident; but Maryland's judiciary provides a Public Case Search tool [26] through the state government's website which users are directed to use to retrieve their case numbers for use in the expungement tool should they not remember their case numbers. Furthermore, MDExpungement.com not only determines eligibility but also helps users update any outdated information and then print, sign, and file their application to the courthouse [28]. But that is not all, The web tool goes one step further in allowing bulk expungements [27] meant for use by advocates or lawyers who are trying to help groups of people clear their records at once.

Montana: Judnich law Office in Montana which according to their website specializes in personal injury representation, DUI defense, private criminal defense representation, and family law matters, has produced an expungement eligibility web tool for records in Montana which is available at judnichlaw.com/montana-expungement-eligibility [23]. The tool works by asking yes/no questions one at a time to determine whether the user is eligible for expungement.

Texas: "Texas Law Help" is a free and anonymous web application developed by students of Georgetown University's Law Center, that helps determine if users are eligible for expungement in Texas. The web tool is accessible at Texas-LawHelp.org [20] and works by asking yes/no questions to determine whether the user is eligible for expungement. But the app is built as a no-code system through the Neota Logic platform. Which means that the software is created and configured through a Graphical User Interfaces (GUI) instead of being programmed. Therefore, as all no-code systems, it has less flexibility for undergoing major changes easily but has the advantage that it is maintainable by non-developers.

To the best knowledge of the authors, no national level tool has been developed nor attempted due to the vast complexity of the expungement law/logic which is unique for each state. Hence, the development of a national expungement eligibility tool is a huge undertaking yet grossly overdue.

6   Paper Prison Expungement Tool

There is a necessity to research and create unique logic flows for each eligible state in order to cater to their distinct laws. The flow logic is implemented in Javascript and the UI is purely built by HTML and CSS. The application accepts a JavaScript Object Notation (JSON) file for each state that is manually assembled from the specific state laws and is used to extract the question flow for that state. The JSON file is built as a decision tree in memory where each tree node contains a question and each response to the question is modeled on an edge that leads to the next node (and hence next question) until an eligible or not eligible leaf node is reached.

For ease of development, the Expungement application is hosted on the Heroku platform which is a platform-as-a-service (PaaS) that enables seamless cloud based build and deployment. Currently, the tool is only functional for New York and Washington State, but eventually the web application will be expanded to all 50 States. The system allows for an easy translation of law based decision trees to a web application which follows the answers given to questions in order to find whether the person is eligible for expungment of changes. There are multiple challenges associated with carrying out this work. First, each state has different laws regarding records relief and these laws are frequently changing.

7   Methodology

The PaperPrisons expungement tool asks a sequence of questions that determine whether individuals are eligible or ineligible to have their former criminal records expunged. This is done through a web based application, where the questions take a yes/no or "select all that apply" format. The user is presented with answers that they can select. Based on the answer they selected they are presented with a new question according to the tree diagram. This approach is chosen because it offers the greatest ease of use. Users will often not know what specific charge they were given, or the technical law terms that are used to determine eligibility. However, they will have enough of an idea to accurately answer yes/no questions regarding their charges. When there is sufficient information on the user's eligibility it will stop loading questions and let the user know if they are eligible or not. To minimize the number of redundant questions that need to be answered by the user, the questions follow a decision tree optimized for each state based on their laws. Therefore, through the pruning of the decision tree during the traversal through it, users skip questions that do not pertain to their situation. For example, if a person has committed first-degree murder in the state of New York, they do not have to provide additional details as that crime makes them ineligible to apply for expungement or sealing of anything in their record.

8   Implications and Impact

The punitive effects of a criminal record on a person's ability to obtain and hold a job are both long lasting and large in scale. Not only does a criminal record hinder the well being of an ex-convict, it also hinders the well being of their dependents [25].

On a macroeconomic scale, the prohibitive effects of a criminal record lowers the overall employment rate by 0.8%, according to the Center for Economic and Policy Research [31]. This effects up to 1.7 million workers across the country. If this tool allows even a fraction of workers to regain their ability to work, this will have positive effects on local economies. Of course, just because a crime is expunged in the eyes of the law, it doesn't mean that crime is free from the grasps of the press and the internet. When an article is published by the press regarding a crime, it is subject to first amendment rights, and a judge cannot easily force the publisher to remove the article [5]. That means that after an expungement is ordered, a crime might be removed from a state's database, but it is rarely truly gone. However, for the purpose of helping a rehabilitated individual to regain their ability to obtain a job, a loan, or an apartment, a crime doesn't necessarily have to be removed from all records for there to be significant positive change. Especially since the state databases are the most important sources for background checks.

9   Work in Progress

9.1   Addition of More States

In addition to Washington [17] and New York [15], as of the time of this writing, the Paper Prisons Project has prepared reports and summaries of the law ("concise statements") for Connecticut [14], Iowa [9], Minnesota [11], Missouri [12], North Carolina [13], Oregon [16], Rhode Island [10], and South Carolina [8], making them good candidates for addition to the expungement tool. The logic flows for these states are currently under development and once completed will be translated into code for the addition to the expungement tool.

9.2   Automated Expungement Paperwork Preparation

An important feature under development is providing users the option to automatically fill expungement forms for their state or county courts. If the user is willing to temporarily provide more information, the tool can help complete the entire application for them without storing their personal data in the system. Even though, it will be ensured that such generated forms will be as accurate as possible, a disclaimer will warn users that they must review the provided document and should seek help from a legal advocate before submitting it to the court. This feature would save time for people who are planning to file an expungement application as well as the advocates helping clients prepare such applications.

9.3   Chatbot Functionality

A chat bot functionality is envisioned to accompany the expungement tool in order to provide a more accessible experience for users. If a person is unsure of their specific charge, the chat bot can ask further questions to help determine that for them. This functionality will also provide a more efficient and dynamic means of evaluating eligibility for users.

Acknowledgements. Many thanks are due to Santa Clara University Law School Professor Colleen Chien - who originated the concept of the Second Chance Gap and founded the Paper Prisons initiative. To the many law students working in the initiative including Evan Hastings, Charlie Duggan, and Katie Rabago whose work on creating concise statements of the law and logic flows provided the basis for the expungement tool. To undergraduate student Alexandra George for her tireless research and data acquisition work for the Paper Prisons project. And lastly to the Frugal Innovation Hub as well as the departments of Mathematics & Computer Science, Computer Science & Engineering, and Information Systems & Analytics for their continued support of the criminal history expungement tool's development at the Ethical, Pragmatic, and Intelligent Computing (EPIC) Laboratory by faculty and students from all three departments.

References

1. Nation behind bars: A human rights solution (2014). https://www.hrw.org
2. Bala, N., Roehl, K.: The case for clean slate in North Carolina (2020). https://www.rstreet.org/wp-content/uploads/2020/03/Short-No.-85-NC-Clean-Slate.pdf
3. Bucknor, C., Barber, A., et al.: The price we pay: economic costs of barriers to employment for former prisoners and people convicted of felonies. Technical report, Center for Economic and Policy Research (CEPR) (2016)
4. Calvert, C., Bruno, J.: When cleansing criminal history clashes with the first amendment and online journalism. J. Commun. Law Policy **19**(1), 123–148 (2010). https://heinonline.org/HOL/P?h=hein.journals/cconsp19&i=133
5. Calvert, C., Bruno, J.: When cleansing criminal history clashes with the first amendment and online journalism: are expungement statutes irrelevant in the digital age? (2010). https://scholarship.law.edu/commlaw/vol19/iss1/5

6. Chien, C.V.: The second chance gap. Michigan Law Rev. (2019). https://papers. ssrn.com/sol3/Papers.cfm?abstract_id=3265335
7. Chien, C.V.: America's paper prisons: the second chance gap. Michigan Law Rev. **119**(3), 519–612 (2020). https://repository.law.umich.edu/cgi/viewcontent. cgi?article=7068&context=mlr
8. Chien, C.V., Duggan, C., Huang, Z., George, A., Shaghaghi, N.: The South Carolina second chance expungement gap (2020). https://paperprisons.org/states/SC. html
9. Chien, C.V., Duggan, C., Pingale, P., Shaghaghi, N.: The Iowa second chance expungement gap (2020). https://paperprisons.org/states/IA.html
10. Chien, C.V., Duggan, C., Pingale, P., Shaghaghi, N.: The Rhode Island second chance expungement gap (2020). https://paperprisons.org/states/RI.html
11. Chien, C.V., Hastings, E., Bathala, H., Shaghaghi, N.: The Minnesota second chance expungement gap (2020). https://paperprisons.org/states/MN.html
12. Chien, C.V., Hastings, E., Bathala, H., Shaghaghi, N.: The Missouri second chance expungement gap (2020). https://paperprisons.org/states/MO.html
13. Chien, C.V., Hastings, E., Huang, Z., Wu, J., Shaghaghi, N.: The North Carolina second chance expunction gap (2020). https://paperprisons.org/states/NC.html
14. Chien, C.V., Kreitzberg, E., Duggan, C., Pingale, P., Shaghaghi, N.: The Connecticut second chance pardon gap (2020). https://paperprisons.org/states/CT. html
15. Chien, C.V., Shaghaghi, N., Hastings, E., Bathala, H.: The New York second chance sealing gap (2020). https://paperprisons.org/states/NY.html
16. Chien, C.V., Shaghaghi, N., Hastings, E., Huang, Z., Bathala, H.: The Oregon second chance expungement gap (2020). https://paperprisons.org/states/OR.html
17. Chien, C.V., Zuyan, H., Kuykendall, J., Rabago, K.: The Washington v. state second chance expungement gap (2020). https://paperprisons.org/states/WA.html
18. Code for America: Apply to clear my record. https://www.clearmyrecord.org
19. Federal Bureau of Prisons: Offenses - statistics (2020). https://www.bop.gov/ about/statistics/statistics_inmate_offenses.jsp
20. Georgetown University Law Center: Texas fresh start guide. https://georgetown. neotalogic.com/a/FS-Example-temporarylink
21. Hill, G.: West's encyclopedia of American law (2008). https://legal-dictionary. thefreedictionary.com/charge
22. Johnston, A.J.: Project clean slate report - Detroit (2019). https://detroitmi.gov/ departments/law-department/project-clean-slate
23. Judnich Law Office: Check your Montana expungement eligibility. https://www. judnichlaw.com/montana-expungement-eligibility
24. Koerner, G., Kettani, H.: Privacy concerns on expungement laws in the digital world. In: Proceedings of the 2019 International Conference on Information System and System Management, ISSM 2019, pp. 11–16. Association for Computing Machinery, New York (2019). https://doi.org/10.1145/3394788.3394791
25. Lee, M.: Do criminal background checks in hiring punish? (2017). https:// openscholarship.wustl.edu/cgi/viewcontent.cgi?article=1162&context=law_jurisprudence
26. Maryland Judiciary: Maryland judiciary case search. http://casesearch.courts. state.md.us/casesearch
27. Maryland Legal Apps, LLC: Bulk Expungements (2016). https://www. mdexpungement.com/bulk.php
28. Maryland Legal Apps, LLC: Maryland expungement determination and form completion (2016). https://www.mdexpungement.com

29. Paper Prisons Project: Second chance gap sizing methodology (2020). https:// paperprisons.org/methodology.html
30. Prescott, J., Starr, S.B.: Expungement of criminal convictions: an empirical study. Harvard Law Rev. **19**(8), 2460–555 (2020)
31. Schmitt, J., Warner, K.: Ex-offenders and the labor market (2010). https://cepr. net/documents/publications/ex-offenders-2010-11.pdf
32. The People's Law Dictionary: Sealing of Records (2005). https://legal-dictionary. thefreedictionary.com/sealing+of+records
33. The   Warnock   Foundation: Expungemaryland.org   [beta].   http://www. expungemaryland.org/b0
34. United States Department of Justice: Prisoners and prisoner re-entry. https:// www.justice.gov/archive/fbci/progmenu_reentry.html
35. World Prison Brief: Highest to lowest - prison population total. https:// www.prisonstudies.org/highest-to-lowest/prison-population-total?field_region_ taxonomy_tid=All

Machine Learning, Education and Training

Is Learning by Teaching an Effective Approach in Mixed-Reality Robotic Training Systems?

Filippo Gabriele Pratticò$^{(\boxtimes)}$ ⓘ, Francisco Navarro Merino,
and Fabrizio Lamberti ⓘ

Dipartimento di Automatica e Informatica, Politecnico di Torino, Turin, Italy
{filippogabriele.prattico,fabrizio.lamberti}@polito.it,
s263600@studenti.polito.it

Abstract. In recent years, there has been an increasing interest in the
extended reality training systems (XRTSs), including an expanding integration of such systems in actual training programs of industry and educational institutions. Despite pedagogists had developed multiple didactic models with the aim of ameliorating the effectiveness of knowledge
transfer, the vast majority of XRTSs are sticking to the practice of adapting the traditional model approach. Besides, other approaches are started
to be considered, like the Learning by Teaching (LBT), but for other
kinds of intelligent training systems like those involving service robots.
In the presented work, a mixed-reality robotic training system (MRRTS)
devised with the capability of supporting the LBT is presented. A study
involving electronic engineering students with the aim of evaluating the
effectiveness of the LBT pedagogical model when applied to a MRRTS
by comparing it with a consolidated approach is performed. Results indicated that while both approaches granted a good knowledge transfer, the
LBT was far superior in terms of long-term retention of the information
at the cost of a higher time spent in training.

Keywords: Mixed-reality robotic training system · Learning by
teaching · Human-Robot Interaction · Robotic teachable agent

1 Introduction and Background

The advancements experienced by the eXtended Reality (XR) related technologies over the last decade is unprecedented for this family of media. The availability of cost-effective hardware solutions is promoting its diffusion at the consumer-
level. Thus both industry and academy are dedicating significant effort to help
XR mediums attain maturity in a variety of contexts and in fields as diverse as
engineering, arts, design, architecture, medicine, education, and many more [5].

This work has been partially supported by the VR@POLITO initiative.

N. Shaghaghi et al. (Eds.): INTETAIN 2020, LNICST 377, pp. 177–190, 2021.
https://doi.org/10.1007/978-3-030-76426-5_12

Since the first days, for both Virtual Reality (VR) and Mixed Reality (MR), one application field suddenly attracting a great amount of interest was training. This is even more true nowadays were XRTSs are moving from the laboratories to the industries, being more and more frequently integrated into the companies training programs [8], especially for the practical and manual task that could benefit from a learning-by-doing setting. Despite the growing body of literature in the field, and the potential of the medium, the vast majority of studies and applications stick to the traditional learning (TL) approach. In traditional learning, a lecturer teaches something to one or more students, possibly using also additional materials such as books, blackboards, or slides. In a common XRTS, the teacher is replaced by the piece of software (not necessarily by a teacher avatar) that guides the trainee in the experience, for instance by providing step-by-step instructions [16]. Even tough the intrinsic engaging nature of VR and MR already boost the training effectiveness through embodiment, there is so much more that can be done. Since the 50', pedagogists have endowed significant effort in developing didactical models to help students climb the learning pyramids [15] effectively. On the opposite side of traditional learning w.r.t the didactic model spectrum, there is the so-called learning by teaching. It grounds on the naïve practice of peer-tutoring, in which students tutor other students by teaching each other self-learned domain knowledge from traditional (or not) sources. In spite of the fact that in normal conditions (humans teaches humans) LBT has proven to be much more effective compared to TL [6,14], especially for long-term retention of the acquired knowledge, it also suffers from some drawbacks. Besides of being more inefficient (time-consuming) w.r.t TL, the training effectiveness depends on the role taken by the student in a given moment (teacher or tutee) and the two roles are dependable of different kinds of feedbacks and stimuli [10,18]. The need to replace the tutee peer has led to the rise of the so-called teachable agents (TA). These are (computer) agents that learners can teach about a subject domain, and while doing so, gain a deeper understanding of the subject matter [3]. In other words, the ultimate goal is not to actually program the agent, but exploiting it to stimulate the mental process involved in the LBT approach, letting the learner gain a better understating of the topic through the process of teaching to someone else. Considering that empathy and other several social factors [6] are crucial in the LBT, one of the most promising implementations of teachable agents takes advantage of service robots [20]. Robotic Teachable Agents (RTA) have been investigated by several studies and proved to be equally or even more effective than the TL (still employing robots) [17], and capable of activating the required mental processes needed for an effective LBT experience [17]. Nevertheless, an intelligent training system (ITS) using just a robotic teachable agent is usually limited in terms of modality, being voice explanation from the learner the main (and often only) form of Human-Robot Interaction (HRI) involved in the experience [9]. To extend the potential of the RTA-based learning by teaching intelligent training systems, some researchers begun to use an MR environment together with the RTA. To now, there is a handful of studies on the topic. In a first study [11] a

Fig. 1. Anki Cozmo

mobile robot along with a spatial MR setup was employed to teach a geometry related topic. In the study was found that learners reacted differently based on the social attribution feedback (positive or negative connotation, and different subject) from the robot, suggesting that the MR environment doesn't affected significantly the social interaction. However, no direct comparison with a TL version was investigated. In a second study [19] employing the same MR robotic training platform, was studied if the physical RTA constitutes a real advantage in terms of learning effectiveness compared to a digital replica of it (just MR) and to a desktop-like application (no MR, no robot). This reflects a key challenge in designing MR robotic experiences, in which the augmented content could take over at the point that having a physical robot may be useless [13]. No significant differences were reported among the three versions of the experience from the learning gains point-of-view, thus indicating the announced problem could have affected the MR intelligent training system.

With the aim of better clarifying if the MR addition could be detrimental to the robot's features that enable the LBT approach, and by seizing the call to action from the research community [2,20], in this paper is presented a preliminary study to evaluate the training effectiveness of a MRRTS implementing the learning by teaching paradigm compared to a traditional learning version.

2   Materials and Methods

The MRRTS was implemented by adopting a table-top projected spatial MR setup together with a commercial off-the-shelf programmable toy robot.

2.1   Technologies

More specifically the *Anki Cosmo*[1] robot was selected among others, due to its popularity and because it has several anthropomorphic features that strengths

---

[1] Anki Cozmo: https://anki.com/en-us/cozmo.html.

its emotional connotation and supporting social behaviours (Fig. 1). The manufacturer provides an official SDK[2] for programming it in Python. Cozmo is a non-holonomic robot with a minimum size of $6 \times 7 \times 11$ cm and includes two moving parts (in addition to wheels). A first moving part, which can be considered as the "head" of Cozmo, has one rotational degree of freedom (DOF), and can rotate by 20° downward and 45° upward. The head of Cozmo is completed by a "face" implemented through a 2×2 cm LED matrix display, which shows a simplified anthropomorphic facial expression using eye-like animations (which can be selected from a pre-defined list using the SDK). Beneath the display, there is a 60° wide field of view 640×480 pixels RGB camera (although the image accessible through the SDK is limited to a 320×240 grayscale image). A feature of the SDK allow to use this camera to let Cozmo automatically follow the user face (by orienting the robot and the "head" of the robot) simulating a look-at behavior. The second moving part is a front lifter (one positional DOF, likewise controllable through the SDK), which is primarily designed to interact with the bundled tangible objects (interactive cubes not used in this project) but beside of that can also be used in custom ways if programmed, for instance to simulate a robot interaction with the projected environment [13] (tap-like animation). Cozmo is also equipped with WiFi capabilities and a built-in speaker that could benefit from the Text-To-Speech (TTS) functionality included in the SDK. The SDK is designed using an event-driven approach and is rich in features (for the sake of brevity, in this review only the subset of features that were actually used for the implementation were mentioned).

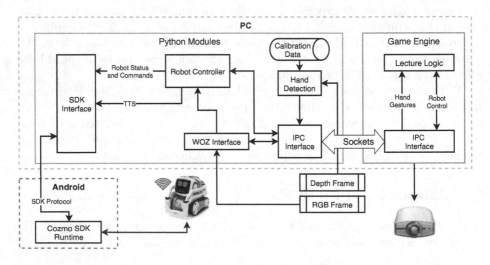

Fig. 2. Architecture of the MRRTS.

---

[2] Cozmo's SDK: http://cozmosdk.anki.com/docs/index.html.

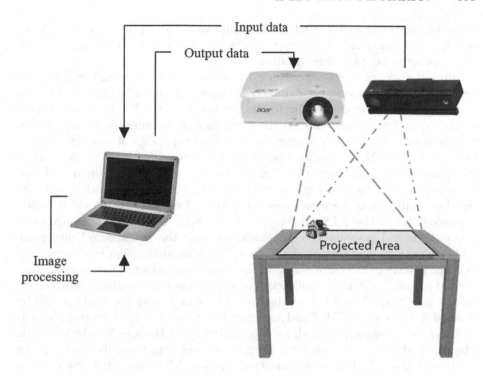

Fig. 3. Setup of the MRRTS.

The whole high-level architecture of the MRRTS system exploited in this work is illustrated in Fig. 2, and includes: Cozmo, a RGB-D camera, a projector, an Android smartphone and a PC. As said, the MR selected for the system is a spatial MR setup, and the augmented digital contents are table-top projected. Since this setup, depicted in Fig. 3, was selected as one of the most used one in the literature [13], and is exploited also by already referred previous works on the topic of LBT with RTA [11,19], just a brief description of our implementation is given in the following. The projector was mounted near the ceiling in order to project the image on the table from the top. To improve the quality of the projected image, the table was covered using a black cardboard of size 85×65 cm, which is also the size of the projected surface. Because of the fact that was decided to provide the user with the ability to interact with the MR environment using natural gestures [13], in the immediate nearby of the projector it was mounted a Microsoft Kinect v2. For this specific setup, both the 1920×1080 pixels, 30 fps RGB camera and the depth sensing 512×424 pixels camera were used. The first is used by the Wizard-of-Oz (WOZ) interface that will described in Sect. 2.2, while the second for hand gesture recognition to enable a touch-based interaction with the projected surface. The depth image is processed using well-known computer vision techniques (background subtraction, depth level thresholding, opening, contour detection). The module is implemented using the OpenCV (v3.2) library and can detect the position of the hand as well as its configuration (i.e. open or closed), and is able to distinguish three touch gestures, i.e. tap, slide and drag.

Since the accuracy of Cozmo's built-in estimated odometry isn't sufficient for the devised application scenario, mostly because suffering of drift related issues, a depth image processing similar to the one used for the hand-gestures is performed to endow the system with the capability of tracking the robot position in a *outside-in* fashion. On average, the tracking capability of this algorithm is $\overline{Err} = 0.81 \pm 0.62$ cm. A calibration phase (performed before the game starts) was required to synchronize the Cozmo's internal coordinate system with the coordinate system used by the external tracking and by the projection, computing the required transformation matrices. Voice feedback was provided (when requested) using the TTS capabilities of the SDK in English language. The lecture logic and graphics were implemented using the well-known Unity game engine (v2018.3), and were deployed to a Windows application running on the PC. The gesture detection module and the robot control logic were instead implemented in another Python application, accessing the functionalities provided by the Cozmo's SDK. The WOZ interface was developed using a webpage served by Flask and written in HTML5 and Javscript language. The inter-process communication (IPC) among the modules was implemented through ZeroMQ sockets. The Android phone is required for the SDK to work since run its runtime. The smartphone, which has to be connected to the PC running the applications through USB cable, communicates with Cozmo by using a WiFi network hosted by the robot itself.

2.2   Experience Design and Implemented Variants

As said, the aim of this work is to compare the learning effectiveness of TL and LBT didactic models in a MRRTS. To this aim, a new training experience named *MireLab* was designed and implemented in two variants.

Topic. The chosen training topic for MireLab is the *Thèvenin Theorem*, from the electronic engineering domain. Due to the fact that the selected target audience was undergraduate students from electronic engineering, it was necessary to select a topic not too basic in order to keep the engagement of the participants, but also not excessively complicated such that the learners have the right level of previous knowledge on the domain thus not being overwhelmed. In particular, are given for granted as background knowledge at least the ohm's laws and the Kirchhoff's Circuit Laws. *MireLab* was designed by getting inspiration from a possible lecture that could take place in an electronic laboratory thus additional lecture material, in that case, would have been slides, paper sheet for notes/calculation, and of course a test bench with components to assemble a circuit and testing the acquiring knowledge.

Common Foundation. In order to minimize the differences, both variants exploit a common foundation about the projected environment (interface) and robot features exploited. MireLab was designed taking into account state-of-the-art guidelines for MR-based robotic experiences [13]. The main interface (Fig. 4a) is made of 3 areas. The first (top-left), occupying the main space of the screen, is constituted by a whiteboard space where the circuits are created and other information can be introduced (equation, pictures, etc.). On the right, there is a *components area*, where both the robot and the user can select the desired components for the circuit. The selection is performed using a coherent gesture: a finger-tap for the user and a tap-animation (using the lever) for the robot. When a component is selected, it appears on a buffer space (bottom-right) where it can be valorized, using the dropdown list which shows coherent values. A few additional option are available in the bottom-left button panel, such as the possibility to erase the whiteboard or orienting the component in the buffer. The component can be then placed in the whiteboard space by a drag-and-drop gesture (as before coherently for both the user and the robot). Finally, when all desired elements are on the panel, they can be connected (wiring) by clicking the cable button and later selecting the adequate terminals of the components. There is also a pop-up input tool that can be used as calculator or as an input tool in the LBT variant. As already announced the robot can move all-over the projected environment and interaction are meant to emulate the counterpart performed by the user. Also, the robot is constantly fed with micro-choreography inputs thus fostering the sense of a living being. The robot can communicate to the user using the TTS features, or by showing elements on the shared projection.

Traditional Learning. In this variant, the user assumes the role of the tutee while the robot acts as the teacher. Well established practices are implemented in that case. The robot is controlled by the software based on an FSM logic. The delegation pattern I-do, We-check, You-practice, is adopted from the robot as teaching style, managing the lecture pace through milestone advancement and feedbacks to the tutee. Hence, Cozmo explains the concept, shows and solve example while speaking to carefully make it clear for the tutee. Moreover, it also asks the tutee for collaboration at some points like choosing the values of the components or removing certain elements suggested by the robot. These little interactions are introduced in order to keep the tutee's attention high during the explanation resulting in a more engaging experience and active learning.

Learning by Teaching. As said, in LBT the learner (user) acts as a teacher lecturing the RTA. To design this variant, we kept in mind that, according to the literature, there are 4 key steps that the learner must undergo and were proved to be effective to maximize learning gains [7]:

1. Preparing to teach (expectation to teach)
2. Explaining to others/RTA (teaching)
3. Interacting with others/RTA (Q&A, feedback to RTA)
4. Observing the RTA spending the acquired knowledge (recursive feedback)[12]

In MireLab, for the first step, a one-sheet long paper is provided to the learner [11,19] that has to study it on its own and prepare the lecture. The cheat sheet, available for download[3], contains a synthetic explanation of the topic that matches the contents that are provided by the robot in the TL variant. Its structure has been designed to suggest the learner a specific order to use later when teaching, however some points bring a certain level of freedom so the learner can lead the lecture in their own way. All the equations, circuits, and images contained are referred with a numerical code. This code can be used by the learner to rapidly add to the whiteboard these snippet elements during the lecture, using the input tool feature.

Afterwhile, the learner uses the MireLab interface to take the lecture and while doing so interacting with the RTA (steps 2 and 3). Hereby, the learner uses the whiteboard to clearly explain the topic and interacts with the robot through the voice and the MR environment. On the other hand, the robot will follow the lesson asking questions and performing the tasks that the learner command in order to increase its inclusion grade on the experience and not being unnoticed [13].

Finally, a prerecorded video of the robot, solving an exercise on the lecture topic while interacting on its own with the MireLab interface, is shown to the learner (step 4). It was decided to use the same prerecorded video for all the participants of the study to minimize bias.

In this LBT variant the robot is no more acting autonomously but its behavior is controlled using a WOZ approach. This was decided because of the complex interaction that the RTA is asked for, considering the fact that none to little AI are already available for that specific purpose, and building such an AI is out of the scope of the presented study.

Wizard of Oz: As can be seen in Fig. 4b, the WOZ interface implementation provide the wizard with the ability to perform exactly the same actions the robot was capable of when relying on the AI (in the TL) and, therefore, act in a comparable manner. Moreover, the control of the robot is not entirely manual, but some assisted features are provided to the wizard to both facilitate it and minimize the interaction discrepancies w.r.t. the TL robot behavior. By remotely observing the MR environment, through the Kinect RGB camera feed, the wizard can teleoperate the robot with keyboard and mouse input, directly controlling it or by clicking at a point of the camera feed (in that case, the robot will automatically reach the point by the shortest path). Particular efforts were devoted to standardizing some possible frequent questions and answers that the RTA could be in the situation to speak to the learner. The list is included in the interface and once selected the item, its text can be edited, or multiple items combined together, before sending the final phrase to the robot's TTS engine. Furthermore, several predefined animations encoding different emotions and reactions

---

[3] Input tool manual and Thèvenin's theorem cheat-sheet http://tiny.cc/s8utsz.

can be triggered by the wizard. Finally, there has been included some buttons to trigger specific events to the application. This capability is essential to simulate the feeling that the robot is actually interacting with the MR environment. For example, if the robot is asked to remove a component from a circuit it will have to touch it performing the required gesture (double-tap) and then the wizard trigger this event to let the system act accordingly (remove or short circuit such component).

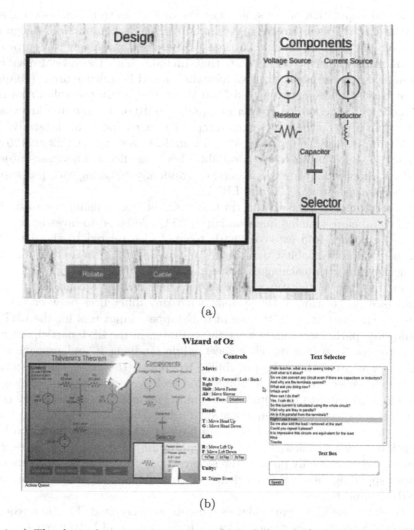

Fig. 4. a) The devised projected interface of MireLab and b) the WOZ interface as seen from the Wizard point of view

3   Experimental Results

This section presents an discusses the results of a preliminary user study that was carried out by using the devised system to compare the training effectiveness of the TL and LBT approach in a MRRTS scenario.

3.1   Experiment Design

The selected population of the study was the one of electronic engineering students that met the requirements of having sufficient background knowledge but scant about the topic (Thévenin Theorem). Therefore, volunteers were provided with a multiple-choice screening test, that includes both theoretical questions and practical exercise about the two aforementioned knowledge areas (10 questions on background knowledge and 5 on the topic). Only the volunteers that scored coherently, i.e. scored greater or equal to $6/10$ on background knowledge and less than $6/10$ on the topic, were accepted as participants of the study. The so-made sample included 6 participants (all males) aged between 22 and 25 y.o. ($\mu = 23.83, \sigma = 1.07$). Due to the (desirable) learning effects, a between-subjects design was adopted for the experiments, by randomly assigning each participant to two equal-sized groups (TL and LBT).

Prior of being exposed to the training, all the participants were asked to respond to a before-training questionnaire (BTQ) designed to investigate: their previous knowledge and expertise with technologies related to those used in MireLab; their study habits; their behavior while learning in a class; and how familiar they are with teaching other people.

After that, the participant received a tutorial given by a confederate about the interface and feature of the system, with tiny differences between the two groups (mostly pertaining to the use of the snippets input tool for the LBT).

Following, participants underwent the training. In the LBT participant were allowed to take notes on the cheatsheet while studying it and preparing the lecture. It was given them the possibility to consult the notes while lecturing the robot, however, they were recommended to leave it on the table (aside the projected area) hand to have just a few quick look at it, otherwise, they could have used the sheet as a communication barrier (by holding it in one hand) between them and the robot, which could have been a negative impact on HRI. In addition, they were allowed to check the notes for a maximum of 5 times, thus preventing to superficially prepare the lecture/study. Finally, the video showing the robot spending the taught knowledge was viewed in another room away from the MRRTS and the robot.

Instead, for the TL no particular expedients were adopted. The time required to complete each step was recorded for each participant of both groups.

After the training was administered a post-experience questionnaire (PEQ), containing: all the items of the *System Usability Scale* tool [4]; the godspeed questionnaire [1], to analyze the learner perception of the robot, complemented by custom additional statement pertaining the specificities of the experiment; and few self-efficacy items to investigate the perceived learning gains. Objective learning gains were evaluated later by administering a post-training test (PTT), which is an extended version of the screening test (13 questions, including the 5 of the screening test). After that, was administered a final questionnaire (FQ) to investigate the perceived quality of the training and the satisfaction with it.

Since one of the key advantages acknowledged by the literature to the LBT w.r.t. TL is the enhanced long-term retention of the acquired information, a retention test (RT) was considered in the study. Participants were asked to answer the same quiz of the PTT after one week, during this time they were not exposed to any information related to the topic. All the devised tests and questionnaires are available for download[4].

3.2   Results and Discussion

Collected data were analyzed using MS Excel with the Real-Statistics add-on (v7.1). Comparative analyses were performed on the two groups using the two-tailed Mann-Whitney U-test and, considering the limited sample size, the significance threshold was set as $p \leq 0.10$. Regarding the BTQ, no significant differences were found between the two groups for the analyzed aspect. More in-depth, on average participants were used to play videogames occasionally and were very accustomed to touch screen interfaces. On the contrary, they were little to none familiar with neither service nor toy robots. Also, 5 participants reported teaching other people at least once a month while 1 never or rarely (belonging to the LBT group).

About the PEQ, no significant difference was spotted about the 5 dimensions of the godspeed questionnaire (anthropomorphism $p = 0.70$, animacy $p = 1.00$, likeability $p = 1.00$, perceived intelligence $p = 0.70$, perceived safety $p = 0.40$), suggesting that the robot behavior was perceived similarly in both groups. This fact also seems to support the statement that the implementation adopted for the WOZ in the LBT didn't biased the comparison. Regarding overall usability, according to SUS results both variants were rated as barely acceptable TL ($M = 68.3$, $SD = 14.6$), LBT ($M = 61.7$, $SD = 7.2$), however, no significant difference was reported ($p = 0.70$). According to the open-feedback collected, these relatively low scores were mainly due to the sluggish feeling of the touch surface compared to what they were accustomed to (tablet and smartphone devices).

About the self-efficacy, it was significantly higher in the LBT ($M = 4.0$, $SD = 0.00$) w.r.t. TL ($M = 3.11$, $SD = 0.38$), as well as the participant confidence about "*successfully pass a test on a thévenin's theorem without further training*", LBT ($M = 4.0$, $SD = 0.00$) vs. TL ($M = 2.33$, $SD = 0.58$). Whereas, no significant differences were reported for the FQ items, suggesting comparable satisfaction levels and perceived quality of the training.

Objective Learning Gains: Fig. 5 illustrates the objective results about learning gains (score normalized at 10). All participants were able to successfully pass the test after been trained by the MRRTS, independently of the group. In particular,

---

[4] Questionnaires and Tests: http://tiny.cc/p9utsz.

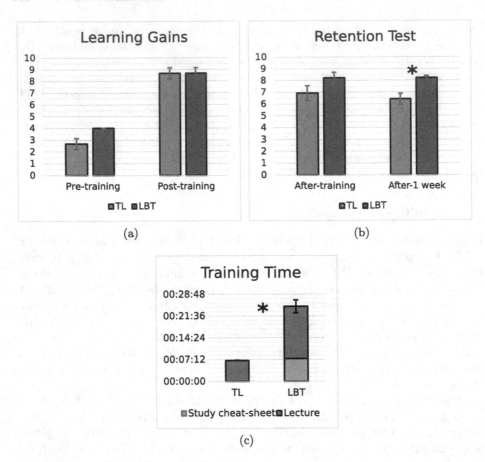

Fig. 5. Objective results of the study. All scores are normalized to 10 and significant comparisons (p-values ≤ 0.1) are marked with *

by comparing common items of the screening test and PTT (Fig. 5a) were found significant and marked learning gains (pre-post training scores) for both groups, meaning that both variants were effective. Also, even if the score of the full PTT is higher for the LBT, the difference w.r.t TL was not significant (Fig. 5b). This fact seems to encourage that the intrinsically interactive nature of MRTTS, and a good implementation of the best practice are able to minimize the differences between the two approaches w.r.t what happen with other mediums. However, this result is probably influenced by the limited sample size. Nevertheless, a significant difference is observable in the retention test (PTT scores, immediately after training and after one week from the exposure). In that case (Fig. 5b), the loss of information was lower in the LBT group, also, all participants from LBT group were able to successfully pass the test after the retention period with a minimum score of 7.7, whereas for the TL this was the maximum score obtained and one of the participants did not reach a sufficient mark (5.4). This confirms that LBT is a superior approach in terms of granting long-term retention. Being this results in agreement with previous studies on LBT, this suggests also that the MRRTS was able to stimulate the required mental process, and that the addition of MR was not too detrimental in that way. The Scheirer–Ray–Hare Test applied to the retention test results highlighted that this difference can be attributable mainly to the training approach. In fact, not significant interaction effects were reported between the approach and the exposure time ($p = 0.80$), and is improbable that this difference is only affected by the exposure time ($p = 0.46$), instead a striking significance was found for the training kind ($p = 0.003$). Lastly, considering the efficiency of the training, our results are similar to those obtained in previous works (Fig. 5c), being the LBT significantly more time consuming (almost 4 times) than TL. This is for sure due to the time invested in studying the cheat-sheet, but also largely ascribable to the higher time spent interacting with the robot (teaching).

4   Conclusions and Future Work

In this paper was presented a study with the goal of evaluating the effectiveness of the LBT pedagogical model when applied to a MRRTS by comparing it with a consolidated model (TL). The select topic of the training was the Thévenin Theorem from the electronic domain and the population of the study was one of the electronic engineering students.

Obtained results outlined that both approaches were able to provide sufficient knowledge transfer to the learner. In spite of the limited sample size of the presented preliminary study, it was observed that, at the cost of a higher time consumed in the process, students that underwent the LBT training were able to retain the acquired information better than those trained with TL. This poses LBT as a promising model also in MRRTS scenarios that worth the attention of the community. That considered, future works should focus on validating the preliminary findings with a larger sample size by encompassing also different target populations (K-12, High School, etc.), on developing tools and AI to autonomously control the RTA with believable and emphatic behavior, and by investing in the direction of natural HRI which is key to improve the efficiency and the effectiveness of this particular kind of MRRTS.

References

1. Bartneck, C., Kulić, D., Croft, E., Zoghbi, S.: Measurement instruments for the anthropomorphism, animacy, likeability, perceived intelligence, and perceived safety of robots. Int. J. Soc. Robotics 1(1), 71–81 (2009). https://doi.org/10.1007/s12369-008-0001-3
2. Baylor, A.L.: Three research directions for affective learning technologies. International Society of the Learning Sciences, Inc. [ISLS] (2018)
3. Biswas, G., Leelawong, K., Schwartz, D., Vye, N., The Teachable Agents Group at Vanderbilt: Learning by teaching: a new agent paradigm for educational software. Appl. Artif. Intell. 19(3–4), 363–392 (2005)

4. Brooke, J., et al.: SUS-a quick and dirty usability scale. Usability Eval. Ind. **189**(194), 4–7 (1996)
5. Chuah, S.H.W.: Why and who will adopt extended reality technology? Literature review, synthesis, and future research agenda. Literature Review, Synthesis, and Future Research Agenda, 13 December 2018 (2018)
6. Duran, D.: Learning-by-teaching. Evidence and implications as a pedagogical mechanism. Innov. Educ. Teach. Inter. **54**(5), 476–484 (2017)
7. Fiorella, L., Mayer, R.E.: Role of expectations and explanations in learning by teaching. Contemp. Educ. Psychol. **39**(2), 75–85 (2014)
8. Hurkmans, B., Rajagopal, K.: The use of extended reality technologies for learning in industry. In: EdMedia+ Innovate Learning, pp. 900–903. Association for the Advancement of Computing in Education (AACE) (2020)
9. Lamberti, F., Prattic\`o, F.G., Calandra, D., Piumatti, G., Bazzano, F., Villani, T.R.: Robotic gaming and user interaction: impact of autonomous behaviors and emotional features. In: 2018 IEEE Games, Entertainment, Media Conference (GEM), pp. 1–9. IEEE (2018)
10. Moreno, R.: Decreasing cognitive load for novice students: effects of explanatory versus corrective feedback in discovery-based multimedia. Instr. Sci. **32**(1–2), 99–113 (2004). https://doi.org/10.1023/B:TRUC.0000021811.66966.1d
11. Muldner, K., Girotto, V., Lozano, C., Burleson, W., Walker, E.A.: The impact of a social robot's attributions for success and failure in a teachable agent framework. International Society of the Learning Sciences, Boulder, CO (2014)
12. Okita, S.Y., Schwartz, D.L.: Learning by teaching human pupils and teachable agents: the importance of recursive feedback. J. Learn. Sci. **22**(3), 375–412 (2013)
13. Prattic\`o, F.G., Lamberti, F.: Mixed-reality robotic games: design guidelines for effective entertainment with consumer robots. IEEE Consum. Electron. Mag. **10**, 6–16 (2020)
14. Roscoe, R.D., Chi, M.T.: Understanding tutor learning: knowledge-building and knowledge-telling in peer tutors' explanations and questions. Rev. Educ. Res. **77**(4), 534–574 (2007)
15. Sprawls, P.: Evolving models for medical physics education and training: a global perspective. Biomed. Imaging Interv. J. **4**(1), e16 (2008)
16. Strada, F., Bottino, A., Lamberti, F., Mormando, G., Ingrassia, P.L.: Holo-BLSD-A holographic tool for self-training and self-evaluation of emergency response skills. IEEE Trans. Emerg. Top. Comput. (2019, in press). https://doi.org/10.1109/TETC.2019.2925777
17. Tanaka, F., Matsuzoe, S.: Children teach a care-receiving robot to promote their learning: field experiments in a classroom for vocabulary learning. J. Hum.-Robot Interact. **1**(1), 78–95 (2012)
18. Topping, K.J., Dehkinet, R., Blanch, S., Corcelles, M., Duran, D.: Paradoxical effects of feedback in international online reciprocal peer tutoring. Comput. Educ. **61**, 225–231 (2013)
19. Walker, E., Girotto, V., Kim, Y., Muldner, K.: The effects of physical form and embodied action in a teachable robot for geometry learning. In: 2016 IEEE 16th International Conference on Advanced Learning Technologies (ICALT), pp. 381–385. IEEE (2016)
20. Werfel, J.: Embodied teachable agents: Learning by teaching robots. In: The 13th International Conference on Intelligent Autonomous Systems (2013)

Neuroevolution vs Reinforcement Learning for Training Non Player Characters in Games: The Case of a Self Driving Car

Kristián Kovalský(✉) and George Palamas

Aalborg University, A. C. Meyers Vænge 15, 2450 Copenhagen, Denmark
aau@aau.dk
https://www.cph.aau.dk

Abstract. The aim of this project is to compare two popular machine learning methods, a non-gradient-based algorithm such as neuro-evolution with a gradient-based reinforcement learning on an irregular task of training a car to self-drive around 3D circuits with varying complexity. A series of 3D circuits with a physics based car model were modeled using the Unity game engine. The data collected during evaluation show that neuro-evolution converges faster to a solution when compared to the reinforcement learning approach. However, when the reinforcement learning approach is allowed to train for long enough, it outperforms the neuro-evolution in terms of car speed and lap times achieved by the trained model of the car.

Keywords: Neuroevolution · Reinforcement learning · Neural network · Evolutionary algorithm · Autonomous systems · Self driving car · Unity · Games · Non player character · NPC

1 Introduction

Autonomous systems are capable of observing and evaluating a situation on a complex and unstructured environment [3] and suggest the most optimal path for the driver or in self driving cars that use image recognition and decision making in order to function [2]. In the field of entertainment, machine learning (ML) is capable of defining game logic and mimicking the actions and behaviour of real players. Artificial intelligence (AI) plays an integral part of video games where it is used for controlling non-player characters (NPCs). These can be very simple such as ghosts in Pac-Man acting according to a certain pattern at various stages of the game [30] to a more complex examples such as neural network (NN) controlled drivatars in the racing series of Forza games [18]. However, some of the most powerful AI bots such as AlphaGo developed by DeepMind require several days of training on an extremely powerful hardware [23].

© ICST Institute for Computer Sciences, Social Informatics and Telecommunications Engineering 2021
Published by Springer Nature Switzerland AG 2021. All Rights Reserved
N. Shaghaghi et al. (Eds.): INTETAIN 2020, LNICST 377, pp. 191–206, 2021.
https://doi.org/10.1007/978-3-030-76426-5_13

The issue with traditional ML algorithms that use gradient-based learning such as back-propagation is that they only work well when presented with big enough training data and sufficient computing resources [13,16,21]. The solution to this might be a global optimizer such as the evolutionary algorithm. Neuroevolution (NE) is an evolutionary approach that uses a genetic algorithm (GA) for optimizing a set of weights describing a NN instead of using stochastic gradient descent methods to train these weights. Several studies have shown that there are cases in which NE can outperform traditional ML algorithms such as reinforcement learning (RL) [9,17,24].

This assumption is going to be investigated in this paper by testing the performance of a NE algorithm against a traditional RL algorithm. A simulation is going to be performed on a series of 3D racing circuits, in Unity3D game engine, with a task of training a car to autonomously drive around these circuits. Their performance will be compared in terms of training time, average and maximum speed the car reaches on these circuits and average and shortest lap time.

2 Background

2.1 Reinforcement Learning

There are three main components of every reinforcement learning algorithm: *agent*, *environment* and *reward*. The agents are placed in an environment and they can interact with it by observing the current state, taking an action and getting a reward (positive or negative) for their action. After the reward is given to the agent, it is again presented with the new state of the environment and it needs to decide on its next action. After certain time, the agent starts to develop a certain set of rules according which it acts. This strategy that is constantly being updated is called the policy [27].

Agent always needs to consider the most immediate reward it will receive and also what is the next state it will go into. RL agents are usually aiming to achieve the highest long-term reward possible. This means that the agent must sometime decide to take an action with smaller immediate reward in order to try to survive for longer periods [5].

The process of calculation of the future rewards is done by summing up the rewards that the agent acquired when it took a similar action at some point before. This sum is multiplied by a variable called *discount factor* that is predefined by the developer (between 0 and 1). This dilemma of whether immediate or future reward should be the main focus of the agent is called the credit assignment problem [5].

One way to solve this problem are value functions. The main two value functions are: *state-value function* and *action-value function*. The state-value function only looks at the current state of the agent within the environment when calculating the expected return whereas the action-value function needs to consider the action as well. The policy π which could be explained as probability $\pi(a|s)$ of the agent deciding to take a certain action a when being in a state s is taken into consideration as well [27].

$$V_\pi(s) = E_\pi \left[\sum_{k=0}^{\infty} \gamma + R_{t+k+1} | S_t = s \right] \tag{1}$$

The above equation describes a state-value function, where $E_\pi[]$ represents the expected return value the agent would receive if it would act according to policy π.

Another problem associated with RL is the one of exploration versus exploitation dilemma [31]. Since the RL algorithm only sees state vectors and based on those it outputs certain action vectors that yield a reward, it sometimes might lead to the algorithm finding solutions which are far from what is desired. However, since the agent is getting rewarded, it keeps doing the same actions. This means that the agent is getting stuck in a local optimum. There have been several approaches attempting to solve this issue, however, none of them are performing consistently on every possible task [4].

Last but not least, RL algorithms have to also deal with the problem of over-fitting. This problem occurs when the agent performs at sufficient level during the training process, however it fails to generalize properly and fails to perform when introduced to a new environment. The main causes of over-fitting are either that the data used for training are not sufficient to train the agent properly, or the agent is too complex for the given task and finds patterns in the training data that might be just noise [5].

2.2 Neuro-Evolution

When dealing with a problem where the optimal topology of the NN is unknown or when there is no training data available to train it with the traditional method of back-propagation, evolutionary algorithms can be used instead as an alternative. This way, the entire topology and weights of a NN can be evolved simultaneously without needing to know what specific setup to use beforehand [12,24]. Neuro-evolution algorithm follows the basic steps of the genetic algorithm as seen on the Fig. 1 where the genomes are weights of a NN [29].

Because of the nature of NE, searching for the right behaviour instead of a value function, it tends to be more suitable for problems where state space is continuous and high-dimensional [6,7].

Genetic Algorithms. Genetic algorithms are a part of bigger group referred to as *evolutionary algorithms* that belong to the class of *evolutionary computation*. The original genetic algorithm was first introduced by John Holland in 1960s [10]. At the beginning of every GA, a random set of possible solutions with high variability, called initial population, is generated. The algorithm then assigns a fitness value to each member of the population based on how well it is suited as an optimal solution to the current problem. Reproduction promotes the survival of the fittest through a selection mechanism which favours solutions with higher

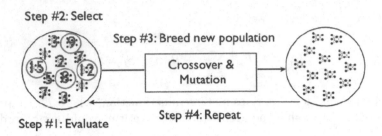

Fig. 1. The basic neuro-evolution loop. The GA is used to evolve both neural network topologies and weights [29].

fitness values [15]. A mutation operation ensures that the offsprings will be significantly different from their parents, thus avoiding local minima stemming from a premature convergence to a solution.

2.3 State of the Art

Deep Neuro-Evolution. In their paper, Such et al. [26] describe how a non-gradient-based evolutionary algorithm can replace already established gradient-based learning algorithms during the training phase of Deep artificial neural networks (DNNs). Their GA was used to evolve weights of a DNN. The evaluation of the approach was performed by comparing the performance of the GA to other contemporary algorithms such as Q-learning, random search (RS) or novelty search applied to deep RL, against a set of Atari games. The GA was performing very well when compared to DQN, A3C and ES. There were some games in which the GA performed significantly worse which only goes to prove how some families of algorithms are more suitable to be used in deep RL for certain tasks. What is interesting is that the GA was able to find a better solution to many games than DQN much quicker. Afterwards, the GA was tested against RS to confirm that the GA is doing something more than just plain random search. The results showed that GA outperformed RS in every single game [26].

Neuroevolution of Augmented Topologies (NEAT). This was first presented by Stanley and Miikkulainen in 2002 [25]. The idea behind NEAT is to evolve not just weights of NNs but also their topology at the same time. This enables NEAT to perform exceptionally well when faced with problems with limited domain knowledge and it also makes NEAT very good at generalizing. The process of optimizing NN with NEAT starts by producing a population of networks with no hidden layers and weights and connections that are chosen randomly. As the algorithm progresses, hidden layers are added through the mutation and crossover processes of the GA [25].

Evaluation of NEAT was performed on two different tasks: simple building of an XOR network and more complex task of balancing two poles on a cart. In terms of the first task, NEAT produced very satisfactory results without any trouble. The networks produced very minimal topology. The second task showed more noticeable advantage of NEAT. NE methods have proved to be able to outperform standard RL methods applied to the double pole balancing problem [17,25].

Neuroevolution as Game Mechanics. A notable example of a practical application of NEAT is the game called EvoCommander developed by Jallov et al. [12]. In EvoCommander, NE is used to evolve NNs, however, these trained networks are then not used for controlling NPCs, but they are given to the players and they can use these networks to take control of their character. There are several behaviours that players need to train their agent to do first, such as ranged attacks, melee attacks, fleeing, etc. [12]. This approach, called "brain switching", showed that the players found the game mechanics engaging in both single-player and multi-player game modes [12].

Reinforcement Policy Learning. One of the finest examples of RL is the bot trained to play the game of Go [22]. The game has been notoriously difficult for AI to master. However, by combining supervised learning and reinforcement learning, AlphaGo has been able to reach win-rate of 99,8% by winning 494 of 495 games played against other computer Go programs that were considered as one of the strongest at that time [22]. Jaderberg et al. [11] used 3D game Quake III Arena to concurrently train multiple independent RL agents. They demonstrate how a RL agent can achieve human-level performance by training on pixels and game score as inputs. Pan et al. [20] proposed a novel method for transitioning from virtual space to real space when it comes to developing driving policy learning with RL, and show promising results of the RL adapting to real world driving. A project by Haarnoja et al. [8] also aimed to address the issue with transitioning from digital simulation space to real world space. Their approach was able to train a real-world Minitaur robot to learn a pattern of steps in order to be able to walk and generalize without issues. Moreover, different NE controllers, based on the concept of pro-prioception, have been compared for efficiency in balancing 3D biped characters in the complex and dynamic environment of a game [1].

All of the above indicate that GA tends to perform better in spaces that are irregular and poorly characterized. On the other hand, RL algorithms feel more comfortable at dealing with tasks that can be solved by creating a grid which maps states to actions.

3   Experimental Setup

The entire project was created using Unity3D game engine. The circuits were created by using the Bézier Path Creator asset from Unity Assets Store. A small green rectangle was put at the same position as the starting position of the car in order to determine the start/finish line. The model consists of a simple 3D car with four wheel colliders that are used for controlling the speed and steering.

The problem of exploitation over exploration also appeared in this project where the agent ended up finding parts of the circuit that were wide enough for the car to turn around and drive back to the start where it would turn around again and head back, thus creating a policy that kept driving in a small loop. This problem was solved by adding checkpoints to the circuits used for the training of the RL algorithm. Adding a sequence of sub-goals has been an efficient method for global optimization problems such as autonomous navigation [19]. By decreasing the reward for the distance traveled and instead giving the agent a reward for driving through checkpoints, the agent learned that in order to get higher long term reward, it needs to keep driving forward and keep collecting rewards from checkpoints instead of driving around in the same place of the circuit indefinitely (Fig. 2).

Fig. 2. The car placed on a circuit with its five ray-casts displayed for debugging purposes. Bright green line in front of the car is the start/finish line (Color figure online)

The first circuit (Circuit 1) is the simplest of the three. The surface is completely flat with no elevations and the shape of it is a plain circle. The second circuit (Circuit 2) is also flat but it consists of multiple turns that were freely drawn by hand. The turns vary between left and right turns as well as long and fast corners to slow and almost 180° hairpins (Fig. 3).

The third and last circuit (Circuit 3) is the most complex. There are only four turns but the first part of the circuit has a variety of successive hills with a steep inclines and declines (Fig. 4).

3.1   Neuroevolution of an Autonomous Car Controller

For this simulation, a standard NE algorithm was used instead of more complex such as the NEAT. The reason behind this was the fact that the aim of this

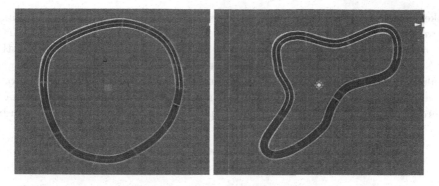

Fig. 3. The first (left) and second (right) circuits used for the evaluation. Checkpoints used for RL algorithm are visible as hollow rectangles with green outline only for visualization purposes. Bright green line marks the start/finish line (Color figure online)

Fig. 4. The third circuit used for the evaluation. Checkpoints used for the RL algorithm are visible as hollow rectangles with green outline only for visualization purposes. Bright green line marks the start/finish line. The right image shows various levels of elevation (Color figure online)

project was to compare training approaches. Both NE and RL use different methods for optimizing the weights of a NN. By using NEAT, the topology of the NN would be changed during the process as well, possibly creating unwanted biases.

The car controller contains methods for resetting the car and its properties when it collides with a wall, method for applying forces to the car's wheel colliders in order to control the acceleration and steering of the car, method for placing the ray-casts on the car and lastly a method for calculating the fitness of the car.

The fitness function is based on 3 variables: the distance traveled by the car, average speed of the car and distance readings from the ray-casts. Each of these variables has also their own multiplier that makes it possible to assign higher or lower importance to certain variables. Once the car collides with a wall, properties of that particular genome are saved, it is subsequently killed and new genome is spawned. The script for the NN builds a functioning neural network from scratch. The output of the NN are values for actions that the car makes: acceleration and steering. The acceleration value is constrained to values between 0 and 1 and steering value is constrained between −1 and 1. The activation functions used are sigmoid for acceleration and tanh for steering. Lastly, the script for GA contains methods for creating an initial random population, creating new population of children, sorting and picking the best members of a population, crossover, mutation and method for when a genome dies and calls the reset method of the car controller script. Training settings of the NE can be seen in Table 1.

Table 1. Training settings of the NE algorithm

Initial population	50
Mutation rate	0.055
Best agents for crossover	8
Worst agents for crossover	3
Number to crossover	39
Distance multiplier	1
Average speed multiplier	0.5
Raycast multiplier	0.1
Number of raycasts	5
Number of hidden layers	3
Number of hidden neurons	15

3.2   Reinforcement Learning of an Autonomous Car Controller

The Unity Machine Learning Agents Toolkit *ML-Agents*, developed by Unity Technologies, was used for this implementation [28]. The car is presented with information about its immediate velocity on all three axes X, Y and Z, its local position and immediate angle of its front wheels. It also receives observations from five ray-casts that are cast from the middle of the car forward and to the sides at 30° angle steps. There are two actions that the agent can perform: *acceleration* and *steering*. The form of actions is continuous, meaning that the action is presented to the agent in an array of floating point numbers between 0 (no acceleration) and 1 (full acceleration) for acceleration and between -1 (left) and 1 (right) for steering. The final acceleration force applied is calculated by multiplying the output of the acceleration action with the motor torque of the wheels. The steering angle is calculated by multiplying the output of the steering action with a maximum steering angle allowed for the wheels which is −45° to the left and +45° to the right.

The agent is awarded 0.2 points every time it collides with any of the 15 checkpoints evenly distributed around each circuit. Positive reward is also given to the agent based on its immediate velocity on Z axis (forward and backward) divided by 2000. A tiny negative reward is given to the agent at each step in order to motivate it to move forward and seek higher reward. A big negative reward of -1 point is given to the agent when it collides with any of the walls. Hitting walls also ends the current episode, resets the agent to its initial starting location, reward is set back to zero and new episode is started. At the start of each episode, the agent is placed on the same position coordinates, however the rotation of the agent is picked randomly from a range of 0 to 60° from its initial rotation in order to support exploration and introduce some variation. Training settings of the RL can be seen in Table 2.

Table 2. Training settings of the RL algorithm

Vector space size	8
Action space type	Continuous
Action space size	2
Number of raycasts	5
Trainer	PPO
Number of hidden layers	2
Number of hidden neurons	128
Learning rate	0.0003
Maximum steps	9.0e6

3.3   Data Collection

Training times and rewards/fitness scores were collected at the end of training session. The trained models were then used to drive around the same circuit in order to collect additional measurements. During this secondary data collection, the car was first let to complete one full lap in order to acquire some speed. At the start of the second lap, data about the car's speed and elapsed time started being recorded. The car was then let to drive for three more laps.

4   Results

First of all, it should be mentioned that neither NE nor RL algorithms were able to complete the Circuit 3. Therefore, only the results from Circuits 1 and 2 are going to be presented. The average training time of the NE algorithm on Circuit 1 was 43.42 s. The condition for successful training was met on average during generation 7. The left graph in Fig. 5 displays the progression of the fitness function during one of the fastest runs that performed well already during the second generation. The average training time of the NE algorithm on Circuit 2 was 1 min and 21 s. The condition for successful training was met on average also during generation 7. The right graph in Fig. 5 displays run that found the right solution quite soon during generation 4. When it came to training with the RL algorithm, the criteria for successful training on Circuit 1 was met after 8 h and 25 min. The model went through 3950000 steps in order to reach the solution. The top graph in Fig. 6 displays how the entropy of the model was changing. It can be seen that the randomness of the choices was generally decreasing during the training. The bottom graph displays the increasing rewards achieved by the agent at certain steps. Training the model with the RL algorithm on the more complex Circuit 2 took 15 h and 10 min. The model completed 7050000 steps until the right policy was found. The top graph in Fig. 7 shows slightly unstable entropy in the first half of the training, however it starts to decrease more stably in the second half. The bottom graph shows the overall increase of the accumulated rewards of the agent, mainly in the second half of the training period.

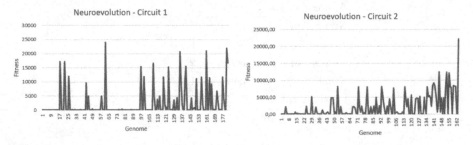

Fig. 5. Fitness scores across genomes during training of the NE on the first (left) and second (right) circuit

Trained Model Results. Data collected from the trained models show that the NE algorithm on Circuit 1 reached the best lap time of 17.52 s. The average time after three laps was 20.16 s. Additionally, as it can be seen on Fig. 8 (top), the maximum speed reached on Circuit 1 was 27.57 and the average speed was 20.83. When the model trained with RL algorithm was tested on Circuit 1 it achieved the best lap time of 15.66 s and the average lap time of 17.15 s. Moreover, the top speed on Circuit 1 was measured at 30.57 with the average speed over all frames being 25.66 (see Fig. 8 bottom).

The NE model trained on Circuit 2 achieved the best lap time of 31.18 s and the average lap time after three laps was 33.63 s. The top speed reached on Circuit 2 was 15.35 and the average speed during three laps was 12.47 (see Fig. 9 top). The RL trained model on Circuit 2 achieved the best lap time of 32.01 s and the average lap time over three laps was 32.82 s. The maximum speed the car reached on Circuit 2 was 18.29 with the average being 12.52 (see Fig. 9 bottom). Now that all the raw data were presented, it allows for their discussion and reasoning of why certain algorithms behaved the way they did.

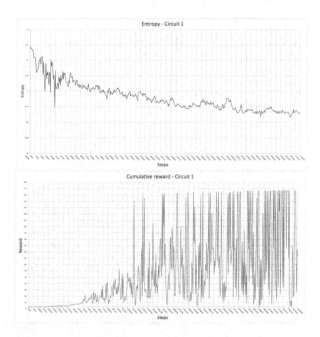

Fig. 6. Top graph shows the change in entropy during training of the RL model on the first circuit while bottom graph shows the change in accumulated reward

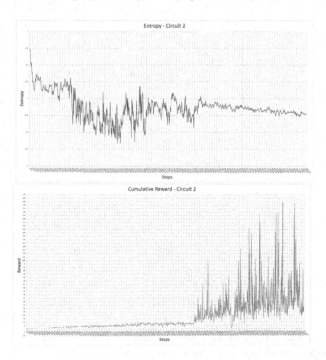

Fig. 7. Top graph shows the change in entropy during training of the RL model on the second circuit while bottom graph shows the change in accumulated reward

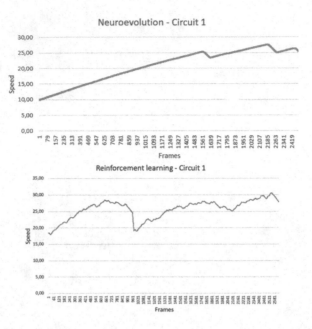

Fig. 8. Speed of the NE (top) and RL (bottom) trained car models at each frame during three laps in play mode on the first circuit

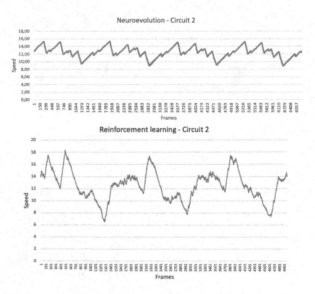

Fig. 9. Speed of the NE (top) and RL (bottom) trained car models at each frame during three laps in play mode on the second circuit

5   Discussion

The difference in training times is quite obvious. The GA and in turn NE was expected to perform better than the RL, however the difference is very substantial and noticeable. Training of the NE on Circuit 1 took 43.42 s on average compared to 8 h and 25 min of the RL. Training of the NE on Circuit 2 took 1 min 21 s on average compared to 15 h 10 min of the RL. The NE algorithm, through complete accident, happened to find a network that managed to drive several laps around a circuit on its first attempt. This only goes to support the claims and findings stated in the Background section (see Sect. 2) that NE is more suitable for problems that are irregular and not so clearly defined. On the other hand, comparing the lap times and speed achieved by the agents show that the RL trained model was able to outperform the NE model in all four measured examples. On Circuit 1, the NE model took on average 20.16 s to complete a lap compared to 17.15 s of the RL model. Average speed on Circuit 1 was also around 20% higher for the RL model at 25.66 compared to 20.83 of the NE model. On Circuit 2, the differences between the two models were not as noticeable. The average lap time of the NE model was 33.63 s and the average lap time of the RL model was 32.82 s, making the difference between them less than 1 s. The difference is even smaller for average speed, where NE model reached value of 12.47 and RL model reached value of 12.52.

5.1   Biases

There are several factors that might have affected the way the results turned out for both training and play parts of the algorithms. The difference in topologies of the NNs used in both algorithms could have caused an unfair advantage of one over the other. The NN used in NE algorithm consisted of 3 hidden layers and 15 hidden neurons, whereas the NN used in the RL algorithm consisted of 2 hidden layers and 128 hidden neurons. Experimenting with finding a middle ground between the two setups could have resulted in different performance of either of the two algorithms. Additionally, the mutation rate and crossover rate of the NE have a great impact on the ability of the NE to find optimal solutions. Figure 5 shows how unstable the outputs of the NE algorithm are during the training. Lowering the mutation rate or increasing the number of better performing individuals to be used for crossover could potentially improve the stability of the NE algorithm.

Another difference between the two algorithms is the way they are awarded for their actions. In case of the NE algorithm, the agent is awarded the fitness score based on the sum of various weighted variables: distance traveled, average speed and ray-cast readings. On the other hand, the RL agents gets higher positive reward the faster it is moving forward and passing through checkpoints. The checkpoints were added to the RL algorithm to fight the well known issue of RL algorithms called exploitation. However, adding them on the NE circuits or adding rewards to the RL algorithm based on the same way as they are given to the NE algorithm would make the comparison more fair.

Lastly, the acceleration action of both algorithms was constrained to be always within the realm of positive numbers. This means that the agents were basically told that moving forward is the right and the only direction they should be moving. If the agents would be able to reverse, the results would almost definitely look different. However, the problem of exploitation of the RL algorithm becomes more prominent again. The lack of braking force also contributed to the fact that neither of the two algorithms managed to successfully train on Circuit 3.

6   Conclusion

The aim of this project was to see whether a neuro-evolution algorithm can outperform a traditional reinforcement learning algorithm when applied on a task of training a car to drive around various circuits in terms of training time, maximum and average speed reached as well as their lap times. The results of different metrics collected both during training and after the training during play mode showed that while the neuro-evolution is capable of finding the optimal solution much faster than reinforcement learning, the solution found by reinforcement learning performs better during play mode. The speeds that were reached by the model trained with the reinforcement algorithm as well as the lap times were consistently better than the ones reached by the model trained with the neuro-evolution algorithm.

Due to some inconsistencies in the implementation, neither of the two algorithms managed to solve the most complex circuit that was presented to them. Potential solutions to this problem as well as biases caused by differences in the topologies of the neural networks and the way algorithms were awarding their agents are going to be presented in the following section. There is definitely room for improving both algorithms either by doing minor adjustments to the parameters of the algorithm or by introducing more complex and robust techniques such as NEAT or recurrent neural networks.

7   Future Works

The very first step at improving the performance of the algorithms would be to introduce braking to the agents. This could possibly extend the training times, but it would most definitely benefit the agents in the long run and help in conquering Circuit 3. Next step would be to introduce a recurrent neural networks. Recurrent neural networks are capable of remembering several past observations and therefore they can deal better with temporal series of events [14]. Another property that should be evaluated is how well the trained models adapt to new environments. Generalization is greatly essential for a network when faced with completely new and unknown environments. Models that fail to generalize properly very often suffer from over-fitting [5]. Last but not least, a more complex version of the NE algorithm such as NEAT could be implemented [25].

References

1. Carlsen, C.S., Palamas, G.: Evolving balancing controllers for biped characters in games. In: Rojas, I., Joya, G., Catala, A. (eds.) IWANN 2019. LNCS, vol. 11507, pp. 869–880. Springer, Cham (2019). https://doi.org/10.1007/978-3-030-20518-8_72
2. Chen, S., Zhang, S., Shang, J., Chen, B., Zheng, N.: Brain-inspired cognitive model with attention for self-driving cars. IEEE Trans. Cogn. Dev. Syst. **11**(1), 13–25 (2017)
3. Cui, Y., Ge, S.S.: Autonomous vehicle positioning with GPS in urban canyon environments. IEEE Trans. Robot. Autom. **19**(1), 15–25 (2003)
4. Duff, M.O.: Q-learning for bandit problems. In: Machine Learning Proceedings 1995, pp. 209–217. Elsevier (1995)
5. Géron, A.: Hands-On Machine Learning with Scikit-Learn, Keras, and TensorFlow: Concepts, Tools, and Techniques to Build Intelligent Systems. O'Reilly Media, Sebastopol (2019)
6. Gomez, F., Miikkulainen, R.: Learning robust nonlinear control with neuroevolution. Technical report, Technical Report AI01-292, Department of Computer Sciences, The University (2001)
7. Gomez, F.J., Miikkulainen, R.: Solving non-Markovian control tasks with neuroevolution. In: IJCAI, vol. 99, pp. 1356–1361 (1999)
8. Haarnoja, T., Ha, S., Zhou, A., Tan, J., Tucker, G., Levine, S.: Learning to walk via deep reinforcement learning. arXiv preprint arXiv:1812.11103 (2018)
9. Hausknecht, M., Lehman, J., Miikkulainen, R., Stone, P.: A neuroevolution approach to general atari game playing. IEEE Trans. Comput. Intell. AI Games **6**(4), 355–366 (2014)
10. Holland, J.H.: Genetic algorithms: computer programs that "evolve" in ways that resemble natural selection can solve complex problems even their creators do not fully understand. Sci. Am. **267**, 1992 (2005)
11. Jaderberg, M., et al.: Human-level performance in 3D multiplayer games with population-based reinforcement learning. Science **364**(6443), 859–865 (2019)
12. Jallov, D., Risi, S., Togelius, J.: EvoCommander: a novel game based on evolving and switching between artificial brains. IEEE Trans. Comput. Intell. AI in Games **9**(2), 181–191 (2017)
13. Krizhevsky, A., Sutskever, I., Hinton, G.E.: ImageNet classification with deep convolutional neural networks. In: Advances in Neural Information Processing Systems, pp. 1097–1105 (2012)
14. Mikolov, T., Karafiát, M., Burget, L., Černocký, J., Khudanpur, S.: Recurrent neural network based language model. In: Eleventh Annual Conference of the International Speech Communication Association (2010)
15. Mitchell, M.: An Introduction to Genetic Algorithms. MIT Press, Cambridge (1998)
16. Mnih, V.: Human-level control through deep reinforcement learning. Nature **518**(7540), 529–533 (2015)
17. Moriarty, D.E., Mikkulainen, R.: Efficient reinforcement learning through symbiotic evolution. Mach. Learn. **22**(1–3), 11–32 (1996). https://doi.org/10.1023/A:1018004120707
18. Muñoz, J., Gutierrez, G., Sanchis, A.: A human-like TORCS controller for the simulated car racing championship. In: Proceedings of the 2010 IEEE Conference on Computational Intelligence and Games, pp. 473–480. IEEE (2010)

19. Palamas, G., Ware, J.A.: Sub-goal based robot visual navigation through sensorial space tesselation. Int. J. Adv. Res. Artif. Intell. **2**(11), (2013)
20. Pan, X., You, Y., Wang, Z., Lu, C.: Virtual to real reinforcement learning for autonomous driving. arXiv preprint arXiv:1704.03952 (2017)
21. Seide, F., Li, G., Yu, D.: Conversational speech transcription using context-dependent deep neural networks. In: Twelfth Annual Conference of the International Speech Communication Association (2011)
22. Silver, D., et al.: Mastering the game of go with deep neural networks and tree search. Nature **529**(7587), 484 (2016)
23. Silver, D., et al.: Mastering the game of go without human knowledge. Nature **550**(7676), 354–359 (2017)
24. Stanley, K.O., Clune, J., Lehman, J., Miikkulainen, R.: Designing neural networks through neuroevolution. Nat. Mach. Intell. **1**(1), 24–35 (2019)
25. Stanley, K.O., Miikkulainen, R.: Evolving neural networks through augmenting topologies. Evol. Comput. **10**(2), 99–127 (2002)
26. Such, F.P., Madhavan, V., Conti, E., Lehman, J., Stanley, K.O., Clune, J.: Deep neuroevolution: genetic algorithms are a competitive alternative for training deep neural networks for reinforcement learning. arXiv preprint arXiv:1712.06567 (2017)
27. Sutton, R.S., Barto, A.G.: Reinforcement Learning: An Introduction. MIT Press, Cambridge (2018)
28. Unity Technologies: Unity ML-Agents Toolkit (2020). https://github.com/Unity-Technologies/ml-agents. Accessed 25 May 2020
29. Whiteson, S.: Evolutionary computation for reinforcement learning. In: Wiering, M., van Otterlo, M. (eds.) Reinforcement Learning, vol. 12, pp. 325–355. Springer, Heidelberg (2012). https://doi.org/10.1007/978-3-642-27645-3_10
30. Wittkamp, M., Barone, L., Hingston, P.: Using neat for continuous adaptation and teamwork formation in pacman. In: 2008 IEEE Symposium On Computational Intelligence and Games, pp. 234–242. IEEE (2008)
31. Yogeswaran, M., Ponnambalam, S.: Reinforcement learning: exploration-exploitation dilemma in multi-agent foraging task. Opsearch **49**(3), 223–236 (2012). https://doi.org/10.1007/s12597-012-0077-2

Training Medical Communication Skills with Virtual Patients: Literature Review and Directions for Future Research

Edoardo Battegazzorre$^{(\boxtimes)}$, Andrea Bottino , and Fabrizio Lamberti

DAUIN, Politecnico di Torino, Corso Duca degli Abruzzi 24, 10143 Torino, Italy
{edoardo.battegazzorre,andrea.bottino,fabrizio.lamberti}@polito.it

Abstract. Effective communication is a crucial skill for healthcare providers since it leads to better patient health, satisfaction and avoids malpractice claims. In standard medical education, students' communication skills are trained with role-playing and Standardized Patients (SPs), i.e., actors. However, SPs are difficult to standardize, and are very resource consuming. Virtual Patients (VPs) are interactive computer-based systems that represent a valuable alternative to SPs. VPs are capable of portraying patients in realistic clinical scenarios and engage learners in realistic conversations. Approaching medical communication skill training with VPs has been an active research area in the last ten years. As a result, the number of works in this field has grown significantly. The objective of this work is to survey the recent literature, assessing the state of the art of this technology with a specific focus on the instructional and technical design of VP simulations. After having classified and analysed the VPs selected for our research, we identified several areas that require further investigation, and we drafted practical recommendations for VP developers on design aspects that, based on our findings, are pivotal to create novel and effective VP simulations or improve existing ones.

Keywords: Virtual patient · Embodied conversational agent · Provider-patient communication · Instructional design · Technical design

1 Introduction

The communication between patients and doctors is a central component of health care practice. On the one hand, good doctor-patient communication help physicians better identify patient's needs, perceptions and expectations [22]. On the other hand, it is not surprising that patients rate open communication as one of the most important aspects of their relationship with the physicians [12]. Research has shown that an effective, patient-centered communication is important to increase patient satisfaction [17,20,24,34,39,49,61]. It can have also beneficial effects on patient's health, improving physiologic measures as blood pressure and glucose levels [62], increasing understanding and adherence to therapy

[36], and even creating a placebo effect in some cases [35]. Conversely, a poor grasp of communication skills can be detrimental to both the patient's and their relatives' health [33,34], and may lead to malpractice accusations.

Communication is a complex phenomenon that's not restricted to the verbal domain. As outlined in [34], there are several critical aspects that have been subject to patients' complaints. They include elements of non-verbal communication (e.g., lack of eye-contact, negative facial expressions, use of "improper" prosodic features), inappropriate choice of words, lack of pauses to let patients ask questions, lack of listening, issues with the information given, and lack of empathy or even disrespect and poor attitudes.

Given the relevance of the problem, a primary goal in healthcare is training clinicians and healthcare providers in developing effective communication skills. Today, standardized patients (SP, i.e., actors who are instructed to represent a patient during a clinical encounter with a healthcare provider) are considered the gold standard in such training programs. SPs provide students with the opportunity to learn and practice both technical and non-technical skills in an environment capable of reproducing the realism of the doctor-patient relationship. These simulated environments are less stressful for the students, who are not required to interact with a real patient [18,38]. However, SPs are difficult to standardize, since their performance heavily depend on the actors' skills, and their recruitment and training can become very costly [46].

A practical alternative to SPs is represented by virtual patients (VPs), i.e., interactive computer simulations capable of portraying a patient in a clinical scenario in a realistic way. VPs are virtual agents that have a human appearance and the ability to respond to users and engage in communication patterns typical of a real conversation. They can be equipped with external sensors capable of capturing a wide range of non-verbal clues (user's gestures and motions, expressions and line of sight) and use them to modulate the evolution of the conversation. In the field of communication skill learning, VPs have the same advantages over SPs and are characterized by comparable learning outcomes [53]. They are cost-effective solutions since they can be developed once and used many times. They can be deployed as in-class or self-learning tools that students can use at their own pace and at any place. They can also be integrated into sophisticated software platforms that include automatic learner assessment, feedback and debriefing sessions. Finally, VP simulations can present, with reasonable accuracy, difficult or rare cases with a high degree of repeatability [65] and, compared to SPs, are also easier to standardize [57].

VPs for provider-patient communication have been surveyed in several works. Bearman et al. [6] conducted a systematic review on VPs focused on developing empathy-related skills, but the Authors did not extend their analysis to communication as a whole. A more recent review [55] investigated the specific context of pharmacist-patient counselling, focusing on the development of knowledge, skills, confidence, engagement with learning, and user satisfaction. However, the work did not discuss in depth the effects of specific design choices. Another integrative review [51] focused on non-technical skills like situational awareness, decision-making, teamwork, leadership, and communication, but did not consider the technical perspective and, like the previous one, it did not elaborate on the impact of specific instructional or design features. Finally, the Authors of [41] performed a systematic review on VPs focused on communication, analyzing which features of instructional design (i.e., the definition of methods, processes and strategies that guide learners to achieve the training objectives) and technical design (i.e., the definition of the technological components aimed to support and implement the envisaged instructional design) are most effective in VP simulations. Unfortunately, the time span of the survey was limited to 2006–2018, and the number of studies remaining from the application of the inclusion and exclusion criteria was rather small (14 works, with only eight discussed in detail).

Based on the above analysis, it was our opinion that a thorough analysis of the instructional and technical design elements as well as of the technological components (sensory system, speech understanding, interaction devices, virtual reality, VR, and augmented reality, AR, etc.) and related relevant concepts (like immersion and presence) that are involved in the development of the considered learning tools was actually missing. Hence, we tried to fill this gap through the review reported in the present paper. Similarly to [41], our study is centered on the instructional and technical design of VP simulations. However, we propose a different approach to the analysis of these two components, by performing in particular a deeper investigation of the technical aspects. Then, based on our findings, we also identify current limitations and potentially unexplored areas with the aim to foster further research and developments in the field.

The rest of the paper is organized as follows. In Sect. 2, the literature review protocol is first introduced. Afterwards, Sect. 3 presents and discusses the research results. Section 4 highlights the gaps that we identified and the directions that future studies could take in order to address them. Finally, conclusions are given in Sect. 5.

2   Literature Review Protocol

As illustrated in the previous section, we performed a literature review to document the current state-of-the-art of the use of VPs for medical communication skill learning and to identify possible areas where further research is needed. The purpose of this review was to understand the instructional and technical design principles and the efficacy of these elements in achieving the expected learning outcomes. To this end, we developed the following guiding questions in order to help focusing information extraction.

- RQ1: What are the latest technical developments in the field of communication-oriented VPs?
- RQ2: Which instructional and technical design features are employed most commonly in VP design?
- RQ3: Which instructional and technical VP design features are more effective for learning communication skills? And which of these features are most appreciated by the users?

The search process, carried out mainly between March and May 2020, started with an automated approach targeting four scientific paper databases, namely Scopus, PubMed, ACM Digital Library and IEEE Xplore. For each database we performed a search based on the main and derivative keywords (virtual patient OR (serious game AND healthcare)) AND (communication), limiting the results to papers published from 2015 onward. The choice of this date was made with the aim to survey only the most recent developments in the field and avoid excessive overlaps with previous literature reviews (e.g., with [51] and [41]).

The papers found were post-processed in order to remove repeated entries and exclude reviews, editorials, abstracts, posters and panel discussions. The remaining 306 papers were analyzed by reading over their title, abstract, and introduction, and classified as either relevant or irrelevant based on the following criteria: (i) does the study relate to any of the design elements of interest (instructional or technical)? and, (ii) does the study disclose at least some of the design choices made by the Authors? If the answer to any of these questions was no, then the paper was excluded. After this step, each of the 70 accepted papers was read completely by at least one reviewer, who also assessed its quality. Its references were also analyzed according to the aforementioned screening process.

At the end of the search process, we selected a total of 28 papers. Among them, we identified a number of works that referred to the same VP, but in different experimental settings or in different phases of the development process. Since our interest was in analyzing the VP design rather than the detailed outcomes of possible experiments, papers sharing the same VP were grouped together, obtaining a total of 21 VPs (17 of them had not been discussed in previous surveys, and only four of them were in common with [41], namely Banszki [4,53], CynthiaYoungVP [19], MPathic-VR [21,40], and NERVE [25,26,37]).

In order to capture the main characteristics of problems and solutions discussed in these papers, we introduced a taxonomy of terms for the instructional and technical design elements, whose initial version was defined based on the Authors' expertise. Based on intermediate findings, this taxonomy was further refined into the final one introduced in Sect. 3. All the Authors categorized the selected VPs according to this taxonomy, and any disagreement was solved by discussion. Finally, as a last step, we searched for references related to the open problems and potential areas of research identified during the analysis.

3   Results and Discussion

In this section, we present the result of our research. As stated in Sect. 2, the selected VPs have been labeled according to the taxonomy of terms summarized in Tables 1 and 2. The definition of the identified categories (which differs to a large extent from the one presented in [41]) is introduced in the following subsections, where we also discuss the survey results relative to each group. We first introduce the instructional design elements, which are connected to the technical elements necessary to realize them; afterwards, we discuss the design choices related to the technical and technological components of the simulations.

Table 1. Synopsis of the reviewed VPs for each instructional design category

Instructional design		
Category	Subcategory	Virtual patients
Structure	*Narrative*	HOLLIE [1], AtRiskInPrimaryCare [2], Dupuy [15], CynthiaYoungVP [19], Jacklin [28,29], MPathic-VR [21,40], Communicate! [31], Marei [44], Ochs [47], Szilas [63]
	Narrative + Problem solving	Banszki [4,53], NERVE [25,26,37], Maicher [43], Suicide Prevention [48], VSPR [50,52], Richardson [54], CESTOLVRClinic [59], Schoenthaler [60], Washburn [66], UTTimePortal [68,69], Zlotos [70]
Unfolding	*Closed-option*	HOLLIE [1], AtRiskInPrimaryCare [2], Dupuy [15], MPathic-VR [21,40], NERVE [25,26,37], Jacklin [28,29], Communicate! [31], Marei [44], Suicide Prevention [48], VSPR [50,52], Richardson [54], CESTOLVRClinic [59], Schoenthaler [60], Szilas [63], UTTimePortal [68,69], Zlotos [70]
	Open-option	Banszki [4,53], CynthiaYoungVP[19], NERVE [25,26,37], Maicher [43], Washburn [66]
	Hybrid	Ochs [47]
Feedback	*Replay feature*	Dupuy [15], Communicate! [31], Ochs [47], VSPR [50,52], Zlotos [70]
	Virtual instructor	At-Risk in Primary Care [2], Suicide Prevention [48], Schoenthaler [60]
	Multiple session structure	MPathic-VR [21,40]
	Quantitative emotional feedback	At-Risk in Primary Care [2], Schoenthaler [60]
	Qualitative personalized post-feedback	Jacklin [28,29], Richardson [54]
	Empathy feedback	CynthiaYoungVP [19]
	Clinical discoveries available	NERVE [25,26,37]
	Game elements	Dupuy [15], MPathic-VR [21,40], Communicate! [31], Schoenthaler [60], UT-Time Portal [68,69]
Gamification	*Scoring system*	Dupuy [15], MPathic-VR [21,40], Communicate! [31], Schoenthaler [60], UT-Time Portal [68,69]
	Badge system	UTTimePortal [68,69]
	Countdown timed events	HOLLIE [1]

Finally, we discuss the experimental evidences related to the effectiveness of the identified design elements.

3.1 Instructional Design

This category encompasses various instructional design aspects implemented in the VP scenario, such as how the VP delivers (and facilitates) learning activities and if (and how) it provides scaffolded support to improve learner's performance.

Structure. The *structure* defines the hierarchical organization and presentation of VP-related information within the simulation. According to [5], two

Table 2. Synopsis of the reviewed VPs for each technical design category

Technical design Category	Subcategory	Virtual patients
Presentation format	Image	HOLLIE [1], Marei [44]
	Video	CynthiaYoungVP [19], Suicide Prevention [48], VSPR [50,52]
	Desktop VR	AtRiskInPrimaryCare [2], MPathic-VR [21,40], NERVE [25,26,37], Jacklin [28,29], Communicate! [31], Richardson [54], Schoenthaler [60], Szilas [63], UTTimePortal [68,69], Zlotos [70]
	Large volume display	Dupuy [15], Banszki [4,53], Maicher [43], Washburn [66]
	Immersive VR	Ochs [47], CESTOLVRClinic [59]
Input interface	Typed	HOLLIE [1], AtRiskInPrimaryCare [2], CynthiaYoungVP [19], NERVE [25,26,37], Jacklin [28,29], Communicate! [31], Maicher [43], Marei [44], Suicide Prevention [48], VSPR [50,52], Richardson [54], CESTOLVRClinic [59], Schoenthaler [60], Szilas [63], UTTimePortal [68,69], Zlotos [70]
	Voice-controlled	Banszki [4,53], Dupuy [15], MPathic-VR [21,40], Maicher [43], Ochs [47], CESTOLVRClinic [59]
	Hybrid	Washburn [66]
	Non-verbal	Banszki [4,53], Dupuy [15], MPathic-VR [21,40], Maicher [43], CESTOLVRClinic [59]
Distribution	Standalone	Banszki [4,53], Dupuy [15], MPathic-VR [21,40], Maicher [43], Marei [44], Ochs [47], CESTOLVRClinic [59], Szilas [63], Washburn [66]
	Web-based	HOLLIE [1], AtRiskInPrimaryCare [2], CynthiaYoungVP [19], NERVE [25,26,37], Jacklin [28,29], Maicher [43], Suicide Prevention [48], VSPR [50,52], Richardson [54], UTTimePortal [68,69], Zlotos [70]
	Undisclosed	Communicate! [31], Schoenthaler [60]

non-mutually exclusive approaches (i.e., *narrative* and *problem solving*) can be defined. The narrative VPs are characterized by a coherent storyline, with a focus on cause-effect decisions that have a direct impact on the evolution of the simulation. These VPs present the patient as more than a mere collection of data and statistics, and devote a certain degree of attention to interpersonal and communication aspects of the provider-patient interaction. On the contrary, the *problem solving* VPs are mainly used to support inquiry-based learning scenarios such as teaching clinical reasoning, differential diagnosis, and history-taking skills. These contexts do not usually concern portraying authentic communicative acts, since they mainly involve making questions and observations.

Scholars and researchers recognize the power of *narrative* design in the creation of meaningful learning experiences [5,44]. Narrative-based simulations that reflect the consequences of the choices and the actions made by the learner can lead to the development of more effective VPs. In particular, for VPs used to teach communication skills, experimental evidence supports the value of *narrative* design [5]. Thus, it is not surprising that all the VPs presented in the selected works are based on this approach. Nevertheless, it is interesting to note that 10 out the 21 VPs analyzed integrate the *narrative* design with a *problem solving* component. This component aims to teach particular skills like history-taking (Cynthia Young VP [19], NERVE [25,26,37], Maicher [43]), clinical reasoning (VSPR [50,52], Richardson [54], Washburn [66], UT-Time Portal [68,69], Zlotos [70]), physical examinations (HOLLIE [1], NERVE [25,26,37], CESTOL VR Clinic [59]), compilation and consultation of electronic medical records (HOLLIE [1], Maicher [43]), and medication administration (HOLLIE [1]).

Unfolding. Given the prominence of narrative design in the development of VPs for communication skill training, another relevant design element is defining how the narrative may unfold, and how the simulation can evolve between different states. A preliminary subdivision can be made among *linear* and *non-linear* narratives. In the former design, VPs have a linear path to follow and the decisions, questions and options possibly presented to the learner do not influence the simulation outcome. It is clear that this design severely limits learning effectiveness, and none of the works included in this survey implemented it.

On the contrary, the *non-linear* navigational structure of VPs offers learners a greater flexibility, and an higher degrees of interactivity and control. In this case, two further choices are possible. In the *closed-option* design, the simulation advances to the next state by selecting one of the possible alternatives or explicit paths offered to learners. Simulation states are organized in a hierarchical structure (similar to that of the "choose your own adventure" books), which stresses the cause effect relation of the user's choices. The *open-option* design (sometimes referred in the literature as "free-text" [28,30,45] or "open-chat" [26]) can be used to develop free-form simulations where states are organized in a partially or fully interconnected structure, and users are free to interact with the VP as they wish, thus emulating the flow of a real conversation. As we will discuss more in detail in Sect. 3.2, learners can formulate questions and statements by either typing or having their speech transcribed into written words using speech-to-text software. Then, the application parses the text and elaborates a proper response. The VP state progression can be influenced also by non-verbal cues such as gestures, body posture, expressions and sight.

The *closed-option* design characterizes most of the analyzed VPs (15), with only four works based on an *open-option* design; as for the remaining, one VP implemented both options (NERVE [25,26,37]), whereas the other one can be considered an hybrid between the two designs (Ochs [47]). One explanation for this result is the lower complexity of the *closed-option* implementation, although some Authors [9,28] argued that a such an approach may be more suitable for novices who, for example, may still be inexperienced about the procedures to follow in a patient encounter. However, other works reported that many students feel restricted by the *closed-option* interface [15,26,28,52], preferring either an *open-option* structure or the possibility to chose between the two variants. It is worth noting that implementing both options allows the use of the same VP in different educational settings. For instance, in NERVE [25,26,37], the less stress-inducing *closed-option* variant is used in the learning sessions, while rehearsal sessions leverage the less restrictive *open-option* setting.

Another interesting approach is the hybrid model implemented in Ochs [47], where the user can freely interact through voice with the VP. Then, a human facilitator selects, from a set of possible closed-options, the utterance that semantically resembles the original phrase the most, prompting the appropriate response from the patient. The advantage of this approach is that it ease the development burden of what appears to learners as an *open-option* VP, with the clear disadvantage of preventing its use as a self-learning and self-evaluation tool.

Feedback. With the term *feedback* we refer to any form of instructional scaffolding enclosed in the simulation itself (i.e., we exclude any feedback external to the simulation, such as post-simulation debrief and reflection sessions with mentors and peers).

Feedback can be given in many different forms, from explicit messages to discoveries made, questions answered, and visual representations of the current VP state.

While researchers recognize the relevance of immediate and after-action feedback as an essential feature in communication-based VPs [1,29,44,50,53], it is surprising that six of the VPs surveyed (Banszki [4,53], Maicher [43], Marei [44], Szilas [63], Washburn [66], CESTOLVRClinic [59]) do not embed any type of built-in feedback. The remaining works take different approaches. Four VPs (Dupuy [15], Communicate! [31], VSPR [50,52], Zlotos [70]) offer the possibility, after the simulation is completed, to *replay* some of its parts and analyze the outcome of different choices. Three simulations (At-Risk in Primary Care [2], Suicide Prevention [48], Schoenthaler [60]) include a *virtual instructor*, i.e., a virtual tutor that gives advice or feedback based on the user's choices. MPathic-VR [21,40] employs a *multiple session structure*, where the first run acts as a learning phase, concluded by an automated and complete feedback provided by the system, whereas the second run (set in the same scenario) serves as an evaluation phase. This type of structure appears to be highly appreciated by students since they can immediately put into practice what they learned during the first phase, taking into account the feedback received. Two VPs (At-Risk in Primary Care [2], Schoenthaler [60]) feature *quantitative emotional feedback* in the form of an on-screen trust meter that indicates users how effective their communication choices were at building a relation with the patient. Two VPs (Jacklin [28,29], Richardson [54]) offer learners a *personalized qualitative feedback* at the end of the simulation. CynthiaYoungVP [19] uses an hybrid approach between automated and human feedback. At the end of the simulation, the students can access a web page containing *empathy feedback* and scores for each response given, where scores are manually assigned by human experts. The approach adopted in NERVE [25,26,37] is to inform learners about the number of *clinical discoveries* and empathic responses available, thus providing inexperienced users with useful guidelines on how to proceed with the conversation. Although it has not been implemented yet, the work in [25] put forth the proposition of providing "cumulative feedback" on how users are developing their skills across multiple patient scenarios. Authors suggest that this feature could both encourage repeated use of the system and act as a motivator for performance improvement. Finally, there is a number of VPs (HOLLIE [1], Dupuy [15], Communicate! [31], MPathic-VR [21,40], Schoenthaler [60], UT-Time Portal [68,69]) that leverage *game elements* as feedback. Since the introduction of game elements is a relevant design feature, it is discussed in detail in the following subsection.

Gamification. The idea of introducing game mechanics in any learning experience is to make them more enjoyable and engaging. Researchers and practitioners recognize that game mechanics contribute to making the learning experience more effective, fostering self-improvement and healthy competition between peers [7,16]. The mechanics used the most in "gamified" experiences are *scores*, *badges* and *leaderboards*. Scores are a quantitative and immediate form of feedback that acts as an extrinsic motivator to foster users to improve their performance. *Scoring systems* can be found in Dupuy [15], Communicate! [31], MPathic-VR [21,40], Schoenthaler [60] and UT-Time Portal [68,69]. In particular, Communicate! [31] and Schoenthaler [60] provide separate scores for each learning goal (e.g., empathy control, language clarity, and pick up of patient's concerns). Such a feature can help learners to tell the areas in which they are already proficient, distinguishing them from those needing improvement.

Badges are visual representations used in games to prove that the player has reached an intermediate goal on his/her road to mastery. Their purpose is twofold: they are a form of gratification to the learners, and they allow trainees to share achievements with peers and educators. Thus, they also represent an extrinsic motivator for improvement. In our survey, the only simulation we found that implements a *badge system* is UT-Time Portal [68,69]. VSPR [50,52] features a system of certificates issued to users at the end of each learning module which shall be regarded as an "intrinsic-only" motivator, since there is no overarching structure that enables users to see each others' achievements.

Finally, leaderboards (or rankings) are a primarily extrinsic motivator that leverage competition with peers when they compare their performance to that of others (it should be noted that, for highly competitive individuals, the act of "climbing the leaderboard" can also be seen as a relevant intrinsic motivator independent of the context). Surprisingly, despite their demonstrated benefits for learning, in our survey, we found no example of public ranking and leaderboards.

A final note is for HOLLIE [1], which implements the very peculiar idea of a Tamagotchi-style VP the learners have to care for (adequately, at regular intervals and in real-time) over two weeks. Here, the leading game mechanics (constant care over a long period) reproduces quite accurately the daily tasks of a nurse leveraging the innate sense of responsibility in the players.

3.2 Technical Features

This category explores, from a technical perspective, the different solutions that can support (and implement) the choices made in the instructional design, i.e., which are the technical features that enable the accomplishment of the envisioned learning activities. These features include the physical devices required to guarantee the exchange of information between the learner and the system, and the possible communication infrastructure needed to run the simulation.

Presentation Format. The surveyed works provide learners with different types of outputs aimed to deliver VP information to the learner and presenting the VP itself. A first rough subdivision is between *text-based* and *graphic* representations. In screen-based text simulators, the VP is presented mainly in the form of a collection of text and structured data, with the possible inclusion of images portraying a static patient or exam results. However, the lack of a graphic component capable of displaying a patient that can express emotions as the simulation unfolds (and, consequently, change posture and facial expressions according to its current state) is one of the main limitations of these approaches. Therefore, researchers started extending text-based simulations into learning activities with a relevant graphic component.

All the VPs surveyed in this work fall in the *graphic* category, which can be further classified in *image, video* and *3D*. VPs in the *image* subclass are presented through a series of static images (either photographs or drawings), such as HOLLIE [1] and Marei [44]. Some VPs present their case using *video*, either in the form of live footage (Suicide Prevention [48], VSPR [50,52]) or as a computer-generated offline video (Cynthia Young VP [19]). However, a clear limitation of this approach is its lack of flexibility, since the actor video cannot be re-purposed to portray a different clinical case.

The majority of surveyed simulations fall in the *3D* subclass and present the patient and the environment as 3D models rendered in real-time. Their main advantage is that tweaking and expanding a simulation using 3D characters can be done in a much more modular fashion than with *image* and *video*-based VPs. Another advantage is that the sense of immersion and presence are greater than those that can be delivered by *image* and *video*-based VPs.

Most of the 3D approaches rely on standard *desktop VR* (DVR) settings (10, namely AtRiskInPrimaryCare [2], MPathic-VR [21,40], NERVE [25,26,37], Jacklin [28,29], Communicate! [31], Richardson [54], Schoenthaler [60], Szilas [63], UTTimePortal [68,69], Zlotos [70]). However, since trying to maximize the feeling of immersion and presence is extremely relevant for engaging learners and helping them achieve the expected learning outcomes, some works integrate (partially or fully) immersive technologies. Four of them (Dupuy [15], Banszki [4,53], Maicher [43], Washburn [66]) take advantage of *large volume displays* to portray a life-sized and more natural interaction with the patient, and CESTOL VR Clinic [59] uses an HMD for the same purpose. In Ochs [47], three different setups (DVR, immersive VR with an HMD, and immersive VR in a CAVE) are compared to analyze their effect on the sense of presence. The outcome of this experiment demonstrates that immersive environments improve the sense of presence and perception of the VP, with the CAVE scoring slightly better than the HMD. It should be noted, however, that while *immersive VR* (IVR) offers a higher degree of immersion and presence over DVR, there are still accessibility issues that limit its use, in particular when the VP is intended for self-learning and self-training.

Input Interface. This category describes the input methods through which the user influences the unfolding of the VP simulation. In the case of *typed* interfaces, user's textual intents are entered by typing on a keyboard or selecting an item in a predefined list of choices. *Voice-controlled* simulations use natural language, which is then parsed into text through a speech-to-text module, usually offered by external Natural Language Processing (NLP) APIs [19,43]. Finally, the integration within the simulation of Natural User Interfaces (NUI) allows to influence the VP state evolution through additional *non-verbal* input cues such as eye contact, distance, facial expression, gestures and body posture, which can be captured with cameras and other hardware.

Among the analyzed VPs, 14 feature a *typed*-only input, only five are *voice-controlled* (Banszki [4,53], Dupuy [15], MPathic-VR [21,40], Ochs [47], CESTOL VR Clinic [59]), Maicher [43] has both options, and Washburn [66] can be considered as a hybrid solution since a human facilitator transcribes the spoken commands through a *typed* interface. One of the reasons behind the limited use of voice controls is the fear, expressed by some Authors [43,47], that NLP systems may be technically hard to implement and prone to wrong transcriptions, which may lead to misunderstandings or unrecognized utterances, break the sense of immersion and cause frustration in the user [8]. This is why some Authors (e.g., Banszki [4,53], Ochs [47], and Washburn [66]) decided to have a human facilitator taking over the function of the NLP module. Moreover, a VP featuring only voice controls cannot be used by learners with speech impairments [43]. However, it should be stressed that, nowadays, speech-to-text APIs have become widely available, and their quality keeps improving; thus, problems related to imprecise transcriptions should be less and less daunting in the coming years. As for the impaired people, a smart solution to achieve maximum flexibility and accessibility could be to let the users choose between *typed* and *voice-controlled* interfaces freely. It should also be noted that IVR environments favour the use of *voice-controlled* interfaces over alternative solutions such as virtual keyboards or situation-specific control boards [59], which are likely to break the sense of immersion and presence and are often cumbersome to use.

Among the analyzed VPs, five of them support also *non-verbal* input, by either leveraging NUI-based approaches (e.g., using RGBD sensors, like in MPathic-VR [21,40] and Maicher [43], or standard RGB cameras, like in Dupuy [15]) or having a human controller that observes the user interacting with the VP and updates the VP's response accordingly in terms of gestures and facial expressions (like in Banszki [4,53]). However, apart from Banszki [4,53], it appears that this information is largely underutilized to influence the VP's behavior. In Dupuy [15], the users' facial expressions are detected to merely assess their emotional state at the end of the simulation. In Maicher [43], the tracked user position is simply used to adjust the agent's gaze, and there is no specific mention of the way the simulation exploits gestures. Finally, in MPathic-VR [21,40], instead of continuously capturing *non-verbal* communication, learners are forced to assume specific expressions and poses when prompted by the system. In summary, the above discussion highlights that sounder ways of using *non-verbal* inputs are sorely needed in this particular research field.

Distribution. One relevant technological parameter of the VP simulation is the way the application is distributed (and how learners can access it). In principle, there are two main options. The first option is to deploy the VP as a *web-based* application that can be accessed over the Internet. Such a simulation often runs inside a web browser (which makes it device-independent), and generally requires a low amount of computational resources. This flexibility can also foster self-learning (since simulations can be accessed at places and times convenient for the learner) and helps reduce costs (since learning can be carried out online). However, since *web-based* applications are required to be portable on many devices (including mobile ones), they generally sacrifice technical characteristics and computational complexity in favour of accessibility. On the other hand, *standalone* applications are deployed locally on a computer or workstation. These simulations can implement more advanced and complex features since they can leverage the full computational power of a dedicated machine, and integrate external devices or sensors (such as high-quality cameras and microphones).

In our survey, we found a total of ten *web-based* and eight *standalone* applications; in two cases, this information was undisclosed in the paper, whereas in one case (Maicher [43]), the VP was deployed in both variants. This latter work is interesting since it shows how a *standalone* version can trade off some of the flexibility of the web one with a broad array of features (such as voice control and gesture/posture detection). The Authors observed that students were significantly more engaged with the *standalone* VP, whereas in the web version they had to focus on typing and reading, which make them be less prone to notice the subtle non-verbal cues manifested by the patient.

Nonetheless, it should be stressed that technology is advancing rapidly, and personal devices come equipped with ever better microphones, cameras and computational power, which can reduce the technological gap between (desktop-only) *standalone* applications and *web-based* ones. Further discussions on this topic are included in Sect. 4.

3.3   Effectiveness of Design Elements

The general effectiveness of VPs on developing communication skills has been discussed by several Authors [41,51,55]. A common complaint in VP-related literature is the lack of a standardized terminology that, coupled with a considerable heterogeneity in study design, makes the retrieval and evaluation of relevant works a troublesome task. Despite this situation, both [41] and [51] concluded that, when appropriately contextualized in a well thought out educational context, VPs are indeed useful for developing, practising and building confidence about communication and other skills like, e.g., decision making and teamwork.

Based on these findings, one possible question arising from our review is if the surveyed papers provide pieces of evidence about the effects on learning outcomes and efficacy of the simulation of the different instructional design elements and the technical features available. Unfortunately, the answer is negative. In most of the analyzed works, the Authors reported only users' feedback or comments about a particular element/feature, and a direct comparison between different design choices is missing. The only notable exceptions are three. The first one is represented by [47], in which different presentation formats were assessed, showing that immersive VR technologies yield superior results when compared to non-immersive ones. The second one concerns the distribution method [43]. The Authors found that a standalone application can provide a considerably higher level of engagement than its web-based counterpart thanks to the possibility to leverage advanced technical features (voice-controlled input and large volume displays) to increase immersion and focus on the task at hand. The third one compared closed and open-option unfolding designs, highlighting the advantages and disadvantages of each variant [26].

4   Open Areas of Research

The surveyed papers show that, despite exciting results obtained, fully understanding how to develop effective VPs for patient-doctor communication training requires further work. Reasons are related to the fact that either the technological components have not been fully explored yet or results are still inadequate to fully assess the effectiveness of different design approaches. Thus, in this section, we briefly discuss some open problems and present areas requiring further research.

Assessment of Design Elements. As discussed in Sect. 3.3, the current literature lacks a thorough evaluation of the effectiveness of alternative designs. This observation highlights the fact that further work has to be done to develop a better understanding of instructional elements and technical features that VP simulations can offer in order to achieve the desired learning outcomes.

Scope. Another comment can be made on the specific communication learning context. While several core skill domains jointly contribute to a patient's health and satisfaction (like relationship building, information gathering, patient education, shared decision making and breaking bad news [56]), most of the surveyed VP simulations focus only on one specific domain. This observation highlights the need to develop novel approaches capable of addressing simultaneously the multiple communication challenges one has to face when interacting with a real patient, thus helping to improve the overall learner's communication skills.

Authoring Tools. Implementing VPs is a cumbersome and complicated process, which requires taking into account several different elements (NLP, emotion modelling, affective computing, 3D animations, etc.), which, in turn, involve specific technological and technical skills. Usually, the development of a VP is a cyclical process of research, refinement and validation with experts that can take a considerable amount of time [58]. Thus, there is the need to develop simple (and effective) authoring tools that can allow developers to support clinical educators in the rapid design, prototyping and deploying of VPs in a variety of use cases. Examples of authoring tools for narrative-style VPs with 3D graphics are very scarce in the literature. The work presented in [31] integrates a scenario builder that allows clinical educators to design the unfolding of their cases. This authoring tool exploits a domain reasoner where the response of the virtual agent is determined not only by the previous dialogue that the user chose, but also by other parameters like the agent's current emotional state. However, this tool lacks the possibility to customize the virtual environment or the VP's aesthetics. The NERVE VP [25, 26, 37] is built upon the Virtual People Factory [58], a web application that enables the users to build conversational models using an un-annotated corpus retrieval approach based on keyword matching. Another interesting example is SIDNIE (Scaffolded Interviews Developed by Nurses in Education [14]). This tool allows clinical educators to edit the patient's medical status, dialogue options and physical appearance. However, to our knowledge, SIDNIE has not been deployed in any publicly available form, and appears to be aimed exclusively at nurse training scenarios.

In other application areas (such as building clinical skills and problem-solving abilities), the extensive use of tools such as DecisionSim, OpenLabyrinth and Web-SP [13] is a clear demonstration of the fact that an easy-to-use authoring tool is a determinant factor for the success of a VP application. However, compared to these areas, the specific context of patient-doctor communication training involves more complex systems, with 3D visuals and branched narratives offering a more realistic interaction, which makes the development of authoring tools in this area much more challenging [64].

Emerging Web Technologies. In the previous sections, we highlighted that personal devices are coming with better and better hardware and computational power, thus helping to narrow the gap between standalone and web-based applications. Another contribution will inevitably come from recent advances in web-based technology, like, e.g., WebXR[1]. WebXR is a device-independent framework that allows users to develop and share VR and AR applications over the Internet, with considerable support for different hardware and web browsers. In addition, game-streaming platforms such as Google Stadia[2] are a very promising workaround for the limited computational capabilities of personal devices. With these platforms, the bulk of the computation is processed on the server side, then the pre-rendered output is streamed to the final user's device. The implementation of such technological solutions in the immediate future will enable the applications to combine the accessibility of current web-based software with the computational complexity of standalone applications run on a dedicated machine.

Multiple Virtual Humans. Interacting with a relative or another health care provider are considered crucial aspects of a clinician's communication skills [23, 34]. However, VP simulations usually include only two actors: the

---

[1] https://www.w3.org/TR/webxr/.
[2] https://stadia.google.com/.

learner (possibly represented by an avatar) and a unique Non-Playable Character (NPC), i.e., a virtual human not controlled by the trainee that represents the patient. The only two examples that include more than one NPC besides the patient are the Medical Interview Episode of the UTTimePortal [68,69] (which incorporates a patient and a caregiver), and MPathic-VR [21,40] (which includes a patient's relative and a nurse). Beyond this observation, we should also note that another interesting future development (still untouched in the field of VPs for patient-doctor communication skills, to the best of our knowledge) could be to provide the possibility of interacting (within the simulation) with other human-controlled avatars, in a way similar to that proposed by approaches focused on inter-professional communication in emergency medical situations [3].

Immersive VR and AR. There is a general understanding among researchers that increasing the level of immersion and realism of the simulations (e.g., using large volume displays, HMDs, spatialized 3D audio, higher fidelity graphics and animations) leads to more believable human-computer interactions [10,32], which in turns help improve the users' communication and empathic skills [47,67] and, ultimatley, the learning outcomes in general [42]. However, surprisingly, the use of IVR technologies in this specific context appears to be quite limited. Only two VPs out of 21, i.e., Ochs [47] and CESTOL VR Clinic [59], mention the use of IVR, and AR appears to be completely unexplored. The primary obstacles to the adoption of IVR or AR in VP simulations seem to be the complexity, challenges and costs of development steps [67].

Fortunately, things are going to change rapidly. In recent years, the availability and quality of VR devices have increased considerably, and their cost has decreased dramatically. These factors contribute (together with the availability of high-end development platforms such as Unity or Unreal engine) to reducing overall costs and efforts for developing IVR and AR applications. Furthermore, IVR offers currently a truly immersive, unbroken environment that can shift the cognitive load directed on imagining oneself "being there" in VR towards solving the task at hand. In turn, higher immersion and visual fidelity can have positive effects on learning [11,27]. Thus, we expect that, soon, VR and AR will contribute to improving the state of the art in this research field.

Fully-Fledged Non-verbal Input. In our opinion, this is a major lack in current designs. The unfolding of the simulation's narrative should be dictated (in tandem) by both user's verbal and non-verbal behaviours. To this end, developers of future VPs should attempt to fully leverage non-verbal cues as a factor that actively influences the state of the agent. For instance, the same utterance should have a different outcome if the user maintains eye contact with the patient, looks in another direction, and is fidgeting or exhibiting an incoherent facial expression. The extraction of para-linguistic factors such as tone of voice, loudness, inflection, rhythm, and pitch can provide information about the actual emotional states of the other peer in the communication. Prosody must be addressed with great attention since it is one of the main ways to express empathy and can have a considerable impact in increasing patient satisfaction [34]. Thus, computational mechanisms capable of extracting these variables from the analysis of the user's voice are sorely needed. The same para-linguistic factors should be also available to modulate the VP response according to its emotional states. In fact, one of the problems with present text-to-speech libraries is that they pronounce everything with the same tone, which makes it impossible to communicate feelings through voice.

5   Conclusion

In our research we found many different examples of VPs focused on provider-patient communication and various approaches to their design. However, we feel that there is not a single VP that realizes the full potential of this learning tool. Some research areas still need to be explored further. The broad range of educational use cases in healthcare suggests that VP applications should be as modular and adaptable as possible. Effective and user-friendly authoring tools are very rarely implemented while being, in our opinion, a crucial feature to ensure the adoption of a VP simulation by clinical educators. The use of technologies such as VR, AR, and advanced NLP also needs to be explored more in depth, as they may give VP simulations the edge they need to be effectively used in daily practice. We also feel that recent developments in web-based technologies will also reduce those compromises between accessibility and advanced technical possibilities that today are still required in many situations.

References

1. Adefila, A., Opie, J., Ball, S., Bluteau, P.: Students' engagement and learning experiences using virtual patient simulation in a computer supported collaborative learning environment. Innov. Educ. Teach. Int. **57**(1), 50–61 (2020)
2. Albright, G., Bryan, C., Adam, C., McMillan, J., Shockley, K.: Using virtual patient simulations to prepare primary health care professionals to conduct substance use and mental health screening and brief intervention. J. Am. Psychiatr. Nurses Assoc. **24**(3), 247–259 (2018)
3. Anbro, S.J., et al.: Using virtual simulations to assess situational awareness and communication in medical and nursing education: a technical feasibility study. J. Organ. Behav. Manag. 1–11 (2020)
4. Bánszki, F., Beilby, J., Quail, M., Allen, P., Brundage, S., Spitalnick, J.: A clinical educator's experience using a virtual patient to teach communication and interpersonal skills. Australas. J. Educ. Technol. **34**(3) (2018)
5. Bearman, M., Cesnik, B., Liddell, M.: Random comparison of 'virtual patient' models in the context of teaching clinical communication skills. Med. Educ. **35**(9), 824–832 (2001)
6. Bearman, M., Palermo, C., Allen, L.M., Williams, B.: Learning empathy through simulation: a systematic literature review. Simul. Healthcare **10**(5), 308–319 (2015)
7. Benedict, N., Schonder, K., McGee, J.: Promotion of self-directed learning using virtual patient cases. Am. J. Pharm. Educ. **77**(7) (2013)
8. Bloodworth, T., et al.: Initial evaluation of a virtual pediatric patient system (2010)

9. Carnell, S., Halan, S., Crary, M., Madhavan, A., Lok, B.: Adapting virtual patient interviews for interviewing skills training of novice healthcare students. In: Brinkman, W.-P., Broekens, J., Heylen, D. (eds.) IVA 2015. LNCS (LNAI), vol. 9238, pp. 50–59. Springer, Cham (2015). https://doi.org/10.1007/978-3-319-21996-7_5
10. Chuah, J.H., et al.: Exploring agent physicality and social presence for medical team training. Presence Teleoper. Virtual Environ. **22**(2), 141–170 (2013)
11. Coulter, R., Saland, L., Caudell, T., Goldsmith, T.E., Alverson, D.: The effect of degree of immersion upon learning performance in virtual reality simulations for medical education. InMed. Meets Virtual Real. **15**, 155 (2007)
12. Dibbelt, S., Schaidhammer, M., Fleischer, C., Greitemann, B.: Patient-doctor interaction in rehabilitation: is there a relationship between perceived interaction quality and long term treatment results? Die Rehabil. **49**(5), 315–325 (2010)
13. Doloca, A., Țănculescu, O., Ciongradi, I., Trandafir, L., Stoleriu, S., Ifteni, G.: Comparative study of virtual patient applications. Proc. Romanian Acad. Ser. A **16**(3), 466–473 (2015)
14. Dukes, L.C., Meehan, N., Hodges, L.F.: Participatory design of a pediatric virtual patient creation tool. In: 2016 IEEE International Conference on Healthcare Informatics (ICHI), pp. 449–455. IEEE (2016)
15. Dupuy, L., et al.: Evaluation of a virtual agent to train medical students conducting psychiatric interviews for diagnosing major depressive disorders. J. Affect. Disord. **263**, 1–8 (2020)
16. Festinger, L.: A theory of social comparison processes. Hum. Relat. **7**(2), 117–140 (1954)
17. Fiscella, K., et al.: Patient trust: is it related to patient-centered behavior of primary care physicians? Med. Care 1049–1055 (2004)
18. Forrest, K., McKimm, J., Edgar, S.: Essential Simulation in Clinical Education. Wiley, Hoboken (2013)
19. Foster, A., et al.: Using virtual patients to teach empathy: a randomized controlled study to enhance medical students' empathic communication. Simul. Healthcare **11**(3), 181–189 (2016)
20. Franks, P., et al.: Are patients' ratings of their physicians related to health outcomes? Ann. Family Med. **3**(3), 229–234 (2005)
21. Guetterman, T.C., et al.: Medical students' experiences and outcomes using a virtual human simulation to improve communication skills: mixed methods study. J. Med. Internet Res. **21**(11) (2019)
22. Ha, J.F., Longnecker, N.: Doctor-patient communication: a review. Ochsner J. **10**(1), 38–43 (2010)
23. Hallin, K., Henriksson, P., Dalén, N., Kiessling, A.: Effects of interprofessional education on patient perceived quality of care. Med. Teach. **33**(1), e22–e26 (2011)
24. Hickson, G.B., Federspiel, C.F., Pichert, J.W., Miller, C.S., Gauld-Jaeger, J., Bost, P.: Patient complaints and malpractice risk. JAMA **287**(22), 2951–2957 (2002)
25. Hirumi, A., et al.: Advancing virtual patient simulations through design research and interplay: part ii–integration and field test. Educ. Tech. Res. Dev. **64**(6), 1301–1335 (2016)
26. Hirumi, A., et al.: Advancing virtual patient simulations through design research and interplay: part i: design and development. Educ. Tech. Res. Dev. **64**(4), 763–785 (2016)
27. Huerta, R.: Measuring the impact of narrative on player's presence and immersion in a first person game environment. The University of Texas-Pan American (2012)

28. Jacklin, S., Chapman, S., Maskrey, N.: Virtual patient educational intervention for the development of shared decision-making skills: a pilot study. BMJ Simul. Technol. Enhanced Learn. **5**(4), 215–217 (2019)
29. Jacklin, S., Maskrey, N., Chapman, S.: Improving shared decision making between patients and clinicians: design and development of a virtual patient simulation tool. JMIR Medi. Educ. **4**(2) (2018)
30. Janda, M.S., et al.: Simulation of patient encounters using a virtual patient in periodontology instruction of dental students: design, usability, and learning effect in history-taking skills. Eur. J. Dent. Educ. **8**(3), 111–119 (2004)
31. Jeuring, J., et al.: Communicate!—a serious game for communication skills —. In: Conole, G., Klobučar, T., Rensing, C., Konert, J., Lavoué, É. (eds.) EC-TEL 2015. LNCS, vol. 9307, pp. 513–517. Springer, Cham (2015). https://doi.org/10.1007/978-3-319-24258-3_49
32. Johnsen, K., Lok, B.: An evaluation of immersive displays for virtual human experiences. In: 2008 IEEE Virtual Reality Conference, pp. 133–136. IEEE (2008)
33. Judge, T.A., Ilies, R.: Affect and job satisfaction: a study of their relationship at work and at home. J. Appl. Psychol. **89**(4), 661 (2004)
34. Kee, J.W., Khoo, H.S., Lim, I., Koh, M.Y.: Communication skills in patient-doctor interactions: learning from patient complaints. Health Prof. Educ. **4**(2), 97–106 (2018)
35. Kelley, J.M., et al.: Patient and practitioner influences on the placebo effect in irritable bowel syndrome. Psychosom. Med. **71**(7), 789 (2009)
36. King, A., Hoppe, R.B.: "Best practice" for patient-centered communication: a narrative review. J. Graduate Med. Educ. **5**(3), 385–393 (2013). https://doi.org/10.4300/jgme-d-13-00072.1
37. Kleinsmith, A., Rivera-Gutierrez, D., Finney, G., Cendan, J., Lok, B.: Understanding empathy training with virtual patients. Comput. Hum. Behav. **52**, 151–158 (2015)
38. Kneebone, R., et al.: The human face of simulation: patient-focused simulation training. Acad. Med. **81**(10), 919–924 (2006)
39. Kohatsu, N.D., Gould, D., Ross, L.K., Fox, P.J.: Characteristics associated with physician discipline: a case-control study. Arch. Intern. Med. **164**(6), 653–658 (2004)
40. Kron, F.W., et al.: Using a computer simulation for teaching communication skills: a blinded multisite mixed methods randomized controlled trial. Patient Educ. Couns. **100**(4), 748–759 (2017)
41. Lee, J., Kim, H., Kim, K.H., Jung, D., Jowsey, T., Webster, C.: Effective virtual patient simulators for medical communication training: a systematic review. Med. Educ. **54**, 786–795 (2020)
42. Limniou, M., Roberts, D., Papadopoulos, N.: Full immersive virtual environment CAVETM in chemistry education. Comput. Educ. **51**(2), 584–593 (2008)
43. Maicher, K., et al.: Developing a conversational virtual standardized patient to enable students to practice history-taking skills. Simul. Healthcare **12**(2), 124–131 (2017)
44. Marei, H., Al-Eraky, M., Almasoud, N., Donkers, J., Van Merrienboer, J.: The use of virtual patient scenarios as a vehicle for teaching professionalism. Eur. J. Dent. Educ. **22**(2), e253–e260 (2018)
45. McCoy, L., Pettit, R.K., Lewis, J.H., Allgood, J.A., Bay, C., Schwartz, F.N.: Evaluating medical student engagement during virtual patient simulations: a sequential, mixed methods study. BMC Med. Educ. **16**(1), 20 (2016)

46. Nestel, D., et al.: Key challenges in simulated patient programs: an international comparative case study. BMC Med. Educ. **11**(1) (2011). https://doi.org/10.1186/1472-6920-11-69
47. Ochs, M., et al.: Training doctors' social skills to break bad news: evaluation of the impact of virtual environment displays on the sense of presence. J. Multimodal User Interfaces **13**(1), 41–51 (2019)
48. O'Brien, K.H.M., et al.: Suicide risk assessment training using an online virtual patient simulation. Mhealth **5** (2019)
49. Papadakis, M.A., et al.: Disciplinary action by medical boards and prior behavior in medical school. N. Engl. J. Med. **353**(25), 2673–2682 (2005)
50. Peddle, M., Bearman, M., Mckenna, L., Nestel, D.: Exploring undergraduate nursing student interactions with virtual patients to develop 'non-technical skills' through case study methodology. Adv. Simul. **4**(1), 2 (2019)
51. Peddle, M., Bearman, M., Nestel, D.: Virtual patients and nontechnical skills in undergraduate health professional education: an integrative review. Clin. Simul. Nurs. **12**(9), 400–410 (2016)
52. Peddle, M., Mckenna, L., Bearman, M., Nestel, D.: Development of non-technical skills through virtual patients for undergraduate nursing students: an exploratory study. Nurse Educ. Today **73**, 94–101 (2019)
53. Quail, M., Brundage, S.B., Spitalnick, J., Allen, P.J., Beilby, J.: Student self-reported communication skills, knowledge and confidence across standardised patient, virtual and traditional clinical learning environments. BMC Med. Educ. **16**(1), 73 (2016)
54. Richardson, C.L., Chapman, S., White, S.: Virtual patient educational programme to teach counselling to clinical pharmacists: development and proof of concept. BMJ Simul. Technol. Enhanced Learn. **5**(3), 167–169 (2019)
55. Richardson, C.L., White, S., Chapman, S.: Virtual patient technology to educate pharmacists and pharmacy students on patient communication: a systematic review. BMJ Simul. Technol. Enhanced Learn. (2019)
56. Riedl, D., Schüßler, G.: The influence of doctor-patient communication on health outcomes: a systematic review. Z. Psychosom. Med. Psychother. **63**(2), 131–150 (2017)
57. Rogers, L.: Developing simulations in multi-user virtual environments to enhance healthcare education. Br. J. Edu. Technol. **42**(4), 608–615 (2011)
58. Rossen, B., Lind, S., Lok, B.: Human-centered distributed conversational modeling: efficient modeling of robust virtual human conversations. In: Ruttkay, Z., Kipp, M., Nijholt, A., Vilhjálmsson, H.H. (eds.) IVA 2009. LNCS (LNAI), vol. 5773, pp. 474–481. Springer, Heidelberg (2009). https://doi.org/10.1007/978-3-642-04380-2_52
59. Sapkaroski, D., Baird, M., McInerney, J., Dimmock, M.R.: The implementation of a haptic feedback virtual reality simulation clinic with dynamic patient interaction and communication for medical imaging students. J. Med. Radiat. Sci. **65**(3), 218–225 (2018)
60. Schoenthaler, A., Albright, G., Hibbard, J., Goldman, R.: Simulated conversations with virtual humans to improve patient-provider communication and reduce unnecessary prescriptions for antibiotics: a repeated measure pilot study. JMIR Med. Educ. **3**(1) (2017)
61. Stelfox, H.T., Gandhi, T.K., Orav, E.J., Gustafson, M.L.: The relation of patient satisfaction with complaints against physicians and malpractice lawsuits. Am. J. Med. **118**(10), 1126–1133 (2005)

62. Stewart, A.M.: Effective physician-patient communication and health outcomes: a review. CMAJ: Can. Med. Assoc. J. = journal de l'Association medicale canadienne 1423–1433 (1995)
63. Szilas, N., Chauveau, L., Andkjaer, K., Luiu, A.L., Bétrancourt, M., Ehrler, F.: Virtual patient interaction via communicative acts. In: Proceedings of the 19th ACM International Conference on Intelligent Virtual Agents, pp. 91–93 (2019)
64. Talbot, T.B., Sagae, K., John, B., Rizzo, A.A.: Sorting out the virtual patient: how to exploit artificial intelligence, game technology and sound educational practices to create engaging role-playing simulations. Int. J. Gaming Comput.-Mediated Simul. (IJGCMS) 4(3), 1–19 (2012)
65. Urresti-Gundlach, M., Tolks, D., Kiessling, C., Wagner-Menghin, M., Härtl, A., Hege, I.: Do virtual patients prepare medical students for the real world? development and application of a framework to compare a virtual patient collection with population data. BMC Med. Educ. 17(1), 174 (2017)
66. Washburn, M., Parrish, D.E., Bordnick, P.S.: Virtual patient simulations for brief assessment of mental health disorders in integrated care settings. Soc. Work. Ment. Health 18(2), 121–148 (2020)
67. Zielke, M.A., et al.: Developing virtual patients with VR/AR for a natural user interface in medical teaching. In: 2017 IEEE 5th International Conference on Serious Games and Applications for Health (SeGAH), pp. 1–8. IEEE (2017)
68. Zielke, M.A., Zakhidov, D., Jacob, D., Hardee, G.: Beyond fun and games: toward an adaptive and emergent learning platform for pre-med students with the UT time portal. In: 2016 IEEE International Conference on Serious Games and Applications for Health (SeGAH), pp. 1–8. IEEE (2016)
69. Zielke, M.A., Zakhidov, D., Jacob, D., Lenox, S.: Using qualitative data analysis to measure user experience in a serious game for premed students. In: Lackey, S., Shumaker, R. (eds.) VAMR 2016. LNCS, vol. 9740, pp. 92–103. Springer, Cham (2016). https://doi.org/10.1007/978-3-319-39907-2_9
70. Zlotos, L., Power, A., Hill, D., Chapman, P.: A scenario-based virtual patient program to support substance misuse education. Am. J. Pharm. Educ. 80(3) (2016)

XR and HCI

Handheld vs. Head-Mounted AR Interaction Patterns for Museums or Guided Tours

Yu Liu[(⊠)], Ulrike Spierling, Linda Rau, and Ralf Dörner

Hochschule RheinMain, Unter den Eichen 5, 65195 Wiesbaden, Germany
{yu.liu,ulrike.spierling,linda.rau,ralf.doerner}@hs-rm.de

Abstract. In recent years, Augmented Reality (AR) technology has been adopted in various fields. The development of handheld devices (HHD) such as smartphones and tablets gives people more chances to use AR technology in their daily lives. However, AR applications using head-mounted devices (HMD) such as Microsoft HoloLens or Magic Leap provide stronger presence experiences than HHD, so that users can immerse themselves better in AR scenarios. While currently there already exist prototypical examples of HMD in museum contexts, widely used interaction patterns are not yet well established, although they would play an important role for accessibility by large user groups. This paper explores existing and potential interaction patterns for guided tours in museums, led by the question how to reconcile AR interaction patterns on HHD and HMD. We use an existing museum showcase for handheld AR from the project "Spirit" to transfer its interaction patterns to an HMD, such as the MS HoloLens. Technical constraints and usability criteria regarding the potential overlaps and applicability have been analyzed in this paper.

Keywords: Augmented Reality · Handheld devices · Head-mounted devices · User interaction patterns · User experience design · Cultural heritage

1 Introduction

In recent years, smart technologies have changed not only working environments, but also private use of gadgets for living and entertainment. For example, the emergence of Augmented Reality (AR) technology evoked higher expectations for visit experiences in museums and exhibitions. However, while people benefit from new technologies, they are also under pressure to use them properly. Therefore, providing reasonable and understandable interfaces and interaction patterns to enhance the usability of AR devices is important, especially for laypersons.

For tour guide applications and storytelling in a cultural heritage context, such as in a museum, AR applications have been researched for decades and recently already produced for the App market. Most of these applications are developed for handheld devices (HHD) like smartphones or tablets, which are available off-the-shelf. However, head-mounted devices (HMD) such as Microsoft HoloLens or Magic Leap provide a much stronger immersive presence experience than handheld AR, while more directly

© ICST Institute for Computer Sciences, Social Informatics and Telecommunications Engineering 2021
Published by Springer Nature Switzerland AG 2021. All Rights Reserved
N. Shaghaghi et al. (Eds.): INTETAIN 2020, LNICST 377, pp. 229–242, 2021.
https://doi.org/10.1007/978-3-030-76426-5_15

exploring the digitally enhanced natural environments, making use of more integrated sensors, including gesture and speech input. Thus, although HMD-AR so far has been successfully applied mainly to hands-free maintenance and assembly support applications, there is only little established common-sense regarding interaction patterns for guided tours. There is a gap between existing scenarios of handheld AR for laypersons and head-mounted AR for professional work, which still needs further investigation.

Our applied research goal in the long run is to develop AR content that can be shared between HHD and HMD. The contribution in this paper is to first identify possible interaction patterns for both HHD and HMD by analyzing their interaction styles and technical affordances based on cultural heritage related use cases. Further, we use an existing museum showcase for handheld AR to discuss the possibility and challenge of transferring its interaction patterns to a head-mounted AR device like the HoloLens. We analyze technical constraints regarding their potential overlaps and applicability and identify gaps for further research.

2   State of the Art

AR technology has been investigated by various industries in the past decades. Marker-based AR technology is widely used on handheld devices; its technical solutions of mixing the digital content with the real world are successfully explored in entertainment [1], production [2] and cultural heritage context [3]. One step in the development of AR applications is interaction design. Pattern approaches have been taken by many software developers and designers to identify and solve problems in the development phase [4–6]. For AR based guided tour applications, many researchers explored the potential possibilities of AR technology in the cultural heritage context with HHD [7]. However, HMD interaction design approaches are not yet sufficiently explored in this application area. While it is often postulated that HMD-based AR enriches user experience by engaging and motivating their imagination through interactive storytelling, gaming and learning [8], there are not many prototypes nor design guidelines that can be used if a new project starts. The technology potential of HMD for cultural heritage recently just gains interest in avant-garde artistic research projects [9, 10], while general interaction patterns are not discussed yet in these.

This paper is concerned with comparing interaction patterns used in exhibitions, museums, or cultural heritage learning, exploiting the possibilities of the HoloLens. In Sect. 3, we compare interaction styles and technical solutions of both HHD and HMD based on cultural heritage related use cases. In Sect. 4, we use an existing showcase from the "Spirit" project [11] to analyze the possibilities of transferring its digital content from HHD to HMD.

2.1   Interaction Patterns

Although many researchers believe that so-called natural user interfaces can ease difficulties to use a new product, people often still must learn basic interaction methods when facing a new interface. [12] Thus, as HHD-based AR applications become more and more popular in daily life, providing understandable interfaces and more widely-used interaction patterns for laymen has become an important topic for development teams.

The first pattern theory was introduced by Christopher Alexander in the 1970s. The purpose of his pattern language was to provide laypersons with a vocabulary to explain their ideas and designs, and to communicate with professionals in the architecture domain [13]. Baltzer et al. adopted the pattern theory from Alexander for their interaction pattern analysis. They point out that patterns are approved solution strategies to repeat known problems and describe the core of the solutions in a way that can be used repeatedly in our daily life [4]. Thus, from the conclusion of Baltzer et al., creating an interaction pattern requires application designers to identify repeatable problems and solutions from a certain task.

In general, the user manipulates the interface with certain interaction styles such as click, swipe, pinch, etc., and it often requires a sequence of repeatable manipulations to finish a specific task. As a pattern offers a vocabulary to explain the problem and solution, an understandable interaction pattern can for example offer a meaningful metaphor that helps users to remember multiple complex manipulations [14].

Understanding use cases can also help designers and software developers to invent new interaction patterns. Constantine [15] points out that from the view of software developers, use cases guide the design of communicating objects to satisfy functional requirements, and use cases provide a straightforward and logical means for modeling workflow. Rumbaugh [16] also indicates that a use case is a sequence of actions, including variant sequences and error sequences. Therefore, we conclude that interaction patterns offer meaningful metaphors to explain the actions within use cases.

In AR application design, actions within use cases are mainly formulated by physical interaction styles and technical solutions. For instance, users need to understand whether they should tap on a screen or move their device to finish a certain task, and, if they will use marker recognition or location detection to activate the digital content. Thus, to create a meaningful metaphor for an interaction pattern, related interaction styles and technical solutions of both HHD and HMD must be explained at the beginning.

3 Comparing Interaction Styles and Technical Solutions of HHD and HMD with Cultural Heritage Use Cases

Research results from Constantine [15] and Rumbaugh [16] suggest that workflows of use cases are often differentiated by different technical solutions. Besides, interaction styles are another important factor that influence the workflow [15]. Therefore, interaction styles and technical solutions from both HHD and HMD will be discussed in the following.

3.1 General Interaction Styles of HHD and HMD

Since smartphones become popular in our daily life, screen-based interactions have been investigated by many researchers. For the handheld device, the user interacts with digital content mainly via press (touch), swipe, pinch, etc. The HMD (such as the HoloLens) offers new interaction styles to manipulate 3D content. According to the Microsoft Mixed Reality design guideline [17], three interaction models have been proposed for developers: hands and motion controllers, hands-free, and gaze and commit. The user interacts with the digital content via various gesture controls such as "air tap", "tap and hold" or with voice input like saying "select" or "back". Yet the different interaction styles from HHD and HMD may share similar manipulation actions in the same task. For example, while the user manipulates digital content on a tablet by "touch" and select, on HoloLens the user will use "air tap" for selection instead. Other important hardware aspects are that the HoloLens and tablet (depending on its configuration) may indeed share some of their internal equipment and sensors, such as a display, sound in/output, camera, and movement tracking/gyroscope. Each platform has specific hardware solutions and restrictions that influence the potential implementations of interaction styles (see Fig. 1).

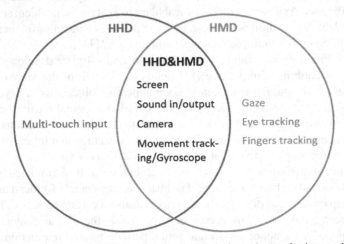

Fig. 1. Overlaps and differences in hardware design relevant for interaction.

Although the HoloLens provides different interaction styles such air tapping and air scrolling, these interaction styles share similar logical input methods with those from a tablet. Thus, it should be possible to adopt at least some use cases from a tablet for a HoloLens. However, the HoloLens also offers new input methods, for example "Gaze and Dwell" by analyzing head position and gaze direction. For a specific use case such as selecting an object in 3D space, the HoloLens then provides more options to manipulate digital content.

3.2   Technical Solutions of Mixing Virtual Objects with the Real World

Augmented Reality is able to integrate the perception of interactive 3D virtual objects within the impression of users' real surrounding environments in real-time [18]. Marker recognition is just one solution to trigger and position AR content within the physical world. To get an overview of the existing market solutions of mixing digital content with the physical world for HHDs, we recently compared and tested 80 popular AR applications with several kinds of categories from App stores.

The result shows the following: Out of 80 applications, 29 used visual marker recognition to trigger content; for example the OTE Museum AR application shows further information about an artefact when the marker is triggered by the camera. 4 applications used face recognition to show AR content; for instance, Instagram uses face recognition to overlay virtual effects once a face is identified. 36 applications used surface detection to let users place AR content by tapping on the screen, while the camera is directed at (mostly) horizontal planes; one example is IKEA Place that requires user to identify a suitable surface to place digital furniture augmenting their home. 11 applications used location detection; such as Car Finder AR that shows a 3D icon to guide the user to the parking place. Table 1 provides an overview.

Table 1. Four technical solutions to apply AR content on HHD

Technical solution	Steps	Example application
Marker recognition	1. Activate the camera 2. The camera focuses on the target marker (or Image) 3. Showing related digital content	OTE Museum AR [19] (Showing virtual object in the real world)
Face recognition	1. Activate the camera 2. The camera focuses on a face 3. Add digital content on the face	Instagram [20] (Add filters or masks on the face)
Surface detection	1. Activate the camera 2. The camera focuses on a flat surface 3. Confirm the flat surface 4. Showing the digital content	IKEA [21] (Select an efficient surface to place the digital content)
Location detection	1. Activate the GPS sensor 2. Detect and calculate the distance 3. Towards the target destination 4. Showing the related digital content	Car Finder AR (Navigation system)

The table above shows four principles of activating and placing AR content on the HHD. With surface detection, the application requires the user to pick up a relatively empty surface to place AR content. Mostly no other specific sensor is required for this solution, as users will place digital content manually. With marker recognition, when image recognition software recognizes a pictorial marker through the camera, the system activates digital content staying registered to that marker. Face recognition works similar, in that once a face pattern is recognized, digital content will be overlayed on the detected face. Locative applications work with distance and location sensors, such as GPS, WiFi or beacons, triggering content when the user gets close to a specific hot spot created during an authoring process.

The HoloLens shares many of these technical solutions for activating and registering AR content, documented in the Microsoft Mixed Reality design guideline [17]. However, the HoloLens does for example not offer GPS in its hardware unit, which means, it is comparably difficult to implement outdoor location detection on the HoloLens as easily as on HHD. Therefore, developers may need to use other technical solutions to implement location detection related use cases. Besides, for placing AR content on a horizontal surface, the HoloLens provides different (and better) solutions than most HHD. The HoloLens uses SLAM technology including room scanning, scene understanding, spatial anchors, spatial mapping, etc. to integrate digital content with the physical world [17]. For instance, the camera sensors on the HoloLens scan the environment consistently and convert the acquired spatial data to an updated digital 3D environment. Based on its unique spatial mapping algorithm, digital content can be automatically anchored to this newly created digital 3D environment.

To sum up, compared with HHD solutions, the HoloLens provides different options, such as spatial mapping algorithms and hand gesture tracking, to allow users operating the AR content. Thus, creating an understandable and reasonable interaction pattern on HoloLens, developers need to combine the advantages of its specific interaction styles and AR-specific technology.

3.3 Identifying General Repeatable Use Cases in a Museum Visit

One goal of this paper is to explore shared potential interaction patterns for both HHD and HMD in a cultural heritage context. To start, we identified typical repeatable use cases from general museum visits.

Visiting processes and user behaviors in museums have been focused on by many researchers. Litvak proposed two states for their interface design based on the visitors' guiding process (compare Fig. 2). When visitors position themselves within the boundaries of a point of interest (POI), all relevant information concerning this POI will be presented within the visitors' view. When attendees leave one POI and return to the main path, the system will change to a navigation state [3]. In general, the digital content of a guided tour includes multiple locations and information about various artefacts. In a tour, visitors may explore artefacts in a certain sequence or by searching for certain POIs to get through an exhibition. We identified an overall visiting pattern with two alternating use cases, based on the exploring behavior in museums which can be further investigated for potential use cases in the cultural heritage context.

3.4 Current Interaction Patterns in a Cultural Heritage Context

Most guided tour applications have focused on the two modes shown above, whereas recently, especially those in the state of current AR research prototypes, may only offer the "exploring" mode. This may be because most research publications are still concerned more with the technical functioning of the AR-related prototype (like tackling the problems of tracking accuracy) than with the overall end-user experience. For example, Chiu et al. [22] proposed an AR guiding system on HHD to guide visitors to walk through the Baoan Temple. The prototype uses marker recognition for showing a virtual object. The visitor first focuses on a mural art piece with the camera. Once the system recognizes the content, more detailed information about the art piece will be triggered and be shown to the visitor. However, the system does not include a navigation function, therefore the visitor must tap on the smartphone screen to operate further visit flows.

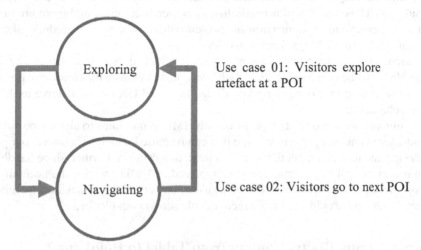

Fig. 2. Visiting pattern of a general museum visit.

Hammady et al. [8] introduced a system loop in the prototype for their museum guidance system "Museum Eye" to test and evaluate the design integrity. The prototype works with a HoloLens and it consists of three stations and other nine stops in the tour. Once the visitor triggers one station, a scene will be generated and mapped on top of the physical environment. Visitors will explore different scenarios without a predefined specific order, so that they receive an authority to control and jump from one scene to another.

Unlike the above, Litvak [3] proposed a guiding system for smart glasses based on location-dependent interactions. Once the user arrives at one POI, related information will be triggered and shown to the user. The system includes both a wearable and a handheld device. The user will follow AR navigation marks (e.g. arrows) popping up in the view to find the way between POIs. When the user arrives at a POI spot, an audio alert will be triggered on arrival. Further, additional information regarding each POI will be presented to the user.

For many "real" cases found in app stores for specific museums that are designed for smartphones, QR markers or similar signs are positioned in the physical environment. Users have then the task to find and move towards the sign, as well as point their camera at it, to access further information. Since we can expect a broader user community to easily get familiar with this pattern, it is often repeated. However, not only technical functioning and interaction patterns affect the visiting experience, as the thematic background of exhibitions and use cases from storylines may also influence the expectations of visitors.

There are only a few experimental projects yet on usable/end-user tested HMD guided tour or museum applications, although some of the very first seminal research endeavors in AR combined HMD and cultural heritage, such as Touring Machine [23] and Archeoguide [24]. However, because of their feature for hands-free interaction, in the following HMD have preferably been developed towards professional industrial applications, mainly in the fields of maintenance or assembly. Currently, the penetration of consumer markets with smartphones and tablets is another reason to use these in museums, which is a matter of accessibility. However, users more and more are fascinated by the experience of immersion and presence that new hardware products like the Microsoft HoloLens or Magic Leap can offer.

Brancati et al. [25] performed a usability study with end-users in a Naples city tour with an HMD, while Hammady et al. [8], who designed a tour with the HoloLens, pointed out that the current lack of existing knowledge in spatial UX made effective usability design a challenge.

In summary, there are too few projects with HMD in museums to already be able to see end-user interaction patterns emerge that can be reused widely. Therefore, our goal is to design and research potential suitable interaction patterns. Further, since handheld AR in museums will most certainly not be replaced by HMDs, we see the necessity to develop guided tour content only once and use it on both kinds of devices. Resulting interaction patterns would need to be reconcilable across both platforms.

4   Transferring Digital Content from Tablet to HoloLens 2

As a start, in order to explore the applicability of existing content designed for tablets and smartphones towards experiencing it on the HoloLens 2, we use a showcase built within the project "Spirit" [11]. The goal of this showcase was once described to achieve a feeling of "presence" [26] at a historical place, in this case a Roman Fort. However, the requirement was to use HHD target platforms (tablets) that were available off-the-shelf in 2016. The AR app placed re-enacted historical scenes of Roman village inhabitants between the mural remains that are still visible.

Although the HoloLens hardware is not optimized to be used in outdoor scenarios, we want to transfer this project to this HMD because of several reasons. First, we estimate a greater experience of "presence" for the encounter with the ghost-like impressions of the "spirits", and want to explore the chances and limitations of placing video characters into the real environment. Further, we estimate that future HMD may have enhanced features (e.g., GPS) and we use this experiment as a step into the future. Finally, we already have access to all the content and authoring elements of this previous project. The scenario is complete in the sense of providing a guided tour and providing suitable content (both general museum use cases of Navigation and Exploration), which allows us to experiment with all the necessary situations for users and explore limitations.

4.1   Example: Interaction Pattern in the Spirit Project

The showcase application from the "Spirit" project was designed to follow a metaphor of "magic equipment" in that interaction design and interactive narrative design were strongly intertwined [27]. The user had to track down the "spirits" of people that once lived by the Roman Fort, represented by filmed actors in historical costumes. While a fictional story built the backbone of the whole interaction, also factual knowledge in form of readable text should be made accessible. The user metaphorically had to find places that the main character of the story, Aurelia, remembered. In the meta-dialogue with Aurelia, she showed blurry memory outlines of buildings that the user had to go to in the following (called "stencils"). That way, several locations could be visited. The app used GPS and image recognition to trigger parts of the story, once the user has found the right position at the "next" location. Additionally, at each position, the user was urged to look around and experience the real environment, such as meaningful geographic directions or relationships to other places around. Using the gyro sensor of the tablet, the device tracked the user's turning movement and thus triggered more "spirits" appearances to the left and to the right, which in total resulted in a pseudo 3-dimensional stage around the user. Because of the intended impression of "presence" of historical figures in the real environment, we assume that using a head-mounted device such as the HoloLens 2 would increase that feeling.

Figure 3 and Fig. 4 show example scenes of the Spirit application. While the app follows the main general visiting pattern explained in Sect. 3.3, it is structured into three modes. Only one of these provides the actual AR experience of an encounter with spirits. Apart from the navigation mode "Search", there is also non-AR content displaying facts as readable text (mode "Read"). Thus, the Spirit concept separates re-enacted, partially fictional historical drama, which is the main AR content, from explanatory text that can be more conveniently read based on the users' demand.

Figure 3 illustrates the three modes in the project "Spirit":

1. Search (Fig. 3, left and middle)
2. Encounter (Fig. 4)
3. Read (Fig. 3, right)

Fig. 3. Spirit example showcase. Left and middle: "Search" mode with map and stencil ("memory image"). Right: "Read/Touch" mode to be used at the user's convenience in between (non-AR content) [11].

4.2 Options for Transferring the Interaction Pattern from HHD to HMD

As mentioned in Sect. 2.1, to create a meaningful metaphor for an interaction pattern, it is necessary to evaluate both interaction styles and technical solutions in the Spirit

Fig. 4. Spirit example showcase. "Encounter" mode: One location with different characters to the left, front and right. GPS plus image markers trigger the first video of a scene. Users need to pan the tablet (turn around 90 degrees) between dialogue pieces to experience the whole scene. The gyro sensor triggers and starts further videos [11].

Table 2. Interaction styles and technical solutions in the Spirit project

Interaction styles	1. Touching on the screen to operate the application 2. Turning the tablet to left and right to trigger further hidden digital information
Technical solutions	1. GPS units for tracking real time location coordinates 2. Marker recognition for triggering digital information 3. Gyro sensor for triggering further digital information at the same location

application to analyze the possibility of transferring its interaction patterns from the tablet to a HoloLens 2 (see Table 2).

The Spirit concept involves several interaction styles and specific technical solutions of a HHD for its interaction patterns, which are not easily transferred to a Hololens. In the "Search" mode, it uses GPS for map navigation feedback as users know it from usual navigation tasks with a handheld. The second mode "Encounter" employs image recognition and events from the Gyro sensor to trigger film scenes with virtual characters surrounding the user (see Fig. 5). In the third mode "Read", the application runs by a familiar touch interaction to scroll text and operate a menu. Users hold the tablet horizontally, while they can also make a short break and sit down for reading.

The HoloLens provides different interaction styles compared to a tablet, although there are at least overlaps in the hardware configuration (see Fig. 1). Therefore, it is partly impossible or unsuitable to transfer the complete designed interaction pattern from the tablet to the HoloLens 2. For example, in the Read mode, it is technically possible to transfer the facts text from the tablet to the HoloLens, but not resulting in a familiar or convenient reading experience.

Further, the HoloLens has no built-in GPS, which means, the "Searching on the map" interaction pattern must be skipped or redesigned to adapt to other technical solutions. Instead of GPS navigation, the HoloLens uses SLAM technology to track the nearby environment consistently. This is acknowledged to work well for indoor activities, but

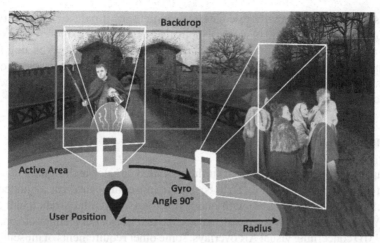

Fig. 5. Spirit triggers for the Encounter mode on the tablet (GPS, backdrop marker recognition, gyro sensor). [28]

only with limitations for outdoors, especially in unstructured environments without walls and for far distances. For the "Encounter" mode that needs recognition of a "backdrop" for a scene and changes in the users gaze direction, the HoloLens is also equipped with a RGBD-camera and gyroscope to support almost the same metaphors as on the tablet. Panning with the tablet to the left and right can be transformed so that users just turn their heads. However, if this is combined with triggering the starting videos, it feels unnatural and may cause physical inconvenience due to the repetition. It is also questionable whether this action is as intuitive as pointing a camera device explicitly into a certain direction for scanning. Currently, the implementation is ongoing work, while we also explore the limitations of so-called natural interfaces [12].

This study aimed at exploring the possibility of transferring interaction patterns from HHD to HMD. After analyzing the specific interaction patterns used within the Spirit project, we see the potential of implementing the same metaphor on the HoloLens in principle. It may save time and money to adopt existing video data from the tablet platform. However, the HoloLens offers more options, as it could offer an even stronger presence experience in that virtual characters could be shown in 3D. Visitors could be able to experience more immersive scenes with spirits, for example viewing a ghost who accompanies them flying through the building while communicating with the users. In contrast, in the Spirit project, all characters were realized as pre-recorded videos, as this was sufficient for the target platform, a 2D screen. The existing 2D videos could still be placed in the 3D environment at a decent distance to the viewer to have a similar "ghost" experience as in the Spirit project. However, one disappointing effect could be that visitors will think of it as "Fake" experiences, as there is no stereo effect and there is greater awareness of the two-dimensionality.

Therefore, in order to optimize the usability and user experience, based on interaction styles and the technical solutions of the HoloLens, novel interaction patterns should be designed when transferring the general concept from the tablet to HoloLens. This would also lead to the necessity to create new content, as it reduces reusability. New interaction patterns making use of gestural input need to be further explored, for example, "waving arms" or "snapping fingers" could remind at a wizard who is casting a spell. Further, because the HoloLens performs poorly for outdoor activities, conceiving outdoor use cases could be limited to a confined radius. Thus, the entire concept of the Spirit application would have to be adapted for optimum fit with the HoloLens.

5 Conclusion

In this paper, we lay the ground for our further research targeted at designing interaction patterns for HMDs like the HoloLens to be used in museum contexts or in guided tours, and which need to be compatible with interactions possible with current handheld AR devices. While we expect that users will experience much stronger feelings of "presence" with an HMD concerning visual AR overlays, some other requirements of museum tours, such as acquiring plain text information and map navigation, may need to be adjusted in specially designed interfaces.

While related work often focuses on solving mainly still challenging technical issues of AR, and there are too few HMD related projects with the focus on meaningful interaction patterns in the cultural heritage context, the state of the art is not ready yet to illustrate efficient interaction patterns for both HHD and HMD. However, from analyzing interaction styles and technical solutions of HHD and HMD, we conclude that although it is possible to transfer the interactive AR content from HHD to HMD, the interaction style of HMD like the HoloLens offers different input methods such as air tapping or air scrolling to manipulate the digital content. It is necessary to redesign new interaction patterns for HMD like HoloLens 2. For cultural heritage content, because of the lacking GPS sensor on HoloLens 2, outdoor-based use cases may not fit the HoloLens 2 well, or, this may require developers and designers to find other technical solutions such as using marker recognition for outdoor tracking.

In the future, museums and exhibitions may be visited with different devices at the same time. Therefore, future work is needed on reconciling the different worlds of HHD and HMD to design one content for several possible devices.

Acknowledgments. This work has been funded (in part) by the German Federal Ministry of Education and Research (BMBF), funding program Forschung an Fachhochschulen, contract number 13FH181PX8.

References

1. Itzstein, S., Thomas, B., Smith, R.: Augmented reality entertainment: taking gaming out of the box. In: Lee, N. (ed.) Encyclopaedia of Computer Graphics and Games. Springer, Heidelberg (2017). https://doi.org/10.1007/978-3-319-08234-9_81-1
2. Zhang, Y., Kwok, T.: Design and interaction interface using augmented reality for smart manufacturing. Procedia Manuf. **26**, 1278–1286 (2018)

3. Litvak, E., Kuflik, T.: Enhancing cultural heritage outdoor experience with augmented-reality smart glasses. Pers. Ubiquit. Comput. **24**(6), 873–886 (2020). https://doi.org/10.1007/s00779-020-01366-7
4. Baltzer, M.C.A., López, D., Flemisch, F.: Towards an interaction pattern language for human machine cooperation and cooperative movement. Cogn. Technol. Work **21**(4), 593–606 (2019). https://doi.org/10.1007/s10111-019-00561-8
5. Fogli, D., Parasiliti Provenza, L., Bernareggi, C.: A universal design resource for rich Internet applications based on design patterns. Univ. Access Inf. Soc. **13**(2), 205–226 (2013). https://doi.org/10.1007/s10209-013-0291-6
6. Yuan, S.-T., Hsu, S.-T.: Enhancing service system design: an entity interaction pattern approach. Inf. Syst. Front. **19**(3), 481–507 (2015). https://doi.org/10.1007/s10796-015-9604-z
7. Bekele, M., Pierdicca, R., Frontoni, E., Malinverni, E., Gain, J.: A survey of augmented, virtual, and mixed reality for cultural heritage. ACM, J. Comput. Cultural Heritage (2018)
8. Hammady, R., Ma, M., Strathern, C., Mohamad, M.: Design and development of a spatial mixed reality touring guide to the Egyptian museum. Multimedia Tools Appl. **79**(5–6), 3465–3494 (2019). https://doi.org/10.1007/s11042-019-08026-w
9. Dixon, S.: Nomad project webpage. https://sophie-dixon.com/project/nomad. Accessed 11 Dec 2020
10. Woodbridge, P.: Immersive Storytelling Experiences, Research Symposium, https://www.curiousmagic.co.uk/immersive-storytelling-experiences. Accessed 11 Dec 2020
11. Spierling, U., Winzer, P., Massarczyk, E.: Experiencing the presence of historical stories with location-based augmented reality. In: Nunes, N., Oakley, I., Nisi, V. (eds.) ICIDS 2017. LNCS, vol. 10690, pp. 49–62. Springer, Cham (2017). https://doi.org/10.1007/978-3-319-71027-3_5
12. Norman, D.A.: Natural User Interfaces Are Not Natural. Northwestern University, KAIST Industrial Design, Nielsen Norman Group (2010)
13. Alexander, C.: The Timeless Way of Building. Oxford University Press (1979)
14. Hey, J., Linsey, J., Agogino, A.M., Wood, K.L.: Analogies and metaphors in creative design. Int. J. Eng. Educ. **24**(2), 283–294 (2008)
15. Constantine, L.L., Lockwood, L.A.: Structure and Style in Use Cases for User Interface Design. Object-Modeling and User Interface Design: Designing Interactive Systems, pp. 245–279. Addison-Wesley (2001)
16. Rumbaugh, J., Jacobson, I., Booch, G.: The Unified Modeling Language Reference Manual. Chapter 5: Use Case View, pp. 63–64. Addison Wesley (1999)
17. Microsoft Design Guideline. https://docs.microsoft.com/en-us/windows/mixed-reality/interaction-fundamentals. Accessed 11 Dec 2020
18. Liarokapis, F.: An augmented reality interface for visualizing and interacting with virtual content. Virtual Reality **11**, 23–43 (2007)
19. Müller, M., Brunotte, J.: Augmented Reality im Museum. Culture To Go Agency Blogpost (in German). https://culture-to-go.com/mediathek/augmented-reality-im-museum. Accessed 11 Dec 2020
20. Priadana, A., Habibi, M.: Face detection using Haar cascades to filter selfie face image on Instagram. In: Proceedings of International Conference of Artificial Intelligence and Information Technology (ICAIIT), pp. 6–9. IEEE (2019)
21. Stumpp, S., Knopf, T., Michelis, D.: User experience design with augmented reality (AR). In: Proceedings of the ECIE 2019 14th European Conference on Innovation and Entrepreneurship (2019)
22. Chiu, C., Wei, W., Lee, L., Lu, J.: Augmented reality system for tourism using image-based recognition. Microsystem Technol. (2019)

23. Feiner, S., MacIntyre, B., Höllerer, T., Webster, A.: A touring machine: prototyping 3D mobile augmented reality systems for exploring the urban environment. In: Proceedings of the First International Symposium on Wearable Computers (ISWC 97), pp. 74–81. Cambridge, Massachusetts, USA (1997)

24. Vlahakis, V., et al.: Archeoguide: first results of an augmented reality mobile computing system in cultural heritage sites. In: Proceedings of International Symposium on Virtual Reality, Archaeology and Cultural Heritage, VAST 2001, pp. 131–139. Glyfada, Greece (2001)

25. Brancati, N., Caggianese, G., Pietro, G., Frucci, M., Gallo, L., Neroni, P.: Usability Evaluation of a wearable augmented reality system for the enjoyment of the cultural heritage. In: Proceedings of 11th International Conference on Signal-Image Technology & Internet-Based Systems (SITIS). IEEE (2015)

26. MacIntyre, B., Bolter, J., Gandy, M.: Presence and the aura of meaningful places. Presence: Teleoperators Virtual Environ. **6**(2), 197–206 (2004)

27. Spierling, U., Kampa, A., Stöbener, K.: Magic equipment: integrating digital narrative and interaction design in an augmented reality quest. In: Proceedings of International Conference on Culture & Computer Science ICCCS 2016, pp. 56–61. Windhoek, Namibia (2016)

28. Spierling, U., Kampa, A.: An extensible system and its design constraints for location-based serious games with augmented reality. In: Alcañiz, M. et al. (eds.) Serious Games, Proceedings, JCSG 2017. LNCS, vol. 10622, pp. 60–72. Springer, Cham (2017)

Design and Analysis of a Virtual Reality Game to Address Issues in Introductory Programming Learning

Chyanna Wee(✉) ⓘ and Kian Meng Yap ⓘ

Sunway University, 47500 Subang Jaya, Selangor, Malaysia
15060197@imail.sunway.edu.my, kmyap@sunway.edu.my

Abstract. The field of computer science has not shied away from employing game-based learning and virtual reality techniques for computer programming education. While a plethora of game-based, virtual reality or combinations of both solutions exist, most are developed as an alternative to traditional lessons where students focus on learning programming concepts or languages. However, these solutions do not cater to problems students face when learning programming that is mainly caused by the abstract nature of programming, misconceptions of programming concepts and lack of learning motivation. Hence, in this paper, a framework to address the abstract nature of programming, common programming misconceptions and motivational issues is developed. The framework consists of three modules that correspond to each issue powered by a simulation engine. To address the abstract nature of programming, programming concepts will be represented with concrete objects in the virtual environment. Furthermore, to address common programming misconceptions, simulation techniques such as interactions and player perspective will be utilised. Lastly, motivational game elements will be employed into the simulation to engage students when learning through the system. Results gathered from questionnaires indicated that users were generally satisfied with the virtual experience developed from the framework.

Keywords: Computer science education · Educational games · Virtual reality

1 Introduction

By the year 2024, it is predicted that the availability of computing-related jobs would increase by twelve-point five percent [1]. This fact is also reflected in the enrolment rates for computing-based courses where student admissions have increased by seven percent from the year 2017 to 2019 [2]. However, recent reports show that the dropout rates for computing courses is at nine-point eight percent which is the highest between other Science, Technology, Engineering and Mathematics (STEM) based courses [3].

This is an issue that has concerned many researchers and has sparked and initiated various studies to determine reasons for the high non-continuation rates. The reasons commonly attributed to student dropouts have ranged from substandard teaching,

N. Shaghaghi et al. (Eds.): INTETAIN 2020, LNICST 377, pp. 243–254, 2021.
https://doi.org/10.1007/978-3-030-76426-5_16

negative experiences and low sense of belonging [4]. Furthermore, students who have un-realistic expectations prior to joining a computing course can also contribute to the decrease in retention rates because often, they fail to fulfil these expectations [5]. Consequently, researchers like Tan, Ting and Ling [6] and Medeiros [7] have taken a different approach and went on to investigate dropout factors from a learning perspective instead. More specifically, these studies analysed issues that students face when learning computer programming. Some of the main issues include the lack of learning motivation, the abstract nature of computer programming concepts and misconceptions of programming concepts.

Due to the use of high-level programming languages that are designed to provide a certain degree of abstraction from the details of the computer to the user, students often find it difficult to understand programming concepts. Particularly, students find it hard to relate programming concepts to real-life and how learning these concepts can solve real world problems [8]. Due to this, students may feel unmotivated to continue and participate in programming lessons. Moreover, students are also more prone to developing misconceptions if they do not fully understand the programming concepts introduced to them. This in turn, can cause unwarranted syntax errors when students attempt to develop a program which further decreases motivation and ultimately leads to student dropouts [9].

Over the years, researchers have come up with different solutions to make computer programming lessons more engaging. For instance, the Game-Based Learning (GBL) technique is commonly utilised where games are incorporated into the learning process. This makes for a highly engaging way to encourage learning and has been proven to lead to knowledge acquisition [10]. Other than that, virtual reality (VR) simulations are also prominent for developing immersive lessons for the whole classroom. More recently, researchers have also employed both techniques to develop solutions that maximise the advantages of both GBL and VR.

However, existing GBL and VR applications are mainly focused on introducing programming concepts and programming syntax. While this is good for students to acquire the "gist" of programming, it does not help students understand how abstract concepts like variables, lists and arrays works. Particularly, how these data structures are stored and accessed in the computer memory. To further aid in the understanding of abstract data structures, visualization and analogies are also necessary. This is important to offload cognitive loads to better incorporate programming concepts into the mental models of students [11]. Other than that, existing applications also do not address common misconceptions to students. This is important as unaddressed misconceptions may lead to problems as the student progresses through the course. Hence, this paper aims to reduce the abstractness of programming concepts and address misconceptions in a motivational and engaging manner.

2   Related Works

This section aims to highlight past works that are closely related to the system. More specifically, applications that employ both GBL and VR will be reviewed. Along with this, research gaps will be identified.

2.1 Virtual Reality and Game-Based Learning

Related works presented in this section will feature VR applications developed to aid in learning computer programming that incorporates game elements. In this context, game elements refer to objectives that are presented to users. This can range from making users complete challenges such as getting from one point to another for the sake of progressing through the experience.

For instance, Vincur et al. [12] developed a VR experience called "Cubely". Cubely employs block-based programming in hopes to make learning programming seem more approachable to new learners. The system features interactable cube blocks that can be used to build small programs. These blocks are labelled with typical programming statements such as for, if and else. The programs built with these blocks will then act as commands to control an animated character in overcoming various challenges. To test the feasibility of the system, a total of nineteen participants were recruited. The system garnered positive feedback in terms of user friendliness and its immersive quality compared to online code camps.

To aid in the learning of Object Oriented Programming (OOP) concepts, Bouali et al. [13] developed a VR game known as "Imikode". The basis of the system is to allow users to program and observe how a specific set of code affects the virtual world. The system allows learners to visualize concepts such as object instantiation, method calls and get/set commands in the virtual environment. For instance, a fox appears in the virtual environment when an object instantiation of a fox is made. The system also features a character that issues out challenges and helps users throughout the experience. As of now, there are no tests done yet to determine the feasibility of the system.

Similarly, Chen et al. [14] also developed a system that employed VR and GBL techniques to help students learn programming. Essentially, the system encourages programming learning in two ways. Firstly, the system allows users to utilize code in creating obstacles for game levels in the virtual environment. Secondly, users can also progress through the game by completing programming-based tasks. This means that users that are tasked with the role of the level designer will first employ "enemy robots" in the virtual scene with commands that bares similarity to the Java programming language. Users who then go through the experience must progress through the game by acquiring hints and answering programming questions while overcoming obstructions that is set up by the level designer. To determine the feasibility of the system, the authors organized a bootcamp where the application is showcased. Results showed that out of fifty-three participants of age nine to thirteen, fifty-two participants found that the system was engaging and promoted learning effectiveness.

Segura et al. [15] also utilized block-based programming in developing a VR game called "VR-OCKS". The game requires users to complete puzzles by controlling an ingame character. Users progress through the game by building programs that acts as commands to get from one point to another while avoiding obstacles. The commands are built with action blocks that represents basic programming concepts and such as for loops, while loops and conditional statements. There are also blocks that represents simple actions such as turn and move forward. Essentially, users place and combine various blocks in the virtual environment to control the character. This allows users to witness how the program that they have built works, fostering programming skills. To test the feasibility of the system, a total of forty participants were recruited. The participants are then broken up where twenty of them have used the system while the other twenty acted as the control group. Each group were then further divided to try out the "Kodu" and "Blockly" block-based programming applications. The results from the experiment showed that those who had experience with VR-OCKS completed twenty five percent more levels than those who didn't.

2.2 Research Gaps

There are three apparent research gaps that can be determined from literature reviewed in the previous section. Firstly, all existing VR applications employing GBL are mainly focused on introducing programming concepts with a heavy emphasis on syntax. This means that there is a paucity of solutions when it comes to addressing common issues faced by students when learning introductory programming. As established, the abstract nature of programming can make understanding concepts a gruelling task if one is unable to form correct mental models. This can cause further issues such as misconceptions and loss of learning motivation. Hence, a solution that addresses these issues are necessary to enhance understanding of programming concepts beyond just learning the syntax of a particular language.

3 Methodology

In order to reduce the abstractness of programming concepts and address misconceptions related to programming in an engaging manner, we propose a virtual reality game. The system mainly consists of three modules that is built with Unity 3D for the Oculus Rift. Figure 1 shows a general framework of the system which consists of the abstract module followed by the misconception module and the motivational module. Sects. 3.2 to 3.3 explains each module in better detail. However, considerations and reasons for developing the system in a certain way is first discussed in Sect. 3.1.

3.1 System Considerations

Like any other system, some choices are made during the development process. These ranges from the type of interactions to employ, the medium of instruction and the simulation perspective. Figure 2 shows these in more detail. Firstly, there are predominantly two type of interactions present in virtual reality simulations. Some systems employ direct interactions with natural hand gestures such as grabbing and pointing while others only allow indirect interaction through a user interface. Secondly, systems developed for use in computing education can deliver interactive lessons with either a text-based or block-based medium. The default medium for teaching programming is text-based. The most popular system that employs block-based programming is Scratch where users build small programs with command blocks. Thirdly, virtual simulations can be developed in the first perspective where the user control themselves and the third perspective where the user controls another character.

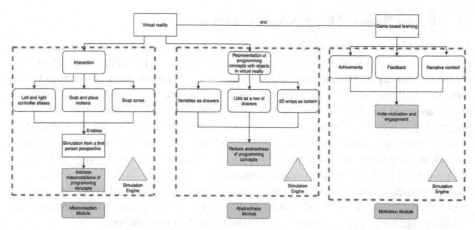

Fig. 1. Framework of proposed methodology.

According to Norris et al. [16], direct interactions with the environment can improve knowledge acquisition. Consequently, Nederveen et al. [17] acknowledged that learning through a first-person perspective can also improve knowledge acquisition. Hence, to improve knowledge acquisition the system will employ direct interactions and will be developed in the first-person perspective. To avoid the need to re-learn syntax, all tasks presented to the user will be delivered with the text-based medium of instruction.

The system is developed with Unity 3D for the Oculus Rift. Frameworks such as the Oculus Integration Package and the Virtual Reality Toolkit (VRTK) are used to implement elements such as teleportation (locomotion), hand presence, interaction and audio. Both frameworks provide useful scripts that speeds up the development process.

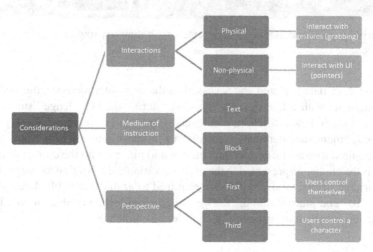

Fig. 2. System considerations.

3.2 Abstract Nature of Programming Concepts

As seen in Figure 1, concepts such as variables, lists and arrays are represented in the virtual environment with real-life objects to aid in the understanding of abstract programming concepts. To determine suitable objects that can be used to represent each concept, attributes such as the ability to label (to mirror how variable, list and array names are used to "label" associated data) and store items (to mirror how values are assigned to a variable, list and array) are taken into consideration. While objects like buckets, envelopes and honeycombs are considered, drawers and lockers are picked instead because it is more conventional to label and store objects in drawers and lockers as opposed to buckets, envelopes and honeycombs. Figure 3 shows how the concepts are represented in the virtual environment where variables, lists and 2D arrays are represented with drawers, a row of drawers and lockers consecutively. This allow students to form concrete analogies to better understand the abstract concepts.

Fig. 3. Variables, lists and 2D arrays represented with drawers, row of drawers and lockers respectively.

To show how data is stored and accessed in the computer memory, the system first presents students with a line of code. This will act as the "challenge" students must complete to unlock new challenges and levels. Particularly, students will be presented with an assignment statement which consists of a data structure and a value. Students are then required to grab the correct data blocks and place it into the correct drawer. For example, if the challenge presented to the user is a variable declaration to assign the value 10 to a variable named total, students are required to grab the data block labelled with the value "10" and place it into the drawer labelled with the variable "total". Figure 4 shows the actions taken to successfully complete a challenge.

3.3 Misconceptions of Programming Concepts

As seen in Figure 1, the ability to interact with objects in the virtual environment in the first-person perspective largely enables the misconception module to address common

Fig. 4. Steps taken to complete a challenge: (1) Assignment statement presented as the "challenge", (2) Data blocks represent values, (3) Drawer representing the variable with purple snap zones that act as visual aids. (Color figure online)

misconceptions. Firstly, to allow students to feel a real sense of presence, left and right-hand aliases that resemble real-life hands are employed into the system. With the use of the default Oculus Rift touch controllers, natural hand gestures in the virtual environment such as grabbing and placing objects are possible. Consequently, snap zones provide visual interaction cues to further facilitate interaction. This enables students to efficiently carry out the tasks presented to them.

For the case of addressing programming misconceptions, the necessary actions taken to complete the challenge is similar to the one described in the previous section. However, instead of just placing data blocks into corresponding drawers or lockers, students must first identify whether the code presented to them possess any syntax errors. If so, students must identify the mistake and place the corresponding "error message" block onto the output station. For example, if the code presented to the user is 5 = count, students must grab the error message block labelled with "wrong assignment" and place it onto the output station (Fig. 5). Since this is a first-person simulation, students who initially could not identify why the code given is incorrect would eventually realise their mistake. For instance, if the student attempts to place the data block labelled with "count" into a drawer labelled with 5, the system simply does not allow this to happen. Consequently, by enforcing the action of placing the data block into the drawer, students can more easily comprehend why the structure of an assignment statement is declared a certain way.

Fig. 5. Misconception example: (1) Code presented to user is syntactically incorrect, (2) Error message blocks, (3) Output station where error message blocks are placed.

3.4 Motivation

As seen in Fig. 1, game elements such as a narrative context, instantaneous feedback and achievements are employed into the system to incite motivation. Firstly, a narrative context is introduced to students before they embark on any challenges in the tutorial scene. Students will be informed that they are currently in the computer's memory where data is stored. Then students would be told that their job is to act as the computer's "assistant" to manage incoming code that is entered by a user. Particularly, students are required to manage how data is stored and accessed in the computer's memory. This gives student's a sense of purpose, making it easier for students to participate in the simulation.

Secondly, instantaneous feedback is present in the system in the form of audio cues. Quite simply, the actions taken by the student is guided through both positive and negative audio ques. While the negative audio cues are used to indicate mistakes made, positive cues are employed to provide a confidence boost which can increase motivation to finish off tasks presented by the system.

Lastly, the system also features an achievement system that rewards students with virtual "trophies" after successful completion of challenges for a particular concept (Fig. 6). This acts as an indication of progress, as well as to foster user engagement.

Fig. 6. Trophies that can be earned during the course of the simulation.

4 System Evaluation

The system was evaluated with the aid of 13 participants between ages 17 to 20, of which 11 were female and 2 were male. 6 of the participants have had taken general computer science courses and were quite knowledgeable in some programming concepts albeit having no actual programming experience. On the other hand, 7 of the participants have never taken any computing-based courses. Hence, they were first briefed on some of the concepts that will be introduced in the virtual experience such as variables, lists and 2D arrays.

The participants were then asked to complete a series of tasks in the virtual environment with the Oculus Rift device equipped with a workstation that is rigged with a NVIDIA GeForce GTX 1080 GPU. After completing all the tasks, questionnaires were given out to assess and evaluate the system. The questionnaire mainly consists of questions that aims to judge user satisfaction and perceived outcomes of the developed system. Table 1 and Table 2 shows a summary of responses gathered from participants that were based on the Likert Scale.

Table 1. Summary of responses from satisfaction survey.

	1 (Strongly dissatisfied)	2 (Dissatisfied)	3 (Neutral)	4 (Satisfied)	5 (Strongly satisfied)	Mean
Representation of variables as drawers in aiding understanding				8	5	4.38
Representation of lists as a row of drawers in aiding understanding				7	6	4.46
Representation of 2D arrays as lockers in aiding understanding				6	7	4.54
Interactions with virtual objects in aiding misconceptions				4	9	4.69
Presence of audio cues in promoting motivation		1	2	4	6	4.15
Presence of achievements in promoting motivation		1	1	4	7	4.31
Presence of narrative role in promoting motivation			4	9		4.69

Table 2. Summary of responses from perceived outcome survey.

	1 (Strongly disagree)	2 (Disagree)	3 (Neutral)	4 (Agree)	5 (Strongly agree)	Mean
I now feel more motivated when learning programming			3	6	4	4.08
I prefer to have analogies presented to me visually in the virtual environment then spoken about in class verbally			2	3	8	4.46
The simulation is a good supplement to lessons taught in a traditional classroom				3	10	4.77
I prefer learning programming through games			1	3	9	4.62
I prefer learning programming through virtual reality experiences				6	7	4.54
I now feel more confident about my programming skills after the experience		1	3	4	5	4.00

5 Discussion

For analysis of the data gathered from the post survey, the average mean is calculated for every question. As seen in Table 1, participants were generally satisfied with the representation of variables, lists and 2D arrays as concrete objects in accordance to aiding their understanding of the concepts. This is mainly due to the fact that common objects such as drawers and lockers were easier to comprehend and the possibility of interacting with the objects made previously abstract concepts more concrete. Participants were also satisfied with the way common misconceptions were simulated and addressed in the virtual experience. For instance, when presented with a syntactically wrong assignment statement, the nature of the simulation requires that the mistake is identified and corrected. This is done with assigning error message blocks to the output station as seen in Fig. 5. Lastly, while satisfaction scores for the presence of a narrative context, trophies and audio cues in promoting motivation were generally satisfactory, some participants expressed disaffection in terms of not getting celebrative cues such as confetti to make trophy collecting a more joyous experience. In terms of audio cues, some felt that the sounds were not loud enough.

Most participants agree that they feel more motivated to continue learning programming and thought that the simulation was a good complement with traditional classes. While most of the responses were positive, some may still prefer traditional lessons over unconventional mediums such as games. This may largely depend on whether the individual is an auditory or visual learner. Most participants also seem keener to learn with virtual reality experiences with some describing the experience as fun and new. In terms of perceived confidence levels, participants who had never taken any computer-based courses were more reluctant when it comes to feeling more confident after the experience. This may be attributed to a lower sense of belonging since they did not have prior knowledge on these concepts compared to those who have taken computing courses.

6   Conclusion and Future Work

This paper outlined several issues related to learning introductory programming. Firstly, is the need to address the abstractness of programming concepts where a framework is proposed to represent programming concepts as concrete objects in a virtual environment. Secondly, is the need to address misconceptions of programming concepts where a simulation design for misconceptions of programming concepts. Thirdly, is the need to incite intrinsic motivation when learning programming. To handle these issues, a framework that combines the potential of virtual reality and game elements was proposed. According to data gathered from questionnaires, we can conclude that the identified issues were mitigated accordingly.

In the future, further work can be done to complement the system. Particularly, in terms of providing more support for different programming languages. This would allow the system to be used by a wider range of audience so as not limit the learning of multiple programming languages. Furthermore, the current framework can also be used to aid understanding of more complex data structures such as trees or graphs. As for further improvements, the current framework can also be combined with other technologies such as haptics. This would aid in considerations regarding the implementation of haptics technology, particularly for education purposes. Lastly, the framework can also be adapted and revised to explain abstract topics in other domains such as engineering, science and mathematics.

References

1. Fayer, S., Lacey, A., Watson, A.: STEM Occupations: Past, Present, And Future. U.S. Bu-reau of Labor Statistics (2017)
2. Higher Education Student Statistics: UK, 2018/19 - Subjects studied, UK (2020)
3. Non-continuation: UK Performance Indicators 2018/19. Higher Education Student Statistics, UK (2020)
4. Giannakos, M.N., Aalberg, T., Divitini, M., Jaccheri, L., Mikalef, P., Pappas, I.O., Sindre, G.: Identifying dropout factors in information technology education: A case study. In: 2017 IEEE Global Engineering Education Conference (EDUCON). pp. 1187–1194. IEEE, Athens, Greece (2017). https://doi.org/10.1109/EDUCON.2017.7942999
5. Pappas, I.O., Giannakos, M.N., Jaccheri, L.: Investigating factors influencing students' intention to dropout computer science studies. In: Proceedings of the 2016 ACM Conference on Innovation and Technology in Computer Science Education - ITiCSE '16. pp. 198–203. ACM Press, Arequipa, Peru (2016). https://doi.org/10.1145/2899415.2899455
6. Tan, P.-H., Ting, C.-Y., Ling, S.-W.: Learning difficulties in programming courses: under-graduates' perspective and perception. In: 2009 International Conference on Computer Technology and Development. pp. 42–46. IEEE, Kota Kinabalu, Malaysia (2009). https://doi.org/10.1109/ICCTD.2009.188
7. Medeiros, R.P., Ramalho, G.L., Falcao, T.P.: A systematic literature review on teaching and learning introductory programming in higher education. IEEE Trans. Educ. 62, 77–90 (2019). https://doi.org/10.1109/TE.2018.2864133
8. Dasuki, S., Quaye, A.: Undergraduate students' failure in programming courses in institutions of higher education in developing countries a Nigerian perspective. Electron. J. Inf. Syst. Dev. Countries 76, 1–18 (2016). https://doi.org/10.1002/j.1681-4835.2016.tb00559.x
9. Kohn, T.: The error behind the message: finding the cause of error messages in Python. In: Proceedings of the 50th ACM Technical Symposium on Computer Science Education - SIGCSE '19, pp. 524–530. ACM Press, Minneapolis (2019). https://doi.org/10.1145/3287324.3287381
10. Perron, B., Schröter, F. (eds.): Video Games and the Mind: Essays on Cognition, Affect and Emotion McFarland & Company Inc. Publishers, Jefferson (2016)
11. Pears, A., et al.: A survey of literature on the teaching of introductory programming. SIGCSE Bull. 39, 204 (2007). https://doi.org/10.1145/1345375.1345441
12. Vincur, J., Konopka, M., Tvarozek, J., Hoang, M., Navrat, P.: Cubely: virtual reality block-based programming environment, pp. 1–2. Association for Computing Machinery (2017)
13. Bouali, N., Nygren, E., Oyelere, S.S., Suhonen, J., Cavalli-Sforza, V.: Imikode: A VR game to introduce OOP concepts. In: Proceedings of the 19th Koli Calling International Conference on Computing Education Research - Koli Calling '19, pp. 1–2. ACM Press, Koli (2019). https://doi.org/10.1145/3364510.3366149
14. Chen, J., Zargham, M.R., Rajendren, M., Cheng, J.: Coding VR games. In: Int'l Conf. Frontiers in Education: CS and CE, pp. 123–127 (2019)
15. Segura, R.J., Pino, F.J., Ogáyar, C.J., Rueda, A.J.: VR- OCKS: a virtual reality game for learning the basic concepts of programming. Comput. Appl. Eng. Educ. 28, 31–41 (2020). https://doi.org/10.1002/cae.22172
16. Norris, E., Shelton, N., Dunsmuir, S., Duke-Williams, O., Stamatakis, E.: Virtual field trips as physically active lessons for children a pilot study. BMC Public Health 15, 366 (2015). https://doi.org/10.1186/s12889-015-1706-5
17. Nederveen, J.P., Thomas, A.C.Q., Parise, G.: Examining the first-person perspective as appropriate prelaboratory preparation. Adv. Physiol. Educ. 43, 317–323 (2019). https://doi.org/10.1152/advan.00213.2018

Low-Complexity Workflow for Digitizing Real-World Structures for Use in VR-Based Personnel Training

Mason Smith[✉], Andre Thomas, Kerrigan Gibbs, and Christopher Morrison

Learning Interactive Visualization Experience (LIVE) Lab, Texas A&M University,
College Station, TX 77843, USA
{masonsmith,cmorr}@tamu.edu, manink@arch.tamu.edu,
klg2799@email.tamu.edu

Abstract. Since the advent of virtual reality (VR), there has existed a need for digital assets to populate virtual environments. Virtual training scenarios have risen in popularity in recent years, increasing the need for digital environments resembling real-world structures. However, established techniques for digitizing real-world structures as VR-ready 3D assets are often expensive, complicated to implement, and offer little to no customization/ To address these problems, a "low-complexity" digitization workflow adapted from existing research and based on procedural modeling is proposed. Procedural modeling allows for non-destructive customization and control over the digital asset throughout the front end of the digitization workflow. A real-world VR training project using this workflow is outlined, demonstrating its advantages over other established digitization techniques.

Keywords: Virtual reality · Procedural modeling · Digitization

1 Introduction

1.1 Virtual Environments and VR-Based Personnel Training

Virtual Reality (VR) is an immersive human-computer interface by which humans can interact with simulated digital environments [5]. In the last decade, VR has risen in popularity as a training platform for various industries, such as construction, oil and gas, law enforcement, and military [20, 27]. Regardless of industry, VR has become increasingly popular as a solution for job safety training and also highly specialized tasks for workers.

The advantages of conducting personnel training in VR are manifold: Bringing a trainee into VR can be easier than taking them to a physical job site or training area. A virtual environment not grounded in the physical world allows the trainee to make mistakes without bringing harm to job equipment, themselves, or others [13]. The interactive nature of virtual environments makes it possible to iterate through or repeat tasks, instantly resetting equipment with a few lines of code.

© ICST Institute for Computer Sciences, Social Informatics and Telecommunications Engineering 2021
Published by Springer Nature Switzerland AG 2021. All Rights Reserved
N. Shaghaghi et al. (Eds.): INTETAIN 2020, LNICST 377, pp. 255–266, 2021.
https://doi.org/10.1007/978-3-030-76426-5_17

Despite its many advantages, VR training applications are still not widely used in some industries. Existing research suggests that an environment's poor graphical quality may hinder the perceived usefulness of VR training applications [6]. In their critical review, Li et al. [19] cite the detail level of job-related digital assets as a potential barrier for accepting VR-mediated training environments. Inaccuracies may lead to "visual discomfort and incorrect geometry perception" and may discourage the use of VR training in industrial settings according to Segura et al. [25].

These findings show that one of the most significant issues in VR training development is how to create job-related digital assets (buildings, structures, equipment) accurately and efficiently. Digitization is the technique by which real-world objects are represented virtually as objects made up of computer code. Because of the highly-specialized and proprietary equipment often used by individual companies, existing repositories of 3D assets are unlikely to include the needed job-related 3D assets for a given VR-mediated training scenario. Companies often update their equipment as technology advances, compounding the need for customizable job-related 3D assets. Therefore, for the purposes of VR training, digitized assets must be accurately represented, be created quickly, possess a high level of detail, and allow for easy customization. This will allow for training scenarios that can be iterated easily as training needs change and real-world equipment are updated.

There exist several techniques for digitizing real-world objects and structures for VR. However, many of these techniques are expensive, time-consuming, require specialized training, and result in assets that are not easily modified at the model level nor easily compatible with VR.

The overall goal of the proposed methodology is to address the questions of customization and complexity when digitizing real-world objects for VR. We propose a hybrid "low-complexity" workflow for digitizing complex industrial structures using procedural modeling. This method relies on image-based reference rather than expensive point cloud data. Using procedural modeling allows us to recreate 3D assets with a high level of detail. The parametric design of procedural-modeling allows for assets that are easily iterated and modified according to the needs of the training scenario. Ultimately, this method is highly suitable for the modular nature of real-world industrial structures and equipment. We aim to present this workflow as an alternative to current widely-used digitization techniques.

Using procedural modeling as its real-world object digitization technique of choice, this research seeks to answer the following questions: How effectively can procedural modeling be used to digitize complex and large-scale industrial structures for VR training? To what extent does procedural modeling address the challenges present in other existing digitization techniques for VR training?

Real-world object digitization for VR is currently being used in several industries, including construction, engineering, oil and gas, city planning, architecture, archaeology, and education. Digital assets based on real-world objects are used not only for training but for heritage conservation, building information modeling (BIM), urban planning, and ecology. Varying asset digitization techniques for each of these purposes exist with varying results. In the following section, real-world object digitization techniques will be outlined.

2 Real-World Object Digitization Techniques

2.1 Photogrammetry and Laser Scanning

Photogrammetry remains one of the most popular and developed techniques for digitizing real-world objects. Photogrammetry involves acquiring several images of a real-world object from several angles. These flat images are interpreted as 3D views of the object when combined by a specialized software. The more comprehensive the image acquisition, the fewer data gaps there will be in the interpreted 3D model. Via photogrammetry, it is possible to "bake" the surface texture and lighting qualities of the real-world object into the digital object. Laser scanning is a similar technique whereby lasers scan objects or environments creating datasets (dubbed "point clouds") of varying resolutions. The point cloud data set may be interpreted and reconstructed as a 3D mesh, similar to photogrammetry [21]. Both techniques have been used to digitize real-world structures with a high degree of structural and surface detail. For example, scanning electron microscopy was used to create 3D representations of Cu-Zn-Al catalytic pellets. A single 3D mesh was made up of 180,000 facets [14].

Achakir, et al. [1], in their paper describing the digitization of the Hassan mosque, presented three criteria for appraising photogrammetrical digitizations and laser point clouds: completeness, resolution, and accuracy. The pursuit of maximizing these criteria has driven much of the recent innovations in photogrammetry/laser scanning.

Besides acquiring images on foot, researchers have experimented with using unmanned aerial vehicles (UAVs) or aerial drones to improve the completeness and accuracy of the resulting data set. Cappelletti used UAVs to carry out forensic scans of engineering sites, arguing that UAVs can accomplish the task much faster than grounded personnel [5]. Dugdale, et al. [9] applied the drone-based method to scan a forest canopy, taking advantage of the resulting 3D models' baked shadow information to study temperature models. Drones were used to non-invasively identify and digitize whales in a 2019 ecological study [15]. UAVs were also used to make 3D maps of urban areas for the purposes of urban disaster planning [16]. Apart from UAV-based image acquisition, researchers have discovered other novel methods for scanning real-world objects, for example using the Microsoft Hololens [4] as a lower-cost alternative to drones or ground-based robots [17].

Existing research has revealed the many caveats and challenges surrounding photogrammetry and laser point cloud scanning. Photogrammetry and laser scanning are often considered to be high-cost, cumbersome processes that take a lot of processing time [8]. Ahmed et al. [2] found photogrammetry and laser scanning too sensitive and costly for the purposes of their heritage preservation project. They also pointed out that highly specialized technology for photogrammetry and laser scanning constitutes a "black box" that lacks accessibility. For Cappelletti et al.'s forensic engineering research, UAV-based image acquisition was most effective when the UAVs travelled in a circular flight plan around the real-world subject [5]. However, circular flight paths might not always be possible. Furthermore, baked texture and shadow information might lead to an unclear or unreadable image if the weather at the time of scanning creates high-contrast shadows. In the case of Kucharczyk et al.'s pre-disaster mapping project [16], significant gaps in the UAV-acquired source images created distorted and inaccurate 3D models. A 2017 study [28] found that harsh real-world environments (for example environments with high levels of vibration), complicate photogrammetry or laser scanning efforts. In the case of the aforementioned research on digitizing catalytic pellets, the photogrammetric technique was useful for capturing the miniscule detail of the pellet components, but not for real-time virtual environments [14]. Indeed, high-resolution 3D meshes are not optimal for 3D VR/AR applications where maintaining an optimal frame rate is crucial to the user experience.

2.2 Manual 3D Modeling

Another common technique for digitizing real-world objects is to manually create the 3D models using flat images as reference. For this technique, the vertex, edge, and face components of a static 3D mesh are manipulated interactively to re-create the shape of the real-world object in question. This is carried out in an interactive 3D graphics software package such as Adobe 3ds Max or Autodesk Maya. This technique is often utilized when assets' geometry need to be optimized for real-time VR/AR applications. For example, Ahmed et al. [2] modeled heritage site structures in 3ds Max, using thousands of acquired images for reference. Poloprutskya et al. [23] adopted a similar image-based approach. Denker and Ahmet [7] developed a virtual recreation of ancient Palmyra, drawing from reference images, drawings, fine art works, and text descriptions. However, a lack of color photographs and incomplete reference descriptions made specifying texture, color, and light information challenging. Osanlou et al. [22] used 3D modeling software to re-create ancient Chinese ceramic artifacts, using their best judgment to create digital assets that resembled the real-world artifacts. However, this technique does not afford the specificity required to bring highly-detailed objects into the digital realm.

2.3 Hybrid Techniques

To avoid some of these challenges, some researchers have adopted hybrid approaches to real-world object digitization, combining photogrammetry and manual 3D modeling [12]. These approaches include "cleaning up" high-density photogrammetry-based meshes or using photogrammetric meshes alongside manually built ones. A 2017 paper on virtually re-creating the Augusteum of ancient Herculaneum mentioned how researchers produced a more VR-friendly 3D model by using 3D software to reduce a 5-million-face mesh to around 20 thousand faces [11]. Manferdini et al.'s project [21] on reconstructing a defaced Roman statue of Nero used a high-density laser-scanned mesh of the remaining sculpture fragments as a basis for reconstructing the statue's form as it may have once stood. In the case of the long-lost Nero statue, existing images, records, and artifacts were used alongside the scanned point cloud as reference for the final result.

These hybrid techniques combining photogrammetry/laser scanning with manual 3D modeling are not without their challenges. Consider Dylla et al.'s "Rome Reborn 2.0" project [10], an attempt to virtually reconstruct the city of Rome as it existed in antiquity. The Rome Reborn 2.0 team used a hybridized digitization technique which involved photogrammetry/scanning of existing buildings, manual 3D modeling, and procedural/parametric modeling. The team's procedural approach involved parametric modeling grammars which were informed by "the well-described rules of Classical architecture". By adopting a hybrid methodology, they were able to reduce the original Rome Reborn 1.0 environment, made up of about 400 million polygons, to a more manageable 9 million polygons. However, the team discovered that details of the scanned structures (such as windows or doors) came from the baked textures of the scanned meshes and did not exist in the mesh's actual geometry. This led to the scanned structures clashing aesthetically with the manually-modeled and procedurally-generated structures. Indeed, Dore et al. [8] state that any digitization process which includes manual 3D modeling or clean-up of assets remains a time-consuming process.

2.4 Parametric/Procedural Modeling

Parametric modeling is an emergent digitization technique where the configuration of a 3D asset is controlled by intrinsic parameters representing physical properties. VR developers have used pre-built parametric CAD models for virtual industrial training [26] and building information modeling (BIM). Dore, et al. [8] suggested procedural modeling as an alternative for BIM-focused parametric CAD modeling. Procedural modeling is an automatic, highly flexible 3D asset digitization technique wherein the attributes of the asset are directly controllable via code. Procedural modeling applications such as Houdini by SideFX allow the 3D artist to interactively create procedural objects and effects, organizing attribute code into nodes.

Procedural modeling avoids the imprecision of manually modeling assets by hand; procedural assets' attributes may be controlled by simulated physics via code. The high level of control inherent to this technique allows 3D artists to optimize asset geometry for VR, potentially avoiding the extraneous vertex count of 3D point cloud data or CAD models. Procedural modeling applications may import diagrams, blueprints, and CAD models for reference, allowing the 3D artist to recreate real-world objects on-spec. The modular code-based configuration of procedural models allows for them to be modified and updated as real-world objects and equipment are updated. Their node-based organization allows 3D artists to flexibly modify the digital assets as needed, re-importing them into the VR development pipeline. Dore et al. [8] described procedural modeling as a possible alternative to traditional parametric modeling techniques used in BIM (Building Information Modeling) because of its high potential for automation and flexible code-based design.

3 Methodology

3.1 The "Low-Complexity Method"

A 2018 paper by Li, et al. [18] described a "low-complexity method" for digitizing hydro-electric generating equipment for a virtual training scenario. The researchers decomposed the needed assets into sets of parts and components as an application of object-oriented thinking. Essential equipment components were digitized and then instantiated as "prefabs" in the Unity game engine to avoid redundancy. By breaking the digitized hydroelectric equipment down into smaller components, the simulation could be easily updated as real-world equipment parts may be updated. They used collected images and

CAD/CAE drawings as specifications for how to create the digital assets. Shaders were used to approximate materials inside the virtual training engine, allowing for further customization and iteration as needed. The result was an efficient asset digitization methodology that allowed for a high degree of customization absent in photogrammetry/laser scanning.

This research proposes a similar workflow to the aforementioned "low-complexity method" to digitize complex job-related equipments and structures. However, while Li et al.'s methodology does not describe exactly how the hydroelectric equipment was digitized into 3D models, ours uses procedural modeling to provide a further level of customization. Here, an outline of the proposed methodology as well as our existing preliminary work will be presented.

Our proposed methodology for efficiently digitizing real-world complex industrial equipment and environments is summarized in Fig. 1. The steps of asset modularization, shader definitions, modular component modeling, and virtual scene creation represent the front-end steps of the workflow. It is in the front-end that most of the customization of the 3D asset occurs. To explain these steps, we will reference an existing VR training project in which a dairy cow milking machine was digitized for virtual reality by a technical artist in the LIVE Lab at Texas A&M University.

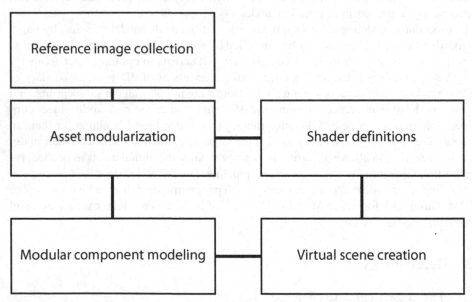

Fig. 1. "Low-complexity" methodology for digitizing complex industrial equipment and structures for use in virtual environments. Lines represent the flow of asset customization between steps in the workflow, front-end and otherwise.

3.2 Reference Image Collection

Researchers were led on a tour of a dairy farming facility near Dallas, Texas, USA and took various photographs of the milking machine. 39 photographs and videos were retained for reference purposes (see Fig. 2). The images included various angles around the milking machine at various levels of closeness to the equipment. They also include images of the machine being occupied by cows and unoccupied. Photographing the milk machine took about an hour.

While the accuracy of photogrammetry is dependent on the comprehensiveness of the image capture, our workflow does not require such comprehensiveness. Here, the goal is to simply capture as few or as many photographs as needed for the digital artist(s) to analyze the appearance and basic operation of the job-related equipment. Acquired photographs may have different levels of exposure from each other or zoom in on a particular component in detail. Unlike photogrammetry, which uses image acquisition as a method for data input, the proposed workflow uses image collection for the benefit of reference and analysis, with photographs being able to be combined with CAD drawings, blueprints, and other technical images to increase understanding of the job-related equipment.

Fig. 2. Example of a collected image for the milking machine project.

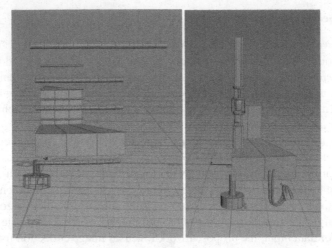

Fig. 3. Procedurally generated milking machine components.

3.3 Asset Modularization and Component Modeling

The technical artist studied the photographs, analyzed the structure of the milking machine, and made determinations on how to break the entire structure down into modular components. Because the machine has a circular structure and is made up of twelve evenly-spaced milking bays, the technical artist determined that only one twelfth of the entire structure needed to be created in 3D. The remaining parts of the structure could be instantiated in the virtual reality engine during the scene creation step.

The components of the milking machine were then modeled procedurally in Houdini by SideFX (see Fig. 3). Houdini allows for nodes, representing chunks of 3D graphics code, to be defined and interconnected to make up a single parameterized object. Changes to the parameters of a single node may affect the appearance of the whole asset. Thus, a high level of customization is achieved for iterative design. The complete 3D model took 13 h and is made up of 16,000 polygonal faces.

3.4 Shader Definitions

Because the milk machine was part of a preliminary experiment, asset textures were achieved with predefined shaders in Substance Painter by Adobe (see Fig. 4). Ideally, these shaders would also be created procedurally to retain the high customization we seek. Texturing the assets using procedural shaders allows technical artists to update or adapt the textures to preferred levels of realism more easily than with baked textures which are not as customizable.

3.5 Virtual Scene Creation

Finally, the many digital assets are imported and assembled in a virtual scene. This may be accomplished in a real-time game engine such as Unreal or Unity. The "low-complexity method" is useful here, because any individual asset may be imported as a

Fig. 4. The complete procedurally-generated milking machine asset with textures.

separate scene object. This allows for complex structures to be constructed out of their smaller components while allowing each component to be modified and re-imported in a way that is non-destructive to the whole virtual environment pipeline. Shaders for texturing 3D assets may also be treated this way. Real-time lighting, easily modified and iterated upon, is also accessible in game engines. Game engines are also useful for rapidly and interactively testing the scene and its objects to suit the needs of the virtual environment.

Once the virtual scene is assembled, it may be manipulated via code to make the digital environment interactive. This interactivity would reflect the functionality of the job-related equipment according to their design and the requirements of the training scenario.

4   Discussion

The proposed methodology for real-world object digitization uses procedural modeling as its technical basis. This methodology is justified by the advantages of using procedural modeling over other techniques such as photogrammetry or manual vertex-based modeling. Procedural modeling allows for a higher level of customization absent from other techniques. Artists creating procedural models may avoid the implicit vertex density and baked light interaction of objects scanned via photogrammetry. The physical appearance and other attributes of a procedurally-modeled 3D object may be parameterized and customized via code. Therefore, the creator of the procedurally generated 3D asset has greater control over the production of the asset. This high level of customization suits the iterative nature of interactive design.

One of the advantages of VR-assisted personnel training is the simulation of functioning job-related equipment. Procedural modeling's ability to organize real-world equipment and structures into groups of individual digital objects allows those objects to be given simulated functionality via computer code. While CAD models of job-related equipment may be available, it is unknown if their object hierarchy is organized in a way that allows for such functionality. For example, a digitized lever on a CAD model may not be able to rotate about its fulcrum without breaking the entire CAD model down in a 3D modeling application, isolating the vertices, edges, and faces that make up the lever, defining a separate object from them, defining the object's rotation axis to be at the lever's fulcrum, and re-exporting the entire CAD model with the new changes. However, using procedural modeling, the lever and its fulcrum may be defined as its own individual object within the hierarchy of the digitized equipment. Later, when imported into the digital scene, the lever may be animated or given functionality via computer code.

The adapted "low-complexity" approach also lends itself well to the specialized nature of development workflows used by creative studios. From a production stand-point, the flow of non-destructive customization in the front-end of the proposed work-flow is highly compatible with the typical studio structure of specialized workers who take charge of each step of the 3D asset creation process i.e. modeling, texturing, lighting, virtual scene assembly, and interaction programming. Any time a job-related 3D asset needs to be updated to reflect changes to the real-world equipment, individual steps of the workflow may be identified for implementing the changes without having to restart the entire digitization process. Specialized workers may then be brought in to the development pipeline as needed. In contrast, a photogrammetric model of job-related equipment would have to undergo costly and time-consuming re-scanning if the 3D model needed to be updated. A procedural modeling-based, low-complexity workflow is advantageous for VR production teams because of its high potential for compartmentalized development steps as the current global COVID-19 pandemic forces more and more businesses to work remotely.

However, this methodology is not without its weakness. The most significant potential weakness may be that of scalability. While our milking machine asset took roughly 16 h for a small team of technical artists to digitize, it is not known how long it would take to digitize an even more complex structure such as an oil platform. At a higher scale, this workflow or parts of it may prove less efficient than other methods. For example, our workflow uses an image-based approach as reference for the real-world objects to be digitized. While the task of photographing the milking machine was logistically simple, gathering images for a larger, more complex structure may prove more difficult. Furthermore, some structures such as oil platforms may be situated in hostile environments that make image gathering difficult. The use of UAVs to take photographs may circumvent the hazards of hostile environments [29]. In such a case, developers may have to use existing reference images, blueprints, and technical drawings (if available) in lieu of gathering images [3].

The efficiency of the proposed procedural modeling-based, "low-complexity" work-flow is yet to be fully evaluated. Therefore, future development of this idea should include user studies assessing VR training scenarios based on our workflow versus those based on photogrammetry, manual 3D modeling, or CAD models. These studies could be for VR production teams assessing the efficiency and level of customization among the different workflows, assessments of the digitized objects by VR users, or feedback from clients inspecting the results of the various digitization techniques. Using such experimental approaches, the barriers of utilizing VR-assisted personnel training cited in paragraph 1.1 may be more comprehensively addressed. Other future works may explore how the proposed workflow lends itself toward cultural heritage and preservation projects. Procedural modeling may be ideal for efficiently digitizing structures for heritage or historical preservation, given that CAD models generally do not exist for such structures. Scalability and stress tests, assessing digitization workflow effectiveness on larger and more complex objects, could reveal weaknesses of individual workflow steps and would also be suitable for future work.

5 Conclusion

A "low-complexity" workflow for digitizing complex real-world objects and environments for interactive virtual scenarios has been presented. This workflow combines image-based reference gathering and procedural modeling to simplify the digitization pipeline and give artists greater control over the 3D assets. The characteristics of the assets are controlled by the artist, not a scanned representation. The result (as demonstrated by our previous milking machine project) are highly customizable, VR-ready 3D assets that are easily updated to suit the needs of the virtual scenario. This approach avoids the ambiguity of "black box" techniques such as photogrammetry. It further reduces complexity by replacing 3D asset creation techniques with procedural modeling, which is more customizable and lends itself better to non-destructive iteration. While there exist implicit weaknesses to this methodology, further development and application will allow us to fully assess its potential.

References

1. Achakir, F., et al.: Digitization of the Hassan mosque. In: 9th International Symposium on Signal, Image, Video and Communications (ISIVC), Las Vegas, pp. 221–226. IEEE (2018)
2. Ahmed, S., et al.: Preserving heritage sites using 3D modeling and virtual reality technology. In: Proceedings of the 3rd International Conference on Cryptography, Security and Privacy, Kuala Lumpur, pp. 267–272. ACM (2019)
3. Avgerinakis, K., et al.: V4design for enhancing architecture and video game creation. In: IEEE International Symposium on Mixed and Augmented Reality Adjunct (ISMAR-Adjunct), Munich, pp. 305–309. IEEE (2018)
4. Bondar, S., Salem, B., Stjepandić, J.: Indoor object reconstruction based on acquisition by low-cost devices. Adv. Transdisciplinary Eng. **7**, 113–122 (2018)
5. Burdea, G.C., Coiffet, P.: Virtual Reality Technology. Wiley, Hoboken (2003)
6. Cappelletti, C., et al.: Forensic engineering surveys with UAV photogrammetry and laser scanning techniques, pp. 227–234 (2019)
7. Chen, L., et al.: Investigating the learning performances between sequence-and context-based teaching designs for virtual reality (VR)-based machine tool operation training. Comput. Appl. Eng. Educ. **27**(5), 1043–1063 (2019)
8. Denker, A.: Rebuilding Palmyra virtually: recreation of its former glory in digital space. Virtual Archaeol. Rev. **8**(17), 20–30 (2017)
9. Dore, C., Murphy, M.: Current state of the art historic building information modelling. Int. Arch. Photogrammetry Remote Sens. Spatial Inf. Sci. **42** (2017)

10. Dugdale, S., Malcolm, I., Hannah, D.: Drone-based Structure-from-Motion provides accurate forest canopy data to assess shading effects in river temperature models. Sci. Total Environ. **678**, 326–340 (2019)
11. Dylla, K., et al.: Rome reborn 2.0: a case study of virtual city reconstruction using procedural modeling techniques. Comput. Graph. World **16**(6), 62–66 (2008)
12. D'Andrea, A., Bosco, A., Barbarino, M.: A 3D environment to rebuild virtually the so-called Augusteum in Herculaneum. Archeologia e Calcolatori **28**(2), 437–446 (2017)
13. Garcia, C., et al.: An approach of training virtual environment for teaching electro-pneumatic systems. IFAC Pap. Online **52**(9), 278–284 (2019)
14. Garcia, C., et al.: An approach of virtual reality environment for technicians training in upstream sector. IFAC Pap. Online **52**(9), 285–291 (2019)
15. Gontard, L., et al.: Accurate 3D characterization of catalytic bodies surface by scanning electron microscopy. ChemCatChem **11**(14), 3171–3177 (2019)
16. Gray, P.C., et al: Drones and convolutional neural networks facilitate automated and accurate cetacean species identification and photogrammetry. Methods Ecol. Evol. **10**(9), 1490–1500 (2019)
17. Kucharczyk, M., Hugenholtz, C.: Pre-disaster mapping with drones: an urban case study in Victoria, British Columbia, Canada. Nat. Hazards Earth Syst. Sci. **19**(9), 2039–2051 (2019)
18. Kurazume, R., et al.: Automatic large-scale three dimensional modeling using cooperative multiple robots. Comput. Vis. Image Underst. **157**, 25–42 (2017)
19. Li, B., et al.: A low-complexity method for authoring an interactive virtual maintenance training system of hydroelectric generating equipment. Comput. Ind. **100**, 159–172 (2018)
20. Li, X., et al.: A critical review of virtual and augmented reality (VR/AR) applications in construction safety. Autom. Constr. **86**, 150–162 (2018)
21. Manferdini, A., et al.: Unveiling Damnatio Memoriae. The use of 3D digital technologies for the virtual reconstruction of archaeological finds and artefacts. Virtual Archaeol. Rev. **7**(15), 9–17 (2016)
22. Martinovic, A., Van Gool, L.: Bayesian grammar learning for inverse procedural modeling. In: Proceedings of the IEEE Conference on Computer Vision and Pattern Recognition, Portland, pp. 201–208. IEEE (2013)
23. Osanlou, A., Wang, S., Excell, P.: 3D re-creation of heritage artefacts using a hybrid of CGI and holography. In: Proceedings of the International Conference on Cyberworlds (CW), Chester. IEEE (2017)
24. Poloprutskýa, Z., Fraštiab, M., Marčišb, M.: 3D digital reconstruction based on archived terrestrial photographs from metric cameras. Acta Polytechnica **59**(4), 384–398 (2019)
25. Samavati, F., Runions, A.: Interactive 3D content modeling for digital earth. Vis. Comput. **32**(10), 1293–1309 (2016)
26. Segura, Á., et al.: Improved virtual reality perception with calibrated stereo and variable focus for industrial use. Int. J. Interact. Des. Manuf. (IJIDeM) **12**(1), 95–103 (2017). https://doi.org/10.1007/s12008-017-0377-0
27. Shamsuzzoha, A., et al.: Digital factory–virtual reality environments for industrial training and maintenance. Interact. Learn. Environ. 1–24 (2019)
28. Teboul, O., et al.: Segmentation of building facades using procedural shape priors. In: Proceedings of the IEEE Computer Society Conference on Computer Vision and Pattern Recognition, San Francisco, pp. 3105–3115. IEEE (2010)
29. Zwierzak, I., Stoddart, D., Hitchens, C.: Imaging solutions for harsh environments. Procedia CIRP **62**, 396–399 (2017)

Acceleration of Therapeutic Use of Brain Computer Interfaces by Development for Gaming

Julia A. Scott[1]([✉]) [iD] and Max Sims[2] [iD]

[1] Santa Clara University, Santa Clara, CA 95053, USA
jscott1@scu.edu
[2] Theia Interactive, Chico, CA 95928, USA

Abstract. Brain computer interfaces (BCI) are the foundation of numerous therapeutic applications that use brain signals to control programs or to translate into feedback. While the technical creation of these systems may be done in the lab with limited design expertise, the translation into a therapeutic calls for the engagement of game designers. This is evermore true for BCI in virtual reality (VR). VR has the potential to elevate BCI in embodiment and immersiveness. These traits are key for neurofeedback therapies for neurobehavioral conditions like anxiety. The cooperation between game designers and scientists overcomes the hurdle in transforming an experiment into a tool. More often than not, BCI on the road to therapeutics or other practical applications are launched in original or adapted games to demonstrate the usability of the platform. In the absence of partnerships like this, slow or stalled progress ensues on the scientific translation. We demonstrate this principle in a range of examples and in-depth with *Mandala Flow State*—a VR neurofeedback system that first served as an interactive installation in an art museum.

Keywords: Virtual reality · Neurofeedback · Brain computer interface

1 Introduction

Brain computer interfaces (BCI) are the modern-day science fact of how our thoughts and intentions are used to control electronic devices. In short, brain signals read in by sensors are processed to distill a discrete and discernable signal that is mapped to control parameters in the computer program [1]. While the primary uses of this technology are for medical purposes, such as control of robotic arms or assistive devices [2], one arm of acceleration for the science has been gaming [3, 4]. In the spirit of keeping with the first video game, the earliest demonstration of BCI was done with a game of pong. It has followed as the proof-of-concept game for emerging BCI technologies, as highlighted in Pong. Mythos exhibition (Germany, 2006–2007). In a few training sessions, a user can implicitly learn to move the paddle right or left with a single electroencephalogram (EEG) channel from the frontal lobe. This beginning then led to BCI for more complex

N. Shaghaghi et al. (Eds.): INTETAIN 2020, LNICST 377, pp. 267–281, 2021.
https://doi.org/10.1007/978-3-030-76426-5_18

games, such as World of Warcraft [5]. The sense of embodiment is promoted when the device controller is removed from the picture.

In furthering the immersive embodiment of the gaming environment, virtual reality (VR) gaming creates a heightened and broadened sensory experience. Imagine the additive perception of engagement if brain signals are used as the controller in a VR first-person game. For example, take the popular Half-life:Alyx and replace the hand controller with built-in EEG sensors such that your intent is translated to digital action. Valve corporation has made the bold statement at GDC 2019 that they are investing in research to integrate EEG into gameplay for a variety of features, not simply substituting the controller. While this makes for a fun experience, the societal benefit is agnostic. However, the same properties of engagement and embodiment can be carried over for therapeutic uses of VR.

VR is one platform for digital therapeutics. Digital therapeutics use monitoring programs and devices to provide user feedback in the management of a medical condition. A longstanding therapeutic is neurofeedback. Neurofeedback therapy gamifies modulation of patterns of brain activity in order to up or down regulate neural pathways that are linked to behaviors [6]. For example, strengthening alpha frequency waves in the frontal lobe is associated with reduction of anxiety [7]. Alpha frequency is visualized in the interface and with practice, the user should be able to change that visualization in the targeted manner. Presently, many research groups, including ours, and some companies are adapting neurofeedback into VR games, though none are to market as of yet. The goal is to improve the potency of neurofeedback with greater engagement in VR.

In this paper, we will explore the role of BCI in recreational gaming, followed by the transformation into gaming for virtual reality applications. Lastly, we will demonstrate how the principles of BCI gaming may be adapted to therapeutic neurobehavioral applications.

2   BCI Gaming

BCI in gaming takes two roads (Fig. 1). One is the identification of mental states by EEG in order to modify the gaming experience in response to these fluctuations in activity. This can be achieved with a few dry electrodes over various locations of the head. A mental state is typically detected by an average signal over seconds of time, typically calculated by a power analysis of frequency bands [8]. This is fairly straight forward in terms of hardware, signal processing and analysis. The second are discrete stimulus-driven responses that are used for specific actions in the games [9]. This depends on more sensitive, numerous and fine-tuned EEG sensors whose signals are converted to event-related potentials (ERP) on the tens of millisecond scale. The key component is isolating reliable signals associated with the intent of the user, in this way substituting for the translation of action through a manual controller. Intent and mental state are two types of distinct signals with categorically different analytical methods. Consequently, they need to be considered separately.

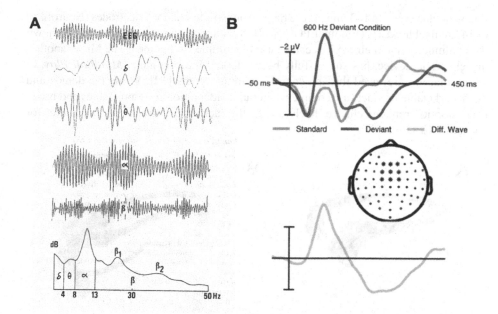

Fig. 1. Examples of EEG analyses used in BCI applications. (A) From raw EEG, frequency bands are separated between 1 and 50 Hz. Then a power analysis is applied to the frequency range. The average over a band is used as the feature for smooth BCI controls. (B) Event related potentials (ERP) are extracted from raw EEG by time-locking to a stimulus provoked response over a set of channels. In this example, mismatch negativity ERP is shown over a 450ms window. ERPs can be used as precise control signals in BCI applications. (a) CC by Albin Michel, Collection "Sciences d'aujourd'hui", Figure 18, page 142, 1987. ISBN: 2226028716. (b) CC by Front. Neurosci., 30 December 2013, Figure 1. https://doi.org/10.3389/fnins.2013.00265.

2.1 Traditional Gaming

A proof-of-concept demonstration of BCI has been well documented by University of Twente [10] and Graz University of Technology researchers [11] in the adaptation of World of Warcraft play with EEG mental imagery or slow wave oscillations. Using EEG channels positioned over sensorimotor cortices, the system learns to recognize directional movements. With practice, users are able to reliably produce these signals as intuitive control of the game play. These groups even incorporated neurofeedback in the form of shapeshifting characters. When indicators of stress were detected, the player changed to a monster-like character. The player would need to relax to return to their default state [11]. This work is nearly a decade old and has not come to market.

The lack of progress is in part due to the limitations in wearable and consumer accessible EEG devices of the time. Significant progress has been made in hardware for consumer EEG headsets and in the algorithm development for signal analysis (Fig. 2). Wireless Bluetooth technology and dry electrode sensors are the two advances that enabled the hardware change from the high-density gel electrode caps wired to preamplifiers then processed through PCs. For software, application of real time signal processing and rapid and adaptable machine learning algorithms have transformed what used to take 30 min in the lab down to 1–3 min. These range from single-channel electrodes (NeuroSky) to 14-channel headsets (Emotiv EPOC X). Both Neurosky and Emotiv have also shown the community that their devices can be used in simple BCI games. The Muse, another dry electrode device, has successfully been adapted into the game *MindBall Play*, in which marbles are raced through complex winding paths [12]. While the demos and even marketable products are completed, iterative adaptation for more games and broad user adoption remains elusive, likely due to the lack of penetration of the market for consumer EEG.

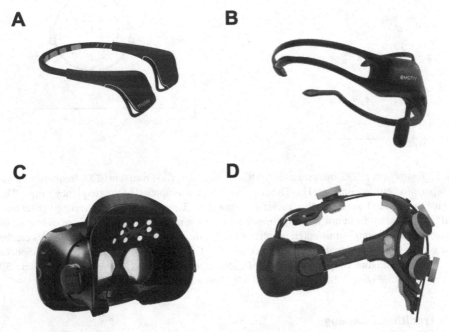

Fig. 2. Consumer devices for EEG and integrated EEG and VR. (A) 5-channel Muse 2, (B) 5-channel Emotiv Insight, (C) Looxid Link affixed to HTC Vive, (D) Neurables HTC Vive with Wearable Sensing electrodes. Each device has different electrode sensor design and distribution over the head. The fit of each is also distinct. For these reasons, the usage in BCI applications are not interchangeable and each have uniquely suited contexts.

Sometimes video games are used to demonstrate a therapeutic proof-of-concept. For example, a functional electrical stimulation (FES) BCI to play Guitar Hero [13]. In this system, electrical signals directly measured from the primary motor cortex are read in and trained to detected combinations of motor messages through mental imagery. This is then mapped to an output of stimulation electrodes to the forearm that activate the combination of muscles associated with the intended movement. The beauty of this demonstration is in the control of each finger in real-time. Now for the paralyzed individual, the function he was most hoping to regain was certainly not Guitar Hero. However, by using the game to train the algorithms for individual finger modulation, further functional movements, like a grasp, can be effectively learned and programmed. Without question, spending hours playing Guitar Hero was more engaging for the patient than repetitively tapping each finger until pattern detection was reached, which is traditional manner to train a BCI controller.

2.2   VR Gaming

The first true BCI VR game, *Awakening*, was developed with Neurable's technology in 2017. Neurable adapted the HTC Vive headset and Wearable Sensing dry electrode EEG to a single piece of hardware. The software analyzes the signals from the parietal and occipital lobes to extract P300 ERPs. The P300 is an indicator of visual attention. Neurable has adapted this signal into a selection tool in the game. So rather than point to or scroll to what you want on the screen, you look at it. For Neurable, gaming is not the primary goal. Their long-term applications are for integration of BCI into simulation training and testing as well as novel devices for more consumer applications. Despite these being their stated goals, investment for this young company first came in the form of VR game development.

Valve Corporation is actively researching how BCI may be used in gaming as revealed at the 2019 Game Development Conference. While the company did present the progressive work of more intuitive control of games through EEG signals paired with eye tracking and gestural control, the focus was on evaluation of mental states during play to adapt the game environment in response to affective dips. For example, a player may become disengaged with the game as noted by decreased attentiveness (lower beta frequency power), which could trigger an exciting turn around the next corner. Difficulty of the game may instead be determined by cognitive load in contrast to a preselected level. In these ways, game play may feel "just right" to the player in this highly personalized and dynamic experience. The adaptive aspect is similar to neurofeedback games, which adjust the difficulty factor based on performance.

The advantages of developing BCI for the context of gaming are that hours of data can be collected from a distributed network of thousands of people. Most research labs do not have the reach or the funds to acquire data at that scale. Individual lab studies typically run for about 15 min and may have a few dozen participants. The great quantity and diversity of data from game play can then drive robust machine learning models for generalization and sensitivity in consumer applications for wellness or market research as cited use cases by Looxid Labs.

Looxid Labs is a relatively young company that is on the forefront of EEG integrated VR. In contrast to Neurable, which positions the electrodes broadly around the scalp, the LooxidLink adheres to the front of the headset with a concentrated set of electrodes over the anterior frontal lobe. This is another example of a gaming introduction to neurofeedback. Their demo games are all driven by classic mental state indices, including the *Mental Playground*. In this game, neon 3D shapes are programmed to rise and fall with fluctuations in concentration. Looxid Labs makes their SDK available for others to develop applications using their hardware and software. For VR BCI that utilizes intrinsic activity, rather than evoked responses, an integrated platform like this may be used for extended training or therapy.

3 Digital Therapeutics

Nearly all current digital therapeutic companies have gamified their therapies. Curiosity, challenge, aesthetics and engagement are critical for a successful implementation of a therapeutic aiming for behavioral change. A handful of companies, highlighted in this section, have shown what can be done with VR to enhance user engagement and efficacy through embodiment, high stimulus environments, reward and challenge. Game designers and software developers are essential players along with the scientists and physicians of therapeutic BCI endeavors, like neurofeedback-integrated VR games. The cooperation between these disciplines are overcoming the hurdles of access to potential benefits of neurofeedback therapy.

3.1 Traditional Neurofeedback

Neurofeedback is a therapeutic adaptation of closed loop BCI. The same components are in place—sensor of brain activity, processer, effector [14]. The user at the center of this loop is learning to control the effector, just like a BCI game or a tool. In stark contrast is the actual goal of the activity. In neurofeedback, the control or modulation of the game is simply an avenue to change the targeted pattern of brain activity. Neurofeedback therapy is agnostic as to what the effector may be, as long as it is effective in engaging the user long enough to make lasting neuroplastic transformations [8]. The reality is that any game or BCI will make changes in the brain as that is what defines learning of all types. Neurofeedback therapy is unique in that its purpose is only relevant as transfer learning. Becoming proficient at the neurofeedback game, must carry over to the behavioral or mood correlate outside of the game. For example, a therapy that targets sustained attention must show that the user then has improved focus at work. Consequently, the bar for performance is greater for the BCI in neurofeedback therapy than in a gaming context.

While specialized neurofeedback programs have been developed for neuropsychiatric clinics like the Drake Institute, these protocols are not accessible to the masses. The personalized therapeutic plan requires high density EEG that is quantitatively mapped [15]. For each patient, the "abnormal" regions are localized and the degree and direction of change is determined. That local signature is then programed as the input to the neurofeedback training game. Over six weeks of daily practice, the brain gradually changes. Assessments are completed to see if the patient has improved upon standardized psychometric scales or may have reduced sensitivity to episodic triggers (as in PTSD). This level of commitment is called for with psychiatric conditions that are debilitating. However, there is an existing need for brain training in subclinical populations and neurobehavioral conditions that interfere with peak performance. This is the concentration of our team's work.

A key democratization of neurofeedback has been the emergence of consumer EEG devices that are sold as part of wellness packages (Fig. 2). The Muse, which is marketed as a meditation aid, is distinctly in the "wellness" market and not for therapeutic use. Emotiv is presented as a tool for a broad set of portable EEG applications, especially research. Emotiv has demonstrated several BCI proof-of-concepts [16]. One of the most outstanding is a demonstration of the Emotiv EPOC used in a serious game for focus training by using the pre-defined mental commands [17]. On average, players showed an 8.25% increase in focus based on EEG measurements compared to keyboard control of the game. As described earlier, Looxid Labs exclusively develops BCI hardware and software for VR with a Unity SDK. The potential for novel and immersive game development is thus open-ended and may be expanded richly by the community at large by partnering with the company. Importantly, each of these companies have devices that run for $300 USD or less, making them an attainable investment.

One example of how a single channel EEG system (MindWave by Neurosky) may be used in treatment of anxiety is shown in the game *Mindlight* [18]. In this game, the frontal alpha and beta frequency ranges are used as different reward parameters in the neurofeedback training to improve self-regulation of anxiety. Targeting 8–16 year-olds with autism spectrum disorders, the game setting is a magical mansion with monsters that are vanquished by the player's light, which is controlled by EEG correlates of focused relaxation. The outcomes of the first trial showed that parents report changes in symptoms, while children do not [19]. While the outcome is not undoubtedly convincing of the effect, the game design in *Mindlight* is on par with simple video games children may otherwise play and were successful in consistent player activity over six weeks, showing strong engagement.

A similar model to what our team is aiming to achieve is practiced by MyndLift [20]. MyndLift uses the Muse EEG device, like we do, and tablet or smart phone delivered neurofeedback system. Any individual may sign up via their website and be paired with a neuro-coach. A subscription fee is collected as an active user. The Muse is a five-channel dry electrode array that is position over anterior frontal and temporal locations. These sites are sufficient to reliably and robustly measure spectral frequencies from 1 to 50 Hz. Standard power analyses are conducted followed by calculation of mental state indices (e.g. "attentiveness"). Either may be used to create a control parameter for the neurofeedback training. The timeline of a therapy is similar, as this is determined by the neurobiology of synaptic remodeling, which takes roughly a month to stabilize. The advantage of the Myndlift system is that it may be practiced at home with easy to use technology. Working under the assumption that a person already has a tablet for general usage, the only specialized hardware needed is the Muse, which is priced lower than a smart phone. Further the monthly subscription fee is a fraction of the cost of an hour with a therapist. This is one path of increasing accessibility to mental health services, which are impacted by limited number of clinicians and cost. While Myndlift is a significant advance in overcoming hurdles of access, the brain training games are graphically simple and gameplay is very one-dimensional, in our opinion. By transforming this model to include a VR option, the user engagement, compliance and efficacy may be improved. We demonstrate a proof-of-concept of this with *Mandala Flow State* as described in Sect. 4.1.

3.2 Enhancement of Digital Therapeutics with VR Features

Gaming in a VR environment enhances the user experience through its immersivity. This is not simply due to the 360-degree views. Rather it is the visual illusion embedded with an array of interactive and sensory dimensions. These affordances are the basis for building a sense of presence and embodiment in the VR environment. The perceptual trickery may be used to more effectively train a BCI for gaming or therapeutic purposes.

The embodiment of the player in a VR space has been adopted into neurorehabiliation interventions [21]. The real time synchronization of an avatar has enabled improved in-home rehabilitation for stroke recovery and pain management. For example, Cognivive recently received FDA clearance for a VR neurorehabilitation system. The stroke recovery training is in the context of a beach resort that includes a social component and puzzle solving in the context of completing physical rehabilitation at home. Likewise, Karuna Labs uses VR therapy for chronic pain management. In this experience, patients are mirroring an avatar to promote virtual embodiment, which lessens the perception of pain during physical therapy. With similar goals, MindMaze is developing a VR headset with integrated EEG for virtual embodiment training for neurorehabilitation [22]. Prior to these VR-based interventions, the options to patients were more limited and difficult to access and painful.

Interactive affordances are a constant innovation in VR gaming. Hand-based gestures to virtually touch something with bare hands or haptic feedback gloves, like those from HaptX, imbue a sense of verisimilitude to the experience. The hand can manipulate and grasp affordances such as switches, dials knob and tools. The tactile simulation may be more convincing in VR rather than screen-based games due to the circumscribed 3D visual field. For interventions targeting conditions with attention challenges or sensory processing, immersivity and presence are critical for efficacy. For instance, by the character of the condition, people with attention deficit disorders are easily distractible by their own thoughts or their environment. Creating a complete audiovisual space with tactile stimulation helps to overcome that distraction by providing sensory input that shields the external world and is more potent than their internal melliu.

These unique affordances of VR may improve the likelihood that users engage with the therapeutic game. Greater engagement does not simply mean spending more time with the game. Engagement can be synonymous with attention. When the goal is to promote self-regulation of attention, the neurofeedback system will train at a faster pace due to this reinforcement. The quicker learning and reward are an encouragement to users, which may motivate users to continue use of the VR game to their therapeutic endpoint of 4–6 weeks.

Gaze direction is readily decoded from a VR headset position or with integrated eye trackers, such as in HP Reverb G2 Omnicept. Gaze is another indicator of directed attention and intent. This may be used in combination with brain signals to reward the learning goals. For example, the gameplay may be a visual search task. When the player fixates on the target and the associated neural correlate increases in conjunction, a pop-up reward may appear (gaining points or prizes). An elegant application of gaze control is demonstrated in *Dreams of Dali* VR experience created for the Dali Museum in St. Petersburg Florida. The visitor simply looks at the glowing orb for three seconds and is then teleported to the next position in an immense world made of his paintings' imagery. This created a seamless teleportation that flies you to your destination. The teleportation illustrates how transitions may feel naturalistic, rather than artificial scene switching. This feature is important for maintaining presence in the virtual environment and concentration on the gameplay.

VR games are rated on immersion and comfort on top of the actual gameplay in contrast to screen-based 2D games. VR games, as a new medium, have links from past titles with modifications for player immersion. The titles can be part of a larger cosmology, such as Star Wars or Harry Potter. The game can also fulfill a filmic narrative within the cosmology allowing the gamer to participate within that world. Star Wars titles done in VR, by the spinoff ILM X Lab, have a character adoption feel that the films could not attain. A narrative is given to promote the player's transformation into the character. For example, the player becomes a fighter pilot for the Rebellion. These games are an expansion in the Universes they create that give a greater sense of belonging. The personalization in the storyline certainly strengthens retention of gameplay, which may be translated into methods for greater engagement in therapeutic VR games. For therapeutics games intended for teens, alternate worlds inspired by popular culture and film may be an effective way for them to connect to the activities and create personalized and elaborate experiences that grow and change over the training period.

For an effective digital therapeutic that is delivered in-home, the importance of user motivation cannot be ignored. Liken this to the info sheet on exercises given to you by your doctor to do at home to reduce back strain. How effective is this intervention? How many people are motivated and organized enough to do boring, repetitive, and sometimes painful and difficult exercises when there is no encouragement or accountability? The same principle applies to any behavioral modification regiment. In-clinic neurofeedback has the advantage of a therapist working with the user in person on a set schedule. Without this structure in place, the factors of the personal motivation and enjoyment weigh heavier. VR capabilities have the potential to make a greater impact on this dimension than other modalities.

4   BCI Neurofeedback in VR

In our opinion, the next milestone in BCI would be to take advantage of the immersive quality of VR to change the way neurobehavioral therapies are conducted. Neurofeedback therapy, as described in previous sections, is a powerful tool when done well—accurately identifying the source signal, adaptive responsiveness of the BCI, and user adherence over six weeks [24, 25]. Unfortunately, the implementation often fails to meet these criteria [8]. The work of our team aims to address some of the weaknesses in the current practices. In particular, user engagement and compliance as well as creation of an environment that promotes the desired effect.

4.1   Mandala Flow State

One of the most reliable EEG signals in the frequency domain is the alpha power over the frontal lobe [23]. This has been used in neurofeedback therapies to improve relaxation, decrease stress and anxiety, and improve focus [23]. Our group has used this signal to drive a VR experience that targets focused relaxation [26] (Fig. 3). The system uses the Muse EEG headset for signal detection and preprocessing. The alpha frequency from the frontal electrodes are extracted and processed into standardized values. The detectable fluctuations in these signals are calibrated with a difficulty factor. The VR application is developed in Unity3D. The processed EEG signal is a control parameter for the game. The VR experience is delivered through an Oculus Rift S headset. This framework opens the door to many variations on a theme of modifying patterns of neural activity and behavior.

In our prototype, we selected a context that would promote a state of focused relaxation via cultural association and sensory experience. The environment created for focused relaxation was thus a mandala, a tried and true meditative visualization aid [27]. The feedback parameter is also an intuitive link to the desired mental state. This version was a procedural mandala that was uniquely generated in each run. The soundscape was an ambient melody layered with 10–12 Hz binaural beats and "Om" chants. The transparency of the mandala and the gain of the chants were parallel feedback channels that changed with alpha power. The first testbed for our prototype was a brief simulation run with pre-recorded EEG. This was run on 38 people over three hours, with a waitlist of 50 people, at the San Francisco Night of Ideas 2019 [28]. The high traffic at our installation showed a significant level of engagement and interest in this platform by the public.

Subsequently, we redesigned the mandala to reflect a more authentic aesthetic and perceptible feedback (Fig. 4). This was achieved with a fog filter over the generative mandala inspired by Tibetan Buddhist mandala architecture. The dynamic aspect of the mandala was how it envelopes the 3D visual space and creates the illusion of traveling movement as the mandala gradually grows from the central point of view. Each instance of the application generates a new design of the mandala from a library of colors and elemental patterns. The soundscape accompanying the visual experience is an original digital composition that follows a template of shifting complexity and dissonance to promote focus and prevent passive viewing. The alpha power from the brain activity was inversely linked to the fog shader in order to figuratively clear the fog from one's mind. The summative reward is to see the complete mandala clearly before it is swept away like sand. Consideration of both the sensory experience and the adaptive, intuitive feedback sets this apart from neurofeedback games that simply levitate a ball or race a car [29] or are exclusively auditory [30].

To date, the system has only been used in an interactive installation at the Asian Art Museum of San Francisco until its closure due to the COVID-19 pandemic (January to March 2020). The details of this project are described in separate manuscript [31]. The formal testing of the system is set to begin once campuses fully reopen and human studies are safe to conduct by IRB criteria.

Truly, the development of the *Mandala Flow State* proof-of-concept digital therapeutic would not have been possible in the absence of interest outside of this area of study. Primary funding for this work came from parties interested in the arts. Students and collaborators emerged from a diverse set of fields, none of which were in science or medicine. Major contributors studied computational creativity, industrial design, religion, music composition, theatre and art history. In the realization of the product—a neurofeedback platform that promotes user engagement and trains the brain towards the targeted goal—the talent and the tools present in the gaming industry became just as critical as the guiding science. This type of partnership is demonstrated by Deep VR and Gaming for Emotional and Mental Health (GEMH) Lab of Radbound University.

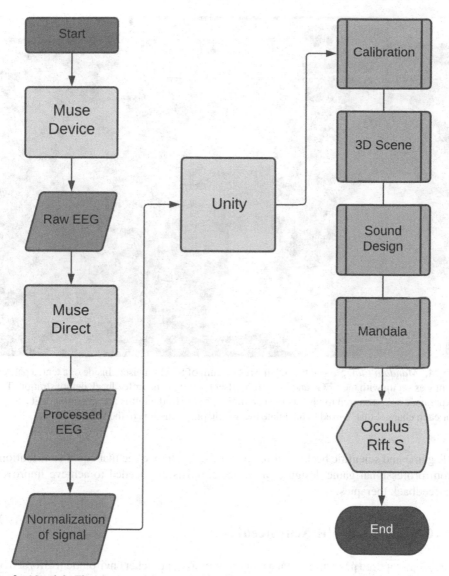

Fig. 3. *Mandala Flow State* workflow. Raw data from the Muse 2 device is read in by the Muse lab software where preprocessing to remove artifact and separate frequency bands is done. Then the absolute alpha power is output to our processing stream to be normalized and input as a control parameter in Unity. The VR display is a layering of the 3D scene, soundscape, the uniquely generated mandala and a fog filter. The alpha power inversely modulates the density of the fog in real time. That convergence is the output to the Oculus Rift S for the person to perceive. The user attempts to relax (or is relaxed by the experience) in order to increase the alpha power, our correlate of focused relaxation.

The product produced is a breathing pattern biofeedback meditative VR game aiming to treat anxiety [32]. The collaboration here led to numerous design and film awards for the

Fig. 4. *Mandala Flow State* at the Asian Art Museum of San Francisco. Inside of a tent, a partici-pant was set up with the EEG band and VR headset try out the neurofeedback demonstration. The experience was mirrored to visitors as seen in the photo. To the left is the streaming EEG signal for each channel that is used to modulate the VR display, which is to the right.

VR game and scientific backing of the methods. Again, we see that equal contributions from professional game designers and the scientists are needed to achieve improved biofeedback therapies.

5 Challenges to VR Neurofeedback

The idea proposed presently is that a more immersive and richer environment afforded by VR will improve the neurofeedback training effects. The alternate effect may be just as likely. The greater complexity of the sensory input may overwhelm attentional systems and detract from the primary function of the game. Efficacy and user experience are yet to be comprehensively tested for any VR delivered neurofeedback construct. Naturally, this is the next step underway for *Mandala Flow State*. Acute effects of the experience will be evaluated by physiological measures of heart rate, heart rate variability, and breathing rate, and user self-report on scales of mood. Full training effects over the course of four weeks will include change in the State-Trait Anxiety Inventory (STAI), survey of perceived effects of the training. The outcome may also be dependent on the quality of the experience design: How well are directions given; Is the experience complex and uncoordinated or harmonious; Can users tolerate extended time in VR without tiring. These questions are yet to be answered by iterative experimentation and must be addressed prior to further investment into VR-based neurofeedback.

Another deterrent in the proposed system of a VR platform for neurofeedback games is the adoption of VR technology broadly. At this time, only 14% (or fewer) of households in the USA have VR headsets [33]. These devices must be paired with "gaming" computers for the sake of the processing speed and graphics card specifications. The current technical requirements of a VR system may make the proposed neurofeedback training out-of-reach for many. However, as progress is made with stand-alone systems, like the Oculus Quest, and the wider use of VR games, more people may be open to adding on a brain training game or two. Game sales are 50% of VR software sales [34]. Again, the gaming industry supports the growth of the therapeutic use of BCI by driving growth in the market for VR. Further, if users are already familiar with BCI as a gaming modality, then the barrier to accepting neurofeedback games is lowered.

Lastly, exclusively EEG-controlled gaming experiences promise to be more intuitive. However, the lack of involvement of the body may counter this feeling. Naturally, we use our bodies to engage with the world. EEG signals are corrupted by the electrical activity of muscle movement, even facial expressions or head rotations. Imagine an excited player, who just achieved a milestone, couldn't express their victory outwardly. Improvements in real-time artifact detection and correction may mitigate these signal artifacts [35]. Unlike a research experiment, users should feel at home in the experience with freedom of movement and without pre-occupation of holding still. While excessive movement may add noise and degrade the detection of the desired pattern of brain activity, robust preprocessing and machine learning algorithms may make the system tolerant of them, thereby rescuing the neurofeedback loop [36]. Another strategy is to make use of both the controller and gestures in combination with the BCI to improve embodiment and engagement. This also allows for more dimensions of interaction with the game.

6   Conclusions

BCI is powerful framework with nearly endless applications [37]. The disciplines that use BCI are interdependent, as in the examples illustrated here. Integration of BCI in entertainment gaming gives a complementary push to therapeutic use of BCI. In particular, closed loop neurofeedback likens to the BCI game controller or modulator. Thus, any aspect of research or investment into BCI games simultaneously builds up the architecture for neurofeedback applications. Inadvertently, the adoption of BCI games in the future will create a ready market for brain training games. This is especially relevant for VR systems as the barrier to purchase said systems is greater.

The work done by our team is in the hope of changing the way neurobehavioral conditions are treated. When fully realized, it promises to give greater agency to the user in having control over their therapy. It reduces the dependency on clinicians and expands access to subclinical populations. By bringing the daily practice home and truly gamifying the therapy, patients for whom getting to the clinic is a challenge will be able to maintain therapy without interruption. What we imagine are adolescents and young adults, who are having difficulty managing their stress or maintaining focus, using the systems that they already have for entertainment and transforming them into therapeutic tool simply by choosing a new game.

References

1. van Gerven, F.: The brain-computer interface cycle. J. Neural Eng. **6**(4), 041001 (2009)
2. Andersen, R.: From thought to action: the brain-machine interface in posterior parietal cortex. Proc. Natl. Acad. Sci. USA **116**(52), 26274–26279 (2019)
3. Rohani, D.: Brain-computer interface using P300 and virtual reality: a gaming approach for treating ADHD. In: 2014 36th Annual International Conference of the IEEE Engineering in Medicine and Biology Society, Chicago, IL (2014)
4. Holz, E.: Brain–computer interface controlled gaming: evaluation of usability by severely motor restricted end-users. Artif. Intell. Med. **59**(2), 111–120 (2013)
5. Scherer, R., Faller, J., Balderas, D.: Brain–computer interfacing: more than the sum of its parts. Soft Comput. **17**, 317–331 (2013)
6. Thibault, R.T., Lifshitz, M., Raz, A.: The self-regulating brain and neurofeedback: experimental science and clinical promise. Cortex **74**, 247–261 (2016)
7. Hammond, D.C.: Neurofeedback treatment of depression and anxiety. J. Adult Dev. **12**(2/3), 131–137 (2005)
8. Orndorff-Plunkett, F., SIngh, F., Aragon, O.R., Pineda, J.: Assessing the effectiveness of neurofeedback training in the context of clinical and social neuroscience. Brain Sci. **7**(96) (2017)
9. Rashid, M., Sulaiman, N., Abdul Majeed, A.P., Musa, R.M.: Current status, challenges, and possible solutions of EEG-based brain-computer interface: a comprehensive review. Front. Neurorobot. **14**(25) (2020)
10. University of Twente, "BMS Lab" (2020). https://bmslab.utwente.nl/
11. Nijholt, A., Plass-Oude Bos, D., Reuderink, B.: Turning shortcomings into challenges: brain-computer interfaces for games. Entertainment Comput. **1**, 85–94 (2009)
12. Interactive Productline Team, "Mindball Play" Interactive Productline IP AB (2018)
13. Gazner, P.D., et al.: Restoring the sense of touch using a sensorimotor demultiplexing neural interface. Cell **181**(4), P763–773 (2020)
14. Sitaram, R., et al.: Closed-loop brain training: the science of neurofeedback. Nat. Rev. Neurosci. **18**(2) (2017)
15. Krepel, N., Egtberts, T., Sack, A.T., Heinrich, H., Ryan, M., Arns, M.: A multicenter effectiveness trial of QEEG-informed neurofeedback in ADHD: replication and treatment prediction. Neuroimage Clin. **28**(102399) (2020)
16. Emotiv, "Emotiv.com" (2020). https://www.emotiv.com/category/independent-studies/. Accessed 5 Oct 2020
17. Alchalabi, A.E., Eddin, A.N., Shirmohammadi, S.: More attention, less deficit: wearable EEG-based serious game for focus improvement. In: IEEE 5th International Conference on Serious Games and Applications for Health (SeGAH), Perth, WA (2017)
18. Wijnhoven, L.A., Creemers, D.H., Engels, R.C., Granic, I.: The effect of the video game Mindlight on anxiety symptoms in children with an Autism Spectrum Disorder. BMC Psychiatry **15**(1), 138 (2015)
19. Wijnhoven, L.A., et al.: Effects of the video game 'Mindlight' on anxiety of children with an autism spectrum disorder: a randomized controlled trial. J. Behav. Ther. Exp. Psychiatry **68**, 101548 (2020)
20. MyndLift, "Myndlift" (2020). https://www.myndlift.com/
21. Perez-Marcos, D.: Virtual reality experiences, embodiment, videogames and their dimensions in neurorehabilitation. NeuroEngineering Rehabil. **15**(113) (2018)
22. "ERA-LEARN". https://www.era-learn.eu/network-information/networks/eurostars/cutoff-11-09-2014/electrophysiological-and-virtual-reality-assembly-for-neurorehabilitation. Accessed 5 Dec 2020

23. Marzbani, H., Marateb, H.R., Mansourian, M.: Methodological note: neurofeedback: a comprehensive review on system design, methodology and clinical applications. Basic Clin. Neurosci. **7**(2), 143–158 (2016)
24. Micoulaud-Franchi, F.A., Geoffroy, P.A., Fond, G., Lopez, R., Bioulac, S., Philip, P.: EEG neurofeedback treatments in children with ADHD: an updated meta-analysis of randomized controlled trials. Front. Hum. Neurosci. **13**(8), 906 (2014)
25. Patel, K., et al.: Effects of neurofeedback in the management of chronic pain: a systematic review and meta-analysis of clinical trials. Eur. J. Pain (2020)
26. Adolfsson, A., Bernal, J., Ackerman, M., Scott, J.: Musical mandala mindfulness: a generative biofeedback experience. In: Musical Metacreation, Charlotte, NC (2019)
27. Harvard University, "Creating a Mandala" (2020). https://pluralism.org/creating-a-mandala
28. "Night of Ideas" (2019). https://www.nightofideassf.com/
29. BrainMaster Technologies (2020). https://www.brainmaster.com/product/zukors-drive-clinical/
30. Interaxon, "ChooseMuse" (2020). www.choosemuse.com
31. Scott, J., Sims, M., Harrold, L., Jacobus, N., Avelar, C.: Transformation of Buddhist Mandalas into a Virtual Reality Installation, Leonardo, submitted
32. Bossenbroek, R., Wols, A., Weerdmeester, J., Lichtwarck-Aschoff, A., Granic, I., van Rooij, M.: Efficacy of a virtual reality biofeedback game (DEEP) to reduce anxiety and disruptive classroom behavior: single-case study. JMIR Ment. Health **7**(3), e16066 (2020)
33. Deloitte, "Digital media trends survey" Deloitte.Insights (2020)
34. Flynt, J.: "3D Insider", 31 May 2019. https://3dinsider.com/virtual-reality-statistics/. Accessed 5 Oct 2020
35. Val-Calvo, M., Alvarez-Sanches, J.R., Ferrandez-Vicente, J.M., Fernandez, E.: Optimization of real-time EEG artifact removal and emotion estimation for human-robot interaction applications. Front. Comput. Neurosci. **13**(80) (2019)
36. Emotiv, "Emotiv.com" (2020). https://www.emotiv.com/our-technology/. Accessed 5 Oct 2020
37. Jackson, M.M., Mappus, R.: Applications for brain-computer interfaces. In: Tan, D., Nijholt, A. (eds.) Brain-Computer Interfaces, pp. 89–103. Springer, London (2010). https://doi.org/10.1007/978-1-84996-272-8_6

KeyLight: VR System for Stage Lighting

Madeline Golliver[✉], Brian Beams, and Navid Shaghaghi

Ethical, Pragmatic, and Intelligent Computing (EPIC) Laboratory,
Santa Clara University, Santa Clara, CA 95053, USA
magolliver@alumni.scu.com, {bmsmith,nshaghaghi}@scu.edu

Abstract. Training in lighting design for theater is increasingly grounded in new technologies. A growing momentum towards the incorporation of new digital tools including computer-based "magic sheets" and digital lighting consoles simplifies the work of lighting designers while also supporting diverse talent through accessibility offerings. As the industry also moves away from traditional classroom education, there is a need for alternative options that will allow future lighting designers to practice their trade.

KeyLight leverages Alexa voice control, Unity Engine visualization, and virtual reality (VR) technologies to train designers to create lighting looks using industry standard terminology and commands. KeyLight's voice user interface (VUI) bypasses the issue of learnability prevalent in other VUIs by enforcing use of theatrical commands that already require specific verbiage in industry contexts.

Through the medium of virtual reality, design students can practice their craft without the constraints of lighting equipment, space, or personnel availability. With this tool, junior lighting designers develop their fundamental technical and communicative skills. Testimonials from industry professionals suggest that KeyLight can supplement the education of aspiring lighting designers by enabling them to practice their communication through digital design work. Through KeyLight, junior lighting designers can learn the fundamental skills of additive color mixing, the efficacy of different lighting angles, the division of lighting fixtures into channels and groups, and to communicate their designs to a board operator. Results also indicate that there are applications of this voice technology to the workflow of professional lighting designers.

Keywords: Lighting design · Theater lighting training · Virtual Reality (VR) · Voice user interface · Unity 3D · Amazon Alexa

1 Introduction

Training in lighting design for theater is increasingly grounded in new technologies [7]. A growing momentum towards the incorporation of new digital tools including computer-based "magic sheets" and digital lighting consoles simplifies the work of lighting designers while also supporting diverse talent through accessibility offerings [4]. As the industry also moves away from traditional classroom

© ICST Institute for Computer Sciences, Social Informatics and Telecommunications Engineering 2021
Published by Springer Nature Switzerland AG 2021. All Rights Reserved
N. Shaghaghi et al. (Eds.): INTETAIN 2020, LNICST 377, pp. 282–296, 2021.
https://doi.org/10.1007/978-3-030-76426-5_19

education, there is a need for alternative options that will allow future lighting designers to practice their trade [4].

1.1 Background

Access to resources, time, and spaces in which theater artists can practice lighting design is an issue for junior theatrical lighting designers and theater students [5]. Tight budgets, small turn-around times between shows, and a lack of equipment and other training resources limits the amount of hands-on experience aspiring designers can have [4].

When training through the classroom, lighting students learn the basics alongside many peers, sharing scarce resources and equipment [5]. Teachers will expose students to lighting equipment, terminology, and basic practice. After learning the basics, students will then be asked to demonstrate their skills through design documentation, written and practical tests, or sometimes even by working on small shows [11]. Experienced staff will expect junior lighting designers to exhibit good design and communication of their ideas, using industry standard terminology [11]; however, many junior lighting designers have few opportunities to practice verbal communication of design in working scenarios [5]. The ability to communicate to a board operator is an integral skill for lighting designers [11], but it can be difficult for students to have access to spaces, peers, and equipment with which to practice these skills in a meaningful way [5]. This tooling provides a new medium through which designers can practice and test their communication skills without said limitations.

1.2 Approach

This project combines virtual reality technology with Alexa voice commands to address gaps in the technical education of lighting designers. The Alexa user interface takes on the role of a board operator. In theater, board operators listen to commands made by the lighting designer and enter each command into a board that controls the lights in the theater. Designers must learn to work effectively with their board operator to create looks and cues for the stage. Designers therefore must learn to communicate their designs. By training with a lighting visualization tool that leverages voice control, designers gain experience creating lighting looks using the same industry standard terminology and commands that they would employ in a real theater.

The use of VR with visualization software does produce some challenges. Computers with powerful graphics cards are currently needed to be able to run VR programs without disruptive frame drops. Not everyone has access to such computers, and the adoption rate of many virtual reality headsets is still relatively low. To address this challenge, KeyLight was designed to also functions without virtual reality equipment (Fig. 1).

Fig. 1. The Keylight stage with a lighting design. The icons show where lights are hung in the space, with different types for the house and stage lights. A large camera icon intersects with a table light near the bottom of the image. This shows where the user sits in virtual reality, next to the board operator at a table in the house.

1.3   Lighting Terminology

Users of the software must have basic theater lighting knowledge. Here are some common definitions for the concepts that appear throughout this paper:

- Channel: An organizational number, assigned by a user of a lighting control board. Essentially serves as a name for some number of dimmers.
- Dimmers: Allow users to change a light's intensity. Connected to lighting fixtures.
- Groups: A group of channel numbers. Allows control of multiple channels at once.
- Light plot: A diagram showing the placement, type, orientation, color, and more of all the lights being use for a production.
- Cyc: A large, blank surface placed on the back of the stage on which lights are focused to create a background effect.
- House: The area where the audience sits in the theater.
- Half: Setting a fixture to fifty percent intensity.
- Full: Setting a fixture to one hundred percent intensity.

1.4   The Magic Sheet

The magic sheet is a "cheat sheet" for a light plot. It provides designers with information about the lights that can be gathered at a quick glance. Groups of lights are separated into multiple miniature plots of the stage. The stage is oriented on the magic sheet as you would see it from the house. Outlines of the set are visible in each square to help orient the designer. The name and number for each group is given above each plot, and available colors are shown as well. Arrows show the direction of the lights, and channel numbers are placed onto the spots where their fixtures will affect the stage. An example of a magic sheet is seen in Fig. 2.

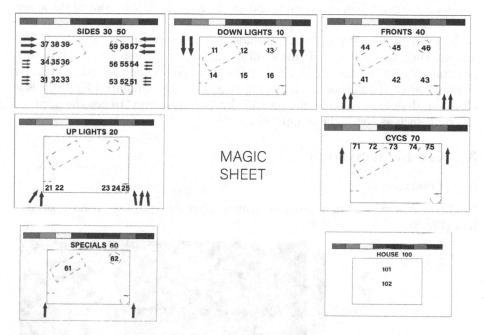

Fig. 2. The magic sheet provided in KeyLight. This is placed on a table in front of the user. Each square shows the stage in miniature with dotted lines indicating the placement of set pieces. Group numbers are next to the name of each group (i.e. the Up Lights are Group 20 and include channels 21–25). Each channel's focus is indicated by its placement on each plot.

2   Related Work

Many lighting visualizers already exist on the market. Software is used by theater professionals to pre-program shows, plan lighting designs, make decisions about where to hang or focus lights, and more. However, popular lighting design tools in the market today do not incorporate a vocal interface [11]. Designs for systems that use voice interfaces to control physical lighting fixtures have already been patented but not incorporated into digital tooling [2]. Designers today use physical or digital inputs to control their lighting consoles or visualization tools.

The addition of a vocal input innovates on top of these previously designed and proven systems.

Virtual reality and other digital tools are becoming more prevalent in theater spaces. Virtual reality is being explored as a tool for visualizing lighting design before events and productions [1]. Large companies such as Vectorworks have created VR visualization tools which can be used to view designs for anything from architecture to set design [12]. Other projects have used VR as a visualization tool, using mechanical controls and motions within VR to control the space [1].

Novel lighting software, which include digital magic sheets or accessibility features such as touch controls and auditory responses, are being explored to support the diverse community of lighting designers [4]. While researching related work, however, the authors found no existing tools that combined lighting visualization, design tools, and voice controls into one program. Hence the need for a system such as KeyLight is apparent.

3   Key Light System

3.1   Overview

KeyLight is a system that provides visualization for lighting within a theater hall (Fig. 3).

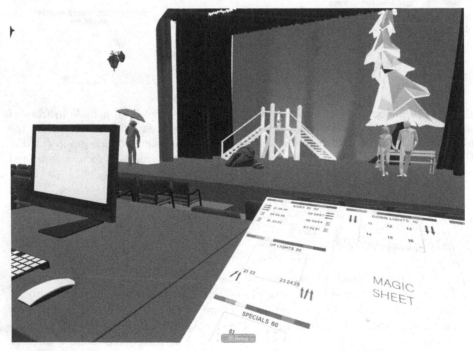

Fig. 3. Users sit at a table in the audience and look out upon the stage they are designing.

The system is designed using Amazon Alexa, AWS Lambda, Amazon Simple Queue Service (SQS), and the Unity Game Engine. Many of the limitations of the system, discussed throughout the paper, could potentially be improved by switching to a different vocal processing tool. A designer utilizing a virtual magic sheet similar to the one shown in Fig. 4a vocalizes a command to a personification of Alexa as seen in Fig. 4b. Alexa then processes the speech as an intent, sending information about the command through the model created in the Developer Console.

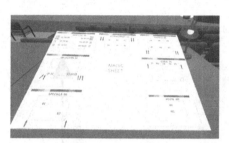

(a) The magic sheet, as displayed in front of the user in VR.

(b) A personified Alexa lighting assistant depicted at the helm of the lighting controls.

Fig. 4. KeyLight work environment

Slots in each intent are filled with keywords, such as the numeric value of a group number as seen in Fig. 5.

Intents / SetChannelColorIntent

Sample Utterances (10)

What might a user say to invoke this intent?

Set channel {channel_number} {color_name}

Change channel {channel_number} to {color_name}

channel {channel_number} {color_name}

Make channel {channel_number} and {channel_number} {color_name}

{color_name} for channel {channel_number}

Fig. 5. An Alexa Intent sheet example, as displayed in the Alexa developer portal.

The Alexa service has a custom AWS Lambda endpoint; all code for handling activated Alexa intents is stored in AWS Lambda and is written in Python. As depicted in Fig. 6 When a valid command is received, such as changing a group of lights to a new color, the command is parsed and sent into an AWS SQS FIFO queue. Unity continually polls the queue to check for new jobs. If one is found, the Unity code removes it from the queue, processes it, and sends the command as an event. Lights in the Unity scene listen for these commands and change their values as directed.

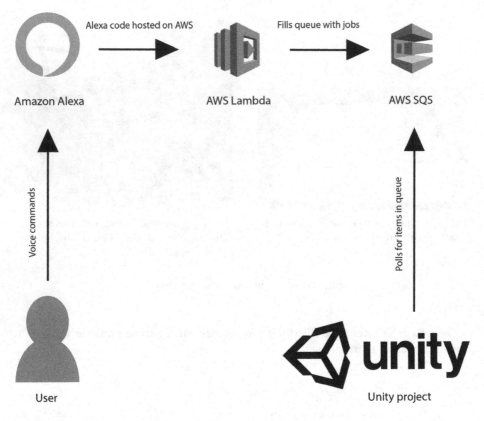

Fig. 6. KeyLight Trainer's backend is built on interactions between Amazon Web Services, user input, Amazon Alexa, and the Unity Engine.

3.2 Current Steps for Use of KeyLight

The steps below describe how the system works in its prototype phase. Future developments would bypass steps I–IV by using any Alexa device; however, Amazon certification for a completed application is needed for this functionality so this will have to be implemented after all development is completed for the project.

I. Sign into the Alexa developer portal using the username and password given.

II. Under Alexa skills, click the skill labeled as "KeyLight".

III. Go to the Test tab.

IV. To interact with Alexa, either hold the microphone button down and talk or type into the terminal.

V. Launch the Alexa component of KeyLight by saying or typing "key light trainer".

VI. Open the Unity executable.

VII. Optional: Put on VR equipment.

VIII. Begin directing Alexa using the lighting commands in Sect. 3.

3.3 Design Choices

Polling Design: Due to Santa Clara University network restrictions on incoming traffic, it was necessary to create a system in which Unity asks the queue for new jobs and receives a JSON response. After lots of trial and error, other models, such as using the Unity Networking packages or using client-server communications, proved unsuitable for this task.

Custom Endpoint: Rather than hosting the Alexa code in the Alexa development console itself, KeyLight uses a custom AWS endpoint in Lambda code. This allowed for easier editing and management of the actual code running behind the scenes to handle the Alexa requests, and the use of Amazon's Simple Queue Service (SQS).

Intents: The commands discussed in Sect. 3.4 have been created as separate intents to clarify their purpose.

Linguistic Limitations

I. At the time of this writing, Alexa is unable to differentiate between intents, based on the input provided. If one intent is formatted to accept channel_number color_name with no other surrounding words, and another is formatted to accept channel_number light_level, Alexa's voice parsers will sometimes plug a command such as "ten red" into the latter of those commands, throwing errors. This could possibly be circumvented with code, but after some time working through this problem, it was decided that KeyLight would enforce a few rules about each command that would still be applicable in traditional lighting design communication. Levels are adjusted by saying "at" (ex. "channel ten at fifty") and colors are changed by saying "to" (ex. "channel ten to red"). If neither word is present, the intent will be processed as a color change, as it is more common to say, "channel ten red" than, "channel ten fifty".

II. Alexa has difficulty processing combined words that should fit into one slot. Thus support for colors such as "red-brown" and "green-blue" were added, but in tests Alexa only processed "red" or "green" and ignored any inputs following that.

HTC VIVE: The program is designed for optional use with the HTC Vive, but as the controllers are not used in KeyLight, it can be easily extended to work on other devices.

Future Simplification of Code: For speed during the prototyping phase, an event listener model was used. The Unity code can be simplified in future versions to use a game object with all the light objects attached, rather than an events system.

3.4 Commands

Each command is associated with a separate intent. The phrase "start key light trainer" invokes the Alexa skill (Table 1).

Table 1. Important Alexa Intents.

Intent Name	Intent Type	Additional Notes
SetGroupColorIntent	Set the color of a group	
SetChannelColorIntent	Set the color of a channel	
SetGroupValueIntent	Set the level of a group	
SetChannelValueIntent	Set the level of a channel	
BlackOutIntent	Turn off all theater and house lights	A small lamp on the designer's table remains on
GroupLevelFade	Add a fade to a group	Not yet supported in Unity and Lambda code
ActionInfoIntent	Request information about available actions	Not yet supported in Unity and Lambda code
DesignInfoIntent	Request information about what to design	Not yet supported in Unity and Lambda code

Intents are comprised of defined phrasing that combines specific utterances with custom slots, which allow for variable speech inputs in an utterance (Table 2).

Table 2. Alexa Slots.

Slot Name	Slot Type	Function	Notes
KeyLightColors	Custom	Defines colors (i.e. light pink, dark purple, white, cyan, grey, etc.)	Colors not natively in Unity were defined to match these words with appropriate values
HalfOrFull	Custom	Set lights to level 50 or 100 using "half" or "full"	
fadeType	Custom	Fade the lights in or out	Not yet supported in Unity and Lambda code
Amazon.Number	Built In	Converts speech to numbers for group numbers, channel numbers, and levels	

Each of these intents has many possible associated commands that Alexa will mark as valid. In the current prototype, users have the ability to change the level (intensity) and color of groups of fixtures or individual fixtures (channels). Supported colors include red, orange, yellow, green, blue, purple, pink, and white.

I. To change a level, a user would say: [**Group/Channel**] [**#**] **at** [**level #**]. For Example:
   "Group [thirty] at [fifty]"
   "Group [thirty] at [half]"
   "Channel [twenty-two] at [one hundred]"
   "Channel [twenty-two] at [full]"
   "Set group [one hundred] to [forty three]"
II. To change a color, a user would say: [**Group/Channel**] [**#**] **to** [**color**]. For Example:
   "Group [ten] [blue]"
   "Channel [twelve] [green]"
   "Change group [ten] to [red]"
   "Set channel [ten] to [yellow]"
   "Let's make channel [thirty one] [purple]"

3.5   Future Developments

These are the planned improvements for the KeyLight Trainer:

- The ability to save stage looks as cues and replay (or load) cues into the scene.
- The ability to ask Alexa to change the set or scenery.
- The ability to choose between different light plots (configurations of lighting fixtures).
- The ability for users to view the current state on an interface within the trainer.
- The ability for users to select additional colors and also make adjustments to those colors.
- The ability for users to change the numbering of channels or groups.
- Further support for transitions and fades.
- Better natural language recognition for communication not relating to commands.
- The use of realistic types of fixtures.
- Expanded dialogue options for the board operator and Alexa.
- Adding additional animations to the model representing Alexa.
- Expanding terminology to match that used outside of the western United States.
- Improvements to visual displays, including communication of state of the fixtures.

4 Results

4.1 Summary of Findings

Four theater industry professionals were presented with a demonstration of the KeyLight Trainer. Those interviewed included Participant 1) a senior product manager at a professional stage lighting company, Participant 2) a Theater Manager for a school district, Participant 3) the Technical Director of Performing Arts at a high school, and Participant 4) a lighting designer.

In a separate demo with Participant 5, who was not formally interviewed and who had no prior lighting experience, testimony indicated that it is particularly important that users have some background knowledge about lighting design and terminology. Participant 5 communicated that they felt uncertainty about how to use the software and a lack of clarity on what might make a design "good". These results focus on the testimony of the four industry professionals, who are closer to the intended audience of this tool (Fig. 7).

Fig. 7. A participant using the Keylight Trainer with a Vive headset.

Of the participants who saw KeyLight in use, 100% thought KeyLight Trainer was a useful tool for lighting designers. All also thought the KeyLight Trainer had novel value. "I think the thing that's different here, is that you're not building the look. You're asking someone else to build the look, and you have to be able to communicate that," said Participant 1 [11]. Participant 3 called KeyLight the "missing link" for students looking to cross over from classroom education to hands-on experience [5]. Participant 3 also noted that the KeyLight project would be beneficial to both professors and students who are often unable to use professional visualization software due to its cost prohibitive nature.

Mentioning the many visualizers available in the market, those interviewed instead reported the success of KeyLight as a communication trainer. "The communication part is something that we don't have, that none of these things have.... The other stuff is already out there. And having a way to talk to a visualizer isn't really that exciting. You already have the visualizer. A way to just learn to talk to a programmer, yeah, that's different," said Participant 2 [11].

All four further discussed the importance of communication skills as a lighting designer, and that the VUI implemented in this software would help designers build upon those skills. "To be able to translate what's in your head into the stage when you're limited by time... when you're trying to explain it to another entity, that means your thoughts have to be organized in such a way that you can communicate them," said Participant 1 [11].

Best applications of the model for this trainer were also discussed. All four participants brought up the different patterns of language and commands used by lighting designers across different lighting boards. There was consensus that the program, if tailored specifically to the language of each board, would provide immense value for learning not only how to communicate but also how to work with specific lighting technologies. They suggested that this would make the trainer more useful for professionals as well. Discussing the generality of the magic sheet and its associated commands, Participant 2 stated, "I like the idea of that in that it's realistic and yet generic. It's not platform specific, it's not Eos but it follows the reality of how those types of software work close enough that you're teaching the concept without getting bogged down" [11]. All four expressed that they liked that the commands programmed in the KeyLight Trainer were more general for student use.

All four also reported a lack of interest in the VR component of KeyLight. While all four had either used or encountered lighting visualizers before, none of them reported using the VR features for any such product.

Only one of the four participants thought that KeyLight was close to bringing value to students and educators in its current state. This participant, a high school teacher and a department head of the theater program at his school, stated that the lights in the virtual space needed to be focused better (reducing lights bleeding unrealistically into areas of the stage) before he would use it with students. This minor improvement is the only feature that he felt impeded effective use of the product, and he stated that he would use the trainer with his theater students if that were to be fixed. The other three participants felt that some major features needed to be added to bring KeyLight into a state where it adds value to students. Describing the value of KeyLight as an educational tool in its current state, Participant 1 stated, "I think it has value. I think it's value is a little bit limited... I think it's cool" [11]. The changes they pointed out are discussed below.

4.2 Improvements Needed

All four participants reported that the trainer needs to include relative brightness to be useful as a teaching tool. This means that the VUI must allow users to communicate level changes such as "Bump up channel thirty by five points" or "Bring down group sixty a little." They felt it was important that future versions also include the ability to change groups of lights according to their names, such as "Fronts at fifty."

State visibility was another critical component that all four professionals felt the current program lacked. There was no way for a designer to check the current levels of any group or channel or to determine which were turned on. The second group of participants suggested that the trainer include another interface on the magic sheet with a visual display of active channels and their levels, as well as the ability to ask the Alexa board operator about these levels.

All four also mentioned color palettes. They expressed that it would be best if users could choose the color of their lights prior to using the tool, or otherwise have a larger selection of basic colors and variations in light warmth.

All four agreed that there should be multiple human targets on the digital stage, and that the ability to switch between set designs would add to the experience. Three expressed interest in the ability to pre-program a set design for potential students and then have the students work in that created space. One thought it was important that the humanoids on the stage also have eye sockets and slightly more realistic features so that students can learn more about the effect of different lighting angles on a subject. Three out of four liked the simplicity of the "cartoony" environment and models.

Debating what would be needed for KeyLight to provide value to theater students, all four also agreed that cues need to be implemented in KeyLight. Users must have the ability to save, replay, and transition between cues or looks on the stage. They agreed that once relative brightness, a display of the system state, cues, and the color palette were expanded, KeyLight would provide great value as an educational tool.

5 Discussion

While pointing out some critical improvements to KeyLight, each professional interviewed also acknowledged the value of KeyLight as both an educational and professional tool. In one testimonial, an interviewee speaking to the immediate application of KeyLight said, "You could go into the theater that's in your [KeyLight] visualizer for the last week of your class and light things using the plot, using the everything. That would be helpful" [11]. Speaking to future applications of the VUI for professionals, another said, "If you had something that would let me voice control a console out there, I would buy it in 30 s. In my world I spend a lot of time at a lighting desk, and I don't have operators that are really very good. I end up having to write my own cues mostly. If I could just sit there and talk into it while I'm watching the stage, suddenly I'm twice as fast. I think there's a product there possibly quite powerful and useful. It's not educational. It's for people who are in smaller venues where your lighting designer has to write cues... I've wanted that for a long time" [11]. In its current state, those interviewed see KeyLight as being a powerful educational tool with future possibilities for professional expansion.

By using a VUI with industry standard language, KeyLight bypasses some challenges posited by voice user interfaces [8,10] by enforcing a model that is both naturally learnable and discoverable for users with training in lighting design. KeyLight also goes beyond this model by requiring users to speak in patterns that reflect those required in their profession. Other research on VUI's has focused on the reliability of a mental model that users build for the program [3], and by focusing on a niche audience KeyLight evades some of the challenges users face while forming one.

Personification of Alexa as the board operator, another aspect of VUI's explored by other researchers [6,9], helps to ground the voice technology and add a sense of realism to this simulation according to those interviewed.

With budget, time constraints, or public health limitations preventing aspiring theater designers from practicing their craft, KeyLight solves access problems in theater education. "Most high schools don't have visualizers," said Participant 2. "Colleges are going to have them but they're probably going to be restricted access as to who gets to do it when. So the idea that you've got something simple built into [KeyLight] is really appealing because anyone can use it and they can see, even if it isn't super fancy visualization, there's something to see that's there and its part of the system" [11]. KeyLight fills a rift in theater education. Many students lack access to the software, spaces, or equipment that will allow them to develop their professional communication skills.

As Keylight continues into later phases, more rigorous evaluation of its efficacy will be needed. After the improvements discussed in this paper are implemented, the intention is to compare both the qualitative and quantitative impact of Keylight versus other lighting software and tooling on junior lighting designers learning lighting through the classroom.

6 Conclusion

KeyLight moves beyond the functionality of similar software in several important ways. As a training program for lighting designers that leverages voice control, KeyLight Trainer helps designers gain experience with an actual method for creating lighting looks, using industry standard terminology and commands. An Alexa voice assistant sits beside the user and takes on the role of a board operator, adding to the immersion of KeyLight Trainer. Finally, while this program uses virtual reality to help designers get comfortable with giving commands in a simulated space, it can also run on any computer without VR equipment.

With KeyLight, junior lighting designers can strengthen their fundamental skills. Users can learn to be more confident communicators as they increase the hours of experience they have designing for the stage. While future expansions to KeyLight have the potential to prepare the trainer for professional use, testimony suggests that this program will increase the comfort, confidence, and competency of both traditional theater students and people entering the industry through new, nontraditional paths.

Acknowledgements. Many thanks are due to the Santa Clara University's Imaginarium for lending a Vive headset without which the development of KeyLight would not have been possible. To those who provided feedback on KeyLight. To Calvin Golliver for being KeyLight's first demo participant. And lastly to the department of Mathematics and Computer Science of the College of Arts and Sciences for their continued support of KeyLight.

References

1. Araújo, J.: Virtual reality for lighting simulation in events. University of Lisbon (2014)
2. Dowling, K.J., Mueller, G.G.: Lighting control using speech recognition. US Patent 7,031,920, 18 April 2006
3. Du, Y., Qin, J., Zhang, S., Cao, S., Dou, J.: Voice user interface interaction design research based on user mental model in autonomous vehicle. In: Kurosu, M. (ed.) HCI 2018. LNCS, vol. 10903, pp. 117–132. Springer, Cham (2018). https://doi.org/10.1007/978-3-319-91250-9_10
4. Duarte, D.: Personal interview, 4 November 2019, including observation of him working on lighting design with a board operator
5. Eriksen, C.: Personal interview, 3 August 2020
6. Haesler, S., Kim, K., Bruder, G., Welch, G.: Seeing is believing: improving the perceived trust in visually embodied Alexa in augmented reality. In: 2018 IEEE International Symposium on Mixed and Augmented Reality Adjunct (ISMAR-Adjunct), pp. 204–205. IEEE (2018)
7. Kuksa, I.: Virtual reality in theatre education and design practice new developments and applications. Art Des. Commun. High. Educ. **7**(2), 73–89 (2009)
8. Lopatovska, I., et al.: Talk to me: Exploring user interactions with the amazon Alexa. J. Librariansh. Inf. Sci. **51**(4), 984–997 (2019)
9. Purington, A., Taft, J.G., Sannon, S., Bazarova, N.N., Taylor, S.H.: "Alexa is my new BFF" social roles, user satisfaction, and personification of the amazon echo. In: Proceedings of the 2017 CHI Conference Extended Abstracts on Human Factors in Computing Systems, pp. 2853–2859 (2017)
10. Schnelle, D., Lyardet, F.: Voice user interface design patterns. In: EuroPLoP, pp. 287–316 (2006)
11. Staiff, M., Sellers, F., Chenault, J.: Personal interview, 10 August 2020
12. Vectorworks: Export web view tutorial for vectorworks 2017, 14 September 2016. https://www.youtube.com/watch?v=zJ-5gX9SyB0

Author Index

Printed in the United States
by Baker & Taylor Publisher Services